M000110719

Ethnonationalist Conflict
in Postcommunist States

NATIONAL AND ETHNIC CONFLICT
IN THE TWENTY-FIRST CENTURY

Brendan O'Leary, Series Editor

Ethnonationalist Conflict
in Postcommunist States

―――――

Varieties of Governance
in Bulgaria, Macedonia, and Kosovo

Maria Koinova

PENN

UNIVERSITY OF PENNSYLVANIA PRESS

PHILADELPHIA

Copyright © 2013 University of Pennsylvania Press

All rights reserved. Except for brief quotations used
for purposes of review or scholarly citation, none of this
book may be reproduced in any form by any means without
written permission from the publisher.

Published by
University of Pennsylvania Press
Philadelphia, Pennsylvania 19104-4112
www.upenn.edu/pennpress

Printed in the United States of America
on acid-free paper

10 9 8 7 6 5 4 3 2 1

Library of Congress Cataloging-in-Publication Data

Koinova, Maria.
    Ethnonationalist conflict in postcommunist states :
varieties of governance in Bulgaria, Macedonia, and
Kosovo / Maria Koinova. — 1st ed.
        p.   cm. — (National and ethnic conflict in the twenty-
first century)
    Includes bibliographical references and index.
    ISBN 978-0-8122-4522-6 (hardcover : alk. paper)
    1. Bulgaria—Ethnic relations—Political aspects.
2. Macedonia (Republic)—Ethnic relations—Political
aspects. 3. Kosovo (Republic)—Ethnic relations—
Political aspects. 4. Ethnic conflict—Bulgaria. 5. Ethnic
conflict—Macedonia (Republic) 6. Ethnic conflict—
Kosovo (Republic) 7. Post-communism—Bulgaria.
8. Post-communism—Macedonia (Republic)
9. Post-communism—Kosovo (Republic) I. Title. II. Series:
National and ethnic conflict in the twenty-first century.
DR93.44.K64   2013
305.8009496—dc23   2013012707

To the memory of my parents Velin and Ivanka,
and to Neda and Elisa

Contents

Abbreviations

AACL: Albanian American Civic League
AAK: Alliance for the Future of Kosovo
ANA: Albanian National Army
BSP: Bulgarian Socialist Party
CSCE: Commission on Security and Cooperation in Europe
DAHR: Democratic Alliance of the Hungarians of Romania
DPA: Democratic Party of the Albanians (Macedonia)
DUI: Democratic Union for Integration (Macedonia)
ECHR: European Court of Human Rights; European Convention on
    Human Rights
ECRML: European Charter on Regional and Minority Languages
EULEX: European Union Rule of Law Mission (Kosovo)
FCPNM: Framework Convention on the Protection of National Minorities
    (Council of Europe)
GERB: Citizens for the European Development of Bulgaria
HCNM: High Commissioner on the National Minorities (OSCE)
HRW: Human Rights Watch
ICCPR: International Covenant on Civil and Political Rights (UN)
ICESCR: International Covenant on Economic, Social, and Cultural Rights
    (UN)
ICFY: International Conference on the Former Yugoslavia
ICTY: International Criminal Tribunal on Former Yugoslavia
KLA: Kosovo Liberation Army
KPC: Kosovo Protection Corps
LDK: Democratic League of Kosovo
LPK: People's Movement of Kosovo
MRF: Movement for Rights and Freedoms (Bulgaria)
NAAC: National Albanian American Council
NCEDI: National Council on Ethnic and Demographic Issues (Bulgaria)

NDP: People's Democratic Party (Macedonia)
NDSV: National Movement Simeon the Second (Bulgaria)
NLA: National Liberation Army (Macedonia)
OFA: Ohrid Framework Agreement
OSCE: Organization for Security and Co-operation in Europe
PACE: Parliamentary Assembly of the Council of Europe
PDK: Democratic Party of Kosovo
PDP: Party for Democratic Prosperity (Macedonia)
PKK: Kurdistan Workers' Party
PMBLA: Liberation Army of Preshevo, Medvedja, Bujanovac
PR: Proportional Representation
RFE/RFL: Radio Free Europe/Radio Liberty
SAA: Stabilization and Association Agreement (EU)
SAO: Serbian Autonomous Oblasts
SCP: Serbian Communist Party
SDSM: Social Democratic Union of Macedonia
SFRY: Socialist Federal Republic of Yugoslavia
SPS: Serbian Socialist Party
SRM: Socialist Republic of Macedonia
SRS: Serbian Radical Party
TDP: Turkish Democratic Party
UDF: Union of Democratic Forces (Bulgaria)
UNMIK: United Nations Interim Administration Mission in Kosovo
UNPREDEP: UN Preventive Deployment Force
UNPROFOR: UN Protective Force
VMRO-DMPNE: Internal Macedonian Revolutionary Organization-
    Democratic Party of Macedonian National Unity

Introduction

Applying Path-Dependence, Timing, and Sequencing in Conflict Analysis

Over the past few decades some Eastern European postcommunist states with large ethnonational minorities managed to participate in nonviolent transitions while in others ethnic conflicts turned into civil wars. Some consolidated their democracies, and by 2007 were full members of the European Union (EU). Others started democratic transitions but did not complete them. Instead, disagreements between majorities and minorities evolved into civil wars, arrested political development, and led to significant loss of life. Despite the EU's mitigating effects on its neighbors, some conflicts displayed remarkable resilience and others developed anew.

The global media reported on the capture of indicted war criminals Radovan Karadzic and Ratko Mladic and their delivery to the International Tribunal on Former Yugoslavia (ICTY), and on multiple counts of criminality and corruption in structures of government. They also covered more mundane topics such as elections and initiatives related to the EU integration of the Western Balkans. But violence continues to be a viable option in this part of the world. Kosovo's declaration of independence from Serbia on February 17, 2008,[1] triggered new riots in the heart of Serbia. The city of Mitrovica in northern Kosovo, divided by the Ibar River into Albanian and Serbian communities, became a new center for violent clashes. Disputes in July 2011 involved the ethnic Albanian-dominated Kosovo government, the ethnic Serb minority, and some NATO troops still deployed there.[2] The dual governance in Mitrovica complicates Kosovo's political development and Serbia's EU aspirations.[3] Kosovo's international status, though not recognized by a majority of the UN General Assembly, also complicates the uneasy peace in Bosnia-Herzegovina, where fears of secession by Republika Srpska, a constituent component, prompted high-ranking Western diplomats to warn: "It's time to pay attention to Bosnia again if we don't want things to get nasty very quickly."[4]

Macedonia is not spared interethnic violence, despite being celebrated as a conflict prevention success story following brief warfare in 2001. Relations between Albanians and Macedonians have been deteriorating. In February 2011 Macedonian and Albanian protesters clashed in Skopje over construction of a museum-church, which Macedonians supported and Albanians opposed.[5] In April 2012 the bodies of five Macedonian men were found near Skopje. Attackers remained unidentified, but the killings triggered violent clashes and numerous demonstrations.[6]

Inter-ethnic peace in Bulgaria prevailed in the 1990s, and was important for the country to join the EU in 2007. Yet the ultranationalist party Ataka emerged in the mid-2000s and challenged this peace. In the streets of Sofia in 2008, one could hear Ataka supporters spreading hate speech against ethnic Turks in a manner rare even in the transition years when relations were fragile. In May and June 2011, Ataka launched demonstrations against the loudspeakers of the central Sofia mosque. Muslim worshippers were attacked and severely beaten.[7]

These examples illustrate the importance of two major questions posed by this book. Why do ethnonationalist conflicts reach different levels of violence? And why do they often persist despite strong international conflict resolution and peace- and institution-building programs? I approach these questions through a decade-long comparative study of three places where majority-minority relations escalated to different degrees of violence after the end of communism: Bulgaria, Macedonia, and the then province of Kosovo in Yugoslavia.[8] Conflicts were characterized by low violence in Bulgaria, mid-range in Macedonia, and high in Kosovo.

Conflict analysis is a well-established field, but with some exceptions, inquiries about the variation in degrees of violence using a joint theoretical framework are not common.[9] This is not surprising given the challenge of coherent comparisons across sub-state conflicts that spread widely after the wars of decolonization in the 1940s and 1970s, and continued with new vigor after the collapse of communism.[10] Scholars are currently divided into two major camps in approaching these conflicts. A large number concentrate on civil wars and other intrastate conflicts where violence is usually high. This interest is also not surprising given the global shift from inter- to intrastate wars after the end of communism: only 7 wars between 1989 and 2004 were between states; the remaining 118 were intrastate.[11] The conflicts in Bosnia-Herzegovina, Chechnya, East Timor, Liberia, Kosovo, Mozambique, Nagorno-Karabakh, the Palestinian territories, Sierra Leone, Sudan, and more recently Iraq, Afghanistan, and the Democratic Republic of Congo have enjoyed much academic attention.

Other scholars, especially in the context of peaceful transformations in Eastern Europe, have concentrated on cases where ethnonational violence remained low. Czechoslovakia split peacefully into the Czech Republic and Slovakia in 1992. Russian minorities in the Baltic republics faced discrimination after the dissolution of the Soviet Union, but did not rebel. Hungarian minorities in Slovakia and Romania mobilized, but not violently. In deeply divided Ukraine, neither Ukrainians nor Russian speakers reached for weapons even when tensions such as the 2005 "Orange Revolution" aimed at toppling an illiberal regime.

Despite methodological criticism that such studies often "select on the dependent variable" and fail to find underlying reasons and mechanisms for a range of outcomes of violence,[12] this focus is understandable because theorizing requires scholars to narrow the pool of relevant cases. Apart from civil wars, important phenomena in ethnonationalism include minority rights, cultural and territorial autonomy, federalism, and secessionist movements. Each tends to be associated with a certain level of violence. Since scholars usually focus on a specific phenomenon, variation in violence is often difficult to find, and researchers move on to other aspects of comparative variation.

The present study shifts the focus from a particular *political phenomenon* to the *relationships* between the agents involved. This approach identifies mechanisms that span ethnonationalist phenomena, and allows for exploring why relationships among major agents in a conflict become more or less violent over time. I concentrate on the evolution of relationships between majority and minority elites and the external factors that may affect them. I seek to understand how agents in these groups associate with the exercise of political power. There are many commonalities, whether the conflicts are driven by minority demands for political and cultural accommodation as in Bulgaria, autonomist claims as in Macedonia, or secessionist claims as in Kosovo. In this sense, this book adds to the emerging body of scholarship on microdynamics of conflicts, approaching conflicts as relational phenomena.[13]

It is puzzling why the conflicts in Kosovo, Macedonia, and Bulgaria reached different degrees of violence after 1989. Retrospectively it sounds commonsensical that these conflicts evolved differently, at least because Bulgaria did not undergo state collapse. But at the outset of the transition process none of this was determined. The countries had some crucial commonalities: the conflicts evolved between Christian Orthodox majorities and Muslim minorities, the communist parties controlled national politics, and there were no effective dissident or other civic movements to create political alternatives. During communism the Turks of Bulgaria experienced brutal assimilation that deprived them of their Arabic names and Islamic religion. Numerous studies indicate that government repression of a communal group is a major source of collective action and organized violent resistance. Initially repression may inspire fear and caution, but it creates long-term resentment and enduring incentives to retaliate.[14] Thus, it is surprising that the Turks of Bulgaria did not retaliate after 1989, but chose a peaceful course of accommodation. It is equally puzzling why the Albanians of Macedonia and Kosovo, who enjoyed many rights in socialist Yugoslavia, encountered more violence during the transition period, and why the levels of violence differed between Macedonia and Kosovo.

The outcomes of violence evolved along specific trajectories. In Bulgaria, relations between the Bulgarian majority and the Turkish minority experienced serious tensions in the early 1990s, but developed peacefully in the long run. The ethnic Turkish Movement for Rights and Freedoms (MRF) became the third parliamentary party with a major say in the formation of governments, although it first entered a governing coalition only in 2001. Nevertheless, in the 2000s the ultranationalist party Ataka capitalized on anti-Turkish, anti-Muslim rhetoric, gained a significant constituency, and became an important parliamentary player, also supporting the formation of a recent government.

In Macedonia, interactions between the Macedonian majority and the Albanian minority were consistently tense. The Albanians were represented in parliament as early as 1990 and belonged to the governing coalitions since 1992, but their demands to be a constituent people of the state were perpetually ignored. Tensions in education and self-government led to peaks of violence in the mid-1990s. Albanian rebels linked to the postconflict environment of wartorn Kosovo staged brief internal warfare in 2001, demanding federalization. In the aftermath, interethnic violence significantly decreased and Macedonia became a candidate for EU membership.

But violence continued. In the first few months of 2012, twenty-five incidents of interethnic violence took place.[15]

In Kosovo, relations between the local Albanian minority and the dominant Serbs, a numerical minority in Kosovo but a political majority in then Yugoslavia, were marred by violence throughout the 1990s. The government systematically repressed the Kosovo Albanians, who declared independence, organized parallel institutions, and launched nonviolent civil resistance. In 1998–1999 the conflict escalated to internal warfare and NATO military intervention, defeat of the Serbian government, and a new period in Kosovo's political development characterized by the rule of the UN Interim Administration Mission in Kosovo (UNMIK) and the presence of NATO peacekeeping forces. During the postconflict period the groups switched positions. Albanians became a political majority in Kosovo, and Serbs a political minority. Violence continued.

The key argument of this book is that the levels and duration of ethnonational violence are rooted in conflict dynamics established between majorities, minorities, and international agents during the formative period at the end of communism (1987/89–1992). At that time, multiple changes in the political and economic environment enabled contingent events to have major consequences and set majority-minority relations on a certain path, foreclosing alternatives that were possible earlier. How timing and sequencing of majority and minority policies took place during this "critical juncture" influenced how the conflict dynamics initially evolved, and how each conflict consolidated at different points on a scale of violence. The international community and kin-states played an important role during this critical juncture as well.[16] Their actual influence decreased after this period ended, because they became adapted to the conflict processes. In the aftermath of the formative period, the relations between majorities, minorities, and international agents became locked in dynamics—conflictual, semiconflictual, or cooperative—that became self-perpetuating and informally institutionalized over time. Constitutions, laws, and other policies officially postulated certain behaviors for majorities and minorities, but the local and international agents acted through the bounded rationality of an entrenched mixture of formal and informal arrangements. Thus, while exogenous shocks and external policy intervention provided opportunities for drastic or gradual change toward lower or higher decrees of violence, the change often related to a single dimension of the majority-minority relationship rather than the dynamic as a whole. This approach accounts for why violence could diminish but still persist even after strong international intervention to resolve conflicts.

This book is situated at the nexus of comparative historical scholarship on path-dependence, timing and sequencing of policies, democratization and conflict, and international intervention. It theorizes about long-term causal processes of continuity and change in conflict dynamics. It shares recent broad recognition among social scientists that "legacies matter" and that social science should better account for both continuity and change, rather than focus on just one, and should certainly not leave the study of continuity primarily to historians. In the next section I elaborate on my perspective, while demonstrating how it presents an alternative way of thinking about continuities and change in the context of conflict and post-conflict processes.

Path-Dependence, Ethnic Conflict, and Violence

Paul Pierson successfully uses a metaphor to juxtapose the ways social scientists think about explaining particular outcomes: that we view the world as if taking "snapshots" or "moving pictures" with a camera.[17] The first approach yields a static frame. Take, for example, one "snapshot" when in 1995 Albanian demonstrators confronted Macedonian police after opening a clandestine university. In this picture, a minority fights for autonomy. The Albanian minority in Macedonia has similar goals to those of the Hungarian minorities of Romania or Slovakia, but not all of them experienced violent encounters with police. A snapshot approach would use these cases for a small-N comparison, or add them to a global pool of instances of minorities fighting for autonomy, conduct a large-N analysis, and seek reasons why interethnic violence varied across cases. It would reveal nothing about the effects of time on the violent episodes.

In a "moving picture" approach, timing and sequencing lie at the heart of analysis. It matters whether the Albanians started to demand autonomy before or after infringement of their rights. It matters whether their demands were addressed or ignored by the Macedonian-dominated government before or after the incidence of violence. A moving picture depicts not only *what* matters and *why*, but *when* it happened and *how* this affects the outcome of interest.[18] Moving picture approach is the mode of thinking for path-dependence scholarship.

"Critical junctures" are important in conceptualizations of path-dependence. These are short periods during which significant changes produce different long-term legacies in different cases.[19] Such junctures are characterized by substantially heightened freedom of political agents to affect the outcome of interest.[20] Junctures become "critical" if they turn out to be choice points between alternatives and if they place institutional arrangements on trajectories that are then difficult to alter.[21] While critical junctures are usually identified retroactively, they can be discerned taking place when there is high volatility in political relationships amid fundamental transformations of institutions and structures, requiring new political strategies and policies. The critical juncture of this study, the end of communism, is identified through policy choices and political strategies that created durable dynamics in the relationships between majorities, minorities, and international agents.

Another underlying consensus in works on path-dependence is that the specific timing and sequencing of events matter. Similar conditions can evolve into different outcomes, large consequences may be invoked from "small" or contingent events, and once introduced a particular course of action may be difficult to reverse, causing agents to become dependent on the path on which they have set out.[22] The major concerns are the types of sequences and how they take place along certain paths. With self-reinforcing sequences—what economists consider "increasing returns"—initial moves of agents in one direction encourage further moves in the same direction through the mechanism of "positive feedback." The path not initially taken becomes increasingly distant over time.[23]

Reactive sequences obey a different logic. These are chains of temporally ordered and causally connected events. The mechanism binding the chain is not positive feedback, but the reaction of each element of a sequence to the antecedent events in the chain. The outcome of interest is typically the final event in this sequence.[24] In the course of this book, we will see both reactive and reinforcing sequences at work in the conflict dynamics of our three cases.

Path-dependence has been championed by "historical institutionalism" in political science. The majority of studies have focused on revolutions, democratization, regime change, and institutional development.[25] Conflict analysis has rarely applied this approach systematically, despite a recent exception.[26] It has been claimed that conflicts are path-dependent, but *why*, *how*, and *when* they become so has been little explored. It has also been asserted that once violence occurs, agents may follow a path-dependent process and resort to further violence more easily than if it has not occurred.[27] Some scholars have begun thinking of intractable conflicts as institutionalized systems of relationships without emphasizing how stable relationships are formed between the local and international agents involved.[28]

This book demonstrates that not just intractable conflicts—such as the Israeli-Palestinian or in Northern Ireland—have stable conflict dynamics, but other conflicts do so as well, regardless of the level of violence. If domestic agents are accommodating toward minority rights reforms, for example, the explanation may be found in the interactions between majorities, minorities, and international agents at a formative period. Thereafter, relationships become largely entrenched, while change occurs either through exogenous shocks or slowly and incrementally, and often does not alter important aspects of the established conflict dynamics.

Rational choice has theorized in a different manner about self-reinforcement processes of conflict dynamics. Here agents operate interdependently, past plays in political "games" exert effects on the next moves, and path-dependence becomes a cumulative outcome.[29] These deductively designed games provide the nuts and bolts of the feedback effects, but they are often insensitive to how contingencies become important during formative periods, and how exogenous shocks—unpredicted, or predicted in a randomized fashion—play an important role in politics.[30] How sequences of exogenous shocks cause specific outcomes is not at the heart of rational choice analysis, but it could be important to the outcomes of interest in specific contexts, as I demonstrate later.

For their part, historical institutionalist accounts, context-bound and often inductively driven, have been traditionally criticized for failing to predict how change occurs incrementally rather than simply by way of exogenous shocks. Recently some scholars have demonstrated that institutional transformation can come both from exogenous shocks and incrementally.[31] Thus, even if durable ethnic conflicts are considered a system of institutionalized relationships, change may still take place in both drastic and incremental ways. The task of the researcher is to delineate the conditions and mechanisms through which continuities endure and changes occur.

A political science study on path-dependence inspired by a comparative historical approach differs from rational choice, but also from a straightforward historical analysis in which detail and narrative provide the flesh and blood for the enterprise. In a path-dependence account, propositions are tested against competing hypotheses to maintain the focus on causality.[32] Ruling out alternative explanations can take place at different stages of the causal process. Timing and sequencing of events at specific moments and relative to each other become important, and time is not linear. Early events may have stronger effects on outcomes than similar events at a later point; they become embedded in the political environment and modify incentive structures and agents' behaviors.[33] They often have lagged effects on phenomena over time.

Definitions, Case Selection, and Methodology

There is an analytical and practical distinction between ethnic conflict and violence. Ethnic conflict occurs on a daily basis in places divided along ethnic lines. With the exception of certain states with little internal diversity such as Japan, Portugal, and Armenia, ethnic conflict is commonplace among individuals, elites, and groups in the world's multicultural societies. Here I adopt a definition of "ethnic conflict" after the understanding of Lewis Coser (1956), a "struggle in which the aim [of the opposing agents] is to gain objectives and simultaneously to neutralize, injure, or eliminate rivals."[34] This broad definition opens space for the concrete understanding of the term "objective," which can vary substantially among the leaderships representing majorities and minorities. To compare political phenomena, I also use a broad definition of "violence." I follow Stathis Kalyvas (2006) who considers violence the "deliberate infliction of harm on people," and add that violence can also be inflicted on physical infrastructure, as many instances of this study demonstrate.[35] Recent studies on civil wars delve deeper into the realm of violence and establish its varieties, from genocide and ethnic expulsion through rape and various corporal mutilations.[36] Such variety is helpful to consider when discussing episodes of internal warfare in Kosovo in 1998–1999 and Macedonia in 2001, but is not enough in other instances of low-intensity violence.

This book operates with a continuum of five degrees of violence. A "nonviolent" outcome indicates that the interests and passions of the conflicting parties are channeled peacefully through the institutional channels of the existing state. "Threatened" violence is the outcome when tensions grow and the majority or minority deploys verbal or physical threats, protests, and boycotts against the other. During "episodic violence" agents of the minority or majority engage in fewer than twenty reported physical attacks against each other on an individual basis over a year. During "extensive violence" such attacks are more than twenty in a given year and include significant injury, death, or damage of property throughout the year. At the extreme end of the continuum is "internal warfare," when actual combat takes place, and members of the dominant or subordinate groups engage in attacks against entire communities of the "other" rather than against individual members.

The three cases investigated here—Kosovo, Macedonia, and Bulgaria—were selected because they provide variation on an explanatory variable, the relative change of minority status, which starts a chain of sequences of majority-minority interactions during a critical juncture. Choosing these cases also controls for a number of factors. All three had Muslim minorities juxtaposed to Slavic majorities of Christian Orthodox faith. The polities shared a common communist past, a similar lack of developed civil society, and similar economic and educational development during communism. Important structural differences—such as a federal state (Yugoslavia) compared with a unitary state (Bulgaria), the spatial distribution of groups, and Kosovo's impoverished economic status compared to other parts of former Yugoslavia—negated the feasibility of a comparative study using a "most-similar systems design."[37]

In addition to the comparative historical method, I chose the "process-tracing" method. As George and Bennett argue, process-tracing "attempts to identify the intervening causal process—the causal chain and causal mechanism—between an explanatory variable (or variables) and the outcome variable."[38] As a "within-case" rather than "across-case" comparison, process-tracing is appropriate in designs where step-by-step sequential logic is the subject of research. It affords the opportunity not only to answer *why* ethnonational violence reached different degrees of violence, but also *how* and *when* it occurred, and to delineate the specific mechanisms of occurrence.[39] Causal mechanisms are "ultimately unobservable physical, social, or psychological processes through which agents with causal capacities operate, but only in specific contexts or conditions, to transfer energy, information, or matter to other entities."[40]

I gathered data during three field visits to Bulgaria, Macedonia, and Kosovo between 2000 and 2008. I conducted more than 150 individual interviews with majority and minority leaders, government agents, members of international governmental and nongovernmental organizations and think-tanks, identified through snowball sampling or secondary resources. Most interviewees remain anonymous. I also consulted secondary sources in a variety of languages.[41]

An Outline of the Argument and Its Contribution

While drawing from historical institutionalist scholarship, this theoretical framework nevertheless differs from an institutional analysis by making three core claims about continuities and change of conflict processes. First, I emphasize the importance of a critical juncture to explain how majority-minority relationships become set on different conflict paths, and especially how international agents and kin-states co-shape these conflict paths at an early stage. Second, I demonstrate how the established conflict dynamics became self-reinforced and informally institutionalized over relatively long periods of time. Third, I point to the importance of exogenous shocks and mechanisms of gradual change that alter aspects of the established conflict dynamics, but often do not change them completely. What follows elaborates on these core claims, highlights the importance of timing and sequencing, and discusses their contributions to the literature.

Importance of the Critical Juncture

The first set of claims pertains to the importance of the critical juncture to set conflicts on different paths. At the end of the Cold War, transition energized ethnic mobilization by opening previously repressed systems for political competition. Outgoing or emerging elites rallied around ethnonational identities as the primary source of identification, especially in these postcommunist societies where class was not a significant social cleavage.[42] During such a major change in the political "rules of the game," ethnic entrepreneurs were limited not by institutions but "by the counter-claims of other suppliers of identity."[43] In this context, the critical juncture became theoretically important not just as an event, but as a combination of political strategies and choices that emerged during this formative period.

This account demonstrates that the minority status change resulted from competition between elites within the majority, who had different visions on how to manage minority status.[44] Two factions were relevant in the Kosovo and Macedonian cases, and three in the Bulgarian case, as will

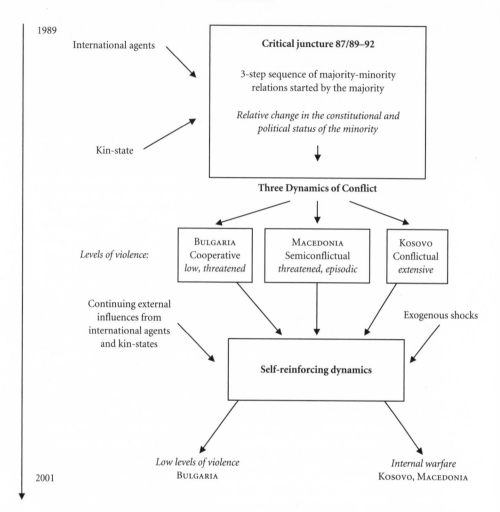

Figure 1. The argument in brief.

be discussed in Chapter 1. The group that won was able to seal its own vision for an altered minority status in specific constitutional provisions. The contingent events during each critical juncture affected which alternative would set the course for majority-minority relations for the longer duration of the transition period. This subargument echoes Gagnon's theme that the long-term struggle between conservatives and reformists in the communist party of Yugoslavia culminated toward the end of the 1980s when these elites were confronted with political pluralism and popular mobilization. Nationalists won that competition.[45] My account demonstrates that choosing the nationalist option was not inevitable, because in Bulgaria the reformists won with their moderate approach on how to deal with the status of the subordinate ethnic Turks.

The sequence of majority-minority relations began with relative decreases or increases in minority status. This is the explanatory variable that started the causal chain leading to the outcome variable, different degrees of ethnonational violence, at the end of the 1990s. In a short time span this first step in the sequence was followed by two others steps: reinforcing government policy to co-opt or coerce the minorities to accept their new status, and a reactive step by the minorities to accept or reject the proposed status. Where lowered minority status was reinforced with coercion (Kosovo) the targets completely rejected the state and opted for secession. Where lowered minority status was reinforced with co-optation (Macedonia), the subordinate group developed a dualistic approach—accepted and rejected the state institutions at different points of time. Where increased minority status was reinforced through co-optation (Bulgaria), the minority accepted the institutions. Through these sequences, three distinct dynamics became established by the end of the critical juncture: conflictual in Kosovo, semiconflictual in Macedonia, and cooperative in Bulgaria.

The *relative* aspect of the minority status change is important rather than the *absolute* scope of minority rights granted by the constitutional changes between 1989 and 1992, as measured by norms of international legislation. The 1991 Bulgarian constitution granted fewer minority rights to the Turkish minority in Bulgaria than the 1991 Macedonian constitution to the Albanians and the 1990 Serbian and 1992 Yugoslavian constitutions to the Kosovo Albanians, but the ethnic Turks experienced a relative upgrade. Bulgaria experienced predominantly nonviolent conflict, unlike Kosovo and Macedonia, where levels of violence surged. The significance of the distinction between relative and absolute rights diminished later slightly, as minority parties and organizations became more aware of their rights in absolute terms via comparative information through human rights channels. Nevertheless, the starting point during the critical juncture was crucial. Starting relatively low on a scale of minority demands foreclosed opportunities for making stronger claims later.

By considering relative status change at the beginning of a causal chain, I present logic close to relative deprivation theories emphasizing that a decrease of minority status, especially autonomy, drove further conflicts.[46] Work by Gurr, Marshall, Walter, and Petersen also attribute explanatory power to the status change relative to a minority's standing in the society, including the majority and other ethnic groups.[47] I emphasize that the *scope* of decrease matters vis-à-vis a minority's established status during communism. A significant status decrease in the form of curtailed autonomy in the Kosovo case triggered higher levels of violence than the slightly diminished constitutional status affecting the Albanians of Macedonia. A relative increase of minority status can lead to nonviolent conflict even if the granted scope of minority rights is minimal compared to others, as in the Bulgarian case.

A new aspect in my work is consideration of how international agents added to the majority-minority relationship when the "rules of the game" were fundamentally redefined. Unlike much scholarship on third-party intervention, focused on strategic interactions and bargaining processes between majorities, minorities, and external agents, my approach emphasizes the importance of the early formation of relationships and the participation of external agents in them. The international community of states and international organizations—not linked to majorities or minorities by identity—promoted democratization and minority rights during the critical juncture. However, this did not mean that they were able to mitigate the evolving conflicts. Rather, it was of crucial importance whether the international community was able or willing to provide three types of guarantees to the domestic elites.

The first related to minority political participation in state institutions. This guarantee was given serious effort in the case of the ethnic Turks in Bulgaria and to a certain degree for the Albanians in Macedonia, but not for the Albanians in Kosovo. The second guarantee was related to the ability to guarantee that domestic or international state sovereignty would not be effectively challenged.[48] This guarantee was enacted in the Bulgarian case, partly in Macedonia, but not in Kosovo. The third guarantee was the international community's own commitment to a long-term presence to achieve conflict resolution. Such a commitment was lacking in Kosovo, unlike Macedonia or Bulgaria. In the latter two cases the type of commitment differed. Security-based institutions such as UN peacekeeping forces and the Organization for Security and Cooperation (OSCE) were early key players in Macedonia; Bulgaria's early agents were democratization-based institutions such as the Council of Europe. While the type of international commitment was certainly influenced by the newly constituted relationship between majorities and minorities, it nevertheless became part of the path-dependent dynamics leading to durable securitization of minority rights in Macedonia and only to some securitization in Bulgaria. Will Kymlicka argues that securitization of minority rights occurs when states view minority claims through the lens of national security and loyalty, rather than fairness and justice.[49]

Kin-states were also involved in providing influences on the majority-minority relationship during the critical juncture. Albania as a kin-state provided mixed stimuli to the Albanians of both Macedonia and Kosovo with its inability to enforce a consistent foreign policy of non-intervention in their conflicts. This lack of consistency occurred not because Albania was openly irredentist, but because it was also undergoing transitions that weakened its institutions and caused it to adopt a two-pronged strategy toward external conflicts. As my previous work (2008) and that of Saideman and Ayres (2008) demonstrate, on the one hand, Albania succumbed to pressure by the international community in the hope of advancing in its own transition, and officially refrained from active support for secessionist and autonomist movements abroad.[50] On the other hand, with limited institutional constraints, some Albanian officials created alliances with discontented leaders across borders based on ideological, clan-based, and particularistic interests. As a result, as early as 1991–1992 some rebels related to the Kosovo struggle had already trained in camps in northern Albania. There was some variation in the subcases of the same kin-state Albania, since clandestine activities were not as clearly pronounced in Macedonia. Nevertheless they existed, and provided stimuli for minority claims for autonomy in 1992. In contrast, there was no transition from communism in Turkey in the early 1990s to further weaken state institutions, so no elites emerged to form alliances and use external movements to legitimize their own existence and claims. Turkey maintained a consistent foreign policy of intervention for strengthening political freedoms of the Turkish minority in Bulgaria, but did not support other claims and so aided early on the rather cooperative majority-minority relations.

Informally Institutionalized Conflict Dynamics and Mechanisms of Conflict Perpetuation

This book advances a second set of theoretical claims pertaining to the establishment and perpetuation of conflict dynamics. Conflictual and cooperative dynamics are considered "vicious" and "virtuous" circles, but often these words are used as metaphors, while concrete aspects of how they operate are buried in historical detail and intuitions about specific cases. Even when systematically examined, these dynamics are generally considered from the perspective of the agents' rational calculations[51] or of density of civic ties that interlock and mutually reinforce each other.[52]

I propose a new way to think about conflict dynamics in the context of transition environments. These are contextually based mixtures of formal and informal arrangements, resembling informal institutions. Helmke and Levitsky define informal institutions as "socially shared rules, usually unwritten, that are created, communicated, and enforced outside officially sanctioned channels."[53] Conflictual and cooperative dynamics are a result of newly adopted formal institutions (constitutional changes), policies to enforce them (co-optation and coercion), and minority responses (acceptance or rejection of the state). After the critical juncture ends, the conflict dynamics consolidate in stable patterns of behavior similar to informal institutions. The contextually bound aspects of these informally institutionalized dynamics establish the bounded rationality that conditions agents' behavior and through which they operate further.

Durable informal arrangements have rarely been considered by conflict analysis, which has focused more on rational interactions among players and change than on continuities. More recently Hassner argued that territorial disputes "become the least desirable institutions in international affairs."[54] Yet durable informal patterns of behavior are empirically important, not only in territorial disputes but in various types of ethnopolitical conflicts. As Helmke and Levitsky noted, in transition environments analysis of formal rules alone will not lead to correct understanding of an outcome. In "the developing and postcommunist world, patterns of clientelism, corruption, and patrimonialism coexist with (and often subvert) new democratic, market, and state institutions."[55] Informal structures often shape the performance of formal institutions, and informal rules trump the formal.[56] Informally institutionalized relationships between majorities, minorities, international agents, and kin-states often provide further incentives to perpetuate the status quo.

Using an example from a formal institutional point of view, the ethnic Turkish minority in Bulgaria had no chance to register as a political party in 1990 or 1991. The political party act and the new 1991 constitution prohibited formation of parties on an ethnic or religious basis. However, facing pressure from the international community, the government strategy of co-optation sought to circumvent the legal rules and register the political formation not as an ethnic party, but as a larger movement. This allowed the de facto ethnic Turkish Movement for Rights and Freedoms (MRF) to enter the political competition and establish itself as an important player in Bulgaria. However, this informal arrangement in which majority-minority relationships were embedded together with their relationship toward the international community is often omitted from the literature. Bulgarian ethnic peace in the 1990s has been attributed to respect for minority rights, tolerance of the Bulgarian nation, lack of state collapse (unlike Yugoslavia), or EU integration.[57]

This book further maintains that conflict dynamics become informally institutionalized through self-reinforcement mechanisms.[58] Four major mechanisms operate across cases and specific majority-minority relationships. "Advantage of political incumbency" refers to a mechanism of positive feedback, where groups able to consolidate early advantage achieve enduring superiority.[59] This mechanism is perpetuated through the policies of the postcommunist elites, who used their early power advantage to create ongoing obstacles to reformist policies in the sphere of minority rights. This mechanism was active soon after the formative period ended and contributed to the initial institutionalization of the conflict dynamics.

"Adaptive expectations" refers to a self-reinforcement mechanism where an initial precedent of what is considered appropriate establishes the basis for future decisions.[60] "Adaptive expectations" sustained many aspects of the conflict dynamics throughout the 1990s and 2000s. In their interactions with one another, majorities, minorities, international agents, and kin-states reinforced the informal rules of appropriateness of behavior established during the critical juncture. These rules were based on the tripartite sequence (minority status increase/decrease, governmental co-optation/coercion, minority acceptance/rejection of the state), and the contextualized ways in which international agents and kin-states related to it. For example, the Albanians of Macedonia adapted to the fact that they could promote legal changes in education and self-government through the parliament and other state institutions, but that they could not advance becoming a constituent people through formal institutions. The international community did not support them on this issue either. In order to pursue their claim to become a constituent people, they adapted their strategy and used a clandestine approach, turning to their kin-state. Albania did not endorse their claim officially either, but unofficially provided multiple opportunities to do so.

"Learning" is the third mechanism of self-perpetuation. Learning effects create amplified reinforcement by assessing the impact of "prior experience with related policies."[61] Usually they are associated with internalization of democratic values. While my account does not reject that democratic values can be learned, it points to negative learning by experience through interactions between majorities and minorities, on the one side, and the international community, on the other, establishing undesirable patterns of behavior. Having experienced repeated policies of the international community neglecting human and minority rights in favor of stability concerns, majorities and minorities learned to employ democratic rhetoric, but in essence to maintain exclusivist nationalist stances that pay off for them. "Learning" started to be active as a mechanism in the 1990s, and has been perpetuated throughout the 2000s.

"Drift" in combination with a "reactive sequence" by the majorities, the fourth mechanism of conflict perpetuation, has been observed primarily throughout the 2000s. Drift designates the divergence from established rules by using the gap between rules and their minimal enforcement.[62] Mahoney and Thelen consider drift a mechanism of gradual change, yet I find that, combined with a reactive sequence by the majorities, it contributes to conflict perpetuation. The lack of serious enforcement of reformed institutional rules prompted the relationship between majorities, minorities, and international agents to consolidate in a realm of "normalization of corruption" to keep political stability intact. This triggered a reaction from majority political groups—usually outside the corrupt political order or having benefited little from it—to raise radical claims and contribute to conflict perpetuation.

These four mechanisms perpetuate a lack of willingness to settle statehood and minority rights questions. Parallel institutions sustained the Kosovo Albanians before 1999; parallel Serbian institutions function in the enclaves in the Kosovo heartland, most notably in the northern part of the divided town of Mitrovica. Also, while the Albanians of Macedonia obtained a large number of constitutional rights with the 2001 Ohrid Framework Agreement, they still voice concern that these changes did not fulfill their expectations. In turn, the Macedonian majority often harbors revisionist tendencies, as the Albanians did before 2001, and has increased its nationalist stances. As a result, the two communities remain seriously divided, despite significant EU and other international presence in the country.[63] In Bulgaria, the increase of linguistic and religious rights is challenged by ultranationalist groups, which in turn are challenged by more radical splinter groups among the Turkish minority.

Sources of Change

A third set of theoretical claims pertains to processes of change. In line with path-dependence logic, this book sees change stemming from two sources: *exogenous shocks* and *incremental change*. Exogenous shocks are sudden events of significant magnitude—such as natural disasters, war and civil unrest in neighboring countries, and volatility in the world economy—that are external to the agents involved, and deviate from periods considered "normal."[64] In my cases, exogenous shocks emerged from a variety of factors external to the established conflict dynamics, and mostly contributed to the escalation of violence. One was the 1995 Dayton Agreement, which ended the war in Bosnia-Herzegovina but did not consider the Kosovo issue. This provided a major external stimulus for radicalism in both Kosovo and its diaspora in Western Europe and the United States. Nevertheless, radicalization of local politics might not have happened had the Dayton Agreement not been followed by the implosion of the Albanian state in 1997, another exogenous shock that enabled Kosovo rebels to obtain previously unavailable weapons. The sequence of two exogenous shocks together in a short time span provided a clear recipe for radicalization. The Albanian diaspora exerted another strong one-time influence on the conflict dynamics in 1998–1999, when it mobilized economic and military resources for the radical Kosovo Liberation Army (KLA). NATO's 1999 intervention ultimately stopped the violence, but became an external shock on the established conflict dynamics in Bulgaria and Macedonia, unleashing causal sequences that contributed to the polarization of majority-minority relations. In Macedonia specifically, this created a fertile ground for Albanian rebels linked to spoiler factions of the KLA in postwar Kosovo to stage a brief uprising in 2001.

Incremental change in the direction of decreasing the level of ethnonational violence took place primarily through what Mahoney and Thelen (2010) consider "displacement" of the existing rules ("replacement" here) and "layering" (introduction of new rules on top of or alongside existing ones).[65] Replacement took place in the aftermath of the 1999 intervention in Kosovo and the 2001 warfare in Macedonia, when new institutions were established. In Kosovo, UNMIK replaced the rule of Serbia with its own institutions and fostered development of local Albanian institutions. In Macedonia, the 2001 Ohrid Framework Agreement fostered changes to the constitution to give more constitutional rights to the Albanians.

Layering is an overarching mechanism that includes *political condition-ality*—attaching specific conditions to distribution of benefits to recipient countries, *socialization* mechanisms with liberal norms, and some *practical attachments* to the new rules, which international agents "layer" on top of or next to existing ones. EU conditionality was relatively effective for the democratic development of Bulgaria as of the mid-1990s and somewhat for Macedonia after 2001. Socialization, usually associated with transfer of lib-eral democratic values and norm promotion, was applied by Western insti-tutions to all three cases, but its effects were often trumped by concerns for security and stability. The mechanism of layering puts conditionality and socialization in perspective. These mechanisms do not necessarily change all political realities, but still contribute to the development of a set of new "rules of the game" to which local agents are introduced and to which they can *develop practical attachments* while the old rules are still in place.

Emphasis on Timing and Sequencing

Research on timing and sequencing of policies is scattered throughout the political science literature.[66] In conflict analysis, Zartman developed the often disputed concept of *ripeness* for conflict resolution, a specific moment of a "hurting stalemate" when belligerents in an ongoing war become ex-hausted and unwilling to continue to fight.[67] The timing of de-escalation of conflicts has concerned a few other scholars.[68] Others point toward the importance of *pace*. Mansfield and Snyder argue that slower-paced transi-tions need to maintain momentum with democratic institution building to keep poorly institutionalized mass politics from degenerating into a nation-alist bidding war.[69] Hassner sees territorial disputes as entrenched rapidly or slowly.[70] While *duration* has been a major concern in studies on civil wars, during the past decade interest in the *onset* of civil wars grew and a number of scholars captured enabling conditions for conflict escalation.[71] Civil war studies treat time-related phenomena as dependent variables to be explained by large-N simultaneous variations. Path-dependence traces processes longitudinally and sees time-related explanatory variables affect-ing an outcome of interest.

Another group of scholars discuss the causal effects of sequencing with regard to democratization and ethnic conflict. Linz and Stepan claim that if at the outset of the transition in a multilevel polity regional elections are held first and all-union elections second, there will be strong incentives for political contestation to focus on anti-state ethnic issues, not on inclusive ones.[72] Snyder argues that the timing of democratization relative to development of the economy and political institutions shapes inclusionary or exclusionary types of nationalism, the latter leading to violence.[73] Mansfield and Snyder argue that to avoid belligerent nationalism in democratizing states, institutions and bureaucratic capacity must be built before popular elections.[74] Bunce claims that if nationalist mobilizations appeared *simultaneously* as the communist regime and a multinational state were disintegrating, rapid transition to democracy took place, as in Estonia, Latvia, Lithuania, Slovenia, Moldova, Russia, and Ukraine. If nationalist demonstrations took place *before* the regime's unraveling, then democratic breakdown or delayed transition to democracy was the outcome, as in Armenia, Croatia, Georgia, Kosovo, Slovakia, and Serbia.[75] Stroschein argues that sequences of events can be "repeated across different trajectories" and can have causal effects over time.[76]

This book adds to this discussion in several ways. For example, it argues that early adoption of a constitution does not guarantee a trouble-free transition. Long-term evolution of conflicts is also affected by whether minorities are given the chance to organize politically before or after major constitutional changes address their status. Kosovo's autonomy was drastically curtailed and the status of the Albanians in Macedonia altered in 1989, *before* the opening of the political system for pluralist competition. Minority claims, full of grievances, were therefore embedded in the programmatic statements of the newly organized minority movements, be they an Albanian party participating in the founding elections in Macedonia in 1990, or the Kosovo parallel structures that boycotted the Serbian electoral process. In contrast, the adoption of the Bulgarian constitution took place *after* ethnic Turks were allowed to organize.

This book also addresses *pace*. The pace of government response to nonterritorial minority demand affects whether the demands broaden in scope and become territorial, leading to escalation of violence in the long run. Minority education is a good example. In Bulgaria pro-Western elites—even if not completely liberal—responded promptly to minority demands; in Macedonia nonreformed postcommunist elites addressed contentious minority educational issues only after Albanians had broadened their appeals and merged them with other demands perceived as territorial. The postcommunist Serbian government halfheartedly addressed Kosovar educational concerns only after they were integrated into the parallel state with its clear agenda pursued initially through nonviolent resistance. The failure of government policy was not simply an effort gone astray, but became one of the factors contributing to minority radicalization and escalation of violence in 1997–1998.

One can argue that concessions to the Turks of Bulgaria, on any matter, functional or territorial, were much less threatening to the Bulgarian majority than concessions to Albanians in Macedonia or Kosovo because of demographic factors such as size and spatial concentration. Let us look at some figures. The last census in Bulgaria (2001) showed 83.6 percent Bulgarians, 9.5 percent Turks, 4.6 percent Roma, and other smaller minorities.[77] The proportions of Bulgarians and Turks were similar to those in 1992. Ethnic Turks have been largely concentrated in the northeastern and southeastern parts of the country. The 2002 census in Macedonia showed 64.18 percent Macedonians, 25.17 percent Albanians, 3.85 percent Turks, 2.66 percent Roma, and 1.78 percent Serbs.[78] There was a slight increase in Albanians in western Macedonia and the capital Skopje. Kosovo has not had a census since 1981, although one is planned. Due to Kosovar nonparticipation in the 1991 Serbia census one cannot be sure of their numbers through the 1990s. Around 95 percent of the almost 1.7 million Albanians in Serbia were concentrated in Kosovo.[79]

While large, concentrated minorities have a better capacity to mobilize than small, dispersed ones, certain configurations of size and distribution of majorities and minorities have been found to be more important for the outcome of violence. Statistical studies show that countries with either very little or a great deal of ethnic diversity are less likely to face high levels of violence.[80] If a country is highly heterogeneous, it is hard to create war alliances and coordinate new wars.[81] The highest risk of large-scale violence is associated with mid-range ethnic diversity, especially when groups are in power parity (close to 50 percent of the entire population), or when a dominant majority confronts a large minority. In such cases societies become polarized, and coordination within groups becomes easier.[82] Toft shows that the highest violence could be expected when an ethnic group is a numerical majority in a territory, not when it is a numerical minority, dispersed, or urban-based.[83]

One should be wary of attributing too much explanatory power to demographic factors. Statistical studies provide evidence for associations between demographic variables and violence, but not for causation. Thus, many studies leave uncertain whether associations are causal or spurious, and whether findings are a priori skewed by the ways datasets are con-structed.[84] Some findings are also challenged by the empirics of this study. Macedonia is the most ethnically diverse of the three societies—Turks, Serbs, Roma, and other minorities live alongside Macedonians and Alba-nians. Nevertheless, violence was higher than in less diverse Bulgaria, and lower than in similarly less diverse Kosovo. Moreover, in all three cases there was ethnic polarization between dyads of Bulgarians-Turks, Macedonians-Albanians, Serbs-Kosovars, but in none of them was there power parity, generally associated with high levels of violence. The effects of concentration patterns fall closer to the predictions. Albanians who mo-bilized for independence were a majority in Kosovo but not Serbia, and Turks who engaged in nonviolent mobilization were dispersed in two re-gions in Bulgaria. Macedonia is an outlier again: Albanians were a majority in western Macedonia, but they did not openly demand independence like the Kosovars.

There is a final argument in this book related to the *timing* of policies. While this study agrees with the general dictum that the long-term horizons of EU and NATO integration created incentives to both minorities and majority-dominated governments to act peacefully,[85] it argues that these horizons were not neutral. Where a country stood in the queue mattered. The EU is now fatigued from its efforts to absorb twelve new Eastern Euro-pean members in 2004–2007. The time horizons are different *before* and *after* 2007 and for the remaining candidates for EU membership. Both Mace-donia and Kosovo are currently geared toward EU integration, but their prospects are uncertain and time horizons have shifted toward the "indefi-nite future." Greece blocks Macedonia's entry because of a long-standing dispute over its constitutionally proclaimed name, Republic of Macedonia. Greece considers this name endangering its historical heritage and state-hood. The veto of Cyprus, Greece, Romania, Slovakia, and Spain on recog-nition of Kosovo's proclaimed independence also affects Kosovo's prospects for EU entry. This fact of political life is well known to local elites. Thus, while often paying lip service to EU integration, they maintain nationalist behaviors inherited from the durable conflict dynamics.

Plan of the Book

This opening chapter presents my theoretical perspective on the formation and perpetuation of informally institutionalized conflict dynamics. Path-dependence accounts do not test hypotheses by ruling out explanations as simultaneous variations. In line with the dictum of comparative historical analysis that eliminates alternative hypotheses systematically at different stages of the process-tracing, the later chapters engage specific clusters of alternative explanations in more depth, and provide far greater empirical detail.

Chapter 1 discusses domestic politics before and during the critical juncture of the end of communism (1987/89–1992). The central discussion addresses patterns of interaction between majorities and minorities during this formative period and the formation of informally institutionalized conflict dynamics. It reviews historical, cultural, and economic explanations and engages security dilemma, credible commitment, and institutionalist explanations. The evolution of the majority-minority relationship during communism established some of the antecedent conditions that informed agents' choices during the critical juncture. Factions among the postcommunist elites advanced different visions of how to address minority status during this formative period. The chapter further examines how minorities were effectively excluded from the constitutional formation process, and how constitutional texts raised or diminished minority status in comparison to the communist period. Sequences of majority-minority interactions resulted in the Turkish minority in Bulgaria choosing to accept existing constitutional rules, while the Albanian minorities in Macedonia and Kosovo did not.

Chapter 2 discusses the self-reinforcement mechanisms that helped consolidate conflict dynamics—*advantage of political incumbency* and *adaptive expectations*—between 1992 and 1999–2001. Nonreformed postcommunist elites, who arrived first on the political scene at the end of communism, bypassed the minorities in policy-making and perpetuated that neglect through much of the 1990s. Minorities and majorities adapted in-group and out-group behavior to the one expected from the out-group. Timely and well-sequenced government responses to nonterritorial minority demands prevented such demands from becoming territorial, as evidenced in the highly contested policy area of minority rights to education in their mother tongue.

Chapter 3 considers how the international community of non-identity-based agents contributed to minority-majority relationship patterns during the critical juncture. It starts with a brief overview of theories on third-party intervention in ethnic conflicts and the importance of early prospects of EU enlargement for the evolution of conflicts. A discussion follows about international legislation on minority rights before the end of communism. Despite their unified approach toward democratization, promotion of minority rights, and de-escalation of conflicts, various politically relevant international organizations and states were successful in mitigating ethnic conflicts only when they managed to provide three credible guarantees to the local agents during the critical juncture: that the minority will politically participate in the state institutions, that the domestic or international sovereignty of the state will not be effectively challenged, and that the international agents will ensure their own long-term presence. Specific policies of the United States, Council of Europe, EU, International Conference on Former Yugoslavia, and OSCE are analyzed in the context of local majority-minority interactions.

Chapter 4 considers international community participation in self-reinforcement processes and change between 1992 and 1999/2001. Contextualized aspects are delineated in the informally institutionalized triangular relationship between the majority, minority, and international agents. International agents' intervention added new elements to the relationship between majority and minority. The contextualized links between agents are rather static and resemble informal institutions that enable and constrain behaviors. Local agents adapted their behavior expecting the international community to take a certain position and vice versa. Through the mechanism of "adaptive expectations" these rules became internalized by the actors involved.

A sequence of exogenous shocks—the 1995 Dayton Agreement followed by the 1997 collapse of Albanian state institutions—provided external stimuli for change toward radicalization of conflict in Kosovo, and NATO's 1999 military intervention in Kosovo polarized majority-minority relationships in Bulgaria and Macedonia. Contagion effects from Kosovo drove the conflict dynamic toward internal warfare in Macedonia in 2001. "Learning" that international stability concerns trump democratization, began in Macedonia and to a certain degree in Bulgaria. The discussion finishes with a presentation of how the evolving process of European integration provided stimuli for keeping the level of conflict low in Bulgaria.

Chapter 5 follows the intervention of identity-based external agents during the 1990s, including the critical juncture, kin-state participation in adaptation processes, and the changes provided by diasporas that affected the level of violence. While kin-states helped design new "rules of the game" between majorities and minorities during the critical juncture, as did the international community, kin-state interventions were less formal and clearly favored minorities. If transition weakened a kin-state's institutions and its elites could not formulate or enforce a coherent foreign policy denying support for irredentism or secessionism abroad, as happened in Albania, then cross-border alliances were formed between the secessionist movement and individual officials in the kin-state, which still contributed to a conflictual dynamic. In contrast, in Turkey, where no transition further weakened state institutions, decisions in the foreign policy realm were enforced with respect to conflicts abroad, and no cross-border alliances were formed with discontented factions of the Turkish minority in Bulgaria.

This chapter also discusses the impact of diasporas on conflict evolution. The timing of Albanian diaspora engagement helped radicalize the conflict when local moderate agents lost popular support because of their inability to achieve the secessionist goal, and when grave violations of human rights took place in the homeland. The Turkish diaspora had little impact on ethnic conflicts in Bulgaria, whose major concern was how to improve its own integration in Turkey.

Chapter 6 elaborates on the changes in conflict dynamics throughout the 2000s. It focuses on the mechanisms of "replacement" of old rules with new ones, and the "layering" of new rules on top of or next to existing ones. Through "replacement" of the established rules of statehood in Kosovo and Macedonia, the status of the Albanians was elevated compared to the 1990s. This contributed significantly to conflict mitigation. Some informal practices in which the majorities, minorities, and international agents were earlier locked were also altered. These concerned international agents' aversion to redefinition of the state and its minimal long-term commitments to conflict resolution and reform, especially in Kosovo and somewhat in Macedonia. Peaceful change occurred also through "layering" of new rules, which were brought in primarily by EU "conditionality" and less by "socialization," but also through practical attachments to new rules while the old rules were still in place.

Chapter 7 addresses the perpetuation of informally institutionalized conflict dynamics throughout the 2000s. Despite multiple international efforts to foster peace and democratization, low to mid-levels of violence continued to exist. The path-dependence approach is discussed along with a review of theories on durability of conflicts from the peace-building and power-sharing literatures. I argue that the earlier discussed changes addressed some aspects of the established conflict dynamics, but did not overturn them in their entirety. Entrenched aspects continued to operate under the surface and to undermine many endeavors. These influences include large-scale corruption, anchored in co-optation and coercion mechanisms of the previous period, which sustains stability but becomes a focal point for nationalist backlash often scapegoating minorities; the lessons from the international community that democratization is secondary to stability and security, encouraging local agents to use reforms to advance nationalist and particularistic agendas; and the clandestine and often disputed influences of kin-states and diasporas. This chapter also offers a discussion of the causal mechanisms that help sustain these conflict dynamics—primarily the effects of "learning" and "drift" in combination with a "reactive sequence" by the majorities.

The conclusion summarizes the utility of a path-dependence approach to conflict analysis, interweaving the three sets of theoretical claims with summarized contextual evidence. It emphasizes the need to analyze the impact of international agents during a critical juncture, often not considered, and elaborates on the seven causal mechanisms of conflict perpetuation and change. A short section discusses the falsifiability and predictive power of this approach, and indicates how researchers might use this approach in the future. The core theoretical claims are subjected to "plausibility probes" for Romania, Bosnia-Herzegovina, and Georgia, and assessed for other conflicts and the transitions in the Middle East during the "Arab Spring" of 2011–2012. The last section points to relevance beyond conflict and postconflict analysis, and for emerging research on long-term legacies in postcommunist societies, EU enlargement toward the Western Balkans, and informal institutions in comparative politics.

A final note voices a call to policy-makers to better understand informally institutionalized conflict dynamics in specific countries in order to target motivational structures of conflict agents, which usually go unnoticed if efforts solely concentrate on formal institutions or agents' rational interests.

Chapter 1

The Majority-Minority Relationship and the Formation of Informally Institutionalized Conflict Dynamics

After defeating communism as an ideology, the liberal creed in the early 1990s appeared to triumph globally. Capturing the Zeitgeist of the time, *institutionalist* accounts offered democratic solutions for mitigating ethnic conflicts by such strategies as respect for minority rights in line with international norms, power-sharing agreements, fair electoral rules and proportional representation, ethnic balance in military and police structures, decentralization, autonomy, and federalization.[1] Principles of respect for diversity, division of power, and competition for power were placed at the core of these solutions.[2]

By the late 1990s some scholars became aware that such institutional solutions might be productive for a more mature polity, but not for a transitional setting. Policies leading to the devolution of power to minority regions—such as decentralization, autonomy, and federalization—were problematized because of their controversial consequences. Sometimes they relieved minority discontent by facilitating representation, but at other times they aided secessionist struggles associated with more violence.[3] The devolution of power to highly concentrated minorities whose loyalties lay outside the state became especially questionable.[4] Aware of such challenges, in the 2000s scholarly voices sang in harmony that transitional regimes were among the most violence prone, especially in polities with highly divided societies.[5]

Transitions can significantly weaken state institutions, which in turn may provide fertile ground for nationalist activities by dominant or subordinate peoples. In Eastern Europe, the transition from communism exerted simultaneous pressures to replace one-party dictatorship with multiparty democracy and a command economy with a market economy, and often to build the state anew, which weakened state institutions.[6] When institutions are weak, using nationalism for instrumentalist purposes faces few constraints. Elites may mobilize the population by evoking ethnicity as "the only politically relevant identity."[7] Public discussion may become skewed by state or monopolistic control of the media, and average citizens may back groups or parties based on incomplete information.[8] Governance suffers: state ability to provide political goods diminishes and corruption rises.[9] Under such conditions, groups that can provide services gain popularity, often invoking a nationalist doctrine while building patron-client relationships.

This chapter focuses on the early transition period (1987/89–1992), when structures and institutions established during communism were fundamentally transformed. Under conditions of high volatility and uncertainty, the choices of majority and minority elites mattered to how the new "rules of the game" of interethnic relations would be defined, and how the ground would be laid for the establishment of conflictual, semiconflictual, and cooperative dynamics.

In this chapter I explore three interrelated questions:

- How did antecedent conditions in Bulgaria, Macedonia, and Serbia influence the options available to majorities and minorities in decision-making during the critical juncture at the end of communism?
- Did the opening of the political system for political competition in each case precede or follow changes in minority status and how did it affect majority-minority relations?
- How did the changes in constitutional status of the Turks of Bulgaria, the Albanians of Macedonia, and the Albanians of Kosovo (Kosovars) create new rules of the game in a transitional environment?

I argue that three factors were highly important for establishing the rules for ethnonational actions during the critical juncture and subsequent development of cooperative (Bulgaria), semiconflictual (Macedonia), and conflictual (Kosovo) dynamics. First, in the volatile late 1980s, communist elites within the dominant ethnic group competed with rival ideas on minority status. When a faction won, it sealed its vision about the minority's status in the newly adopted constitution. I show the importance of the *relative* change in minority rights compared to the communist period, rather than the *absolute* scope of minority rights judged against global or regional normative standards. The relative scope of *decreases* in status also mattered. Constitutional changes created a political threshold that propelled causal chains of majority-minority interactions leading to different degrees of violence over time.

The second factor was a decision-making sequence that aimed at reinforcing the earlier majority decision. Majority elites decided to make minorities comply with these decisions through co-optation or coercion. The third factor, depending on the combinations of majority choices about the type of minority status change (increase/decrease) and strategy for compliance (co-optation/coercion), was the development by the minorities of a reactive sequence of counter-strategies. These took the form of rejection of the state, using state institutions to advance their goals, or both. In Bulgaria, policy liberalization in the form of slightly increased minority constitutional status and co-optation worked to reduce ethnic Turks' demands and minimize subsequent levels of violence. In Macedonia, policy restriction in the form of moderately decreased status combined with co-optation prompted a two-pronged strategy among the Albanians. The level of violence remained low when they pursued their goals through formal state channels, but increased when they engaged in informal clandestine activities. In Kosovo, drastically decreased status, in combination with coercion, triggered the establishment of clandestine minority institutions that clashed regularly with government forces.

Historical, cultural, and economic explanations relevant to the end of communism are also important, and others are woven in later in the chapter, at different stages of process-tracing. Interactions between majorities and minorities during communism created some of the antecedent conditions informing agents' choices during the formative period. Majority-minority relations during the critical juncture have theoretical implications. Competition among communist elites within the dominant ethnic group, timing of minority status change in relation to opening for political liberalization, and the nature of constitutional changes played important roles. Specific reinforcing and reactive sequences helped establish conflictual, semiconflictual, or cooperative dynamics that became ultimately responsible for degrees of ethnonational violence over time. Figure 2 presents this evolution through the 1990s.

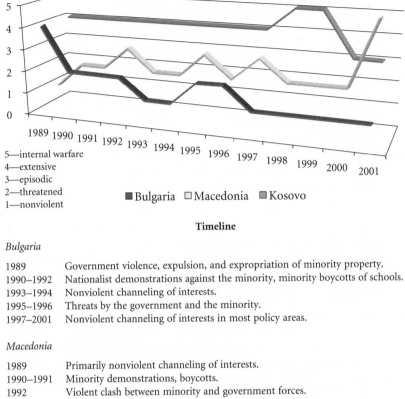

5—internal warfare
4—extensive
3—episodic
2—threatened
1—nonviolent

■ Bulgaria □ Macedonia ■ Kosovo

Timeline

Bulgaria

1989	Government violence, expulsion, and expropriation of minority property.
1990–1992	Nationalist demonstrations against the minority, minority boycotts of schools.
1993–1994	Nonviolent channeling of interests.
1995–1996	Threats by the government and the minority.
1997–2001	Nonviolent channeling of interests in most policy areas.

Macedonia

1989	Primarily nonviolent channeling of interests.
1990–1991	Minority demonstrations, boycotts.
1992	Violent clash between minority and government forces.
1993	Tensions around the discovery of a paramililtary conspiracy.
1993–1994	Minority and governmental threats, constitutional boycott by the minority.
1994	Tensions around elections and in the parliament.
1995	Minority demonstrations crushed by the police.
1996	Tensions around the functioning of a semi-parallel university.
1997	Minority demonstrations crushed and leaders imprisoned.
1998	Tensions around the semi-parallel university.
1999–2000	Tensions related to the Kosovo crisis.
2001	Guerrilla clashes with government forces.

Kosovo

1989	Several violent demonstrations crushed by the police.
1990–1997	Government violence against minority members on a daily basis.
1998–1999	All out clashes between guerrillas and governmental forces involving civilians on a large-scale basis.

Figure 2. Evolution of ethnonational violence, 1989–2001.

Alternative Explanations: Historical,
Cultural, and Economic Factors

Accounts claiming that *ancient hatreds* and *historical enmities* explain violence in the Balkans only perpetuate nineteenth-century ethnic stereotypes
and have been rightfully refuted by sound scholarship.[10] My account adds
more fuel to this fire: Serbs and Albanians, Macedonians and Albanians,
and Bulgarians and Turks harbor many historical enmities, but they did
not have the same levels of violence during the transition period. This holds
true even if we consider "sleeping beauty" theories: that ancient hatreds
dormant during the highly repressive communist regime were awakened
with the end of communism.[11]

Aware of this easy dismissal of hatred-based accounts, a few related
theorists took a step farther. Petersen argued that "hatreds" do not need to
be ancient to lead to violence. Emotions such as fear, hatred, resentment,
and rage are part of the human condition. When triggered by landmark
external events and structural change, they provide the mechanisms driving
groups to violent ethnic mobilization.[12] Kalyvas found that personal ven-
geance is a recurrent motive for participation in civil wars.[13] Kaufman argued that elites cannot mobilize ethnic groups for violence unless deeply
ingrained, socially acceptable "myth-symbolic complexes" justify hostility
against the other group.[14] These accounts go into the mechanisms leading
to ethnonational violence, but they do not explain the situations I am ex-
amining. I do not reject the importance of emotion following constitutional
changes, or of deeply ingrained myths, but I stress that specific sequences
of majority-minority relations laid the foundations for conflict dynamics.

Language is considered a primary culprit for the emergence of contentious politics in the Eastern European context, where nationalism developed along linguistic lines. "Linguistic territoriality" designates the
expectation that "the national space would be mapped by a national language" officially standardized.[15] Language conflicts have their own dynamic
compared with other forms of cultural conflict, civilizational or religious.[16]
Classic works on ethnic conflict observe that language differences can easily
leave politics and become a threat to peace. More recent large-*N* studies
demonstrate exactly the opposite: greater linguistic differences do not lead
to higher levels of violence, but tend to relocate the conflict from the military to the political realm.[17] Language conflict offers only a partial explanation in my cases. Certainly, linguistic tensions exist between minorities that

do not speak Slavic languages (Albanians, Turks) and Slavic-speaking majorities (Serbs, Macedonians, Bulgarians). But these differences did not become politically salient unless they were attached to autonomist or territorial demands. Evidence (see below) supports David Laitin's argument that language grievances are not associated with group violence per se, but can turn dangerous in conjunction with other discriminatory factors such as kin-state support of minority grievances or a rural basis for contention.[18]

Civilizational and *religious* differences are not explanatory either. I side with the critics of the much debated "clash of civilizations" thesis of Samuel Huntington, who argued that after the end of the Cold War the world's conflict lines would be drawn along cleavages of civilization and religion, most notably Christianity and Islam.[19] Although the three minorities of this research are Muslim and the majorities Christian Orthodox, the outcomes in levels of violence vary. Also, while religion was certainly politicized, it did not play a strong nation-building role and was subsumed under other nationalist claims. For example, Albanians have often emphasized that the "religion of Albanians is their Albanianism,"[20] not that Albanians are Muslims.

Economic arguments are also inconclusive. Some scholars find that the determinants for insurgency are primarily based on economic greed, because rebels calculate more expected gains from war than from productive economic activity.[21] Some argue that political grievances and opportunities for violence rather than greed and economic motivations pose better explanations.[22] According to others, economically strong regions do initiate secessionism.[23] Most scholars assert that higher levels of violence are more likely in economically weak states that are also institutionally weak and have difficulty controlling rebellious activity within their borders. There is an association between high poverty and onset of civil war, since poverty reduces the opportunity costs of forgoing productive economic activity for participating in armed rebellion.[24]

Empirical evidence suggests that economic decline and rise in unemployment toward the end of communism are important factors, but they did not always lead to large-scale violence. Kosovo was the poorest region of former Yugoslavia, Macedonia was not far ahead, and both were less affluent than Slovenia, Croatia, or Serbia. In 1988, "the per-capita output in Kosovo was 28 percent of average output in Yugoslavia."[25] As underdeveloped regions, Kosovo and Macedonia received central funding as compensation.[26] During communism the minorities in all three countries were less affluent than the majorities, but the gap was not striking in a command-style system that leveled general economic welfare. The deepening economic crisis at the end of communism did lead to a massive expulsion campaign of ethnic Turks in Bulgaria in 1989 (and an extensive level of violence). But the poverty of the Albanians in Kosovo and Macedonia did not lead immediately to the onset of civil war: intrastate violence took place in Kosovo only in 1989/99 and in Macedonia only in 2001.

Majority-Minority Relations During Communism

Before the collapse of communism, Turks in Bulgaria and Albanians in Macedonia and Kosovo lived in states with different understandings of ethnonational diversity. Bulgaria was a unitary state, highly centralized in decision-making, and ethnocentric in constitutional wording. The 1971 constitution, which remained in force until 1991, did not mention "minorities" or "nationalities," but referred to "citizens of non-Bulgarian origin."[27] The Socialist Federal Republic of Yugoslavia (SFRY), where the Albanians of Kosovo and Macedonia lived, was a federal state in which even smaller nationalities had some constitutional recognition.[28] The 1974 constitution had a three-tier system: "nations," which had republics within the SFRY; "nationalities," with kin-states outside the SFRY; and "ethnic groups," which had neither but were ethnically distinct from nations and nationalities. Albanians were defined as a nationality.

The Albanians of Kosovo and Macedonia were positioned differently under SFRY basic law. Starting in 1974, Kosovo had the status "constituent part of the Socialist Republic of Serbia,"[29] almost a full federal entity short of the right to territorial self-determination.[30] The status of the Albanians of Kosovo was in many ways comparable to that of titular nations of the six other republics, who had representation in the main federal bodies and self-management powers in economic decision-making and even some areas of foreign policy.[31] The Albanians in the Socialist Republic of Macedonia (SRM) were never explicitly defined as a "constituent" element of the republic; their rights were given individually to "persons belonging to a nationality." The 1974 constitution stipulated that Macedonia was "a state of the Macedonian people and the Albanian and Turkish nationalities."[32] Albanians were guaranteed the same rights as Macedonians, including proportional representation in the legislature; they could fly their national flags, and their languages and alphabets were considered of equal status to that of the Macedonians.[33] However, unlike the Albanians of Kosovo, the Albanians of Macedonia did not enjoy territorial autonomy.

Before the 1980s the initiative to alter majority-minority relationships in the SFRY came primarily from the Albanian minorities. After the 1966 removal of Alexander Rankovic as vice-president of Yugoslavia—a pro-Serbian proponent of restrictive policies toward Albanians—strong sentiments surfaced as early as 1968 to promote Kosovo from "province" to "republic" and its status from "nationality" to "nation." Albanians claimed that their total number in the federation far exceeded that of some "nations" who had republics, such as the Slovenes and Macedonians. The 1974 constitution made their status an autonomous province, but not a federal republic. As demands for federalization remained unmet, Albanian nationalist sentiment grew. As Hugh Poulton notes, in 1981 the situation in Kosovo exploded when student demonstrations in Prishtina led to clashes with the police: around 2,000 people were arrested and several killed. Underground groups formed; in 1984 they were accused of arms smuggling, caused nine explosions in Prishtina, and incited an armed uprising. The more republican status seemed unachievable, the more these organizations tended toward violence.[34]

The Albanians of Macedonia backed the demands of their Kosovo brethren, and also challenged the Macedonian republic's status quo. A demonstration in the Albanian-dominated town of Tetovo in 1981 called for Albanian-inhabited areas of Macedonia to join Kosovo as the seventh republic. Underground groups were established, with government sources claiming that in 1983 at least three illegal Albanian "nationalist and irredentist groups" existed in Macedonia.[35] But events only echoed those in Kosovo, and never developed a serious dynamic of their own.

In contrast, in Bulgaria during communism the government and not the Turkish minority initiated minority status changes. The 1947 constitution explicitly favored rights of "national minorities" to develop their cultures.[36] However, a policy to assimilate predominantly Muslim populations—such as Turks and Bulgarian Muslims (Pomaks)—started in the late 1960s, and culminated in the principles underlying the 1971 constitution, which did not mention "minorities." The government inaugurated a brutal assimilation campaign in the mid-1980s that further strengthened its grip. In a "revivalist process" in 1984–1985 the government used tanks and police violence to change the names and religion of the ethnic Turks.

In March 1985, head of state Todor Zhivkov openly declared that "there are no more Turks in Bulgaria." Thereafter some Turks mobilized in a clandestine resistance movement that was unable to grow because its leaders were betrayed and imprisoned.[37]

Despite differences in who initiated status changes, the three minorities did have a common experience: the increasing nationalism of the dominant groups starting in the late 1970s. In Bulgaria, the attempt at total cultural assimilation of the Turks was marked by continued repression. It remains unclear whether the bomb attacks of 1984 and 1986 at the Varna and Plovdiv airport and railway stations respectively were carried out by underground resistance activists or by state security apparatus trying to legitimize the assimilation campaign.[38] But state-sponsored Bulgarian nationalism was clearly in a very aggressive phase. The regime enacted brutal measures: that Turkish not be spoken in public or private, that the practice of Islam be kept to a minimum, that mosques be destroyed or turned into museums, and that medical files with Turkish names be eradicated.[39] Bulgarian nationalism reached its all-time peak in spring 1989, with the expulsion of 300,000–370,000 Turks over a few weeks.[40]

In socialist Yugoslavia, the rise of Serbian nationalism was driven both by a response to growing Albanian nationalism and by the ruling elites. Repressive measures continued in the aftermath of the 1981 Kosovo riots, when 7,000 Albanians—mostly young male students or teachers—were arrested and imprisoned on charges of participating in nationalist activities.[41] Repression of individual political prisoners existed as well. The 1980 death of president Josip Broz Tito—who stood for organization of Yugoslavia on the principle of "Brotherhood and Unity" and equality of nations, and who had generally successfully arbitrated differences among Yugoslav nations, nationalities, and ethnic groups—opened the door for elite change and resurfacing of nationalist sentiments within the republics, which Tito had kept in check.[42] In Serbia specifically, nationalism flourished because the Serbian people had strong emotional attachments to Kosovo as a symbol of their history and statehood, most notably with regard to the traumatic 1389 Battle of Kosovo.[43] During the Balkan wars (1912–1913), for example, thousands of young Serbs volunteered to join the Serbian army to avenge the battle.[44] By 1983 Serbs in Kosovo were openly complaining that they were subject to Albanian attacks and began leaving the province. In 1986 a petition by 2,000 Serbs denounced Albanian nationalism.[45] More important, the same year a nationalist memorandum of the Serbian Academy of

Sciences became public. It claimed that Serbs in Kosovo were subject to "genocide" by the Albanians, and called for policies to reverse the growing Albanian birth rate and downgrade Kosovo's autonomous status.[46] Due to the Albanians' high birth rate, and the migration of Serbs and Albanians within Yugoslavia, the proportion of Albanians in Kosovo increased from 67 percent (1961) to 74 percent (1971).[47] The campaign culminated with the statement of Slobodan Milosevic, deputy president of the Serbian Communist Party, in a speech at Kosovo Polje on April 24, 1987 in response to demonstrating Kosovo Serbs battered by local police: "No one will ever dare beat you again!"[48]

Albanian nationalism was considered a potential threat in Macedonia as well.[49] The authorities believed an irredentist Albanian republic would mean that Macedonia would lose its western territory, inhabited predominantly by Albanians. Moreover, territorial changes would inevitably fuel irredentist ambitions in Macedonia by neighboring Bulgaria, Serbia, and Greece. Thus, Albanian nationalism was considered a threat not only to territorial borders, but also to the existence of the fragile nation.[50] These fears resulted in increasingly harsh sentencing of Albanians in Macedonia compared to Albanians in Kosovo, who had the institutions of autonomy to protect them.[51]

Special measures followed in policy areas where the authorities could easily have an impact, such as cultural politics. In July 1981 syllabi for teaching Albanian were revised and the hours of study of Macedonian increased.[52] In 1983 a number of Albanian teachers were expelled from the League of Communists for not using Macedonian as required.[53] In 1986, the authorities started creating obstacles to registration of Albanian names at birth; in 1988 they initiated restrictions on property ownership, religious teaching, and secondary education.[54] Demonstrations in the Albanian-inhabited towns of Koumanovo and Gostivar against these interventions on educational freedom resulted in arrests, trials, and imprisonment.[55]

When the regimes started to liberalize in 1987–1990, the three minorities and respective majorities had very different expectations of their place in the polities where they resided. The Albanians of Kosovo, who for many years had struggled for a federal republic within Yugoslavia, expected to exercise self-determination by full republican status. They were opposed in equal intensity by Serbian nationalist aspirations for expansion and domination, not simply in Kosovo. The Albanians of Macedonia expected more rights as well, while the government was concerned about how to promote the Macedonian nation. Finally, the Turks of Bulgaria, whose nationality was officially eradicated during communism, had no serious ambitions to collective rights, but wanted emancipation as an ethnic group through recognition of their identity.

Critical Junctures

In path-dependent processes one expects periods of relative openness for change and periods of relative stability.[56] Critical junctures are such short periods, when chance matters, volatility is high, and political agents have substantially heightened freedom to affect the outcome of interest.[57] Their choices may be highly contingent or deeply embedded in antecedent conditions.[58] According to Paul Pierson, such formative periods—viewed ex ante—can produce more than one possible outcome. "Once a particular path gets established, however, self-reinforcement processes are prone to consolidation or institutionalization."[59]

The critical juncture of the end of communism gave significant discretion to the majority and minority elites in these three cases to decide how to approach the minority status change. Their decisions, of course, were informed by antecedent conditions, such as federal versus unitary statehood, constitutional understandings of ethnonational diversity, recent experiences of violence, growing nationalism among dominant nations, and mutually exclusive expectations of future status. But unlike structural accounts that see such conditions as decisively shaping the use of violence, I see them as informing the choices of elites responding to contingent events in the rapidly changing political environment.

It is important to identify a meaningful starting point and time span for a critical juncture. One could argue that the degrees of ethnonational violence in Kosovo, Macedonia, and Bulgaria were actually determined in previous historical periods. For instance, in 1912–1913, when the Albanian state was formed, the London Conference of Ambassadors left half the Albanian population in present-day Kosovo, Macedonia, Montenegro, and the Preshevo Valley in Serbia. The Albanian national narrative often evokes this as the traumatic historical moment in need of redress. The trauma was exacerbated by Serbian attempts to reoccupy Kosovo and expel its population, most notably during the Balkan wars and after World War I.[60] In royal Yugoslavia (1918–1941), Kosovo Albanians were culturally dominated by Serbs, and Kosovo was further colonized. Hopes to join Albania after World

War II did not materialize, and the first two decades of communism were again grim for Kosovo Albanians.[61]

Incomplete national revolutions become a cause for more secessionism, irredentism, and violence, as Philip Roeder argues.[62] While an incomplete revolution thesis is certainly plausible, it does not account for why different national demands emerged among Kosovars and Albanians of Macedonia in the 1990s. The Kosovars aspired to be a full republican unit in federal Yugoslavia, and in 1991 opted for independence; the Albanians of Macedonia remained less ambitious.

A closer point in time could be the violent 1981 Kosovo riots. One could argue that by this stage Serbian elites recognized that Kosovo Albanians were determined not to settle for the autonomy in the 1974 constitution, but to pursue greater territorial power. In addition, the 1981 violence may have permanently changed the trajectory of ethnic conflict in the area. When violence is used, one can expect more violence in the future.[63] The Macedonian elites may have feared that the Kosovo problems could spill over into Macedonia because the Albanians of Kosovo and Macedonia had extended family, educational, and business linkages during communism.[64] These events created insecurity among the ruling elites. This line of reasoning is supported by restrictive measures against Albanians in Kosovo and Macedonia in the late 1980s; it does not explain why minority status was decreased drastically in Kosovo and more moderately in Macedonia when political systems started to liberalize.

Historical memories also shape the experiences of ethnic groups in Bulgaria. Unlike the Serbs, who primarily rallied around the 1389 Battle of Kosovo, Bulgarians rendered the entire period of the Ottoman conquest between the late fourteenth and late nineteenth centuries inherently traumatic. They did not have a strong focal point for political mobilization. For ethnic Turks of Bulgaria, the most salient traumatic moment was the 1989 expulsion campaign, gaining in significance after a century of oscillation between state policies of domination and minimal recognition of rights. I have noted elsewhere that a violent campaign to change Bulgarian Muslims' names took place during the Balkan Wars, and another serious assimilation attempt was launched in the late 1930s. The 1947 constitution guaranteed freedom of conscience, and experimented with some nontraditional attempts to constitutionally recognize the existence of ethnic minorities, but Quranic schools were banned by 1947 and assimilation attempts against Islam intensified in the late 1950s.[65]

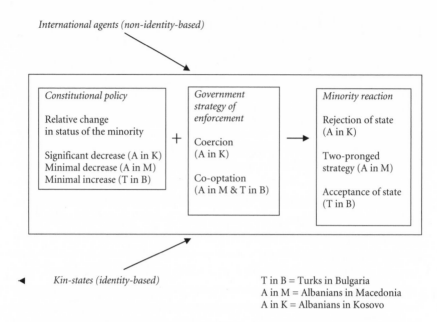

T in B = Turks in Bulgaria
A in M = Albanians in Macedonia
A in K = Albanians in Kosovo

Figure 3. The critical juncture, 1987/89–1992.

I do not deny the importance of historical legacies. They are crucial in shaping the memories of both majorities and minorities and creating narratives serving as focal points for political mobilization. Yet political elites are the ones who use these narratives, and they do so most successfully under conditions of rapid transformation. Under communism, *nomenclatura* circles shaped ways of approaching ethnic diversity; there were no alternative elites. In the 1980s new elites within communist parties started to emerge. I maintain that the decisions of majority and minority elites during the critical juncture from about 1987–1989 to 1992 explain how the new rules of the ethnonational game would be formed, which in turn laid foundations for different conflict dynamics in the three cases examined here.

Competition Between Communist and Reformist Elites

Unlike Hungary, Poland, and the still united Czechoslovakia in the early 1990s, whose dissidents and human rights activists have been called "opposition from below" by democratization scholars, the cases in this study had weak or no strictly liberal democratic opposition. In Bulgaria, there was some ad hoc dissident activity among ecological rights groups after pollution disasters on the Danube River, and among Bulgarian nationals outraged by actions against the Turkish minority. Even less dissident activity existed in Macedonia and Serbia, although, compared to other communist-bloc countries, SFRY allowed freedom of travel, economic self-management, and creative expression through the arts. In all three cases the forces that drove the transitions and changes of minority status were based in communist circles, not outside them.

Two major groups within the Serbian Communist Party (SCP) struggled on the Kosovo Albanian issue, and the nationalists won over a reformist faction with a pro-Yugoslav agenda. An incident related to the death of a Serbian soldier at the hands of an Albanian conscript in 1987 created a highly divisive response in the party.[66] Reformists—such as Dragisha Pavlovic, a high-ranking SCP member and ally of Serbian president Ivan Stambolic, who had a Yugoslavist agenda—were critical of the media inflating an anti-Albanian campaign based on the incident. Milosevic, however, used it to further inflame hatreds through the media, garner support from the military, and rally around "meetings of truth" attended by around three million people as of July 1987. The campaign culminated in a crisis in the Serbian Central Committee in September that year.[67] This was the crucial moment. At that meeting the pro-Yugoslav faction was purged for being "soft" on the Albanian issue, since it was prepared to negotiate a solution with the Albanian leadership.[68] Milosevic and his nationalist communists stood for speedy reversal of Kosovo's status. The defeat of Pavlovic and the inability of Stambolic to protect him led to the latter's resignation a few days later, and paved the way for Milosevic to consolidate his power. Any other choice for tackling the status of the Kosovar Albanians became impossible because he did not want alternatives.[69] He restructured Kosovo's government and institutions in 1989, excluding Albanians and putting the local Serb minority in charge.

Two major alternatives also existed among the outgoing communist elites in Macedonia, where a group advocating liberalization reforms overpowered an alternative advocating Yugoslavia's status quo, and turned nationalist in the process. As Zhidas Daskalovski points out, in the early 1980s Macedonian communist elites favored the status quo or a more decentralized but communist Yugoslavia. But by the mid-1980s a faction emerged around the personalities of Petar Goshev, Branko Crvenkovski, Vasil Tupurkovski, and Georgi Spasov, who advocated liberalization of the communist system.[70] According to Iso Rusi, a few members of the Macedonian Central Committee, still vested in Yugoslavia's federal institutions, opposed redefining Macedonia as a state of the Macedonian people. But this group turned weaker than the one advocating liberalization, which tried to operate independently from the committee and obtained executive power. When Goshev became president of the committee, antagonisms between the two groups further increased.[71]

Attempting to find its place in a liberalizing polity, and following trends toward decentralization of power among Yugoslav republics such as Slovenia, Croatia, and Serbia, the reformist group began transforming itself from communist to nationalist.[72] It was on the motion of the government that the Assembly (Sobranie) in April 1989 passed amendments to the SRM constitution that redefined SRM as the "nation-state of the Macedonian people" instead of the previous "state of the Macedonian people and Albanian and Turkish nationalities."[73] According to Rusi, the role of the opposition groups that emerged at the time, most notably the highly nationalist Internal Macedonian Revolutionary Organization Democratic Party of Macedonian National Unity (VMRO-DMPNE), was marginal because the groups were politically inexperienced. Thus, changes in minority status should be seen as a product of interactions between old communist politicians.[74] In contrast to Serbia, where divisions between Milosevic and pro-Yugoslav factions were pronounced, in Macedonia the groups had internal disputes about how a liberalized Macedonia should be defined, but by 1989 their opinions started converging on how to treat the Albanians. The old communist elites were close to Milosevic and mirrored some of his anti-Albanian policies, while the new elites stood for the primacy of the Macedonian nation.

In Bulgaria, reformists among the communists were more preoccupied with regime change from within their own ranks, and staging a "palace coup" against dictator Todor Zhivkov in November 1989, than with any other political concern. Nevertheless, as Mihail Ivanov, former political adviser to President Zhelyu Zhelev, observes, at the time three major groups within the communist party advanced visions on how to handle the brewing ethnic tensions. The circle around Alexander Lilov was the driving force for reform. Lilov, a Politburo member, was open for reformist policies because he wanted to rescue the socialist system. His group viewed restoring the use of Islamic names by the Turks as a necessary step to reduce the country's isolation resulting from its coercive assimilationist and expulsion campaigns. The second group concentrated around the last communist prime minister, Georgi Atanasov, who supported ousting Zhivkov from power but who advanced his political career by playing a leading role in the "Revivalist Process" of the mid-1980s and the name-changing campaign. This conservative circle was strongly against allowing the Turks to use Muslim names. It organized nationalist rallies against the December 29, 1989, decision of a Communist Party Plenum, prepared by Lilov, which officially stated that Muslim names taken by force should be restored. A third group was connected to Andrey Lukanov, a leading party member. He was considered reformist but was interested in empowering high-ranking communist functionaries to retain power through transforming their political leverage into economic strength. According to Ivanov, Lukanov's circle was behind the creation of two political formations—Bulgarian nationalists and the MRF—to pit them against each other. This tactic narrowed the space for development of democratic political formations, but made the MRF a political subject expected to play an important role in the economic transformation of power. Ethnic relations were thus manipulated to serve the economic interests of the Lukanov circle.[75]

Why did the more democratic alternative prevail in the volatile months of 1990–1991 despite Bulgarian nationalist demonstrations and attempts to restore the previous coercive situation?[76] Ivanov argues that in early January 1990 minister of defense Dobri Dzhurov, who controlled the army, stood openly with the Lilov circle, as did president of the State Council Petar Mladenov. Unlike in Yugoslavia, where Milosevic wanted to preserve political power, in Bulgaria the economically oriented group around Lukanov deliberately ceded certain political appointments to gain time and autonomy to transform the economic system and retain power in its own ranks. Lukanov also sought the collaboration of circles in the democratic opposition for street demonstrations that would pressure party conservatives to accept the desired changes. In late December 1989, round-the-clock "spontaneous" rallies by Bulgarian Muslims took place in front of the parliament. In fact, they were connected to personalities within the Union of Democratic Forces, in support of the supposed reformers to make the crucial decision about Muslim names. These street demonstrations should be viewed not as an independent political alternative but as part of the agenda of the reformist circles in the communist party.[77] In early January 1990 the National Assembly passed a declaration on the national question.[78] Zhivkov was arrested January 18 and charged, inter alia, with inciting ethnic hatreds, but not with further responsibility for the assimilation campaign.[79]

Timing of Minority Status Change

The significance of the *timing* of changes in minority status regarding open-ing political systems to pluralist competition has not been addressed in scholarship so far. There has been some discussion of republican elections conducted before federation-wide elections in multinational federal states, such as Yugoslavia, and their role in legitimizing nationalist parties and triggering state disintegration.[80] I focus on an earlier period when majorities took steps to alter the minority's status, even *before* the opening elections. In Kosovo and Macedonia minority status decreased in 1989, *before* minori-ties were allowed to organize in parties and participate in the founding elections in 1990. In Bulgaria, the Turks' status was minimally improved through reinstating Islamic names, *before* the system became open for polit-ical competition.

The timing of these changes in status structured incentives for minority political participation in different ways. In Kosovo and Macedonia, effective alternation of leadership within the Albanian minority was restricted to those with communist affiliations who had previously held power in federal Yugoslavia. Hence, the minority leaders who created alternative formations and took leadership positions shortly thereafter—intellectual Dr. Ibrahim Rugova and his Democratic League of Kosovo (LDK) and English teacher Nevzat Halili and his Party for Democratic Prosperity (PDP) in Macedo-nia—made the change of minority status a focal point for mobilization. The LDK never participated in Serbia-wide elections, considering Kosovo separate from Serbia. In Macedonia, still part of Yugoslavia, the PDP did participate in the November–December 1990 general elections, together with another small Albanian coalition party, the People's Democratic Party (NDP). The PDP took 25 seats in the 120-seat parliament, becoming the third major political formation after the Macedonian nationalist VMRO-DPMNE and the Social Democratic Union of Macedonia (SDSM).[81] Never-theless, the Albanian parties did not turn cooperative. They refused to par-ticipate in Macedonia's independence referendum in September 1991, disagreeing with the terms on which the new state emerged.[82]

In Bulgaria, the gradual and painful changes toward more minority rights during the formative period reassured the ethnic Turkish MRF that it would be given consideration in politics. The postcommunist government bowed to international pressure, and registered the MRF as a party.[83] Ethnic Turks were the core MRF voters, but the group was officially registered as a political movement with a broad base, not as an ethnic party.[84] This move allowed the MRF to participate in the June 1990 elections for a Grand National Assembly, garner 6 percent of the vote, and become the third-largest formation after the Bulgarian Socialist Party, the former communists' heir, and the Union of Democratic Forces (UDF), the democratic opposition.[85]

Security Dilemmas and Credible Commitments

The emphasis here on the timing of minority status change is theoretically different from arguments based on "security dilemmas" and "credible commitments," which also address majority-minority interactions under high levels of uncertainty. In the "security dilemma" logic, when central authority weakens, minorities fear for their place in the changing polity because of expectations of malign intent by the majority or lack of credible information. Thus, minorities are prone to strike first.[86] Detailed disaggregation of these cases demonstrates that this was not the case. Malign intent by the majority was clear in Serbia, where Milosevic's nationalism was on the rise, and in Macedonia where educational and cultural restrictions were taking place. Ambiguity and fear about intent reigned in the Bulgarian case after the 1989 expulsion campaign. There was indeed ad hoc activism among democratically minded Bulgarians and ethnic Turks to reject the disgraceful communist policies politically, but it was not clear what the real power holders—the party leaders who staged the coup—were interested in.

"Commitment problems" are a variation of the "security dilemma" argument. Minorities initiate preventive war strategies not as a result of miscalculations about the majority's intent, but because the majority did not make a credible commitment not to exploit minorities.[87] From a "credible commitment" perspective, changing the status of minorities before allowing for political organization and founding elections could significantly affect minority perceptions about the majority's credible commitment not to abuse minorities during and after the transition. But a credible commitment argument would exclude the effects of other signals the three minorities received. This section demonstrates how all three minorities were pro forma included, but de facto excluded from the constitution-making process. They received the same message across the board: they would not have an active voice in the new political system.

Despite malign and ambiguous intent, the minorities did not strike first during the early liberalization of the communist polities. It was the dominant majorities who initiated a redefinition of the rules of the game. In this early period, minorities were mostly reactive. The Albanian leadership was ready to negotiate with the reformists in 1987. Immediately following the abolition of autonomy, Kosovo Albanians reacted with three waves of violent demonstrations and strikes—in spring and autumn 1989 and January 1990—and were met by violent response by Serbian authorities ("extensive" level of violence). Nevertheless, the Albanian leadership realized their power asymmetries with the regime's coercive apparatus and in spring 1990 changed to nonviolent means.[88] In Macedonia, before the reduction of the minority's status in 1989, Albanians mainly voiced their discontent over educational and identity policies. Indeed, following events in Kosovo in February 1990 some 2,000 Albanians demanded Albanian-dominated areas be granted independence. They chanted in favor of "Greater Albania," but the police dispersed them quickly and the situation remained relatively calm ("threatened" level of violence), while developments in Kosovo took center stage.[89] In Bulgaria, before the reinstating of Islamic names and religion, Ahmet Dogan, leader of the ethnic Turks, "spoke the same language" with key leaders of the opposition and "played a constructive role in the process."[90] Yet the level of violence remained "threatened" in 1990 due to Bulgarian nationalist demonstrations against the restoration of Islamic names.

The fact that minorities were reactive does not mean they were not considered a threat by the majorities. They were, especially in Macedonia, where Albanian nationalism coupled with the looming disintegration of Yugoslavia had the potential to destroy the fragile Macedonian statehood. Security dilemmas therefore only partly explain the interactions between these majorities and minorities. They do not fully account for why majorities initiated minority status changes, which were at the core of the development of causal chains that led to different degrees of violence in the long run.

Hence, while security dilemmas and credible commitment problems could be at play, they are of secondary importance. Also, they presuppose an intergroup dynamic, whereas my account demonstrates that the minority status change resulted from competition between elites within the majority, with different visions on how to manage minority status during this volatile period. In addition, my argument about timing of the minority status change relates to restructuring of minorities' incentives; it does not predict that minorities will inaugurate preventive war.

Constitutional Changes

There is an ongoing discussion on constitutional formation during the transition process.[91] Constitutional constraints make it more difficult for an assembly and society to change its mind on important questions, binding the behavior of groups and individuals beyond their temporary passions.[92] In the transitions of Central Europe, constitutions were passed prior to communists' departure from power (Hungary) or after the collapse of the regime (Czechoslovakia), or no comprehensive constitutional reform took place at this stage (Poland).[93] While these differences in timing of constitutional adoption did not disturb the prospects for democratic consolidation in Central Europe in the long run, I argue that in the three cases of this research early acceptance of a new constitution did not guarantee a trouble-free transition. Incorporating international minority rights standards into the new constitution did not guarantee interethnic peace. And even if included pro forma in the constitutional formation process, minorities might or might not accept the new constitution.

The *relative* change of constitutional minority status early in the transition rather than the *absolute* scope of rights in the new constitution established the basis for minority acceptance or rejection of the new rules of the game. This proposition is close to "relative deprivation" and "ethnic status reversal" theories, which maintain that a lowering of ethnic status is of particular importance for escalation of violence.[94] There can be a constitutional dimension to what are primarily emotion-based arguments: a relative change of status may be a key political and psychological threshold that triggers resentment.[95] This threshold may not be obvious for all the minorities in my cases because the Albanians of Macedonia explicitly referred to constitutional problems, while the other two made fewer such claims. Nevertheless, the relative change of status created new political rules early in the transition process.

Brand-new constitutions were passed at the outset of the transition—1990–1992—but they did not become guarantees for interethnic peace in the long run. In Bulgaria, they paved the way for peaceful minority-majority interactions, but in Macedonia and Serbia they created focal points for ethnonationalist mobilization.[96] They produced a drastic loss of status for the Kosovo Albanians, a more moderate loss for the Albanians of Macedonia, and a slight increase for the Turks of Bulgaria. The reduced status of Kosovo was sealed with the 1990 Serbian and 1992 Yugoslavian façade constitutions: Kosovo and Vojvodina were given autonomy as provinces, with assemblies and executive bodies, but were placed under the administrative domination of the Belgrade-controlled government. The previously amended status of the Albanians of Macedonia was clearly reinforced in the 1991 Constitutional Preamble, which defined the state as belonging to the Macedonian people alongside other nationalities. The Albanians' status was reduced to that of the Vlach and Roma, who had earlier lacked nationality rights.[97] The Macedonian Orthodox Church was explicitly mentioned, while other religious denominations were broadly defined as "communities and groups."[98] Finally, the increase in status of the Turks in Bulgaria was minimal. In an attempt to redress the assimilationist past, the constitution prohibited "forcible assimilation" on the same footing as torture and cruel and degrading treatment.[99] It also allowed expression of religious and ethnic (rather than "national") identities.[100]

Formal inclusion of minorities in the constitution-building process did not guarantee interethnic peace. All three minorities were represented in the parliaments when the constitutional changes took place, but they did not have a real say in the key provisions. The postcommunist elites from the majorities dominated the process, seeking political space for themselves in the new transition environment. In Bulgaria, the ethnic Turkish MRF participated in some working groups of the Grand National Assembly, but could not overrule the consensus among Bulgarian majority elites—both socialist and newly developed democrats—to prohibit political parties on an ethnic or religious basis.[101] The Macedonian-dominated parliament gave similarly limited access to Albanian parties, already demanding to be a "constituent element" of the state.[102] The 1991 Constitution of the Republic of Macedonia rubber-stamped earlier amendments and redefined Macedonia as a "nation-state of the Macedonian people." Similarly, Kosovo Albanians were present in the Kosovo Assembly in 1989 when the Serbian regime pressured them with tanks and armored vehicles to pass constitutional amendments that effectively gutted Kosovo's autonomy.[103]

Internationally defined standards on minority rights embedded in the new constitutions certainly did not guarantee interethnic peace. Paradoxically, the Bulgarian constitution was the most restrictive of the three. It granted significantly fewer rights to the Turks compared to the Albanians in Macedonia and even in Kosovo. Yet the level of violence in Bulgaria remained low. The most limiting clause was the prohibition of formation of parties on an ethnic, racial, or religious basis.[104] Like the Macedonian constitution, it defined the Eastern Orthodox religion as the traditional denomination, mentioning "religious institutions and communities" in general terms.[105] Although neither allowed for territorial devolution of power, the Bulgarian constitution explicitly prohibited it.[106] It referred vaguely to "citizens whose mother-tongue is not Bulgarian" and gave them the right to "study and use their own language alongside the compulsory study of Bulgarian."[107] The Macedonian constitution allowed more explicitly for education in a minority's mother tongue in primary and secondary school alongside compulsory study of Macedonian.[108] The Serbian constitution granted similar rights.[109] Finally, the Macedonian and Serbian constitutions called for parallel use of minority languages in self-government; the Bulgarian did not.[110]

Self-Reinforcing and Reactive Sequences

Passing these constitutions created a *self-reinforcing sequence* on the side of the majorities and a *reactive sequence* on the side of the minorities. Self-reinforcement occurred via strategies of *coercion* and *co-optation* to pressure the minorities to acquiesce in their new status. Depending on how the relative minority status change was combined with these majority strategies, the minorities diverged in accepting, rejecting, or adopting a two-pronged strategy toward the state. As a result, toward the end of the critical juncture in 1992, opening the political system to include more rights for the Turks in Bulgaria, combined with a co-optation strategy, managed to create a rather cooperative dynamic between majority and minority and keep the level of violence low in the long run ("threatened" or "nonviolent"). In Macedonia a combination of status decline and co-optation gave rise to a two-pronged minority strategy and a dynamic marred by occasional but fairly predictable conflicts. Higher levels of violence ("episodic," "internal warfare") took place in the long run when the Albanians chose the route of clandestine opposition. Lower levels ("threatened") occurred when they occasionally or systematically used threats, but still pursued their claims through institutional channels. A combination of drastically decreased constitutional status and coercion of the Albanians of Kosovo led to large-scale clandestine minority mobilization, a conflictual dynamic on a daily basis,

Table 1. Comparative Framework

Relative change in the status of the minority	Government strategy Co-optation	Government strategy Coercion
Increase	minority responds institutionally	n/a
Decrease	institutional + *clandestine* response by minority	minority responds with *clandestine* activities

and "extensive" levels of violence through the 1990s and "internal warfare" in 1998–1999.

The self-reinforcing sequence is driven by the mechanisms of coercion and co-optation. In O'Leary's account, coercion is a form of "control," where the controllers organize the dominant and disorganize the subordinate, and the dominant community controls the coercive apparatus of the state: its security and policing systems.[111] Coercion refers to exclusive use of negative sanctions to manage ethnic difference, aiming at direct rule over the subordinate.

Coercion as a strategy was employed quickly after Kosovo's autonomy was curtailed in the "emergency measures," a package of 36 laws adopted between 1990 and 1992. The laws were aimed at completely revamping Serbia's domestic legislation and stripping Kosovo Albanians of a large number of rights. A July 1989 law stipulated that citizens of non-Serb origin could sell or obtain property only with the consent of the Ministry of Finance. This law was used as a low-profile tool for "ethnic expulsion" and discrimination in minority-populated areas.[112] Although declared unconstitutional in 1990, it was still enforced.[113] Another law, passed in 1990, placed all public administration and publicly funded enterprises under direct control of Serbian authorities in Belgrade. The former legal system was dissolved; some low-level courts and offices were suspended and judicial institutions handed over to the Serbs.[114] Other legal acts mirrored the constitution to a certain extent. For example, while the 1990 constitution guaranteed the right to a civil service alternative to military conscription, the 1993 Act on the Armed Forces of Yugoslavia restricted this right to recruits called up after November 1993 and was usually applied to non-Albanians.[115]

Co-optation refers to sustained use of manipulative strategies by superordinate elites to neutralize an independent course of action by the subordinates, in a form of indirect rule. The mechanism is often subsumed under the general category "control" strategies to manage ethnic difference, but it involves some degree of consensual politics on the side of the co-opted, exercised in clear power asymmetries. Co-optation takes various forms, for example, patron-client relationships and backdoor deals. Institutional co-optation operates as the co-opted participate in "significant socialization processes leading to conformity with and commitment to a particular set of political norms."[116] Such a practice is aimed at adapting the co-opted to a pre-set world, rather than aspiring to alter it.[117] In Bulgaria and Macedonia co-optation forms merit attention because they facilitated relatively peaceful relations with the minorities without substantially advancing overall respect for minority rights. These cases are not an isolated phenomenon; co-optation and its by-product corruption have become widespread government strategies to deal with opposition in the developing world.

How did co-optation work in our cases? Recent evidence from the opening of communist archives in Bulgaria and long-term knowledge among various individuals in decision-making positions show that MRF leader Ahmet Dogan participated in the underground movement against the assimilation campaign but was also an agent of the former communist security services.[118] In context, this does not mean that he did not have an agenda to promote minority rights during the transition, which he certainly did, but that entanglement with powerful structures and economic interests of the previous regime created serious obstacles to his interethnic interests. From the vantage point of the late 2000s, some of the biggest complaints in Bulgarian society are related to MRF corruption in its entanglements with economic groups that emerged early in the transition process from those same security services.

The path-dependent argument developed here makes sense of all this, if we look back at the formative period when majority elites and the MRF found a modus vivendi to coexist in superficial conflict against an underlying mutual understanding, trumping possibilities for more radical minority agendas. In line with this co-optation dynamic, the Bulgarian majority elites were satisfied that the 1990 Political Party Act and later 1991 constitution prohibited formation of parties on an ethnic basis. This meant that only the MRF could be registered, precluding development of other ethnic parties in the future. The MRF would thus monopolize the ethnic politics of the minority in Bulgaria.[119] Not only formal, visible legal rules but also informal, invisible rules were very much behind the celebrated success of the Bulgarian ethnic peace. Authoritarian corporatism and co-optation, rather than

respect for minority rights or lack of nationalism among Bulgarian elites or
society, were what mattered.

Why, if such evidence does not exist for Macedonia, do I still claim
that during the early transition the Macedonian elites adopted a form of
co-optation toward the Albanians? The most powerful counterargument
would stem from those who consider ethnic politics in Macedonia a
power-sharing arrangement as classically defined by Arend Lijphart.
Lijphart gives five important criteria for a consociational power-sharing
arrangement: (1) grand coalition and inclusion of all minority groups in
government; (2) proportional representation of all major groups in parliament and public administration; (3) inclusion of major ethnic groups in
government; (4) veto rights; and (5) segmental or high degree of autonomy.[120] If we follow parliamentary and government politics only, Macedonian dynamics certainly resemble power sharing even in these early years.
Unlike in Bulgaria, where the MRF remained an important but solely parliamentary player until 2001, Macedonia had a coalition government between Macedonian and Albanian elites as early as 1992.[121] This was not
least because fear of not being able to maintain the territorial integrity of
Macedonia in a volatile political environment prompted the Macedonian
elites to create coalitions with the Albanians to induce their relative loyalty
to the Macedonian state. Indeed, O'Leary points out, in a consociational
arrangement the leaders of communities should fear the consequences of
ethnic war and consider themselves incapable of governing on their own
without sustained challenges.[122]

However, the resemblance to a classic consociational arrangement in
Macedonia drifts away if we analyze further elements. Proportionality
rules were applied to the public sector at least on paper, and Albanians
were given some representation in the judiciary, civil service, and self-
government. Nevertheless, unlike classic consociational democracies, such
as Switzerland and the Netherlands (where proportionality is the principle
of the electoral system as well), in Macedonia—as other parts of former
Yugoslavia—a clear-cut majoritarian electoral formula was adopted for
the founding elections of 1990. The choice of formula indicates the determination of the dominant group to avoid concessions to minorities.[123] As
a result the parliamentary power of majority parties increased, impeding
representation of smaller groups and producing "ethnic fiefdoms" in areas
where ethnic groups were territorially concentrated, such as predominantly Albanian-inhabited western Macedonia.[124] Even with this arrangement, Albanians did not enjoy a high degree of autonomy. This important

consociational element was achieved to a certain degree with the 2001 Ohrid Framework Agreement: Albanians gained the right to autonomy in education and language and territorial decentralization, albeit not territorial autonomy. As in Bulgaria, in the early 1990s the Macedonian elites put little effort into accommodating the Albanian minority beyond the political level. Crucial measures that would have filtered minority rights from elites to the mass level—such as linguistic rights in parliamentary and judicial affairs, self-government, and education—were often ignored or dealt with in minimal ways.

Co-optation as a mechanism worked much less successfully in Macedonia than in Bulgaria, precisely because a decreased minority status preceded it and prompted the Albanians to take more radical measures to alter their status, as discussed shortly. Nevertheless, both majority and minority parties benefitted from the arrangement. For the Macedonian elites, an Albanian party in government gave some leeway to maintain territorial integrity and to trumpet adherence to minority rights and democratic reform internationally. Albanian PDP party leaders, many of them former communist *nomenklatura* functionaries promoted by President Kiro Gligorov, enjoyed their new access to power.[125]

The mechanisms of coercion and co-optation were the second step in a sequence of majority-minority interactions over the duration of the critical junctures following the reconfiguration of minority status. Unlike their *self-reinforcing* property, the next step in the sequence was *reactive* on the side of the minorities. Although initially they all challenged the new constitutional rules, their reactions were qualitatively different.

The Kosovo Albanians went through a twofold reformulation of their national goal in that critical juncture. Much of the literature ignores the fact that the Kosovar response to curtailed autonomy was not to seek independence immediately but to go through an intermediary stage. In June 1990 a number of ethnic Albanian deputies tried to block adoption of the new Serbian constitution using their powers in the Kosovo provincial assembly. As a countermeasure, they proposed a scheme to make Kosovo an independent republic within the SFRY.[126] Since this did not happen, and the Kosovo Assembly was abolished in September 1990, Albanians secretly adopted the so-called "Kacanik" constitution. It is worth noting that this clandestine constitution reiterated that Kosovo was a republic within the Yugoslav framework. It also stated that all laws emanating from Serbia or Yugoslavia would be valid only insofar as they were in harmony with the new constitution.[127]

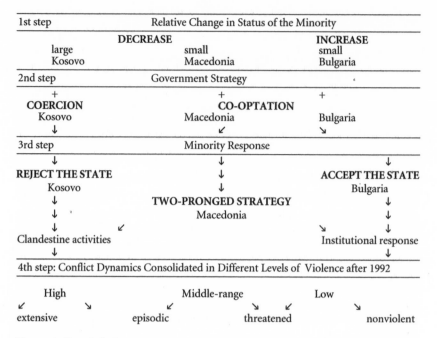

Figure 4. Causal chains.

Only when socialist Yugoslavia collapsed did the Kosovars further reformulate their national goal. On September 22, 1991, as soon as the other SFRY republics declared independence, a shadow parliament of the "Republic of Kosovo" approved a Resolution on Independence and Sovereignty of Kosovo.[128] This decision was voted through a clandestine all-Kosovo Albanian referendum, conducted on September 26–30. The secret vote of the population was reflected in the October "amendment" of the Kacanik constitution, which at that point already envisaged Kosovo as independent. The national goal remained constant until 2008.

The collapse of Yugoslavia is an important factor whose impact on the reformulation of the Kosovar goal of independence has been mentioned in multiple accounts but theoretically underplayed. Rational choice and bargaining models are not easily able to address this matter, because it was neither embedded in the rules of the game nor signaled from an external lobby agent. It was a one-time seismic event, part of the larger political environment. While running counterfactuals is considered a risky enterprise in social science because of the difficulty of projecting alternative futures, in light of Lebow's recent scholarship on "close call counterfactuals" or "minimal rewrites of history close to the event whose outcome we wish to mutate,"[129] it is worth asking whether the Kosovars would have proclaimed independence had Yugoslavia stayed territorially intact.[130]

Proclamation of Kosovo independence in such a scenario seems unlikely for two reasons. First, Kosovo Albanian leaders had cherished republican status since the 1960s and, second, voices for independence were rather marginal. Albanian elites realized the Albanians' situation in Yugoslavia was not likely to generate the same sympathy for self-determination as Slovenia and Croatia. Without outright collapse of Yugoslavia it seems likely therefore that Kosovo Albanians would have stuck to their strategy of seeking republican status.

In Macedonia the Albanian minority adopted a two-pronged strategy toward the state—accepting the state by participating in government or officially boycotting policies while rejecting it by clandestine activities. Although a few clandestine elements outside the PDP had more radical views, the PDP's own stances fluctuated between the two strategies. Initially, challenges to the constitution sought official channels and the level of violence remained low. In 1991 the PDP boycotted the new constitution at the last stages of its drafting, withdrew Albanians from participation in Macedonia's independence referendum and the 1991 census, and refrained from voting on the new constitution.[131] PDP president Muhamed Halili threatened that if pressure for change did not bring results his party would consider the constitution invalid and call for full autonomy.[132] In 1992 the Albanians rejected the new citizenship law requiring fifteen years of residence for naturalization,[133] which stripped many Albanians who worked outside the country from citizenship rights. In early January 1992 the PDP switched gears and called a clandestine referendum in which 74 percent of Albanians voted for the territorial autonomy of western Macedonia.[134] Some radical Albanian nationalists then proclaimed the "Republic of Illirida." They went much farther than the official PDP, claiming that this republic should unify all Albanians of the former Yugoslavia. In the meantime, however, they stood for federalization.[135] International pressure discouraged the PDP from seeking autonomy or constitutional change, and violent police response was averted.[136]

In contrast to the other cases, the constitutional changes in Bulgaria and the co-optation strategy created incentives for the ethnic Turkish MRF to adopt a benign response. This response was in line with its general philosophy as formulated by Dogan, that the movement had to remodel itself quickly from a "destructive force" directed against the totalitarian regime during communism to a "constructive political subject" with "tolerant behavior" that had "obligatorily to be legitimized by the society." In line with these ideas "the movement had to change the strategy to encapsulate the ethnos in order to maintain its survival" for a new strategy intent on opening up, building an ethnoreligious identity, and integrating it into civil society.[137] Thus, even when challenging the constitution the MRF continued to focus on integrating the Turks into Bulgarian society. Many MRF and a number of UDF deputies walked out of parliament in 1991 during the final vote for the 1991 constitution, heavily dominated by the former communist Bulgarian Socialist Party (BSP).[138] It is worth noting, however, that MRF's reasoning was the general BSP domination of the constitution, not the particular provision prohibiting formation of parties on an ethnic or religious basis.[139] This attitude paved the way for only marginal challenges of the constitution later in the transition, as discussed next.

Did the minorities' organizational power before the end of communism affect whether they would accept or reject the state? Certainly, prior organizational strength mattered, as all institutional explanations maintain. In a changing political environment, the *institutional strength* of minorities living in ethnofederations under communism—such as the former Yugoslavia and the Soviet Union—gave them resources for nationalist projects challenging the central state.[140] Ethnic groups that had had autonomy during communism were likely to seek secession in its aftermath; groups with little or no institutional status in the hierarchy of the multinational state usually sought higher status or greater autonomy.[141] After decades of policies aimed at their obliteration in the state, the Turks of Bulgaria were one of the weakest minorities in the postcommunist region. By contrast the Albanians—especially those of Kosovo who earlier had autonomy—had considerable organizational strength.

Organizational strength of the minorities was indeed important for mobilization. I see such accounts as complementary to this analysis, but inconclusive. It is not clear why minority demands translated into wide temporal variation of violence during the transition period. Kosovo's secession did not lead immediately to "internal warfare," but had an "extensive" phase first. The demands of the Albanians of Macedonia did not vary significantly after the transition started, but the levels of violence did, from "threatened" to "episodic" to "internal warfare."

Institutional accounts are also insensitive to the effects of contingency and intermediate steps that channel prior organizational strength through one type of response and not another. Why did the Kosovo Albanians first try to establish a federal republic and only then opt for independence? Because preceding minority choices were important to inform their decisions, because they were looking for allies against Serbs within Yugoslavia, and because they had not fully anticipated Yugoslavia's collapse. Why did the Albanians of Macedonia entertain ideas about independence, but quickly drop them from their menu? Because majority co-optation worked well during the formative period.

One can argue that the Albanian PDP engaged in a voluntary coalition with the Macedonian SDSM. Such an interpretation would be formally true, but it would not reveal the nature of the relationship. The PDP had a fundamental disagreement with the Macedonian parties about the redefined Macedonian state, a stance voiced much less vigorously over time. Significant socialization with a particular vision of the state and pressures leading to official conformity underlay the co-optation mechanism, including the promotion of PDF functionaries by President Gligorov alongside the old communist networks.

Conclusions

Competing alternatives on how to deal with the national question, stemming from factions within the postcommunist elites, were important to how minority status was changed during the critical juncture at the end of communism (1987/89–1992). In light of this finding, at various stages of the process-tracing I argued against or qualified the pertinence of historical, cultural, economic, security dilemma, credible commitment, democratization, constitution-building, and minorities' institutional strength theories.

The *timing* of the opening of the communist system for political pluralism and the relative change of minority status mattered decisively, creating incentives for the minority elites to incorporate more moderate or radical demands into their early electoral behavior. Where minority status was decreased before the opening of the system (Macedonia, Kosovo), minorities integrated their grievances about their diminished status into electoral politics. The Albanians of Kosovo boycotted elections in Serbia; the Albanians of Macedonia integrated their grievance at not being a constituent element of the state in their participation in the first founding elections. In Bulgaria, the Turks' minority status was slightly raised before the opening of the communist system, which made the ethnic Turks open to moderate options in Bulgarian politics.

During the critical juncture three elements led to a cooperative (Bulgaria), semiconflictual (Macedonia), and conflictual dynamics (Kosovo) of majority-minority relations. The first was the *relative change of minority status* compared to the communist period. The second was a *self-reinforcing sequence*, when the governments used strategies of coercion (Kosovo) or co-optation backed by coercion (Bulgaria, Macedonia) to make minorities comply with their new status. The third was a *reactive sequence*, when the minorities chose to accept (Bulgaria), reject (Kosovo), or develop a two-pronged strategy (Macedonia) toward the new regime. Higher levels of violence were expected where minorities rejected the state and engaged in clandestine activities.

The dynamics established during this formative period were based on formal rules—such as constitutions and crucial policies—but also informally on key elements of how majorities and minorities chose to interact with each other early on. How these informal rules became self-perpetuating after the critical juncture ended in 1992 will be discussed in the next chapter.

Chapter 2

Self-Reinforcing Processes
in the Majority-Minority Relationship

Various strands of scholarship have identified the existence of "vicious and virtuous circles" and also that they become self-reinforcing. Repetitive moves in rational choice game theory and density of civic ties offer two of the clearest ways to think about such dynamics.[1] These accounts, however, have not sufficiently considered the role contextual and temporal characteristics play shaping these dynamics. The most advanced qualitative analysis has come from scholars working on intractable conflicts. Ruane and Todd observed that the conflict in Northern Ireland is so durable because of a "system of relationships with different levels which interlock and mutually reinforce each other."[2] A 2006–2007 debate in the journal *International Security* shows how much path-dependent thinking underlies Ron Hassner's approach to the intractability of the Israeli-Palestinian conflict, although his core explanations are informed by constructivism, not historical institutionalism. For him, the "entrenchment path that territorial disputes follow constitutes a process of institutionalization in which disputes take a life and a causal power of their own."[3]

These insights are well taken, but they speak only to conflicts considered intractable, not to a wider range of cases where conflict dynamics are informally institutionalized regardless of the level of violence they consolidate or whether they are primarily territorial. Seemingly peacefully resolved conflicts, such as that between the Turkish minority and Bulgarian majority in the 1990s, can obey a conflict dynamic rooted in contingencies during a formative period of time, and their implications can be observed in later time periods. Hassner's account of the Israeli-Palestinian conflict mentions a variety of entrenchment mechanisms—material, functional, and symbolic—but they relate to territory, not to the durable behavioral aspects of agents in a relationship. Chapter 1 elaborated on important elements—such as antecedent conditions, critical junctures, contingency, and agent behaviors—for establishing these varied conflict dynamics. This chapter demonstrates two self-reinforcement mechanisms that perpetuate them over time. It explores two interrelated questions:

What mechanisms of self-reinforcement of conflict dynamics can be identified in Kosovo, Macedonia, and Bulgaria during the 1990s?

How did the timing and sequencing of government responses to minority demands create incentives that explain subsequent levels of violence?

I argue that after the critical juncture ended in 1992, the new rules of the ethnonational game—established through the tripartite sequence of decrease/increase of minority status, co-optation/coercion of minorities, and minority acceptance/rejection of the state—were consolidated into a range of conflict dynamics, and were reinforced by two causal mechanisms: *advantage of political incumbency* and *adaptive expectations*. Through much of the 1990s this mixture of arrangements, formal (constitutions) and informal (government strategies to ensure minority compliance and minority acceptance/rejection of the state), became informally institutionalized and dictated the rules of the ethnonational game. Timely, well-sequenced government responses to nonterritorial minority demands became important for preventing social and political disputes from turning into territorial ones, and avoiding higher levels of ethnonational violence. The chapter gives a theoretical introduction of the two self-reinforcement mechanisms and their contextual operation in the three cases. It concludes with a discussion of the timing and sequencing of government responses to nonterritorial minority demands.

Self-Reinforcement Mechanisms and Processes

The conflict dynamics established at the end of the critical juncture were cooperative (Bulgaria), semiconflictual (Macedonia), and conflictual (Kosovo), and they spread across a spectrum of low, medium, and high levels of violence. How were these dynamics perpetuated during the 1990s? This section demonstrates the mechanisms and processes of self-reinforcement

of these conflict dynamics, reproduced in political realms of vital importance to minority politics—minority self-government, education, and cultural politics. Self-reinforcement mechanisms often take place through
positive feedback processes—called "increasing returns" in economics—
that give incentives to agents to continue on the path established during
the critical junctures.[4] Previously available alternatives—such as reversal of
minority rights in Bulgaria or return to cooperation with the Serbian state
for the Kosovars—became less attractive and unlikely to succeed even if
briefly considered later in the transition.

One mechanism that has self-reinforcement properties is the *advantage
of political incumbency*. This refers to positive feedback by which groups
able to consolidate early incumbency achieve enduring superiority.[5] As
Kathleen Thelen rightly points out, the positive feedback argument has two
aspects: if one has power one can always use it to induce more power, and
if one arrives first, one will have power, as Pierson argues.[6] While we need
to distinguish these two dynamics, in my cases the outgoing communists
both had power and arrived first on the political scene during the transitions. They shaped the fate of later arrivals in the political game in all three
cases, including minority elites and democratic forces. Where this authority
of power was broken briefly, in the Bulgarian case with the short-lived UDF
government in 1991, minor changes began to alter the dynamic, but slowly
and ineffectively.

Another important mechanism is *adaptive expectations*, which create
positive feedback by "logic of appropriateness."[7] An initial precedent for
what is considered appropriate forms a basis for future decisions on what
is a legitimate action.[8] Constructivist scholarship in international relations
usually associates the "logic of appropriateness" with acquiring and following democratic norms.[9] I argue that such logic can pertain to informal
institutionalization of other types of behaviors as well. In our cases, during
the critical juncture majorities and minorities learned what to expect from
each other—what was considered "appropriate" behavior. Appropriateness
requires an adjustment of ethnic in-group behavior in view of how the out-
group is expected to perform. A minority locked in a relationship with a
majority that co-opts it but has slightly raised its status (Bulgaria), has
different expectations for in-group and out-group behavior from a minority locked with a majority that co-opts it but has downgraded its status
(Macedonia). A majority locked in a relationship with a minority that has
a two-pronged strategy toward the state (Macedonia) has different adaptive

expectations from one locked with a minority that rejects (Kosovo) or accepts it (Bulgaria). The dynamic element of this mechanism stems not from particular fluid bargaining positions of majority and minority, as accounts informed by rational choice would argue, but from the bounded rationality of adaptation to the tripartite sequence established during the critical juncture, which locked the majority-minority relationship into a specific conflict dynamic.

I now turn to contextual evidence for the self-reinforcing capacities of advantage of political incumbency and adaptive expectations.

Advantage of Political Incumbency

First-mover advantage was exercised by postcommunist elites in all three cases, since they had spent considerable time in power throughout the 1990s. Their advantage was reflected in defining the terms of political debate, adopting restrictive minority-related policies and laws, penetrating lower levels of government by overt or covert centralization, and delaying adoption of policies for effective change. Former communists ruled in Bulgaria in 1989–1991 and 1994–1997 and in Macedonia in 1991–1998. They were continuously represented in the Serbian government until Milosevic was ousted in 2000. Rotation of power between new and old elites did take place in Bulgaria with the short UDF rule, and for an entire mandate in 1997–2001, but the rest of the time nonreformed former communists ruled either directly in the cabinet or behind the scenes. A technocratic government (1993–1994) was officially nominated on the mandate of the ethnic Turkish MRF, but former communists were the main force behind it. In Macedonia, rotation between old and new elites from the majority and minority occurred only in 1998. Until then the postcommunist SDSM ruled in coalitions with the Albanian PDP, and the nationalist VMRO-DPMNE with the Democratic Party of the Albanians (DPA), which emerged out of PDP radical circles and ruled until shortly after the 2001 internal warfare. The rotation of power in Albanian minority elites suggests that the initial form of co-optation worked well until 1996–1997, when intra-elite divisions began. Yet co-optation took new forms in the later period, as I will demonstrate; see Table 2.

In Bulgaria, despite the low MRF profile on constitutional challenges, former communists created policies that fed on their earlier resentment

Table 2. Executive Leadership, 1989–2001

Bulgaria

Presidents

1989–1990	*Petar Mladenov*, Bulgarian Communist Party, renamed Bulgarian Socialist Party (BSP), 1990
1990–1997	*Zhelyu Zhelev*, Union of Democratic Forces (UDF), former dissident
1997–2002	*Petar Stoyanov*, UDF

Governments

Feb.–Dec. 1990	*Andrey Lukanov*, Bulgarian Communist Party
Dec. 1990–Nov. 1991	*Iliya Popov*, independent
1991–1992	*Philip Dimitrov*, UDF
1992–1994	*Lyuben Berov*, government of experts
1994–1995	*Reneta Indzhova*, government of experts
1995–1997	*Zhan Videnov*, Bulgarian Socialist Party
1997	*Stefan Sofiyanski*, UDF
1997–2001	*Ivan Kostov*, UDF

Macedonia

Presidents

1991–1999	*Kiro Gligorov*, Social Democratic Union of Macedonia (SDSM)
1999–2004	*Boris Trajkovski*, Internal Macedonian Revolutionary Party-Democratic Party for Macedonian National Unity (VMRO-DPMNE)

Governments

1991–1992	*Nikola Kljusev*, government of experts
1992–1994	*Branko Crvenkovski*, SDSM in coalition with Liberal Party, Socialist Party, & the Albanian Party for Democratic Prosperity (PDP) and People's Democratic Party (NDP)
1994–1998	*Branko Crvenkovski*, Alliance for Macedonia, SDSM (in coalition with the minor Liberal and Socialist parties), and the Albanian PDP and NDP
1998–2001	*Lyubcho Georgievski*, VMRO-DPMNE in coalition with DPA

Table 2. (Continued)

Serbia

President

1989–1997 (of Serbia)	*Slobodan Milosevic*, Socialist Party of Serbia (SPS)
1997–2000 (of FRYugoslavia)	*Slobodan Milosevic*, SPS

Governments

1990–1991	*Dragutin Zelenovic*, SPS
1991–1993	*Radoman Božovic*, SPS
1993–1994	*Nikola Šainovic*, SPS
1994–2000	*Mirko Marjanovic*, SPS

Parallel government of Kosovo

1991–1999	*Ibrahim Rugova*, President, Democratic Movement for Kosovo (LDK)
	Bujar Bukoshi, Prime Minister in exile, LDK
1997–1999	*Hashim Thaci*, Guerrilla Leader of Kosovo Liberation Army

against MRF registration as a political party. These policies were most pronounced at the height of the BSP government (1995–1996), and were associated with a "threatened" level of violence in the form of government threats against Islam and minority schools, and minority protests against these threats. Former communist party members obstructed the constitutional legitimacy of MRF registration on several occasions. The first was when the MRF applied for registration in 1990. Several deputies launched a court challenge on the grounds that the new Political Party Act did not allow formation of parties on an ethnic basis. The Sofia City Court refused to register MRF, but the Supreme Court overruled the decision and paved the way for registration. After the new constitution was adopted in 1991, the MRF encountered serious problems re-registering on the ground that the Political Party Act had expired. In a new round of decisions, the City Court again denied registration and the Supreme Court allowed it.[10] Socialist deputies filed a complaint with the Constitutional Court, claiming that the MRF violated two articles of the new constitution and should be declared "unconstitutional."[11] By a narrow margin, the Court rejected this claim.[12] On return to power in 1994, the Socialists attempted to revert to earlier policies, and inaugurated a new court challenge in 1996. This time, the Constitutional Supreme Court rejected the claim on the basis that it had made a decision on the issue in 1992. In court dealings, president Zhelyu Zhelev (1991–1997), elected on the UDF ticket and supported by the MRF in parliament, had an important say, because he influenced judges and encouraged them to trump decisions of lower courts dominated by BSP loyalists. The political character of these attacks was obvious.

Further restrictions on minority rights in Bulgaria took place in more or less visible ways. The first postcommunist government promised that the Turks would be allowed mother tongue instruction in municipal schools in ethnically mixed areas. But the Grand National Assembly—dominated by barely reformed communists and their nationalist ideology—introduced a moratorium on minority mother tongue education. Just before its dissolution the assembly passed a law prohibiting the use of minority mother tongues in state schools but not municipal ones.[13] In an attempt to reverse policies during the 1995 local elections, the strategic town of Kardzhali in southeast Bulgaria, densely inhabited by ethnic Turks, became a focal point for manipulation by postcommunist authorities. Using their incumbency advantages, they further penetrated lower levels of government, daring to use electoral fraud and threatening to infringe on established local MRF influence. International intervention was important to avert escalation of tensions, as will be discussed in Chapter 5.

In 1995 the BSP government also replaced leading figures in the Muslim religious organization with its own loyalists. Nedim Gendzhev, a participant in the communist-era "Revivalist Process," was restored to office as a Muslim leader, an act that triggered protests by some Muslims in Sofia, fearing their rights would be endangered. In addition, the socialist daily Douma referred to the Turkish minority as an "Islamic threat" to Bulgaria. In January 1996, minister of education Ilcho Dimitrov, another active figure during the 1980s assimilation campaign, declared, "Turkish schools will not be allowed to exist in Bulgaria, this should be clear. If they want Turkish schools, they are free to go to Turkey."[14] The BSP tried to make explicit links between anti-Islamic nationalism and Bulgaria's place in the Bulgarian Orthodox Church, but was not very successful because the church was split between supporters of communist and democratic forces, and could not render monolithic support to the BSP.

Finally, successive postcommunist governments were reluctant to introduce decentralization reforms that would empower the lowest level of government, the municipality. The mayor embodied the government in the municipality, but regional governors—as middle-level executives controlled by the central government—often exercised some mayoral functions.[15] Decentralization took place only in 1999 with a new UDF government.

In Macedonia, the nonreformed SDSM party knew the Albanian grievances needed to be addressed, but held off as long as possible to see how little they could get away with.[16] Pressured by the international community, they reacted to demands about constitutional changes relatively moderately, considered the 1992 Albanian referendum on autonomy invalid, and imposed a tone of "integration" in its aftermath, arguing that autonomy would not serve the Albanians well and would result in their "ghettoization."[17] However, their dominant position allowed them to impede many feasible reforms. They refused to open a pedagogical faculty in the Albanian language, which the Albanians demanded to address their inability to attend higher education in their mother tongue as they had during communism at the University of Prishtina in Kosovo. They resisted a law on higher education, decentralization of power to the local level, and a reformed law on self-government. Instead, they used the advantage of incumbency to impose subtle centralization.

The 1995 Local Government Act increased the number of municipalities, but reduced the number of competences they enjoyed, especially economic powers. The larger municipalities had provided services such as public transportation and water in many neighborhoods. These were often difficult to coordinate among the smaller units.[18] Majority elites in power also resisted opening public administration, local government, police, and army to more Albanians. The three main towns with strong Albanian representation—Tetovo, Gostivar, and Debar—had only three PDP mayors in 1990–1996. In 1996, only 23 mayors of 124 municipalities were Albanian;[19] Albanians made up 80 percent of the citizens in Tetovo, but only 38 percent of the police force.[20]

In addition, both the socialist SDSM and the nationalist VMRO-DPMNE strongly supported the Macedonian Orthodox Church. An important element of Macedonian identity, it played a disproportionately large role in state affairs. Orthodox icons and religious symbols were featured on bills and coins. Eran Frankel gives an interesting example of how the Orthodox religion became embedded in Macedonia's celebration of statehood. During a concert sponsored by the UN Preventive Deployment Force (UN-PREDEP) in the mid-1990s, aimed at recognition of the new state as a country of diversity, the activities of Albanians, Turks, and Roma were featured. But the backdrop for the stage was an Orthodox church.[21] Official recognition of the Macedonian autocephalous church—which split from the Serbian church in the late 1960s but was not recognized by the Serbian church—became a rallying point in local and international activities.

Religion was used to channel security fears shortly after independence and the beginning of the war in Bosnia-Herzegovina. A myth of an "Islamic threat" spread in 1992–1993, with public attacks bringing tension to a "threatened" level of violence. The image of the Muslim "enemy" in the faces of Albanians was used to unite Slavs when major international powers refused to recognize Macedonia as an independent state.[22] The myth slowly began to disappear as of 1994, when Macedonia was recognized by other powers.

In comparison, Milosevic raised the role of the Serbian Orthodox Church to an extreme for nationalist purposes, even though Serbian legislation officially guaranteed equality of all denominations. The regime attacked Kosovo Albanians on "Islamic fundamentalist" grounds rather undeservedly, since they were known for belonging to the Roman Catholic Church as well, and for historically considering religion secondary to national identity. "Evidence" for an Albanian jihad was found in the observation that Muslim clergy participated in demonstrations and other Albanian activities that were political, not religious in nature.[23] Interestingly, such developments were mirrored among Orthodox Christian Serbs. While higher Orthodox clergy made some efforts to reconcile with Croats and Muslims around 1992, ordinary clerics often gave overwhelming support to the Serbian war effort.[24] When Kosovo Orthodox bishop Artemije opposed Milosevic's policies in the late 1990s and actively advocated reconciliation between Albanians and Serbs in Kosovo, the regime punished the Kosovo Serbian Orthodox Church. In 1998 it closed churches and denied permission to build new ones or renovate old ones.[25]

In addition, Milosevic used his incumbency to adopt policies beyond the initial "emergency measures" that purged Albanians from higher education and public administration, prohibited their media, and initially imposed martial law. He used police and judicial actions on a daily basis for intimidation, contributing to an almost permanent "extreme" level of violence in 1990–1998. All independent Kosovo enterprises were merged with similar companies in Serbia. Local radio and television frequencies were taken over.[26] The regime used manipulation of electoral politics in

Kosovo to strengthen its own position at the center. Since Albanians boycotted all the elections, radical political formations gained advantage. For
example, in 1992 the Serbian Socialist Party (SPS) and the Serb Radical
Party (SRS) entered into a silent coalition with each other and with "independent candidate" (and war criminal) Zeljko Raznatovic-Arkan. In December 1993, non-Albanian parties further consolidated power on the basis
of votes from Kosovo, with the SPS winning 21 of the 24 mandates in the
province. In the 1996 federal elections, of the 13 mandates for the Chamber
of Citizens from Kosovo, the ruling SPS won 12 and the SRS 1.[27] The 1996
elections, marred by fraud across Serbia, became particularly so in Kosovo
because the opposition exerted almost no control over the electoral process.
Given that Albanians did not vote, it was inexplicable that the number of
registered voters and valid ballots increased. In the main municipalities of
Prishtina, Mitrovitsa, and Peć the number of valid ballots nearly doubled,
from an average of 30 percent in previous elections to 55.9 percent.[28]

Adaptive Expectations

The mechanism of *adaptive expectations* involves interactions between majorities and minorities. It describes how majorities and minorities learn and
adapt to the unwritten rules of "appropriate behavior" from the in-group
and out-group. This behavior had been conditioned by the sequences of
majority-minority interactions during the critical juncture.

Acting toward a co-opted Turkish minority whose status had been
slightly raised, all majority governments in Bulgaria—postcommunist or
UDF-based—maintained two main political goals. The integrity of the state
should be preserved and no territorially autonomous regions permitted.
Ethnic Turks belonged to the Bulgarian "political" (civic) nation, not to
an ethnic nation, but their cultural freedoms should be guaranteed. Thus
changing the constitutional provision that prohibited registration of parties
on an ethnic basis was not an option.

The pro-liberal UDF-based elites were eager to allow more educational
and cultural freedoms for the Turkish minority but had a tacit agreement
with the postcommunists on the rules of in-group behavior. When in 1991
the UDF had the choice to enter a coalition government with the MRF or
form a government based on its own mandate, it chose to go solo. As Luan
Troxel pointed out, the UDF understood that joining a coalition would
have jeopardized its position in Bulgarian society, as fears would have

increased that Turks would hold political power as during the Ottoman period (a myth very much advocated by postcommunists at the time).[29] Around 1992 the UDF withdrew support for President Zhelyu Zhelev, once elected on its ticket, not least because while president he became critical of the government and closer to the MRF. During its second term, starting in 1997, the UDF made a concerted effort to diminish MRF influence. In particular, it created loyalties with an ethnic Turkish faction called the Movement for Renewal of the MRF and headed by Gyuner Tahir. Like the Socialists, the UDF attempted not to open the political system for registration of parties on an ethnic basis, but to launch another policy of co-optation with this new faction. There was an unwritten agreement in the Bulgarian elites that a slight increase in minority status together with co-optation were tools to preserve the privileged position of the Bulgarian nation while inducing peaceful interactions with the Turkish minority.

For its part, the MRF was aware of the limitations of postcommunists and the UDF and Bulgarian society in general, which created incentives for its own behavior. A 1991 Radio Free Europe/Radio Liberty (RFE/RL) report read that "the movement wants to have an important impact on the political process, but not to govern."[30] Moreover, after a 1992 no-confidence vote for the UDF, the MRF as a parliamentary power had the opportunity to form its own government. It nevertheless supported formation of one based on experts. MRF leadership knew they could not govern alone, since this would bring parliamentary crisis, and chose to remain a decisive power in the parliament.

Locked into its co-optation and monopoly of power in the ethnic realm, the MRF became a weak force to challenge the restrictive constitutional provision. Demands to change this paragraph were voiced in public mainly during the 1998–1999 debate surrounding adoption of the Council of Europe Framework Convention on the Protection of National Minorities. Proposals for constitutional changes had occasionally been voiced by Ibrahim Tatarli, an important functionary in the MRF, but not by MRF leader Ahmed Dogan, whose influence remained strongest. Tatarli claimed that rights for the Turkish minority should be granted in line with the 1947 constitution, which explicitly mentioned "national minorities" and their rights to education and development of culture. But such claims were voiced rarely, never aggressively promoted, and not backed by serious political action.[31] Thus, even challenges to the constitution were relatively benign and contributed to a "nonviolent" outcome to ethnic conflict.

A more aggressive stance toward the constitution was adopted by the Turkish Democratic Party (TDP) and its leader Adem Kenan. This political formation arose in 1992 in opposition to the MRF, as did three other ethnic Turkish factions over the 1990s. The TDP projected a much stronger nationalist stance than the MRF.[32] Its 1992 program declaration insisted that a new Grand National Assembly be called to adopt a new constitution that would not be ethnocentric and would "fit the international requirements for [models] of multi-national states."[33] However, the TDP—along with the other three parties—remained marginalized throughout the 1990s because it was not allowed to register legally, so its public statements had no serious political weight. There was a mutual understanding among the majority elites that this marginalization was appropriate.

In Macedonia, majorities in government—whether SDSM or VMRO-DPMNE—had two political goals: to preserve the Macedonian nation by preserving the newborn state, and to establish a "civic state" with a high degree of protection for cultural diversity.[34] This conveniently meant that there were no legal grounds to favor one minority, the Albanians, over another, for example, the Vlachs.[35] Elevating Albanian status to a "constituent" element of the state was out of the question. Acting toward an Albanian minority that early in the transition had chosen to participate in both government and clandestine activities kept authorities constantly on alert. When clandestine activities surfaced politically, Macedonian elites interpreted them as challenges to the state and repressed them forcibly, leading to "episodic" levels of violence. In January 1994, police arrested a number of PDP members charged with a plot to smuggle weapons into Macedonia and develop an Albanian militia.[36] A major clash took place when radical Albanian activists opened Tetovo University in 1994–1995. Police with riot gear and automatic weapons dispersed a demonstration of more than 500 Albanians in early 1995.[37] In 1997, the DPA used its mayors in Gostivar and Tetovo to raise Albanian and Turkish national flags over the town halls. During this event at least 200 people were injured. Two civilians were killed and one was beaten to death.[38] Military violence was employed as well during the 2001 crisis that turned into brief "internal warfare," discussed in Chapter 4.

The Albanians adapted to the Macedonian elites' reluctance to address their diminished constitutional status and to co-optation by pursuing their two-pronged strategy toward the state and a peculiar pattern of in-group ethnic outbidding.[39] Participating in government coalitions was accompanied by official boycotts, including during the 1993 parliamentary sessions, where UN recognition, new electoral laws, self-government, and education were discussed. The boycotts were somewhat effective in the 1990–1994 parliament, where no single party was able to form a majority.[40] In the 1994–1998 parliament, the SDSM had a nearly absolute majority, and the PDP boycotts and those of a splinter radical group in its ranks no longer had such a strong impact.

On the clandestine side, radicalization among PDP members began gathering momentum after the failed 1992 referendum on territorial autonomy. In 1993, several PDP officials—among them the former secretary general and deputy ministers for health and defense—were arrested and accused of possessing 300 machine guns, planning to create the "Republic of Ilirida," and seeking to join Albania.[41] This plot demonstrated that the PDP had an official and unofficial face from early in the transition process. This became even more obvious in 1994 when a faction arose, led by Arben Xharefi, that began openly advocating "armed revolt."[42]

Unlike in Bulgaria, where ethnic outbidding in the minority sector was de facto impossible because of restrictions on registration of parties on an ethnic basis, it was commonplace in Macedonia and became intertwined with the strategy of co-optation. By including radical Albanian elements in power, the coalition governments enjoyed some years with no serious minority outbidding. However, the lack of resolution to constitutional and other contentious issues encouraged new radical elements to enter political competition. Co-optation worked best when radicals entered governing coalitions and toned down their demands. For example, the radical DPA won local elections in 1996 and did well in general elections in 1998. International and domestic observers feared it would develop radical policies while in power. Instead, its unnatural coalition with another nationalist formation, the Macedonian VMRO-DPMNE, initially resulted in a pro-Western policymaking orientation, and the demand for "constituent element" status was put on hold. This approach opened space for the growth in 2000–2001 of another radical formation, the National Liberation Army (NLA), that claimed domestic origins but enjoyed strong support from splinters of the dismantled KLA in Kosovo. However disputed its motivations to stage "internal warfare" in 2001, the NLA claimed it took up arms to drastically change the Macedonian constitution and demanded federalization.

Facing a secessionist Kosovo Albanian minority, the Serbian authorities—regardless whether represented by Milosevic or his opposition—had one political goal: to preserve Kosovo as a territorial part of Serbia. The government did not hesitate to use force against the Albanians' parallel structures, especially against activities posing a security threat. With respect to the shadow "defense" ministry, in 1993 more than 100 ethnic Albanians were arrested on charges of preparing an armed uprising. Public attention focused on the trial of 19 people who allegedly possessed automatic weapons, grenades, and bombs.[43] A second wave of arrests followed at the end of 1994. The main targets were around 200 former Albanian police officers who had been fired in 1991 and were charged with creating a parallel ministry of interior, stockpiling weapons and police equipment, and spying on the Serbian police and Yugoslav army.[44]

Interestingly, Serbian authorities adapted to the nonreligious character of the Albanian political movement, though on the surface they continued to make claims about its "Islamic fundamentalist" character. During the 1999 ethnic expulsion campaign, Serbian forces destroyed Muslim religious sites and singled out Muslim clerics for harassment. But Albanians were primarily attacked because they were Albanians, not because they were Muslims: Albanians of other religions were subjected to violence as well. In March 1999 Serbian forces did not hesitate to remove around 200 Albanians from a Catholic church in Peć and expel them from the town. Moreover, while Albanian Christians and Muslims received equal mistreatment, Serbian forces did not target other Muslim minorities such as Roma, Turks, and Muslim Slavs.[45]

Scholarship on secessionism is prone to view Kosovo Albanian political activities in the 1990s as a complete rejection of the Serbian state because Kosovars did not participate in elections, boycotted institutions, and formed their own parallel structures and ministries.[46] Nevertheless, they did adapt to realities in a state whose institutions they could not completely ignore. They carried Yugoslav passports and used the Yugoslav post office, telephone company, and dinar. They had to deal with Yugoslav courts, police, and national army troops stationed there.[47] Most notably, Rugova and his LDK realized that they did not have control over weapons, and that the Yugoslav military preponderance would crush their movement unless a strategy of nonviolence and informal shadow institutions was adopted. In a personal interview, former prime minister in exile Bukoshi argued that, although "from the very beginning ministries of interior and defense existed," the shadow government put more emphasis on education, medical care, and internationalization of the conflict. The security ministries became "frozen," but their members maintained contact so as to be able to organize in case of a Serbian attack.[48] Realizing that the Serbian opposition was no less nationalist than the Milosevic government, Kosovo Albanians adapted their expectations and strategies by choosing not to participate in the Serbian elections. A change in government would not have effectively changed the status of Kosovo.[49] On the contrary, through a democratic vote the Albanians would have given domestic and international legitimacy to a new Serbian nationalist government that would be able to prevent them from achieving independence for Kosovo.

Timing and Sequencing: Preventing Nonterritorial Demands from Becoming Territorial

We have seen so far that early adoption of a constitution during the transition process did not guarantee interethnic peace in the long run, and that the timing of the opening of the communist system for political competition, before or after changes in the minority's constitutional and political status, was important in explaining whether peaceful or conflictual dynamics formed.[50] A third dimension of timing—government responses to nonterritorial minority demands—affected whether the demands would broaden to include challenges to the existing territorial order and whether violence would remain low or escalate.

In the Bulgarian case, pro-Western elites in power facilitated a timely response. Responses were stalled in all three cases when nonreformed communist elites were in power. Educational policy is a good example. Some of the most outspoken demands of the Turks of Bulgaria were focused on educational rights in the minority language. Coercively assimilated during communism, many ethnic Turks needed to relearn Turkish. The MRF advocated the introduction of Turkish language education in 1989 and pursued this demand in two stages, asking for mother tongue education as an elective and then a compulsory school subject. In 1989–1990 the postcommunist government made vague promises that such education would be allowed in the future but, as earlier noted, the Grand National Assembly introduced a moratorium. This move led to a widespread boycott of schools endorsed by the MRF and was followed by ethnic Turkish parents and students ("threatened" level of violence). When the Western-oriented UDF came to power several months later, it issued a decree allowing for opening primary and secondary schools for Turkish language education as an elective subject. The normative basis was fixed only in 1994, with a technocratic government that enjoyed strong parliamentary backing from the ethnic Turkish MRF.[51]

The second MRF demand surfaced in 1995. By that time activists were expressing the desire to include language education in the regular curriculum and teach some subjects in Turkish. The MRF viewed the optional study as discriminatory, because parents had to opt explicitly for their children to study their mother tongue. They felt that Turkish faced unequal competition with other world languages, and that children preferred to learn English or Russian instead.[52] It took the MRF four years to change this status. Initially, its demand was met with fierce resistance by the ruling BSP, which voiced threats in the media on numerous occasions in 1995–1996 ("threatened" level of violence). Tensions decreased after the 1997 elections brought another pro-Western government to power. The second UDF government became receptive to pressures from the Council of Europe because of its ambition to advance Bulgaria's accession to the European Union. The parliament adopted the Framework Convention on the Protection of the National Minorities, and in 1999 introduced a law that required education in the mother tongue.

It may seem paradoxical that it took longer for Macedonian governments to address issues related to demands for Albanian university level education, given that Albanians were part of the governing coalitions and represented in the parliament. However, because the initially incumbent Macedonian and Albanian elites shared a postcommunist ideological past, they were not predisposed to think of liberal reforms in the minority rights sphere. Minorities in Macedonia enjoyed many more rights than other minorities in the Balkans, as government officials proudly asserted in official and unofficial communications with representatives of the international community. Albanians, Turks, and Roma had their own media outlets and were schooled in their mother tongues. But these rights were inherited from communism, not an achievement of the transition period. Despite alternation of power after elections, it was only in 1998 that a pro-Western (if not liberal) coalition came to power that was able to open the system to some reforms under international pressure, as is discussed further in Chapter 4.

In the meantime, there was a lack of adequate response to minority demands, which turned the nonterritorial issue of university-level education into a political one with territorial implications. In the early 1990s the

Albanians of Macedonia requested establishment of an Albanian Pedagogical Faculty at Skopje University. After much contemplation, in 1994 the government introduced an affirmative action quota for minority students to enter the state university, but did not consider opening a separate faculty.[53] This decision was a turning point. The escalating spiral of conflict led to an "episodic" level of violence in early 1995, after the Albanians established the semiparallel University of Tetovo, which was proclaimed "unconstitutional," and demonstrations were crushed by the Macedonian-dominated police. Macedonian authorities belatedly decided to open the Pedagogical Faculty in 1996, but the conflict had already engulfed Macedonian society. Ethnic Macedonian university students marched on the streets of Skopje in a violent protest against opening the faculty. And Tetovo University had acquired high nationalist significance for Albanians in west Macedonia, making its dissolution very difficult.

Timing and sequencing of government policies were also important for radicalization in the Kosovo case. The ramifications of the failure of the Education Agreement, signed separately between Milosevic and Rugova in 1996 in response to the Kosovo parallel schooling system, are a case in point. With the formation of Kosovo shadow institutions in 1992, the Albanians merged education with territorial and political demands. The shadow schools performed both a social and political function; they supplied students with knowledge, employed teachers dismissed from state schools, and strengthened the community's nationalist bonds. In the words of Albanian intellectual Shkelzen Maliqi, parallel schooling activities generated a feeling of involving virtually everyone in Kosovo.[54] Since education activities were the most successful, it was no surprise that students and teachers attracted the regime's attention and violent actions ensued. According to the Albanian Teachers Association, by 1994 some 3,300 teachers had been detained and interrogated by the police, and at least two directors of primary schools killed. School children were also subjected to some police abuse. Local educational officials methodically intimidated the population by confiscating education certificates bearing stamps of the "Republic of Kosovo" or testifying that students had completed the parallel education.[55]

The so-called "Rome [Education] Agreement," mediated by the Italian Catholic group Communita di Saint Egidio in 1996, required that Albanian students and teachers be permitted to return to public schools at all levels of education, including some buildings of Prishtina University.[56] To secure the social aspects of education and avoid further politicization, the agreement

addressed access to school buildings and some financial matters. It deliberately remained vague about the precarious subject of the Serbian language
curriculum or precise deadlines and mechanisms for its implementation.
But the agreement failed not just because it was vague. Its vagueness was a
symptom of the lack of desire on both sides to address the core social issue.
The two leaders who signed the agreement appropriated it for political purposes. Rugova used it to claim that Milosevic had recognized him as
Kosovo's legitimate leader. Milosevic used it to demonstrate to the international community that he was ready to negotiate.[57] Milosevic apparently
never intended to advance the agreement, since the implementation commission met only a handful of times and failed to make progress. By the end
of August 1997 it became clear the agreement would not be implemented.

The agreement did not decrease the level of "extensive" violence. Intimidation of Kosovar Albanians continued. The failure added to an existing
political dynamic that fueled sentiments among Albanians against Rugova's
strategy of nonviolence. The lack of prospects for improvement drove Albanian students into the streets. Three demonstrations took place in October
1997; the first turned violent. Rugova did not approve of the demonstrations, arguing that they would impede implementation of the agreement.[58]
But by that time the students had taken matters into their own hands and
secretly established connections with radical diaspora circles and the KLA
abroad.[59] In the words of student demonstration leader Albin Kurti, the
students rebelled not only against Milosevic, but also against Rugova and
"the political class . . . who were enjoying their privileges," and the international community that did not reward the politics of nonviolence, but tried
to silence the students who took to the streets.[60] At that time the entire
student body converged against the strategy of nonviolence.

Conclusions

The self-reinforcing mechanisms and processes regarding the conflict dynamics—conflictual, semiconflictual, and cooperative—were established
during the formative period; they were based on formal rules—such as
constitutions and crucial policies—but also informally on key elements of
policies on how majorities and minorities chose to interact with each other
in that early formative period. After 1992 these dynamics became consolidated by the self-reinforcement of two mechanisms: *advantage of political*

incumbency and *adaptive expectations.* Nonreformed postcommunist elites, who had the advantage of being first on the political scene at the end of communism, bypassed minorities during constitution formation and perpetuated neglect for minorities and their rights through much of the 1990s. This trend was demonstrated by reversal of policies—such as attacks on the constitutionality of the ethnic Turkish MRF in Bulgaria—or deliberate delay of laws that would have increased minority rights in education, self-government, and cultural politics in Bulgaria and Macedonia. In Kosovo the regime used its incumbency to deepen the penetration of the "emergency measures" that subjugated Albanians to Serbian political domination and to use electoral politics in Kosovo, boycotted by the Albanians, to manipulate elections and strengthen Serbian nationalist and radical representation at the central level of politics.

With the second self-reinforcing mechanism—adaptive expectations—majorities and minorities adapted their in-group and out-group behavior to that expected from the out-group. A co-opted Turkish minority in Bulgaria enjoyed a slightly elevated status and knew that no other ethnic party could officially register. It was content to monopolize ethnic Turks' representation, did not develop major challenges to the constitution, and kept a low profile with regard to minority demands. Postcommunist and democratic elites in Bulgaria were allied against constitutional changes and MRF's active participation in government during the 1990s. They preferred perpetual attempts at co-optation of groups in the Turkish minority, knowing that such politics led to comparatively peaceful majority-minority interactions.

A co-opted Albanian minority in Macedonia whose status had slightly decreased, acted differently. It adapted to the realities of Macedonian politics by participating in ethnic outbidding. Albanian political parties could only enact minor policy changes while participating in the government and parliament; they could not address constitutional status, linguistic politics, self-government, and education, and this allowed radical groups to emerge. These groups were in turn co-opted when they entered politics and toned down their demands, which led to the emergence of new radical groups. Macedonian authorities adapted to Albanian demands for change of constitutional status by deliberately ignoring them in official state politics, while violently confronting activities considered disloyal, such as opening Tetovo University, raising Albanian and Turkish flags in Gostivar and Tetovo, and radical NLA activities around the 2001 crisis.

The coerced Kosovo Albanians, a local majority whose status drastically decreased, adapted to the realities of Serbian politics in several ways. First, they chose not to participate in electoral politics, maintaining that Kosovo was no longer part of Serbia after the 1991 declaration of independence. The leadership realized that trying to oust Milosevic from power by the ballot box would not have the desired effect, because Serbian opposition was no less nationalist: there were no prospective Serb allies. Kosovo's leadership also realized that it lacked arms, which created huge power asymmetries with the coercive capacity of the authorities. If it wanted to preserve its brethren, it needed a strategy of nonviolence. The Serbian regime adapted to the idea that there were shadow Kosovo authorities and intimidated them regularly, but did not crush them completely as it later attempted when the radical Albanian KLA became more powerful in 1997.

Finally, I have argued here that timely government response to a nonterritorial minority demand is likely to prevent its being linked to territorial demands, increasing the potential for escalation of violence. In Bulgaria, despite significant resistance, the government responded relatively quickly to the demands of ethnic Turks for mother-tongue education. In Macedonia, a government strategy to hold off opening a faculty for education in Albanian as long as possible made some discontented factions in the community proclaim their own parallel educational institution, which became indirectly linked to claims for territorial autonomy. Violent clashes with the police followed. In Kosovo, the social need for education of the Kosovo Albanian population was not met by the state, so education became quickly incorporated into Kosovo parallel structures. Even when decoupling Kosovar social and territorial demands was possible with the Education Agreement, the government postponed its implementation indefinitely, which aided further radicalization of the conflict, and escalation of violence.

This chapter has sought to elucidate mechanisms that sustained the conflict dynamics and importance of timely responses to minority nonterritorial demands for nonescalation of violence. A discussion of change was not central here because I argue that much of the change was associated with factors exogenous to majority-minority dynamics. Change came primarily from exogenous shocks, policies of the international community, or identity-based agents such as kin-states and diasporas. The following chapters will address these in more detail.

Chapter 3

International Intervention During
the Formative Period

Shortly after the end of the Cold War, scholars considered third-party intervention from the point of view of economic, political, and geostrategic interests of states and international organizations in a world emerging from bipolarity and moving into a multipolar world order where intrastate conflicts prevail. The internal strife in the Balkans, Caucasus, and Africa during the 1990s triggered further interest in how local agents internationalized these conflicts by interconnecting their own interests with those of third parties.[1] With a plethora of new and continuing civil wars in Africa, nationalist strife in the postcommunist space, and sectarian strife in the Middle East, the field matured around schools of thought discussing conflict management, humanitarian military interventions, bargaining between third parties and domestic agents, and the impact of third parties on the onset and duration of civil wars.[2]

Yet scholarship remained dominated by inquiries into militarized disputes, though they have been of smaller proportions than all ethnonationalist conflicts. Other conflicts remained peaceful or became stalled in a no-war/no-peace dynamic. Nonviolent cases, especially in Eastern Europe, were often optimistically portrayed as results of the EU's positive impact on respect for minority rights in countries aspiring for membership. Little research has been done on the impact of third parties on ethnic conflicts that shared many characteristics at the end of communism, but reached different degrees of violence over time. Theorizing across cases about the role of international agents specifically during the critical juncture (1987/89–1992) has been scarce; most accounts focused on interactions between domestic elites.

This chapter aspires to provide initial answers by focusing on the main question of how the international community contributed to the diverging patterns of violence between majorities and minorities, and explores the conflicts in Kosovo, Macedonia, and Bulgaria during the formative period. This requires analysis of a set of interconnected subquestions. How did the international community relate to evolving majority-minority relations during the critical juncture? How did international agents react to the relative changes in the official status of minorities, to government strategies of co-optation or coercion, and to minorities' acceptance or rejection of the state? What were their own interests and how did they get layered on top of existing local relationships? What was the international level of commitment to resolving these conflicts?

From the outset of the transition, the international community—states and international organizations with no identity-based connections to the local agents—was interested in promoting democratic change including promotion of human rights. These goals were laudable, but did not result in the desired low levels of violence. Its influence was, however, crucial during the critical juncture, when these policies had strong implications on how the "rules of the game" on the national question were redefined among the local agents. The international community succeeded in mitigating local conflicts during this formative period if it provided three types of credible guarantees:

- the minority should have political participation in the state institutions;
- the basic premises of statehood (international legal or domestic sovereignty) should not be restructured; and
- the international community should have its own long-term commitment to conflict resolution and reforms.

Only in Bulgaria were these three conditions fully met; they were met partially in Macedonia and not at all in Kosovo. The presence or absence of these conditions became intertwined with the already evolving majority-minority dynamics, creating an informal triangular relationship.

It is important to be more precise about the terms "international community" and "intervention." Apart from designating states and international (governmental and nongovernmental) organizations, which are not bound by kin to the majority or minority, the "international community" refers to what Maoz calls a "politically relevant international environment" to a given conflict.[3] Despite their divergent interests, mandates, and methods of intervention, international agents shared many underlying interests toward postcommunist southeastern Europe. They all sought to preserve regional security and stability by decreasing the intensity of ethnic conflicts and supporting the democratization of these countries. The contrast with international involvement in the Middle East in the past is significant, although the Arab revolutions of 2011–2012 may change that. Traditionally, security and democratization have been important international concerns in the Middle East, but national interests, complicated by oil politics and political ties with Israel and the Arab countries, often lead policies to diverge orthogonally from each other.

"Intervention" designates the multiple modes through which an external power can shape local conflicts. The frameworks of Lake and Rothchild on conflict management and Whitehead and Schmitter on democracy promotion are adapted here.[4] *Coercive regulation* refers to policies primarily backed by negative sanctions: economic and military, and policies such as coercive diplomacy, peacekeeping, monitoring of security arrangements, and humanitarian military interventions.[5] *Consent* refers to consensual interactions between external and domestic groups, which often generate a new normative context. These include mediation as a confidence-building measure, consensual monitoring, and promotion of norms of minority rights through mechanisms of socialization such as learning, social influence, and persuasion. *Co-optation* refers to the socialization of the co-opted, leading to their conformity to a world of pre-set values, rather than engaging them in ways to alter it. *Conditionality* is intervention on the part of multilateral institutions, deliberately attaching conditions of compliance to specific political and economic reforms in exchange for membership or benefits for candidate or recipient countries.[6] Conditionality is especially relevant to our cases where the adoption of minority rights and democratic stability became preconditions for a country's future EU membership. *Contagion* refers to the diffusion of experience and social networks through neutral, often noncoercive and unexpected channels. Contagion takes place without much agency on the part of the international community.

Alternative Explanations: Third-Party Intervention in Ethnic Conflicts

Three streams of thought on third-party intervention provide relevant insights to this study. Scholarship on *timing of international intervention* is

especially significant. Existing works have generated valuable yet inconclusive results. Conflict resolution is most promising at an early stage, *before*
violence has entrenched the conflicting parties' positions.[7] Early military or
economic intervention on behalf of the incumbent government does not
shorten the conflict's duration, but early intervention on behalf of the rebels tends to lengthen it by helping the minority build capabilities and gain
military ground.[8] Others have found new opportune moments for conflict
resolution later in the conflict spiral, *after* belligerents have fought substantially and reached a "ripe moment" or stage of "mutual hurting stalemate,"
when they are willing to put down their guns and return to negotiations.[9]
Studies have argued that the middle of a conflict's lifecycle is the most
propitious time to initiate mediation or early and late stages of intervention.[10] Cease-fires and interim arrangements brokered during the middle of
the conflict may avert further escalations of violence, but may also allow
belligerents space to regroup, and thus contribute to increased duration.[11]
In short, the results are paradoxical and contradictory.

While early intervention is important in the analysis of the three cases
examined here, we must go beyond studying intervention in the lifecycle of
a conflict to understand the political context in which it is embedded. Here
the early stages took place during a critical juncture at the end of communism, when the political "rules of the game" were fundamentally redefined
not simply by the majorities and minorities but by international agents as
well. Analyzing the impact of international agents during this formative
stage is a theoretical necessity.

The second stream of thought focuses on *bargaining processes between
majorities, minorities, and third parties* and their strategic interactions. Jenne's
work demonstrates that an external lobby agent becomes embedded in a
triadic relationship with the majorities and minorities by giving signals of
support or no support to the minority, and thereby contributes to shifts in
minority claims ranging from affirmative action to secessionism. Signals of
external support enhance the minority's bargaining leverage against the central government, while signals of withdrawal make it more accommodating.[12]

Other scholars disagree about the extent to which the prospects of international intervention matter in domestic agents' calculations. Cetinyan
finds that a third party's presence in the bargaining process does not change
the essence of the game between majorities and minorities, though they
may consider the third party in their strategic calculations. He operates
under the assumption that rational agents can obtain perfect information
and therefore anticipate the responses of others.[13] Other scholars assume

that imperfect information is widespread and interpreted unevenly among agents. Thyne argues that if a third party sends costly signals—for example, building military alliances—then the government and the opposition will shift their bargaining positions. Cheap signals—for example, media statements—do not convey the same credibility. The same cheap signal could be interpreted as disingenuous by the government and credible by the opposition.[14] Grigoryan suggests that imminent humanitarian military intervention may perversely create incentives for the majority-dominated government to increase coercive measures against the minority and even resort to "ethnic cleansing," as Milosevic did toward Kosovo Albanians during NATO's 1999 military intervention.[15]

Bargaining models of interventions are valuable for the tasks they accomplish—demonstrating the significant sequentialism in agents' rational choices, how their choices are informed by different access to information, and how they may lead to different outcomes. Yet these studies miss contextual variables—such as existing structures in which agents operate, and often miss exogenous shocks that alter all calculations regardless of previous anticipations of others' strategic responses. A *path-dependence account* is more suited for a theoretically informed discussion of the interactions between agency and structure in volatile environments, and to demonstrate the formation of durable institutionalized relationships between majorities, minorities, and third parties.

A third stream of scholarship is concerned about how *prospects for future EU integration* change the norms and calculations of governments. The mechanisms of EU influence on domestic policy are specified differently in the opposing arguments advanced by rationalists and constructivists in international relations theory, who respectively focus on the "logic of consequences" and the "logic of appropriateness."[16] Viewing EU and local elites as self-interested agents, rationalists emphasize the importance of bargaining under asymmetrical interdependence.[17] Eastern European countries were weaker parties in their relations with the EU but nevertheless were interested in introducing change because of the benefits of compliance with EU standards. Conditionality was the major mechanism because the human and minority rights reforms in the 1993 Copenhagen criteria set standards for future integration.[18] The OSCE, of which potential EU candidates were already members, embedded these criteria in the role of its High Commissioner on the National Minorities (HCNM), who appraised potential candidates. Compliance was challenging, because costs were high for the local elites, especially when EU conditions apparently reduced the security and integrity of the state.[19] Nevertheless, pro-Western governments in Bulgaria, Romania, and Slovakia introduced some resented minority rights reforms, recognizing that the long-term benefits of EU membership outweighed the costs.[20] Domestic change also took place by way of socialization mechanisms. As Kelley points out, by contrast to conditionality, here "the defining feature is that external agents do not link any concrete incentives to behavior but rely solely on the use of norms to persuade, shame, or praise agents into changing their policies."[21] Rationalist and constructivist logics were unified in Kelley's framework, suggesting that EU membership conditionality motivated most policy decisions, but that socialization efforts provided guidance.[22]

While most of these accounts advanced an almost consensual finding that EU integration had positive effects on domestic minority rights reforms, they did not capture the dynamics regarding cases where violence took place.[23] Most scholarship on the impact of the EU so far has derived its findings from Central European countries. We need to scrutinize the relevance of these ideas to Balkan countries, where domestic change in the 1990s took place amid the collapse of Yugoslavia. Conditionality and socialization may be seen as instances of "layering" as a mechanism of change: new rules are introduced on top of or alongside existing ones. How conditionality and socialization coexist with these old rules needs in-depth theoretical inquiry.

Minority Rights Before the End of Communism

Respect for minority rights and democratization became important policies of the international community toward the countries of Eastern Europe after 1989. These norms were rooted in an international legal system that defined minority rights in individualist rather than collective terms. The 1945 UN Charter, the 1948 Universal Declaration on Human Rights (UDHR), and the two major 1966 UN covenants governing human rights—the International Covenant on Civil and Political Rights (ICCPR) and the International Covenant on Social, Economic and Cultural Rights (ICSECR)—developed a strong individual rights focus.

While emphasizing individual rights, the UN legal system nevertheless developed a contradictory relationship between the individual and the state. This tension was embedded in the UN Charter, which prohibits intervention in a domestic jurisdiction, yet allows the Security Council to authorize humanitarian military interventions when threats to international peace arise. These threats have sometimes come to be associated with ethnic expulsion and genocide. The Charter's Chapter VII provisions were invoked with varying degrees of success in military interventions in Bosnia, Rwanda, and Kosovo in the 1990s and Afghanistan in the 2000s.

International policies requiring domestic respect for human rights were rooted in the political Helsinki Process that marked the beginning of the end of communism. The Helsinki Final Act was signed in 1975 by 35 countries, including Yugoslavia and Bulgaria, within the framework of the Conference on Security and Co-operation in Europe (CSCE at the time, later OSCE). It made Western foreign assistance conditional on human rights concessions by the communist regimes. By that time the economic crisis of the mid-1970s had weakened the Soviet Union and its allies in the former communist bloc, so they became increasingly dependent on Western trade and investment. In the aftermath of the Helsinki Accords several important international policy changes took place. The Carter administration for the first time openly embedded human rights in the U.S. foreign policy agenda. The subsequent Reagan administration increased its confrontational approach with the Marxist regimes on the human rights question. Monitoring of human rights increased significantly. The State Department started to publish regular reports, and emerging NGOs such as Amnesty International and Helsinki Watch published occasional reports. As one U.S. participant in this process emphasized, the focus was on respect for "human rights," not minority rights or democratization.[24]

Liberal democracies were critical of the human rights abuses in Yugoslavia and Bulgaria during communism. The U.S. Congress and the European Parliament directly condemned the human rights violations of Kosovo Albanians during the 1968 and 1981 riots. The brutal assimilation campaign against ethnic Turks in Bulgaria in the mid-1980s received special attention because of its magnitude and systematic planning, and because exposing the ills of communism served Western powers. The fact that RFE/RL had a Bulgarian section but not a Yugoslav one, indicated that Western countries were less inclined to expose human rights violations in Yugoslavia. Geopolitically, Bulgaria was the Soviet Union's closest ally in the communist bloc and a staunch supporter of its strict version of communism. In contrast, Yugoslavia was part of the Non-Aligned Movement until 1989, and maintained a more relaxed version of communism. Despite its attention to Bulgaria's human rights violations, the international community was reluctant to adopt any policy in favor of the Turks. Even Turkey and other Islamic countries were unwilling to apply effective political and economic sanctions to force the Bulgarian government to alter its policies.[25] The strongest measures were to include Bulgaria on the negative list of the Organization of the Islamic Conference, and to create restrictions on effective trade. The policies of liberal democracies toward the abuses of the Turks of Bulgaria and Kosovo Albanians did not go beyond diplomatic statements and heated media rhetoric.

International Intervention During the Critical Juncture

Having won the ideological war against communism in 1989, liberal democracies adopted common standards toward the democratizing polities in Eastern Europe. From the outset of the transition they promoted human and minority rights on an individualist basis, and condemned collective nationalist aspirations aimed at secession. This stance was rooted in the contradictions of an international legal system, resilient to alterations despite the vast political and economic changes on multiple levels. While vigilant about human rights violations, the international community, most notably the United States, sought to preserve Yugoslavia as a state. Considering Yugoslav communism as having a human face, they trailed after many of the local political processes tending toward self-determination. Germany, an exception, saw the Cold War's end as a chance to exercise its own right to self-determination and reunite its western and eastern parts. Germany therefore adopted a more sympathetic approach toward the self-determination aspirations of Slovenia and Croatia.[26]

The international community, apart from Germany, had its own agenda for preservation of Yugoslavia as a state. Thus its lukewarm response to the constitutional changes in Kosovo and Macedonia in 1989 was not surprising. The reduction in the constitutional status of the Albanians of Macedonia went almost unnoticed. The international community was slightly more active regarding the 1989 curtailment of Kosovo autonomy, attempting to better understand the situation and stop the violent demonstrations in response to the loss of autonomy. Several diplomatic statements were issued and visits made to the region to obtain information, but with no serious repercussions on government policies. During his first visit to Kosovo, in July 1989, U.S. ambassador Warren Zimmerman criticized the Milosevic government for its use of violence, and the Albanian opposition for boy-cotting all Serbian institutions. He also urged the Albanians to participate in the upcoming elections.[27] The European Parliament issued a resolution condemning the local violence and dispatched a delegation in 1989.[28] The delegation did not succeed because the Serbian government confined its access to government officials only.[29] The only serious concern expressed about the loss of autonomy came from within Yugoslavia—from Slovenia in 1989, where Communist Party head Milan Kucan organized a rally against the unlawful constitutional change.[30]

In contrast, the international community had no need for concern about the preservation of the Bulgarian state, which was unitary and stable. Hence, it became a fierce critic of the human rights violations against the ethnic Turks. In spring and summer 1989, the Todor Zhivkov government inaugurated the campaign to expel more than 300,000 ethnic Turks to Tur-key. The Bulgarian government faced strong criticism by Western media and many Western democracies, in particular the United States. Several days after the first repression in May 1989, the Bush, Sr., administration criticized the use of violence. In June it instructed its embassy to conduct a formal inquiry into the events, and canceled a series of diplomatic meetings in Washington. When in August the number of refugees reached 310,000, ambassador Sol Polanski was recalled to Washington for consultations. Thus, Bulgaria—traditionally receiving little attention in Washington cir-cles—moved quickly up its policy agenda.[31] The CSCE conference on human rights in Paris in June 1989 also criticized the Bulgarian govern-ment. The most vocal critic was Turkish foreign minister Mesut Yilmaz, who stated that Turkey was ready to negotiate an emigration agreement with Bulgaria. Representatives of the U.S. and the German Bundestag backed him.[32]

In all three cases the early international initiatives were critical of the human rights abuses conducted by majority-dominated governments against minorities, but did not go beyond soft mechanisms, such as declara-tions, discussions, diplomatic visits, and some minor straining of diplo-matic ties in the Bulgarian case. Attempts to monitor the situation on the ground in Kosovo inflicted no particular damage on the Milosevic govern-ment, except for harming his already damaged international image. In the Bulgarian case, too, the international response did not advance beyond out-spoken criticism. U.S. policies did not significantly disrupt relations be-tween the two states.[33] The June CSCE conference had no profound domestic impact on Bulgaria.[34] Another CSCE conference, in Sofia in October 1989, paid more attention to the rights of environmental activists than to the abuse of the ethnic Turks.

Thus, while the international community had different political emphases regarding Bulgaria and Yugoslavia at the end of communism, the policy effects on the evolving majority-minority relationship were similar. Adopting a democratization and human rights discourse was laudable but meant little to majorities or minorities. Criticism of human rights violations did not have serious policy repercussions for the majority-dominated governments. Failure to defend the minorities against a constitutional decrease in their rights demonstrated the international community's reluctance to engage in the intrastate dimension of the evolving conflicts.

The antecedent historical conditions, including the international legal system and Yugoslavia's and Bulgaria's positions in the Cold War geopolitical order, shaped how international agents responded to the transformations during the critical juncture: they became proactive in Bulgaria and less active in Yugoslavia. But antecedent conditions did not determine how the conflicts would evolve. Like the domestic policies of majorities and minorities, international intervention was shaped by the contingency of events on the ground. The international community's strategies did not reach deeply into the majority-minority relationships in these early stages of profound and multifaceted political change.

While the relationship between local agents remained primary for establishment of a conflict dynamic, the international community became interconnected with it and helped shape it during this formative stage by providing three types of guarantees. These were not just signals supportive of the minority or the government, but *specific types* of signals with specific content: support for minority political participation in state institutions, respect for the external and domestic sovereignty of the state, and long-term commitment on the part of the international community. The effects of these guarantees, not the motivations, political will, or ability to provide them, are crucial for the present argument.

☐ *Guarantee 1: Minority political participation in state institutions*

The first guarantee was related to the political participation of minorities in the transitioning polities. I emphasize political participation rather than identity politics because political participation is not simply a major

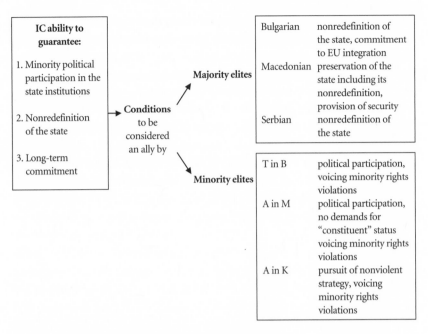

Figure 5. International agents and the critical juncture.

step toward minority accommodation in a democratic polity, as democratization scholars tend to argue. It creates the first crucial element in a
dynamic between the local majority-minority relationship and the international community. If minority political participation is encouraged by international agents, it signals that the minority has an external ally vested
specifically in its state institution participation.

The ethnic Turkish minority in Bulgaria understood as early as 1990
that the international community could be considered an ally for its political participation in state institutions. In previous years international criticism had no significant impact on the majority-minority relationship. But
after the transition that started with the palace coup in November 1989,
international threats to withdraw support for Bulgaria became an effective
political tool. The reformist majority politicians who defeated the conservatives were interested in international backing for Bulgaria on multiple levels, but primarily for economic reforms, and that in turn rendered Bulgaria
more vulnerable to international pressures. As discussed earlier, in 1990 and
1991–1992 the MRF encountered considerable obstacles to registration as a

political party. It was registered only after collaborative pressure from the U.S. and Turkey. U.S. State Department representatives held talks with Bulgarian diplomats in Washington, convincing them that prohibiting the MRF from registering could have negative repercussions on Bulgarian-American relations.[35] In addition, Bulgaria was heavily criticized by the U.S. and most European Community (EC) member state delegations at the 1991 CSCE Moscow Summit. These moves successfully exerted indirect pressure on the domestic courts to register the MRF.[36]

The Albanians of Macedonia faced no similar challenges to registering their political parties. The Albanian PDP and a smaller party, the People's Democratic Party, participated unimpeded in the 1990 elections. However, from the outset of the transition the external intervention to support Albanian political participation was shaped by security concerns generated by Yugoslavia's collapse and Macedonia's state building. In 1990–1991, when constitutional changes were taking place to confirm the 1989 reduction in minority status, and international agents were unwilling or unable to change the course of events, the Albanians became aware of *how* they should consider the international community as their political participation ally. They would receive support when working within the state institutions, but not when they voiced demands to become a constituent element of that state. This lesson was confirmed at high-level political forums, most notably the 1991 Hague Conference, aiming at preserving Yugoslavia, and the Badinter Arbitration Commission established in 1992 by the EC to assess the eligibility of Macedonia for international recognition. These forums stressed human rights, but avoided discussions on constitutional status, instead focusing on security. The 1992 Opinion of the Arbitration Commission gave Macedonia a positive evaluation, since "the Republic had given the necessary guarantees to respect human rights and international peace and security."[37] The Commission decided to recognize that Yugoslavia had dissolved, and insisted on recognizing the territorial integrity of the former republics within Yugoslavia. Hence, it indirectly helped lock the Albanians into Macedonia and Serbia.

It is worth asking what would have been the repercussions on Macedonia's interethnic peace in the long run if international intervention had been exerted to help introduce the principle of concurrent consent (the so-called "Badinter principle" of double majority vote) in the 1991 constitution of the independent republic of Macedonia. This principle was only endorsed ten years later, *after* the 2001 internal warfare, in the Ohrid

Framework Agreement. Had the international community pursued consociational settlement in 1991, the likelihood for escalation of violence would have diminished. In 1991 the Albanians had no institutional mechanism to channel their dissatisfaction with their status reduction from 1989, and were overruled by the Macedonian majority in parliament.[38] This set the course for a grievance to endure and initiated the search for channels outside official politics. The tense situation in Kosovo provided a paragon example that clandestine channeling of grievances is possible when such grievances cannot be properly addressed within the existing state.

In Kosovo, Albanians became aware of the specifics of their relationship with the international community when the 1990 constitutional changes in Serbia sealed the effective elimination of their autonomy. The international community was an ally for defending their human rights, but not for their aspirations to reverse the constitutional changes or alter the internal structure of the state. Indeed, their political participation in state institutions became a subject of contention with the international community. International diplomats encouraged the Democratic League of Kosovo (LDK) to participate in the electoral process. The LDK refrained because it had started to consider Serbia an occupying state, especially after Yugoslavia collapsed in 1991. It raised nationalist demands from republican status to independence. Kosovo Albanians began considering themselves a "people," not a "minority." This secessionism was met with a highly negative response from the international community, apart from the kin-state Albania.

Nevertheless, the international community consistently defended the Kosovars against the human rights violations perpetrated by the Serbian regime. In April 1990 hearings took place in the U.S. Congress. LDK leader Ibrahim Rugova and Veton Suroi, an influential intellectual politician, attended these sessions.[39] Mobilized by Albanian diaspora circles, U.S. senators Dennis DeConcini and Robert Dole arrived in Kosovo leading a group of seven other senators.[40] As Alex Bellamy observed, like their European colleagues, they were given very little information about actual events. In November, Congress issued the so-called "Nickles Amendment," giving Yugoslavia six months to cease repression or risk losing its $U.S.5 million of aid. This document was clearly intended as a mechanism of coercive regulation, but it turned out to be more symbolic than practical. The U.S. realized that if it proceeded to implementation, the lack of aid for Yugoslavia—a state that international powers still wanted to preserve—would impede economic reforms at the federal level.[41]

□ *Guarantee 2: The state will not be internally or externally restructured*

The international community supported the minorities' political participation while ignoring their aspirations for constitutional amendments, but
did not necessarily guarantee that the international legal or domestic sovereignty of the state would not be effectively challenged by the minorities.[42]
Successful guarantees were difficult because Kosovo Albanians proclaimed
independence in 1991, challenging an existing international legal order, and
the war in Bosnia-Herzegovina threatened to spill over into the wider Balkans. Nevertheless, during this formative period the international community acted in clearly statist terms in high diplomatic forums, with mixed
success in turning statements into practice. A gap emerged between policy
and consequences, paving the way for institutionalization of informal relationships with majorities and minorities.

During the critical juncture the international community clearly con-
veyed its intent to preserve the fragile state of Macedonia. The International
Conference on the Former Yugoslavia (ICFY) undertook a successful mediation in reaction to the 1992 Albanian autonomy referendum, challenging
the way political authority was exercised in the state. The ICFY managed to
convince the Albanian elites to cooperate with their Macedonian counter-
parts in a tense international environment. While the long-term impact is
unclear, at the time the mediation was able to prevent further escalation.
The government did not respond with significant violence to such a minority move, surprising given the government's high degree of illiberalism.

The international community had similar aspirations but less success
with Serbia and Kosovo. During major international conferences third parties confirmed that the Serbian state (Yugoslavia) should not be changed
internally or externally. The two conferences aimed at finding solutions to
the collapse of Yugoslavia, in The Hague (1991) and London (1992), and
the Badinter Arbitration Commission considered Kosovo part of Serbia.
Kosovar leaders claimed that the Hague Conference made a fundamental
mistake in recognizing six successor states rather than eight. The additional
two would be Kosovo and Vojvodina, which had de facto republican status
under the old constitutional arrangement.[43] The Badinter Commission considered Kosovo part of Serbia, and so indirectly gave legitimacy to Milosevic's previous maneuvers over the constitution and placed Kosovo in a
"second-tier of international decision-making."[44] The 1992 London Conference—already trying to bring peace to Bosnia-Herzegovina—sidelined
the Kosovar leadership even more bluntly.[45] In a personal interview a

Kosovar participant suggested that the international community was still interested in including a Kosovar delegation at the conference. But its presence would have meant that Milosevic would not cooperate. Thus, a trade-off was considered: in exchange for Kosovo Albanians' nonparticipation a special group focused on Kosovo would be formed within ICFY to act with the Working Group on Ethnic and National Communities and Minorities.[46]

Despite using high-level international conferences to confirm that it would ignore the Kosovars' secessionist demands, the international community was unable to provide guarantees that the state would not be challenged from within. It had no ability to reverse existing secessionist proclamations, and confined itself to co-opting the Kosovars by nurturing their nonviolent strategy. This was simply a strategy of co-optation, in which the status quo was not supposed to change. Yet the international community could co-opt Kosovars about certain policy aspects, but could not convince them to change their goals. Kosovars continued refusing to cooperate with international institutions when participation in local elections was at stake, and when initiatives referred to them as a "minority," not a "people." Though the international community tried to appease Milosevic diplomatically in the hope he would end the war in Bosnia-Herzegovina, it provided no credible guarantees that secessionism would not persist.

In Bulgaria, international agents faced less salient minority challenges, and were more successful in guaranteeing that the state would not be internally restructured. They nevertheless experienced the need to make choices, because an ethnic Turkish faction advocating autonomy—the TDP—surfaced in 1992. International agents refrained from supporting this group, and as a result TDP almost disappeared from the political spectrum at the time. Interestingly enough, the fact that the TDP could not register through legal state channels did not trigger the same vigorous international reaction as the denial of MRF's claim to register only a year earlier. The U.S. embassy and international human rights groups criticized the restrictive constitutional provision prohibiting formation of parties on an ethnic basis, but European governments became reluctant to engage. The international community backed the integrationist minority elite (which was also co-opted), not the one asking for autonomy. Thus, local co-optation of the Turkish minority became politically convenient because it helped avert further security challenges in an already volatile region. Relaxing the international attitude toward a liberal principle of minority rights in the name of international stability provided some informal guarantees to the government that Bulgaria's statehood would not be endangered.

□ *Guarantee 3: Credible long-term commitment to conflict resolution*

How did majority and minority elites know during the early formative period whether the statements of the international community would carry weight in the long run? It is much more challenging to understand when commitments are credible ex ante than ex post. North and Weingast (1989) and Dixit (1996) argue that policy-makers can achieve credibility if they have *reputational capital* from previous interactions. Committing to arrangements incorporating *multiple veto points* to change would be another solution, as would *delegating powers* to an agent with an incentive structure different from that of the principal, such as supranational institutions.[47] Credibility can also stem from whether a third party is a partisan or fair-minded facilitator of agreements, and whether it has a clear plan or is ambiguous or vacillating.[48]

To what extent are these ideas applicable to our three cases? During the critical juncture the international community had not established sufficient reputational capital in an international system undergoing transformation alongside the domestic transitions. External agents did not target the new constitutions to enshrine power sharing, autonomy, or multiple veto points for minority protection. Delegation of powers to an international institution did not actually take place. Processes of reincorporation into European institutions were started to some degree in Bulgaria, but only remotely in Macedonia.

Dispatching peacekeeping forces to Macedonia during the critical juncture allowed for the development of long-term guarantees that the international community would closely monitor majority-minority relations and external threats. Multiple concerns made Macedonian president Kiro Gligorov appeal to the UN in December 1991 to dispatch peacekeeping forces to the country. Following armed confrontations in Croatia in April and May, a contagion of violence to Macedonia seemed almost inevitable, especially against the backdrop of Macedonia's declaration of independence in September. Fears of possible Serbian intervention intensified after the peaceful withdrawal of the Yugoslav National Army, which left the country with no arms or military equipment. Despite Macedonia's declared neutrality regarding hostilities in former Yugoslavia, Macedonian authorities feared that if Serbia gained the upper hand in Bosnia-Herzegovina it would

open a second war against Macedonia.[49] Albanian demands on the new
state exacerbated the insecurities of Macedonian Slavs, who feared that if
full-blown conflict were to erupt in Kosovo, Albanians of Macedonia would
join in and turn the western parts of the country into a base for rebel
incursions from Kosovo.[50]

When speaking of conflict prevention, scholars and practitioners alike
emphasize the positive role of UNPROFOR, the first UN preventive deployment mission dispatched to Macedonia, and the subsequent UN Preventive
Deployment Force (UNPREDEP) mission, which was operational until
1998.[51] As Carment and Rowlands observe, intense early peacekeeping intervention yields cooperative results more quickly.[52] This is especially true
if the force is overwhelmingly powerful and impartial. The dispatch of
peacekeeping forces during the critical juncture affected how the new rules
of the political game were to be redefined. Externally, UNPROFOR's presence in Macedonia had a major deterrent effect on Milosevic in Serbia: a
"line in the sand" regarding the war in Bosnia-Herzegovina. But it affected
the domestic majority-minority relationship as well. Fulfilling the function
of an army, though not mandated with firepower for offense, UNPROFOR
became a neutral arbiter by giving the minorities the security of a watchdog
over government operations, and by assuring the majority that minority
provocations or violent acts would not be tolerated.[53] It helped to contain
initial manifestations of interethnic violence and create a sense of a protected environment in which international agencies could thrive.

Another organization that became active early in the transition was the
OSCE Spillover Mission dispatched in 1992 to Macedonia at President Gligorov's request. The OSCE provided an early commitment to conflict resolution and an important role in addressing domestic ethnic affairs through
more consensual mechanisms. While cooperating with the UNPREDEP,
OSCE was more political.[54] A special office dealt with minority affairs and
held consultations between minority members and government officials.
The OSCE became the most important agent for monitoring elections and
working behind the scenes on crucial minority complaints related to education, media, and self-government.

In contrast, a variety of coercive and consensual international initiatives
exercised only a temporary deterrent effect on the Serbian regime regarding
Kosovo, and did not provide long-term international commitment to conflict resolution. These initiatives were not part of a long-term strategy to
address the Kosovo problem, but ad hoc measures to address contagion

from the war in Bosnia-Herzegovina. Most notable was the so-called "Christmas Ultimatum" of December 1992. This one-sentence cable, issued by the outgoing George Bush, Sr., administration, warned Milosevic that "in the event of conflict in Kosovo caused by Serbian action, the U.S. will be prepared to employ military force against Serbians in Kosovo and Serbia proper."[55] The ultimatum stopped Milosevic from intimidating the Kosovars on a larger scale, and empowered them psychologically. It was confirmed by President Clinton on his arrival in office, but it was not a long-term strategy. It's aim was to keep Kosovo out of the war, not to find long-term solutions.[56]

The credibility of the international commitment suffered as well, because it was unable to establish a long-term presence on the ground in Kosovo. In August 1992 the OSCE dispatched a mission to Kosovo and Vojvodina to monitor human rights violations and open dialogue.[57] This mission was intended to be of long duration, but in 1993 Milosevic refused to extend the visas of its personnel. Milosevic was suspicious of its "international" mediation aspect, since he considered Kosovo an "internal" affair, and became more hostile when a July 1992 Helsinki Summit temporarily suspended Yugoslavia's membership in the OSCE.[58] This mission was much weaker than the OSCE Spillover mission in Macedonia. The effect of its reports was almost negligible, since its findings were not linked to particular enforcement mechanisms such as sanctions or military intervention. Perhaps without the OSCE monitors the government might have engaged in even greater violence: in 1993 large-scale arrests took place immediately after the monitors left Kosovo, and hundreds of families were mistreated.[59] But human rights abuses continued, and violence remained "extensive," even while the OSCE was present.

Finally, the credibility of international commitment failed because the ICFY diplomatic initiatives did not halt the violence in Kosovo. These initiatives lacked the capacity to deliver partly because Milosevic was a key player in the ICFY, which limited international leverage over him. The Working Group on Kosovo avoided dealing with the province's constitutional status, and focused on practical solutions to concrete problems, most notably education.[60]

In Bulgaria international institutions established prospects for a long-term presence as early as 1991. Bulgaria and the European Community signed a Trade and Cooperation Agreement in 1990, and the same year Bulgaria joined EC's PHARE Program.[61] In 1992 Bulgaria was admitted into the Council of Europe, considered an antechamber for future integration into the European Union (EC became EU after 1992). The parliament adopted the European Convention on Human Rights (ECHR), which views minority rights on an individual basis, like the UN covenants, but has stronger implementation mechanisms, legally binding the state to rulings of the European Court of Human Rights provided the convention is fully incorporated into domestic law. Thus a member of a minority whose rights are violated by state institutions has an established channel as an individual to file a legal suit against his or her own state. These early steps toward European integration and legal repercussions from the Council of Europe created binding mechanisms for the Bulgarian government to respect human rights, and for minorities to voice their grievances.

The evidence from these cases demonstrates how important it was to have an *early commitment* by the international community to reduce inter-ethnic tensions during the transition, and to provide credible guarantees by way of neutrality and presence on the ground with peacekeeping forces, mediation, monitoring, and engagement with regional integration initiatives. Scholars working on credible commitments tend to omit the effect of the *type* of long-term commitment on the evolution of conflict trajectories. In my analysis *these types are contextualized and have specific content.* In Macedonia and Bulgaria, where the international community provided long-term guarantees, we clearly see that the type of commitment was different. In Macedonia institutions concerned with security rather than democratization entered the transition process first, while in Bulgaria international organizations were occupied with initiatives for democratization. This analysis does not indicate that grave security concerns for potential contagion effects from the war in Bosnia-Herzegovina could have been averted by a simple focus on democratization. But it does aim to increase awareness of the effects of security-based versus democratization-based informal arrangements on establishing relationships between local and international agents during the formative period.

Conclusion

The major impact of the international community on the ethnonational conflicts in Kosovo, Macedonia, and Bulgaria started during the formative

period (1987/89–1992). At that point the international community adver-
tised its abilities to guarantee minority political participation in state institutions, its assurance that the state would not be restructured internally or
externally, and its long-term commitment to conflict resolution. But only
in Bulgaria did the international community fulfill all three conditions. It
fulfilled them only partially in Macedonia, and not at all in Kosovo. Regardless of its success in follow-through on formal commitments, international
agents became part of a tripartite dynamic relating to majorities and minorities in specific contextualized ways.

As a result of early interventions at the end of the critical juncture,
majority and minority elites became locked into ways of considering the
international community as an ally for their own cause. Domestic and international agents were set on a path of relationship specificities, foreclosing
earlier possible alternatives. Majority elites relied on the international community regarding the nonredefinition of the state, but also for long-term
integration processes (Bulgarian elites), and security and preservation of
the state (Macedonian elites). In all three cases, the minority elites considered the international community an arena where they could voice concerns about rights violations. The Turks of Bulgaria and Albanians of
Macedonia relied on it for protecting their political participation in state
institutions, yet they were also aware of the limits of their chances for support. The Albanians of Macedonia were ignored whenever they raised demands to become a constituent element of the state, and Kosovo Albanians
were expected to confine themselves to nonviolent struggle.

These findings point toward the important causal impact of *timing and
sequencing*. Early intervention by the international community does not
necessarily mean that it mitigates existing conflicts, as some scholarly accounts on conflict resolution assert. The three above-mentioned conditions
of an early intervention, conducive to the de-escalation of conflicts, need to
be present. One could argue that it would be difficult for the international
community to provide similar credible guarantees across different types of
cases, especially because the claims of majorities and minorities are often
different. In Kosovo specifically, claims were mutually exclusive about territory as an indivisible issue, which traditionally poses huge obstacles to negotiated solutions.

While such arguments make sense for discussing phenomena such as
integrationist, autonomist, and secessionist movements, if viewed from the
point of a path-dependent analysis their appeal as a causal explanation

weakens. Despite slightly different geopolitical interests, the international community had similar starting points in each case: promotion of human and minority rights and state stability, and reluctance to engage with local conflicts. While antecedent conditions from the Cold War may have informed the choices of the international community on how to act during the critical juncture, these conditions did not determine how the conflicts would evolve. Contingencies became important during the substantial changes in the formative period. The fact that the international community did not decisively oppose the decrease in status of the Albanians of Kosovo and Macedonia in 1989 created path dependencies that encouraged higher resentment among the minorities in the short and long run. In addition, a lack of credible commitment to conflict resolution in Kosovo was important for how the conflict would evolve. Kosovo Albanians did not proclaim independence until after the collapse of Yugoslavia in 1991, two years after the transition had started and the international community had been passively involved.

While the international community decisively influenced the formation of conflict dynamics during the critical juncture, its impact diminished in subsequent periods of self-reinforcement because its actions were constrained by the vested interests of the three agents locked in the triangular relationship. Chapter 4 will elaborate in more detail on self-reinforcement mechanisms and on processes of change in which external agents were involved.

Chapter 4

International Agents, Self-Reinforcement of Conflict Dynamics, and Processes of Change

We now turn to how non-identity-based third parties contributed to the *duration* of conflicts and their *change*. By delineating specific causal mechanisms of conflict perpetuation, the following adds to established scholarship on third-party interventions. An insightful yet inconclusive quantitative literature on civil wars has analyzed primarily how third parties change the capabilities of the government or opposition on the ground, how they manipulate the information available to local belligerents, and how they relate to achievement of military victory or negotiated settlement.[1] Evidence suggests that military and economic interventions tend to increase the duration of civil wars, but this claim has been disputed.[2] These quantitative studies have established the associations between different variables and the duration of civil wars, but do not address the causal mechanisms in conflict duration. The present qualitative account focuses on self-perpetuating causal mechanisms and processes of change, and theorizes about both violent and nonviolent conflicts beyond civil wars.

How was a tripartite dynamic between majorities, minorities, and the international community perpetuated after the formative period? Where did opportunities for change originate during the 1990s? I argue that mechanisms of "adaptive expectations" and "learning" aided the informal institutionalization of conflictual, semiconflictual, and nonviolent conflict dynamics over time. International agents became absorbed into these dynamics, so their actual influence decreased. Opportunities for change arose from exogenous shocks and long-term regional integration initiatives. Exogenous shocks—the 1995 Dayton Peace Agreement, the 1997 collapse of

Albania, NATO's 1999 intervention in Kosovo and contagion effects in its aftermath—triggered drastic changes, mostly in the direction of conflict escalation. By casting the "long shadow" of future membership in Euro-Atlantic organizations, and using conditionality more than socialization mechanisms, the international community and specifically the European Union contributed to incremental change in the direction of interethnic peace.[3] EU rules were often "layered" on top of existing ones.[4]

Causal mechanisms fostered the development of durable contextualized ways through which agents related to each other in a tripartite relationship. The timing and sequencing of some exogenous shocks became important for the radicalization process in the cases researched here, and also how they contributed to the escalation of conflicts in Kosovo and Macedonia by the end of the 1990s. How prospects for EU integration fostered change without drastic reforms in Bulgaria in the same time period closes the chapter.

Self-Reinforcement Processes and Adaptation in a Triangular Relationship

As in domestic majority-minority relations, *adaptive expectations* were also important mechanisms driving the international community, majorities, and minorities toward self-perpetuating behavior in the mid- to late 1990s. Adaptation offered the opportunity to perpetuate vested interests established during the formative period. Figure 6 shows a triangular relationship resulting from international community intervention early in the formative period, and the contextualized links established between the three parties. The relationship between majority and minority is primary, but the international intervention adds new material. Local agents adapted their behavior expecting the international community to take a certain position, and vice versa. These decisions were not driven simply by rational self-interest or anticipation of rational moves of the other actors. They were embedded in the constraints of the ways the agents were connected to each other. I argue that *the links between agents are more static* than those in studies using bargaining logic and emphasizing a fluid dynamic. Decisions can be made strategically, but in the context of bounded rationality stemming from the *contextualized ways* the informal rules of the ethnonational game consolidated. Through the mechanism of adaptive expectations these rules became

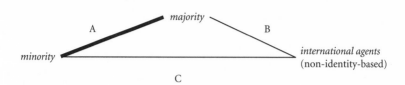

The Structure of the Links

BULGARIA	MACEDONIA	KOSOVO
A—minority—majority: ⇨ Minimal increase of minority status ⇨ Co-optation ⇨ Minority acceptance of the state B—majority—international agents: ⇨ Nonredefinition of the state ⇨ Prospects for EU integration C—minority—international community: ⇨ Political participation ⇨ Voicing of minority rights violations	A—minority—majority: ⇨ Minimal decrease of minority status ⇨ Co-optation ⇨ Two-pronged strategy towards the state B—majority—international agents: ⇨ Non-redefinition of the state ⇨ Provision of security C—minority—international agents: ⇨ Political participation but no demands for becoming a constituent element of the state ⇨ Voicing minority rights violations	A—minority—majority: ⇨ Drastic decrease of status ⇨ Coercion ⇨ Minority rejection of the state B—majority—international agents: ⇨ Nonredefinition of the state C—minority—international agents: ⇨ no political participation, but nonviolent strategy ⇨ Voicing of minority rights violations

Figure 6. A triangular relationship.

internalized and binding, resembling what Helmke and Levitsky would call "informal institutions" that enable and constrain behavior.

Chapter 2 explored the self-perpetuating dynamic of the majority-minority relationship, shown by Link A in Figure 6. In the following pages I discuss the self-reinforcement processes of conflict dynamics in Macedonia (1992–2000), Kosovo (1992–1998), and Bulgaria (1992–1997). I show how "adaptive expectations" became crucial for self-perpetuating behavior regarding the links between the international community and the majority (Link B) and minority (Link C).

Kathleen Thelen argues that once a set of institutions is in place, their structure constrains agents and induces certain kinds of behavior, that agents adapt their strategies to reflect and reinforce the logic of the system.[5] Informal arrangements such as conflict dynamics are often as rigid as formal institutions, and provide legitimacy and constraint to reinforce previous behavior. The minorities in this study had no formal pacts with international organizations, but international interest in global human and minority rights encouraged them to consider the organizations as allies on these issues. The international community remained staunchly opposed to redefinition of the state during this period, constraining minorities from seeking support. They turned instead to kin-states and diasporas.[6] The majorities shared with the international community the conviction that nonredefinition of the state is a legitimate stand in world politics; that is, they defended the Westphalian world order.

☐ *Adaptation between majorities and the international community: minimal adoption of international minority rights*

Because majorities shared an interest with the international community in the nonredefinition of the state, adaptation was not difficult. They adapted to international demands by signing and ratifying international human and minority rights legislation, but implemented it minimally and only insofar as external pressures for democratization were linked to their domestic needs. In Bulgaria, where prospects for EU integration were at stake, the majority elites implemented minority rights legislation only if it advanced the country's candidacy and did not challenge the position of the Bulgarian language or ask for territorially based rights. In Macedonia, the need to preserve the state and maintain security through international peacekeeping forces predominated. Since international support for nonredefinition in the Yugoslavian case was the most ambiguous, the Milosevic regime was the least interested in human and minority rights legislation. Milosevic adapted by maneuvering through the legislative ambiguities created by the collapse of socialist Yugoslavia.

In Bulgaria there was a period of self-reinforcement between 1992, when the formative period ended, and 1997, when the European Commission published its first "opinion" about preparation for future membership.[7] European integration was high on the Bulgarian foreign policy agenda, regardless of the force in power—technocrats (1992–1994), socialists (1994–1996), or democrats (since early 1997). The 1993 Copenhagen criteria demanding minority rights reforms became an important political requirement. Yet, though these criteria were normatively strong and required compliance for accession, they were "weakly defined and poorly elaborated," as Hughes and Sasse commented, and created dilemmas among candidate countries on how to determine whether the conditions had been satisfied.[8] Most notably, ambiguities opened opportunities to avoid compliance. Bulgaria signed a "Europe Agreement" in 1993 and applied for EU membership in 1995, but did not make

Table 3. Adoption of International Human and Minority Rights Legislation

	Years of ratification			
Treaty	Bulgaria	Macedonia	SFRY	FRY
ICCPR/OP1/OP2	1970/92/99	1994/94/95	1971	2001/01/01
ICESCR	1970	1994		2001
CERD	1966	1994		2001
CAT	1986	1994	1991	2001
CPPCG	1950	1994	1950	2001
ECHR	1992	1997	ns	2004
P1/P2/P3/P4/P5	92/92/92/93s-00/92	97/97/97/97/97	ns	2004
FCPNM	1999	1997	ns	2001
ECRML	ns	s1996	ns	ns
Geneva Conventions	1954	s1993		s2001
P1/P2 to the GC	89/89	s93/93		s01/01

Abbreviations:
ICCPR   International Covenant on Civil and Political Rights
OP1/O2   Optional Protocols to ICCPR
ICESCR   International Covenant on Economic, Social and Cultural Rights
CERD   Convention on the Elimination of All Forms of Racial Discrimination
CAT   Convention against Torture and Other Cruel, Inhuman, or Degrading Treatment
         or Punishment
CPPCG   Convention on the Prevention and Punishment of the Crime of Genocide
ECHR   European Convention on Human Rights
P1/P2... Additional Protocols
FCPNM   Framework Convention on the Protection of National Minorities
ECRML   European Charter for Regional and Minority Languages
GC   Geneva Conventions
ns   not signed
s   only signed, but not ratified
s/...   signed during researched period and ratified in indicated year thereafter

significant progress on minority rights until 1997–1998. Major problems existed regarding instruments for linguistic freedoms. Bulgaria ratified instruments with a clear individual-rights focus, such as one of the Additional
Protocols of the European Convention on Human Rights (1993) and the
European Convention for the Prevention of Torture (1994), but hesitated on
conventions considered minority-specific.

The Bulgarian elites refused to sign the European Charter on Regional
and Minority Languages (ECRML), fearing that linguistic rights—especially
if granted to a previously unrecognized Macedonian minority—would

open the door for future territorially based demands. They exploited the policy inconsistency typical of the EU during the accession process, which did not press as hard for adoption of this convention in Bulgaria as elsewhere in Eastern Europe, most notably Slovakia.[9] In the eyes of many local officials this convention lacked legitimacy because Western European countries such as Belgium and France had not ratified it either. Nevertheless, international pressure on the socialist government in 1995 was critical for its decision not to adopt a draft law that envisaged the exclusive use of Bulgarian in public affairs. This was a successful international attempt to stop the trend of giving primacy to the majority language, not a promotion of positive linguistic freedoms.

International pressure to adopt the Council of Europe Framework Convention on the Protection of National Minorities (FCPNM) started building in Eastern Europe after it was opened for signature in 1995. It did not yield results in Bulgaria until it was linked to active conditionality for EU membership and a pro-Western government taking power in 1997. NATO, though a major player in Bulgaria's transition, did not significantly pressure for minority rights reforms.[10] The alliance relied on the monitoring reports of international organizations. As long as the Turkish minority was politically integrated and did not pose a security threat, the country's minority rights record was considered acceptable. For example, the international community was aware in the mid-1990s of MRF complaints that ethnic minority conscripts were placed in construction units and not allowed to carry arms in potential combat units. After the construction units were disbanded, concern for the place of minorities in the army became less pronounced.[11]

The relationship between the Macedonian elites and the international community during the period of self-reinforcement—from the end of the formative period in 1992 to the signing of the EU Accession Agreement in 2000—was locked in two aspects: preservation of the state including its nonredefinition, and security. These elements created a different bounded rationality for action compared to the Bulgarian case. The need to preserve the state and the fragile nation was of utmost importance to the Macedonian elites, and they adapted accordingly to international pressures for democratization. Majorities related positively to personal diplomacy and official pressures from the ICFY and the Council of Europe to conduct an internationally supervised census in 1994, appoint Albanians to the cabinet, and increase media coverage in Albanian on the basis of population percentage.[12] This gave them some international legitimacy.

The Macedonian-dominated parliament adopted international legislation in two rounds, with specific *timing* related to the elites' dire need for international approval for the state-building efforts. The first round took place in 1993, when it adopted a number of UN-based international legal instruments, as demonstrated in Table 3. This move took place soon after Macedonia became a UN member, when it needed to redefine international legal commitments that expired after it proclaimed independence from Yugoslavia. The second round, adoption of Council of Europe conventions, took place in 1996–1997. Macedonia became part of the ECHR and accepted its five Additional Protocols, the FCPNM, and the ECRML. Other countries in Eastern Europe used adoption of these conventions to signal that they were democratizing on the path to EU integration. Macedonia did so because it was striving to be recognized as a state with its self-proclaimed name, the Republic of Macedonia, which was challenged by Greece. It needed to communicate that it could make serious commitments on international treaties.

Surprisingly, unlike Bulgaria and other countries in Eastern Europe, Macedonia had no problems adopting the FCPNM and ECRML at an early stage of development. Given the experience with collective rights in former Yugoslavia, the Macedonian elites did not have to work to persuade their constituencies of the policies' appropriateness. Whether the government planned to implement this international legislation was another question. Some of my interviewees related that the quick adoption of human rights instruments helped elites build a case against critical domestic and international agents seeking to further expand minority rights. The elites argued that the new country had demonstrated its commitments, and that minority rights were broader than in other reforming countries in Eastern Europe.[13]

Like the Macedonian elites, the international community was not primarily focused on advancing minority rights, even though these rights were considered necessary for democratization. Aspiring to preserve security and a peaceful interethnic status quo, it tended to downplay rights violations and act uncritically of the government, which it saw as a stabilizing force in a fragile state and region.[14] Whether international organizations had an explicit mandate in security or democratization, they delivered the same signal: security mattered more than minority rights. As a peacekeeping mission, UNPREDEP had a security-based mandate. It had a political wing interested in democratic reforms, but only on a procedural level; implementation of minority rights was tangential.

The OSCE gained a reputation as the institution concerned with minority rights throughout the 1990s, but faced constraints. Between 1994 and 2000 the OSCE High Commissioner on National Minorities, Max Van der Stoel, played a leading role in developing the legislative and institutional basis for a multicultural university in which Albanians could receive higher education in their own language after 2001.[15] However, the mission continued to reinforce the notion that security mattered more, including the idea that the state should not be redefined. While human rights organizations such as the International Helsinki Federation, Amnesty International, and Human Rights Watch openly criticized the new constitutional status putting the Macedonian nation above other nationalities, the OSCE kept a low profile. During the controversial raising of the Albanian flag on municipal buildings in Tetovo in 1997, the OSCE did not condemn police violence against the demonstrators, instead engaging in diminishing the tensions. As a senior OSCE official mentioned during a personal interview, when the organization went too far in intervening in relations between the Albanian elites and the government, the government reminded OSCE of its mandate to monitor "spillover" with no broader functions.[16]

As a civilian power promoting democracy, the EU had a minimal effect on Macedonia between 1995—when it established diplomatic relations—and the end of internal warfare in 2001. But it too joined the chorus of international organizations emphasizing security and downplaying minority rights. The assistance Macedonia received through the Programme Harmonisé d'Appui au Renforcement de l'Éducation (PHARE) Program—the main EU financial instrument for building institutional and economic capacities in Eastern Europe—was focused on democratization but had little impact on interethnic relations.[17] Until the start of negotiations on the Stabilization and Association Agreement (SAA) in 2000, the EU considered Macedonia mainly in regional initiatives aimed at preserving security in the region, such as the Royamount Process (1996), the Regional Approach (1997), and the Stability Pact for Southeastern Europe (1999).[18] The EU also provided inconsistent monitoring evaluations of respect for minority rights. Gjurcilova points out that an April 1998 European Commission communication mentioned that Macedonia still needed progress on a number of human rights issues, including minority education. Six months later the Commission noted that Macedonia "clearly presents a picture of political maturity" and is a positive example in the region, respecting basic principles of democracy and regional cooperation.[19] This sudden change marked not increased respect for minority rights in Macedonia but the inauguration of an initially pro-Western coalition the international community viewed as having potential to introduce reforms.

What we see in Macedonia is a clear-cut case of "securitization of minority rights." According to Kymlicka, countries in Eastern Europe and the developing world are more inclined than industrialized Western countries to securitize minority rights, that is, to view minority rights through the lens of national security and loyalty, not fairness and justice.[20] Whether such a clear division between the West and the rest indeed exists—especially if we reflect on the increased securitization of discourses on diasporas in Western societies after the 9/11 terrorist attacks—Kymlicka's ideas are well taken and raise two additional points.[21] First, securitization of minority rights was more pronounced in Macedonia than in Bulgaria and other countries of Eastern Europe. In Macedonia and other entities that emerged out of former Yugoslavia, including Kosovo, the transition was dominated by the majority's security concerns rather than democratization. Second, scholars and practitioners have only recently started thinking that the international community itself contributed to this securitization, by conveying the signal that implementation of minority rights should not be taken seriously. I argue that this signal was internalized by the local elites, demonstrating that *learning effects* matter for the perpetuation of conflict dynamics over time.[22] In the cases here, learning this pattern strongly influenced how majorities and minorities related to the international community after major violence.[23]

"Adaptive expectations" worked as a mechanism for both the Milosevic regime and the international community, despite their antagonistic relationship. Milosevic and the international agents continued to perpetuate their joint interest in not restructuring the state internally or externally, even after the critical juncture ended in 1992. Milosevic was considered an ally of the international community for an expected peace deal for Bosnia-Herzegovina even after the 1995 Dayton Agreement. As earlier, the UN and OSCE pressured him fruitlessly for his human rights violations in Kosovo. But UN resolutions and reports had no follow-through, and OSCE monitors left Kosovo in 1993.[24] Milosevic adapted to international pressures by exploiting the international legislative vacuum into which the remainder of Yugoslavia (Serbia and Montenegro) fell after socialist Yugoslavia collapsed. The gap emerged from the fact that the UN considered that the old Yugoslavia ceased to exist in 1992.[25] The new Yugoslavia—like Macedonia—

needed to reconfirm international commitments in its domestic legislative process.

Unlike the leaders of Macedonia, Milosevic had no interest in reconfirming the old Yugoslavia's commitments or abiding by new international human and minority rights legislation. He created a legislative façade with the 1992 constitution, which still postulated some autonomy for the Kosovars. But he enforced coercive "emergency measures" against the Kosovars as previously described. Some specific international decisions indirectly aided his opportunism, like a restriction on OSCE membership and denial of Council of Europe membership as long as his regime lasted.[26] These decisions meant that adopting the Council conventions was off the table. Only after his departure from power in 2000 did the new Serbian governing elites adopt major human and minority rights conventions.

□ *Adaptation between minorities and international community:* *internationalization of minority rights*

Minorities and the international community also acted on "adaptive expectations" regarding each other. Minorities relied on the international community to provide a "voice" for complaining of human rights violations. As Keck and Síkkink as well as Risse, Ropp, and Síkkink observed, in the post-Cold War world international organizations became important allies to local human rights groups for exerting pressure on their own states for domestic change by way of "boomerang" or "spiral" effects.[27] In Bulgaria, Macedonia, and Yugoslavia (Serbia and Montenegro), minority grievances were directed toward government channels—such as regular reports of the U.S. State Department and European institutions— but more toward NGOs with minority rights orientations, such as the Helsinki Federation, Human Rights Watch, Minority Rights Group, and Amnesty International. The Soros Foundation, with local branches in Bulgaria and Macedonia and support for projects on civil society in Kosovo, played an important role in developing awareness of violations. Search for Common Ground and the Greek Helsinki Monitor were especially active in Macedonia, and Oxfam and the Italian Catholic Communita di Saint Egidio in Kosovo.

The "internationalization" of minority rights violations became a clearcut minority strategy along the informal lines established in relationship with the international community. The Turks of Bulgaria became especially vocal when their political participation in the state institutions was endangered. When the BSP was in power (1994–1997), they struggled to maintain even the minimal achievements of the early transition, and struggled to prevent government initiatives to reverse minority rights protections. The MRF strongly internationalized the renewed challenges to its registration and its power in local self-government. The severe manipulation of results in the 1995 local elections in the southeastern town of Kardzhali, densely inhabited by ethnic Turks, became a focal point for contention. The corruption threatened to replace the local legally elected MRF mayor with a socialist one. The Parliamentary Assembly of the Council of Europe (PACE) became an appropriate forum to voice complaints.[28] In addition, MRF leader Ahmet Dogan had long talks with U.S. and EU diplomats, and complained about the BSP to the Socialist International, European Parliament, and other organizations.[29] As a result of international pressure, in April 1996 the Bulgarian Supreme Court overruled a local court decision that declared the elections invalid and reinstalled the mayor elected on the MRF ticket.[30]

The MRF used international channels to voice complaints on a number of other issues of minority rights concern. One was the draft law of 1995–1996 envisaging compulsory use of Bulgarian in public affairs. The MRF alarmed the media and public in Turkey, and submitted its text to PACE and to the U.S. Carnegie Endowment.[31] Another example was the draft broadcasting law that did not envisage programs in Turkish. In addition to U.S. institutions such as the Carnegie Endowment, the local branch of the Soros Foundation became an important channel on this occasion. The MRF also complained to the Council of Europe concerning mother tongue education, arguing that the study of Turkish should be compulsory, not optional.[32]

The international community and the Albanian minority adapted to each other's political limitations in Macedonia as well. Albanians of Macedonia used international channels to voice grievances related to political participation and self-government, but kept a low profile on demands to become a constituent element of the state, where they enjoyed no support from the international community. Complaints about political participation were launched in direct and indirect ways. Minority elites—in government or opposition—argued to international organizations that they did not enjoy enough representation in power structures such as police and defense ministries and local self-government. The OSCE and its High

Commissioner on the National Minorities became allied in an effort to develop legislation on self-government and educational rights. The Council of Europe aided the Albanians on the need for Albanian local self-government and education.[33] The Albanian elites made further indirect claims about political participation by arguing that their actual population was higher than the 1994 census results, which counted only Albanians with Macedonian citizenship. The highly restrictive 1992 citizenship law required fifteen years of residence, and excluded a large number of Albanians. According to their estimates, around 100,000 Albanians had worked in other parts of Yugoslavia during communism and thus did not meet the residency requirements.[34] The numbers game was important to the Albanian elites to prove they deserved more constitutional rights.

The Albanian minority adapted to the international community's expectations that Albanians would not challenge the state by making their demands for constituent status less open and frequent. Such demands surfaced rarely—with the exception of the DPA rise to power in 1997—and subsided quickly. The discussion about the citizenship law—in contrast to those on self-government or education—was also surprisingly muted in Macedonia, especially compared to the heated debates in which the international community was involved in the Baltic republics.

In Kosovo, the Albanian leadership in the shadow state sought internationalization of the nonviolence campaign and of reports on human rights violations. The government-in-exile, founded initially in Slovenia in 1991/ 1992, relocated to Germany and gradually established foreign offices, including in the UK, Sweden, Switzerland, Belgium, Albania, and Turkey. According to former prime minister in exile Bujar Bukoshi, its presence was tolerated in these countries.[35] While lobbying worked more successfully in the U.S., some good relations were fostered with various governments in Europe.[36] LDK's relationship with Germany, in particular, evolved from connections with the Green Party and some parliamentarians to permanent contacts with German foreign ministry officials.[37] With Bukoshi in Bonn and LDK leader Ibrahim Rugova often visiting from Kosovo, discussions with diplomats, international organizations, and diaspora groups were commonplace.

Discussions often evolved around the nonviolence strategy, and self-determination claims were toned down. According to one interviewee, when trying to internationalize the conflict, the Kosovar leadership stressed the plight of Albanians in the human rights area rather than the national question. It feared that if the latter were addressed in a form other than defense of human rights, the international community "could have misunderstood" the Kosovars. The LDK goal was to prove that it was cooperative with the international community, and that by pursuing a strategy of nonviolence the Kosovars were ready to take responsibility for the governance of their nation.[38] The leadership was also trying to prove its pro-Western orientation and avoided links with organizations from the Islamic world.[39]

International governments regularly solicited information from the Kosovo leadership about human rights violations. However, NGOs were the most active on the ground. They recorded and emphasized human rights violations without engaging in the politics of the self-determination struggle. They operated through consensual politics, which were incapable of decreasing the level of violence. Milosevic regarded international NGOs as "enemies," and did not trust their impartiality for mediating between him and the Kosovo leadership. International NGOs with political functions— such as the German Friedrich Ebert Foundation and Bertelsmann Foundation, and the Princeton-based Project on Ethnic Relations—aspired to connect the parties, with no particular success.[40] Other meetings in New York and Paris also did not lead to specific results.[41] The only effort that partially succeeded was the education agreement brokered by the Communita di Saint Egidio, which quickly failed.[42]

In the absence of high-level international initiatives, the most active NGOs in Kosovo engaged with civic projects. The Soros Foundation and Oxfam provided financial support for local projects aimed at physical and psychological survival of the Albanian community. The Mother Teresa Society, part of the parallel structures, was an important local counterpart.[43] WHO and UNICEF launched a polio immunization campaign together with the parallel society and state system to immunize all children of Kosovo. Oxfam developed a program to improve the water supply system in ethnically mixed villages.[44] Although those organizations were highly influential, they did not go beyond voicing human rights concerns.

In a book comparing the internationalization campaigns of the Zapatista uprising in Mexico and the Ogoni movement in Nigeria, Clifford Bob found that successful strategies for local movements depended on how they framed their grievances to match the interests of international organizations.[45] The Kosovo Albanians framed their relationship with the international community largely in terms of nonviolent struggle and the human rights abuses they endured. Yet this did not bring positive change, and nonviolence became associated with corruption of local elites in the face of repression and nonresolution of conflicts.

Forces of Change: Exogenous Shocks and EU Integration

Exogenous shocks occur suddenly and are beyond the control of policy-makers in a particular country.[46] Yet attributing too much explanatory power to them has been rightly criticized because moments of crisis do not simply cause certain outcomes. As Legro points out, earthquakes can have radically different implications depending on factors such as the area where they occur and how strong the buildings are. In the political world, endogenous characteristics—such as ideational constructs by the local agents affected by the shock or political agents' interests and relationships—can strongly affect what kinds of change result from the same shock.[47] We need to reveal the links between the causal mechanisms they launch and how the shocks are processed by political agents.[48]

This section addresses the causal impact of four exogenous shocks that led to internal warfare in Kosovo (1998–1999) and Macedonia (2001): the 1995 Dayton Agreement, the 1997 collapse of Albania, the 1999 NATO military intervention; and the contagion effects of the 2001 Kosovo conflict in Macedonia. These shocks differ in that some were policies induced by the international community (Dayton and the NATO intervention) and others were crises and contagion effects from the political neighborhood. They all belong to the category of exogenous shocks from the viewpoint of key local agents because the shocks were not within their control.

Change in Bulgaria was more incremental. The EU conditionality that gained importance after 1997 inspired the majority elites to adopt major legislative and policy changes in the sphere of minority rights. Socialization with human and minority rights was present, but rationalist logic related to cost-benefit calculations for the European integration process prevailed. EU integration was not a shock but a long-term exogenous process, partially endogenized in the nonviolent conflict dynamic from the early 1990s.

Sequencing of Exogenous Shocks: Dayton Peace Agreement and the Collapse of Albania

The specific *timing and sequencing* of key exogenous shocks had causal implications on the evolution of the Kosovo conflict. The failure of the Dayton

Accords to resolve the Kosovo question in 1995, followed by the collapse of the Albanian state in 1997, *together* contributed to the radicalization of local Kosovo politics.

A number of studies have pointed out that the Dayton Agreement led to the radicalization of Kosovo politics, because it delegitimized Rugova's strategy of nonviolence as incapable of achieving the nationalist goal. The general narrative goes that because a solution for Kosovo was not incorporated, Milosevic received political concessions and the Kosovars were left vulnerable to the Serbian regime. The Agreement mentioned Kosovo only marginally, alongside demands for Serbia's cooperation with the ICTY and in the context of imposing an "outer wall of sanctions" on Serbia.[49] Dayton also showed Kosovo Albanians that their politics of peaceful internationalization had failed, and had opened an opportunity for international recognition and consolidation of Yugoslavia (Serbia and Montenegro), born in 1992. In 1996 the EU recognized this new Yugoslavia, delivering a further blow to the Kosovars.[50]

Dayton certainly triggered the radicalization of Kosovo's domestic politics, but the causal mechanisms linking Dayton and radicalization are only one aspect of an altered conflict dynamic weakening nonviolence as a strategy, and this was not a foregone conclusion. The immediate post-Dayton period had two competitive political alternatives. If the Albanian state had not collapsed in 1997, two years after Dayton, and so added its own impact on change, it is not clear that radicalization would have occurred, or would have occurred as quickly as it did.

One alternative emerging after Dayton has received little attention. It involves scattered individuals and groups, including Rugova to some degree, who continued to pursue a peaceful solution to Kosovo self-determination. They did not rule out some remote rapprochement with Serbia. The 1996 educational agreement was a major step in this direction. Rugova was persuaded to enter talks on the agreement after numerous visits with the pope in Rome and the remote backing of the United States.[51] This was not an easy task, because Rugova refrained from engaging with the Serbian regime to preserve the nationalist goal and his reputation as a leader. At the same time, former political prisoner and head of the Council for Defense of Human Rights Adem Demaci developed a proposal to create a confederal state, "Balkania," to be constituted by Serbia, Montenegro, and Kosovo as equal units. Erin Jenne is among the few scholars to give a good analytical reading of this situation, through the prism of her ethnic

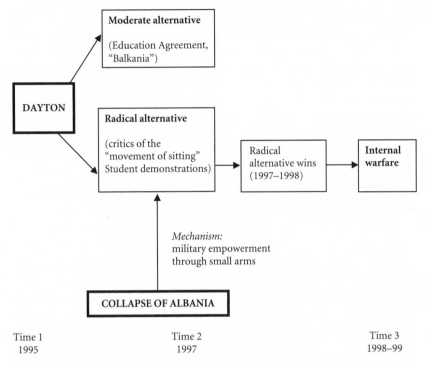

Figure 7. Sequence of exogenous shocks: Dayton 1995, collapse of Albania 1997.

bargaining model. She argued that Serbia signaled its nationalist intent after Dayton, and the international community signaled a lack of interest in the Kosovars, causing Kosovars to perceive their vulnerability and opt for a strategy of moderation.[52]

A second alternative on which the literature has focused was brought forward by local activists growing more discontented with Rugova. Organized in an ad hoc manner, they were frustrated by the inability of Rugova's government-in-exile and the international community to deliver political goods for the Kosovars. The Education Agreement was brokered without the students' consent, which created serious resentment among them, especially in view of the fact that the agreement failed.[53] Demaci turned openly critical and called for protests against the Serbian regime, recalling that nonviolence did not necessarily mean passivity.[54] In Demaci's words, his efforts failed to draw serious attention, even though he had traveled to

numerous European capitals immediately after Dayton to try to raise attention among international diplomats that the situation in Kosovo was becoming explosive.[55] In addition, Rexhep Qosja, the radical opposition party
leader, attacked Rugova for having created a "movement of sitting." He did
not rule out the "possibility of heavier clashes between Albanians and
Serbs."[56] Rumors were propagated in Kosovo society against Rugova, who
it was alleged to use his ties to the international community to benefit
personally from the strategy of nonviolence while the Kosovo people were
suffering under the Serbian regime.

In many accounts the radicalization of the Kosovars became feasible
because weapons were distributed from military barracks after Albania
collapsed in 1997. Kalashnikov rifles sold cheaply through the porous borders
helped arm the Kosovars.[57] This interpretation is generally correct, but political change in the direction of radicalization was strongly related to the *timing
and sequencing* of the collapse of the Albanian state relative to Dayton. Would
the effect of the collapse have been the same had it happened *before* the
Dayton Agreement delegitimized the politics of nonviolence? It is plausible
that some radicalization could have occurred earlier, given the fact that LDK's
strategy of nonviolence was originally designed because Kosovars lacked
weapons. Also, some exiled elements were interested in a second front on
Serbia at the height of the war in Bosnia-Herzegovina in 1993. Yet, one needs
to bear in mind the context of such possible changes: the neighborhood was
explosive, exiled elements had no strong standing within Kosovo, and moderates still held the political upper hand. Although another front would have
been very expensive for Serbia, it was still militarily strong and potentially
capable of suppressing a rebellion within its own borders. It had enough
power to use brutal repression, which did not subside in Kosovo throughout
the 1990s, although Serbia was at war in the first half of the decade. With the
de-legitimization of the nonviolent strategy at Dayton and the international
community's implication in it, the influx of small arms from Albania facilitated overcoming collective action problems, so that the radical KLA quickly
gained overwhelming domestic support.

Albania's collapse in 1997, *after* Dayton, tipped the balance toward the
radicals at a "ripe" moment of the conflict, when the old order had not
completely collapsed but the new one had not yet emerged. The student
demonstrations of October 1997, only months after Albania's implosion,
are a major observable implication of this new trend. Students held demonstrations in opposition to Rugova's wishes.[58] According to their leader,

Albin Kurti, who later led the self-determination radical movement Vete-vendosje, the student demonstrations were held despite foreign diplomats' attempts to stop them, using the argument that the Serbian regime might retaliate. The students acted on the assumption that the international community would only take political agents seriously if they "cause events and not when they are subject to them."[59] The students were already connected to the KLA abroad.[60] On March 5, 1998, Serbian forces killed the entire family of one of the KLA founders, Adem Jashari, in the village of Donjii Prekaz. The massacre became a tipping point for the surge of violence from "extensive" to "internal warfare." The killings increased and included many civilians, violating not only human rights but humanitarian laws in the Geneva Conventions.

Since this period has received good journalistic and scholarly attention, I will refrain from engaging the details here.[61] However, from the point of view of my analysis of durable and changing relationships between the international community and local agents, it is important to emphasize two trends: the international community was still interested in the official nonredefinition of the state, while preserving its concern with defending the Kosovars against human rights violations. Violations led the diverse international community eventually to conclude that the violence must be stopped. International mediation activities, resolutions, and agreements condemned the escalating violence on the ground. As Bellamy observed, when Donji Prekaz was burning, British foreign secretary Robin Cook was in Belgrade, where he threatened Milosevic with isolation from the EU but continued to insist on his good will to implement the already outdated Education Agreement. International mediators managed to convince Rugova to meet Milosevic "in principle" in May 1998, a futile move that only further diminished Rugova's reputation in the Albanian community.

UN Security Council Resolution 1160 of March 1998 condemned both the Serbs and the KLA for the violence. A stronger resolution was passed in September, which more clearly condemned the Serbian regime because of the increase in refugees and internally displaced persons, reaching 100,000–300,000 during the summer. This resolution, like the October 1998 Hoolbroke-Milosevic Agreement and the February 1999 final negotiation agreement from Rambouillet, failed to conceive of Kosovo's status as any different.[62] The international community's biggest step was to enshrine a paragraph in the Rambouillet Agreement stipulating that the future status of Kosovo would be determined by an international conference to be convened in three years.[63] This clause managed to get the divided Kosovo factions to sign the agreement, but made Milosevic even less cooperative.

As a result of the failure of the Rambouillet talks, NATO launched 78 days of airstrikes between March and June 1999, without UN Security Council authorization, which made them controversial. As several accounts have already demonstrated, the Serbian regime responded by increasing ethnic expulsions and triggering massacres of Kosovo Albanians.[64] As the U.S. State Department points out, as the airstrikes started, ethnic cleansing accelerated drastically, with Serbian forces burning 200–600 houses in Djacovica in western Kosovo alone, and expelling more than 90 percent of the Albanian population in Kosovo from their homes. Victims were usually put on trains or other public transport, and those left behind were used as human shields. More than 850,000 refugees fled to Albania, Bosnia-Herzegovina, Macedonia, and Montenegro.[65] The airstrikes eventually brought these humanitarian law violations to a stop by helping defeat the Milosevic government militarily. NATO troops entered Kosovo, paving the way for a new period in Kosovo's political development.

NATO 1999 Intervention in Kosovo and Contagion Effects

NATO's military intervention has been thoroughly examined in terms of controversial issues with global implications. Specific attention has been given to whether the campaign was driven by humanitarian or geopolitical reasons, to what extent international norms of non-intervention were redefined in the face of ethnic expulsions and massacres, and how this unauthorized military intervention set a precedent for future conflicts.[66] But the intervention has not been sufficiently explored in terms of the causal mechanisms it unleashed. The NATO intervention was an exogenous shock for Macedonia and Bulgaria. It directly affected majority-minority relations by polarizing them, and indirectly changed them by weakening Serbia and creating opportunities for contagion effects for Macedonia. It also gave the Bulgarian government the opportunity to accelerate the country's entry into the EU and NATO, while reinforcing an earlier aspect of the conflict dynamic: little concern for profound minority rights reforms.

Both the Bulgarian and Macedonian governments backed NATO military intervention. Bulgaria's pro-Western government under Ivan Kostov allowed NATO to use the country's airspace for military operations. The pro-Western government of Lyubcho Georgievski and Arben Xhaferi in

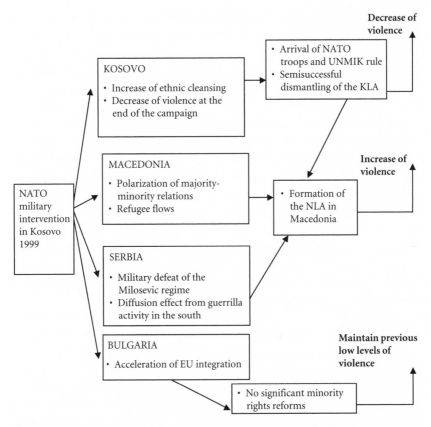

Figure 8. NATO 1999 military intervention as an exogenous shock.

Macedonia also supported the alliance. Tensions surged in the ruling coalition, but were mitigated by diplomatic intervention.[67] In addition, in 1998 the coalition government of Macedonia had asked for a replacement of the UNPREDEP peacekeeping forces with NATO troops as a preventive measure against possible external attack while the conflict in Kosovo was escalating. Bringing NATO on the ground was considered "bringing discipline" to the local agents, as Frckoski put it, and facilitating a "choice between Serbia and Europe," as Arifi claimed.[68]

The NATO intervention brought polarization of in-group/out-group relations to countries in the region. The cultural theories discussed earlier would suggest that it reinforced clear-cut conflict lines between Slavic majorities (Serbs, Macedonians, and Bulgarians) and non-Slavic minorities

(Albanians and Turks) on the community level. The former condemned the campaign, while the latter supported it. Polarization did not have the same effects on the three cases, weakening the determinism of cultural theories but still accounting for why Slavic majorities and non-Slavic minorities reacted differently. The Turks of Bulgaria had no particular stake in the Kosovo conflict apart from their willingness to demonstrate solidarity and use the occasion to reassert their own right to political freedom in Bulgaria. As earlier mentioned, in Kosovo existing polarization was reinforced by NATO's campaign, which led to Serb-driven ethnic expulsions and subsequent Albanian-led reprisals. Only in Macedonia did polarization have causal repercussions on the communal level in the long run. The Albanians of Macedonia found the campaign to be a moment of truth; they cheered it and so further alienated the Macedonians. Both local Macedonians and Serbs demonstrated in opposition to the airstrikes. Georgieva argued that although the demonstrators were not an influential segment of Macedonian society, they still voiced widespread fear of a possible "Greater Albania option."[69]

NATO's intervention also triggered refugee flows from Kosovo. During the airstrikes, 200,000–245,000 Kosovo Albanian refugees entered Macedonia. The fact that most were placed in temporary refugee camps and only a few with local Albanian families helped reduce the potential of direct contagion, and the relations between local Albanians and Macedonians remained surprisingly nonviolent. Several street beatings in Skopje and Tetovo were minor exceptions.[70] Most refugees returned to Kosovo relatively quickly after the defeat of the Milosevic regime. According to government statistics, only around 2,000 remained in the country in 2000. This low number prevented a change in the ethnic composition of Macedonia.[71]

NATO's airstrikes contributed to the polarization of interethnic relations in Macedonia, though to a much lesser extent than in other conflict-ridden regions. Recently scholars have argued that refugee flows are not simply a consequence of conflicts, but may also cause them by importing combatants, arms, and ideologies.[72] There were reports, for example, that KLA fighters attempted to mingle with refugees and local Albanians in the village of Janice in 1999.[73] However, the activities of the Kosovo Albanians in the camps did not play the same catalytic role in the growth of radicalism in Macedonia as in other comparable cases globally. For example, the Palestinian refugee camps in Lebanon became a hub of radicalism in the early 1970s, which eventually contributed to the onset of the Lebanese civil war

(1975–1990). Nor did radicalism in Macedonia grow because humanitarian aid was absorbed by radicals in the camps and used for military training purposes, as Lisher observed among the refugee camps in the Democratic Republic of Congo after the 1994 Rwandan genocide.[74] In Macedonia fears of the refugee crisis and the joint efforts of the ruling coalition and international community to prevent the crisis from spilling over were enormous and rather successful.[75] As mentioned, the numbers of displaced were rather low. Indirectly, however, the refugee crisis further eroded the already fragile Macedonian state and made it susceptible to contagion effects from the neighborhood.

Contagion took place by two mechanisms: the demonstration effect of the KLA success by inducing political change using violent methods, and the diffusion effect of connectedness between former KLA fighters across the porous borders. These effects manifested themselves through the emergence of two new guerrilla groups: the Liberation Army of Preshevo, Medvedja, Bujanovac (PMBLA) in early 2000 in southern Serbia, and the NLA in early 2001 in Macedonia. The PMBLA aimed to liberate territories taken from Kosovo after World War II.[76] These radicals were linked to the Kosovo liberation struggle, and some were former KLA fighters. They saw a political opportunity to achieve their goal after NATO weakened Serbia by defeating it militarily and created a "ground safety zone" to separate NATO ground troops in Kosovo from Serbian military forces.[77] The PMBLA used the political vacuum in this territory to launch more than 300 attacks in 2000. Negotiations between Serbia and NATO eventually restored the status quo. They allowed the Yugoslav Army to enter the Preshevo Valley in exchange for amnesty for the rebels and surrender of their weapons. While a number of rebels took advantage of this offer in 2001, they had already set a new example of radicalism for the Albanians of Macedonia and established connections with some of the most discontented. A new guerrilla group emerged from this group, the NLA, which launched attacks and caused the surge of violence in Macedonia in early 2001.

The internal warfare in Macedonia was caused by the coupling of a contagion effect with three enabling conditions: long-standing grievances against decreased constitutional status, large-scale corruption that led to the informal division of the state around 2000–2001, as Hislope points out, and embarking on the path to the EU without previously changing the constitution. Connectedness in rebel networks took place through two channels. One was the long-standing unity among Albanians challenging the status quo in former Yugoslavia. The NLA leadership was part of the anti-Yugoslav People's Movement of Kosovo in the 1980s, and was present at the formation of the KLA in 1993. Its ties were reinvigorated in 1999 when NLA leader Ali Mehmeti and his circle decided to transplant the Kosovo struggle onto Macedonian territory and looked for an opportune moment to do so.[78] The second channel was NATO's failure to disband the KLA completely, though demobilization took place and the Kosovo Protection Corps (KPC) was formed to incorporate former KLA fighters. Fighters who did not become part of the KPC found a livelihood in the Preshevo Valley, and were later recruited for the Albanian struggle in Macedonia. Belonging to a generation of fighters taking part in the armed conflicts of collapsing Yugoslavia, they were "unemployed" but possessed weapons they wanted to use.[79] In addition, individuals in the KPC were caught rendering logistical support to the NLA rebels, and NATO expelled them accordingly.[80]

Long-term constitutional grievances provided the NLA rebels with a moral platform to launch their violent campaign in January 2001. The NLA's clear-cut demand for federalization of Macedonia from March 2001 tipped the balance of the conflict. At that point the government for the first time responded with a full-fledged military operation and quickly claimed victory over the rebels. Yet by the end of April violence had resumed.[81] Under international pressure, all four major parties (two ethnic Macedonian and two ethnic Albanian) formed a coalition government. However, ethnic Macedonian prime minister Georgievski threatened to declare war in June. The NLA forces became more aggressive and seized the town of Aracinovo, just a few kilometers from the capital Skopje, triggering strong fears among Macedonians that their state was on the brink of collapse. Seven weeks of negotiations, mediated heavily by EU and U.S. envoys, stretched over several broken ceasefires until the fighting parties agreed to sign an agreement in mid-August 2001 in the Macedonian town of Ohrid.

Informal attempts to divide the country along ethnic lines before 2001 had created another facilitating condition for internal warfare. Hislope argues that the NLA military incursions into Macedonia succeeded because the interethnic coalition was highly corrupt and had divided the country into spheres of patronage to conduct shady businesses. The VMRO-DPMNE controlled Skopje and Eastern Macedonia, and the DPA controlled Tetovo and western Macedonia.[82] Indeed, in the midst of the 2001 conflict, the Macedonian Academy of Arts and Sciences issued a proposal to make a territorial and population exchange, and Georgievski neither condemned nor promoted this proposal. Rumors of a 1998 secret deal between Xhaferi and Georgievski to divide Macedonia spread in 2005: Xhaferi confirmed them, while Georgievski denied them.[83]

The corruption also created resentment among ordinary Albanians in Macedonia. While some DPA leaders allegedly held a prominent place in organized crime rings linking Macedonia, Albania, and Kosovo, and became richer after their arrival in power in 1998, average Albanians remained challenged to make ends meet. Selective employment in illicit networks did not fill the gap between rich and poor. The NLA emerged as the noncorrupt alternative. It also carried the torch of the nationalist goal to change the constitution, a goal the DPA had already set aside.

If the Albanians of Macedonia had believed that following a path to European integration with the 2000 Stabilization and Association Agreement would guarantee a change of constitutional status, the NLA would probably have not found the community support it did. Alongside Albanians' general mistrust of Europe (and trust in the U.S.), Albanians of Macedonia wanted to see substantial political changes before they set out on the road to Europe. The NLA picked the right *timing*, and behaviorally resembled a "spoiler" in peace processes by launching violence before it was too late to change the rules of the game, and before agreements consolidated.[84]

NATO's military intervention was also an exogenous shock for the Bulgarian case. Here, it did not trigger escalation of violence but consolidated the previously established dynamics of avoiding minority rights reforms. The key to this development was the government's clear alignment with NATO. This was a new signal the Bulgarian authorities delivered to the international community, and Kostov's Union of Democratic Forces government supported NATO's military intervention despite disapproval of large parts of the Bulgarian population. In consequence, the country's accession to NATO and EU membership accelerated. As Noutcheva and Bechev observed, the European Commission was initially reluctant to open accession negotiations with Bulgaria and Romania during the Helsinki European Council in December 1999. It considered them lagging behind other East European countries in meeting the Copenhagen conditionality criteria, including economic performance and reform of minority rights. However,

Western policy makers wanted to reward Bulgaria and Romania for their support for the intervention, and to signal that a peaceful transition pays off. Pressured by the UK—a major NATO member—the Commission opened negotiations with Bulgaria. Thus, geopolitical reasons rather than clear performance on reforms made Bulgaria and Romania eligible to begin negotiations together with Latvia, Lithuania, Malta, and Slovakia in February 2000.[85]

EU Conditionality and Long-Term Change

By accelerating Bulgaria's accession negotiations, NATO's military intervention in Kosovo turned out to be an exogenous shock that indirectly facilitated further consolidation of a nonviolent outcome in the majority-minority relationship. Further moves in this direction took place more directly as a result of EU conditionality pressure. Vachudova calls it "active leverage" to distinguish it from the "passive leverage" characteristic of the early 1990s, when the EU had traction on domestic politics "merely by virtue of its existence and its conduct" rather than by actual policy pressure on Eastern European governments.[86] In a milestone decision in 1999, the Bulgarian parliament, dominated by the pro-Western UDF, adopted the controversial FCPNM. Although both democratic and socialist majority elites had previously opposed this convention, this time they realized that the EU pressure was real. The 1997 Luxembourg European Council had not included Bulgaria (or Romania) with the first group of countries to start accession negotiations.[87] Remarks critical of Bulgaria's minority rights record continued to be included in the EC monitoring reports in 1997. The Bulgarian elites recognized that adoption of the FCPNM was a necessary trade-off for further advancement on the path to Europe.

The Bulgarian elites acted in line with a "logic of consequences" or cost-benefit calculations rather than a "logic of appropriateness" or internalized liberal values of multiculturalism resulting from socialization. They promulgated the convention together with a special declaration that cautiously mentioned the need to protect the "human rights and tolerance of persons belonging to minorities" and stipulated that the convention should not imply "any right to engage in any activity violating the territorial integrity and sovereignty of the unitary Bulgarian state, its internal and international security."[88] While change was taking place with the convention's promulgation, residues of the older contextualized ways of relating remained between majorities and the international community to protect the nonredefinition of the state. As Csergo observed, the convention specified a number of minority rights to be protected in an individualist UN-based paradigm, not on a collective basis. It explicitly stated that nothing in the convention should be interpreted as implying permission for any activity against international law, state sovereignty, and territorial integrity.[89] The FCPNM also allowed states to give their own interpretation of the term "minority," creating ambiguities on how to treat minorities and develop future policies. The Bulgarian government signed this convention by attaching exactly such an ambiguous declaration. By 2004 only Azerbaijan had adopted a similar declaration.[90]

This posture shows that securitization of minority rights remained visible. New EU rules were "layered" over existing ones, and the old rules continued to coexist.[91] The convention was also scarcely implemented, apart from the 1999 change of mother tongue instruction in Turkish from "optional" to a "compulsory-to-be-chosen" subject, a media law in 2000 that created the possibility of mother-tongue broadcasts, and several media programs. Legislation and policies related to economic development of minority areas, wider public use of minority languages, and placement of minorities in government and structures of power remained underdeveloped.

Like the majority elites, the ethnic Turkish leadership also had a strong interest in European integration. In a 1991 statement, MRF leader Dogan had stipulated that "Bulgaria's way to Europe goes first via the Bosphorus," that is, through Turkey.[92] But by 2000 he had changed his stance, proclaiming that "only Bulgaria's integration into NATO and the EU is able to guarantee the defense mechanism for the rights and freedoms of the minorities in Bulgaria." In fact, the European integration processes did for the MRF some minority rights work it was uninterested in doing for itself. An anonymous MRF leader argued in 2001 that European requirements on minority rights surpassed those of the MRF, and that if the EU imposed a minority language in public administration, MRF leaders and voters would gladly accept it. He also claimed that only EU integration could make Bulgarian society accept such policies.[93]

This statement indicates a rather passive approach in expectation of positive pressures from the EU. In addition, going farther on the path to Europe gave the MRF and individuals in the ethnic Turkish minority confidence to use the litigation procedures of the ECHR. For example, in October 2000 the ECHR sued the Bulgarian state on behalf of two senior religious functionaries, who in 1996 had filed a complaint against the socialist government that had imposed new leadership on the Islamic religious community. This act of state meddling in religious affairs was addressed earlier through notes of protest to Turkey, international human rights NGOs, and the Council of Europe. But it was only through the 2000 ECHR intervention that an ultimate solution was found. The decision stipulated that the Bulgarian state had violated some articles of the European Convention on Human Rights, and ordered the country to pay compensation of 10,000 leva, around U.S.$5,000.[94]

Toward the end of the 1990s the level of ethnonational violence in Bulgaria remained low, but the pace of minority rights reforms was slow. The latter phenomenon was explained not just by government reluctance to introduce reforms and a passive Turkish minority leadership. General failures of EU policies toward the countries of Eastern Europe accounted for the lack of genuine minority rights reforms. Rechel summarized several major EU deficits: lack of minority standards within the EU, including double standards applicable to old and aspiring members; superficial monitoring of candidate states; and lack of concern for human and minority rights compared with priority given to the *acquis communautaire*, the body of more than 80,000 pages of EU legislation the new entrants needed to internalize in their domestic legislation.[95] Some of these deficits continued throughout the 2000s, and became important for Macedonia as well.

Conclusions

While the international community decisively influenced the evolution of conflicts during the formative period, its impact diminished during periods of self-reinforcement because its actions were constrained by the contextualized ways in which all three agents became locked in the triangular relationship. Self-perpetuating processes were sustained by the mechanisms of "adaptive expectations," and partly by "learning." Exogenous shocks—the 1995 Dayton Accords, Albania's 1997 implosion, NATO's 1999 military intervention (for Bulgaria and Macedonia), and contagion effects—altered some aspects of these conflict dynamics, including minorities' nonviolent strategies and military capabilities, and therefore led to the escalation of violence to "internal warfare" in both Kosovo (1998–1999) and Macedonia (2001). In contrast, the NATO intervention and EU integration processes led to consolidation of a nonviolent outcome in the Bulgarian case by the end of the 1990s, but also to consolidation of decreased interest in minority rights reforms, perpetuating an earlier aspect of the triangular relationship.

These findings speak to the existing scholarly accounts on conflict analysis and resolution in several ways. First, causal mechanisms of self-perpetuation consolidated the formal and informal rules between majorities, minorities, and the international community, established during the formative period. In this path-dependence account, the nature of the triangular relationship is seen as more *static* than in bargaining accounts, which see it as more dynamic. Once conflict dynamics are established, they become embedded in specific contextualized ways through which the agents relate. The causal mechanisms perpetuate these ways and facilitate how the specific links between agents become informally institutionalized. These relationships then constrain the agents' behavior. Hence, actors use bounded rationality to assert their claims, and are not driven only by rational and utility-based calculations. If, for example, the link between the minority and the international community in Macedonia was established on the premise that Albanians had the ability to voice minority rights violations through international community channels but not on demands to become a constituent element of the state, then further minority actions became constrained by the nature of this link.

This account has also demonstrated that the exogenous shocks that played a role in the Kosovo case—the 1995 Dayton Accord and Albania's collapse in 1997—did not simply lead to the radicalization of domestic politics. It was the *timing and sequencing* in which they occurred that mattered, so that radical factions received overwhelming support from the Kosovo Albanian population. Dayton occurred first and weakened the legitimacy of the LDK pursuing nonviolent resistance. Albania's collapse took place second, allowing for the purchase of cheap weapons. This tilted the balance toward a radical alternative that was competing with a moderate one for whom some remote rapprochement with Serbia was considered.

Exogenous shocks do not simply trigger certain payoffs among the local agents, but launch entire causal chains that lead to the outcomes of interest, in our cases to "internal warfare" (Kosovo, Macedonia) or consolidation of "nonviolence" (Bulgaria). These include agents' strategies—such as a government's strategic decision to support NATO intervention as in Macedonia and Bulgaria, or to launch attacks against a weakened Serbian state in the political vacuum of a little governed territory (the Preshevo Valley), as did the PMBLA. These causal chains contain other structural elements such as polarization of communal relations, which became crucial for the outcome of violence in the Macedonian case. This path-dependence account combines the effects of structure and agency rather than focusing on just one of them. Using the onset of the internal warfare in Macedonia as an example, I also demonstrated that a *ripe moment* need not necessarily be considered only in terms of possibilities for conflict resolution. A ripe moment can also be used to increase the level of conflict. The concatenation of several factors—such as contagion effects from a nearby neighborhood, informal divisions of a country because of corruption, and embarking on European integration without first addressing long-term constitutional grievances—was conducive to the escalation of violence in Macedonia. The NLA tried to break the status quo before the rules of the game were fully consolidated.

This chapter drew attention to the phenomenon of securitization of minority rights, where local elites learn that informal rules of the primacy of security take precedence over formal ones of democratization. "Learning" crystalized only during the process of self-reinforcement, when the adoption of international legislation of minority rights and their policy implementation became relevant for majorities and minorities as adaptive strategies within the established triangular relationship. Majorities used minority rights to advance their own integrationist (Bulgaria), state-building (Macedonia), or state-preservation (Serbia/Kosovo) agendas. Minorities used them to advance nationalist goals to the extent possible within the bounded rationality established with the international community.

In fact, however, these international agents were not very concerned with minority rights per se. This fact had unintended consequences, rendering the concept of minority rights hollow, allowing it to become hijacked by security and stability concerns, and marring it by the disbelief of all concerned agents. Although all the agents talked about minority rights, they acted on select rights and strove for completely different political agendas. Understanding how identity-based actors—kin-states and diasporas—support these agendas will be discussed next.

Chapter 5

Intervention of Identity-Based Agents:
Kin-States and Diasporas

Kin-states and diasporas are important external agents in ethnic conflicts because of their close identity-based ties with domestic agents. During the nation-state formation era in the late eighteenth to early twentieth centuries, kin-states sought to incorporate their ethnic brethren in neighboring states. Irredentism continued to flourish during the First and Second World Wars, but a bipolar world order during the Cold War suppressed many of these movements.[1] After the Cold War ended, conflicts did not resume in the same manner because the nature of irredentism had changed. In the second half of the twentieth century, pressures to redraw territorial borders came from external secessionist movements rather than from within the irredentist kin-states.[2] As Horowitz observed, the "foreign policy goals [of an irredentist state] were thought to be better achieved by encouraging secessionist movements . . . than by encouraging irredentism."[3] Ethnic brethren had been considered victims of injustice inflicted by the Great Powers during the drawing of new international borders, but after 1989 diasporas gained more capacity to influence their original homelands, especially if they lived in distant locations. Anderson has called members of such diasporas "long-distance nationalists." They often act "irresponsibly" toward the original homeland, because they do not bear the consequences of their actions.[4]

Scholarship on kin-state intervention is better developed than that on diasporas. Since the mid-1990s some researchers have argued that irredentist crises are more deadly than non-irredentist ones;[5] that kin-states intervene because of affinity ties, instrumentalist reasons, and structural considerations;[6] and that interventions are driven by domestic political calculations[7] and consideration of international institutions that might offer financial aid or "club membership."[8] The impact of kin-states has been discussed in the context of the large-scale violence after the break-up of former Yugoslavia and the Soviet Union or nonviolent minority-majority interactions in Eastern Europe. Almost no theoretical accounts exist about the gray zone, when kin-states do not clearly make irredentist claims but still facilitate escalation of ethnonational conflict. Saideman and Ayres make a welcome exception by focusing on why some states in the postcommunist space pursue irredentism while others do not.[9]

Here we see that the intervention of identity-based agents on ethnic conflicts that had similar characteristics at the end of communism facilitated the development of specific contextualized relationships between identity-based agents, minorities, and the international community. This chapter addresses how kin-states and diasporas contributed to diverging patterns of violence in Kosovo, Macedonia, and Bulgaria in 1987/89–1999/2001. It focuses on Albania's kin-state interventions in the conflicts in Kosovo and Macedonia, Turkey's intervention in Bulgaria, and the interventions of the Albanian and Turkish diasporas. I identify processes of continuity and change in the informally institutionalized conflict dynamics and compare the involvement of identity-based agents and the international community.

What processes facilitated or constrained intervention of identity-based agents? When did kin-state and diaspora agents use affinity-based logic and when instrumentalist calculations? How were initial relationships established during the critical juncture and how did they change? I argue that kin-states participated in delineating the "rules of the game" between majorities and minorities during the formative period, but that compared to international community interventions theirs were less formal and clearly favored the minorities. Domestic political processes affecting the institutional strength of kin-states influenced whether they formulated a coherent and enforceable foreign policy toward external conflicts or mixed official policy and clandestine strategies.

As a state undergoing transition, Albania was exposed to both pressures from the international community and its need for domestic reform, which radically weakened its institutions. As a result, Albania exhibited a Janus-faced foreign policy toward the ethnic conflicts in Kosovo and Macedonia. Officially, it gave in to international community pressures to maintain a non-interventionist stance. Informally, it pursued an interventionist agenda. With limited institutional constraints, some state officials established alliances with secessionist and autonomist movements across borders that matched their ideological, clan-based, and other particularistic interests. Albania's variation in treatment of Albanians in Macedonia and Kosovo in the 1990s is largely explained by the relationships established during the formative period. The end of communism opened opportunities for the Albanian population in former Yugoslavia to reconnect with their ethnic brethren in Albania, which had pursued staunch isolationism during the Cold War. Officials could form transborder alliances more easily with Kosovo's clandestine separatist institutions, which needed external protection and experienced more human rights abuse, than with Albanians in Macedonia, who were severely discontented with their diminished constitutional status but still part of a coalition government.

Turkey, a kin-state that did not undergo transition from communism, was less likely to intervene in the conflict in Bulgaria. Throughout the 1990s Turkey remained under military guardianship, so arguably its government was less affected by domestic pressures that otherwise might have arisen to protect Turks in the European neighborhood. With no need for drastic domestic reforms, Turkey was less vulnerable to international pressures and could maintain the institutional strength to implement a coherent foreign policy toward the Turkish minority in Bulgaria. Furthermore, there were no significant emerging elites that might use external secessionist and autonomist movements to legitimize their own domestic agendas.[10]

The intervention of the Albanian and Turkish diasporas in the majority-minority relationships during the critical juncture was less pronounced, but it became more important over time, especially in the Albanian case. Little interventionism during the formative period occurred because diasporas and their ethnic brethren were largely disconnected during the Cold War, and there was little sustained organization of expatriate circles. During the critical juncture diasporas were rather sporadic agents of initial engagement and did not actively shape the majority-minority relationship, compared to the international community and kin-states. The diaspora role grew, however, driven by new waves of emigration and more transnational connectivity over the years. An overwhelming diaspora support for radicalism exerted external pressures on the informally institutionalized conflict dynamic in Kosovo in 1998–1999, and provided opportunities for change in the direction of higher levels of violence. In line with my interest in theorizing about timing, I also argue that the Albanian diaspora intervention occurred when moderate local agents started losing support for their nonviolent struggle and grave human rights violations took place against ethnic brethren in the original homeland.[11]

It is important to clarify the terms "kin-state intervention," "diaspora," and "diaspora intervention." For kin-state intervention, I adapt a definition of Ganguli: a "kin-state can offer tangible support to its ethnic kin, including military and material aid, access to transportation, media, communications, and intelligence networks, and political and diplomatic support including statements of concern, support for international governmental organizations, diplomatic pressure, publicity campaigns and diplomatic recognition, services which may be rendered either inside or outside the secessionist region."[12] For diaspora, I adapt a definition of Adamson and Demetriou: a cross-border social collectivity that sustains a collective national, cultural, or religious identity through ties with a real or imagined homeland, and has the ability to address the collective interests of its members through developed organizational frameworks and transnational links.[13] Diaspora intervention can take place through "contained" or "transgressive" contention, to adapt concepts of McAdam et al., who have worked on transnational social movements.[14] In diaspora politics, contained diasporic repertoire includes nonviolent rhetoric, lobbying, petitions, publications, nonviolent demonstrations, and others. A transgressive diasporic repertoire includes boycotts, violent demonstrations, recruiting of fighters, purchase of arms, and fund-raising for radical domestic factions.[15]

Alternative Explanations

Kin-State Intervention

Official Albania was not outwardly irredentist toward the Albanians of Kosovo and Macedonia; neither was Turkey as a kin-state to the ethnic Turks in Bulgaria. Why then did Albania contribute significantly to ethnic conflict in Kosovo during the 1990s, but less in Macedonia, whereas Turkey did not contribute to ethnic conflict in Bulgaria? The most obvious explanation is that Albania intervened in Kosovo for humanitarian reasons: the Kosovars endured severe human rights violations from the Serbian regime and needed backing from abroad. The Albanians of Macedonia and the Turks of Bulgaria had much more peaceful interactions with their majorities. This explanation makes sense, but it considers only the need for intervention, not the mechanisms involved. Many humanitarian crises, such as those in Rwanda, Somalia, Sudan, and the Congo, have demonstrated that the need for humanitarian intervention rarely translates into action. If Albania were acting primarily on humanitarian grounds, it could have taken a much stronger stance. In the late 1980s and early 1990s, when the Turks of Bulgaria were subjected to severe cultural assimilation and expulsion, Turkey reacted much more boldly on the diplomatic front than Albania did in the 1990s vis-à-vis Kosovo.

Historical experiences may have affected outcomes. Defeat in wars in the early twentieth century taught many kin-states the high cost of irredentism.[16] Invaded by Italy in 1939, Albania became a de facto protectorate. A puppet regime pursued the "Greater Albania" agenda, including governance over the territories of Kosovo and parts of western Macedonia.[17] However, given that Albania was itself occupied, it would be hard to claim that it learned by defeat. Nor would this explanation account for why Albania contributed to more violence in Kosovo than in Macedonia. Yet this explanation is partially relevant to Turkey. Turkey emerged as the successor state of the collapsed Ottoman Empire in 1923, and went into an introspective phase of virulent domestic nationalism under Kemal Atatürk that did not expose minorities abroad to the same nationalist pressures as in Turkey.[18] Pan-Turkism grew as a phenomenon, but Turkey maintained neutrality for most of World War II, entering the war at its very end on the side of the victorious Allies. Yet, defeat in war does not explain why Turkey openly or tacitly challenged the governance of the former Ottoman *villayet* of Mosul, lost to Iraq in 1926, or why it invaded Cyprus in 1974.

Kin-states may be careful about supporting secessionist or autonomist movements abroad because they are themselves ethnically diverse and may feel vulnerable to secessionism from their own population.[19] Albania might have felt vulnerability, because Greece and Macedonia historically have had claims on their ethnic brethren inside Albania. But Albania nevertheless intervened in Kosovo and Macedonia. Turkey, might have felt vulnerability, because it was heavily criticized about its mistreatment of the Kurds. But Turkey's stances were selective with regard to its neighbors, involving carefully calculated and executed foreign policy. In general Turkey was driven by non-interventionist logic throughout the 1990s, but maintained its troops in occupied Cyprus[20] and openly or tacitly supported the Turkmen of Iraq, seeking to balance the Kurdistan Workers' Party (PKK), which used northern Iraq to launch attacks against Turkey.[21]

Turkey's official foreign policy was not interested in balancing in Bulgaria. It took a conservative stance toward radical claims and recognition of self-determination movements in the postcommunist space. It was among the states that did not favor the collapse of Yugoslavia and the Soviet Union, and only followed suit after major international powers recognized the successor republics. It was even more cautious not to recognize second-tier secessionist movements, such as the proclaimed Republic of Kosovo and Republic of Chechnya. Even when warfare broke out in Yugoslavia, Turkey was cautious not to aid the Bosnian Muslims unilaterally, but to stay close to the political line of the United States.[22] It also intervened on behalf of Azerbaijan to suppress the secessionist movement in Nagorno-Karabakh, more as a balancing act, since the region has been inhabited by the Armenians, age-old geopolitical rivals. Turkey was even cautious toward Chechnya. Diasporic communities of Chechen descent mobilized in support of Chechnya.[23] But both Turkey and various activists were cautious not to push Russia too much. A 1996 ferry hijacking was condemned by both Turkey and Russia as a "terrorist act."[24] Turkey's interest in Russian gas and oil was an important reason why multiple visits by Chechen leaders during the second Chechen war in 1999 did not yield major policy outcomes.

Two models have explored dynamic relationships between kin-states and domestic agents. From a constructivist perspective, Brubaker argued that minorities, "nationalizing states," and kin-states are bound in a triadic nexus, where each closely monitors the change in stance of the others and reacts accordingly.[25] Jenne, by comparison, has presented a bargaining model in which minorities become empowered or disempowered by the external lobby agent (the functional equivalent of the kin-state) position, which may vary over time.[26] While these two approaches emphasize the dynamics of relationships and establish the importance of connectivity among these three agents, the account presented here offers *a more static path-dependent perspective*, arguing that relationships are established at an early stage of the transition process, informally institutionalized in specific ways of engagement, and perpetuated over time.

More recent studies have emphasized the ways domestic and international politics enable and constrain kin-states' behavior. Saideman and Ayres argue that domestic politics are highly relevant to whether a country's politicians formulate a foreign policy that would (1) do nothing regarding an external minority, (2) develop assertive foreign policies, or (3) go to war, which explains why some kin-states are more irredentist than others.[27] This approach offers important meso-level theorizing about kin-state intervention, but assumes that when a foreign policy is formulated, it will be enforced, and neglects the fact that a state may present itself as pursuing one policy while following another. Albania demonstrates that a foreign policy may be largely formulated in non-interventionist terms, but those terms are not enforced because weak institutions allow alternative approaches to flourish. Several other accounts derived from the Central European context make similar assumptions. Either domestic elite competition in the transition countries,[28] or the EU and other international institutions are taken to provide constraints for kin-states behavior.[29] These studies pay little attention to the fact that the transition process may severely weaken state institutions and capacity for implementing domestic and foreign policy. When institutions are weak, clandestine transborder alliances can occur in parallel to official policies.[30]

Diaspora Intervention

The field of diaspora intervention in ethnic conflicts has emerged more recently. A growing body of scholarship has demonstrated that mobilized diasporas abroad can sustain intrastate conflicts, but systematic comparisons of diaspora mobilization, and mechanisms of intervention are scarce.[31] Three major explanations compete in addressing a major question for this chapter: how did the Albanian and Turkish diasporas contribute to the levels of violence in the ethnic conflicts in Kosovo, Macedonia, and Bulgaria? These explanations relate to conflict-generated identities, diaspora organizational level, and diasporas as economic resources for rebels in civil wars.

Traumatic identities of conflict-generated diasporas are potentially a reason why diasporas might be more inclined to radicalize conflicts in their original homelands. These are not voluntary migrants, but refugees or their descendants. Their trauma of displacement and intent to return may freeze their identities and make them difficult to change.[32] These identities could then drive the functioning of diaspora institutions, which in turn perpetuate them, because conflict resolution would render these institutions obsolete.[33]

The Albanian and Turkish diasporas have segments that are conflict-generated and segments that are not. On various junctures throughout the twentieth century, violence by Serbs toward Albanians made Albanians leave. Because of the more open border policy of socialist Yugoslavia during communism thousands of Albanians from Kosovo, Macedonia, and Montenegro took advantage of guest worker opportunities in Western countries during the 1970s.[34] They formed communities, most notably in Germany and Switzerland, which later hosted political exiles from the violent events in Kosovo in 1981 and the refugee waves of the 1990s. A conflict-generated identity became superimposed on other identities rooted in guest worker status and predominantly rural origins.

Conflict-generated identities were important for the evolution of diaspora support, but cannot explain why in 1998–1999 the Albanian diaspora contributed to significant radicalization of the local conflict in Kosovo, and not in Macedonia. Conflict-generated identities are not a cause for radicalization per se. One needs to understand the mobilization process and specific conflict dynamics already established in the original homelands as the backdrop to which diaspora members intervene.

In contrast, the diaspora of the ethnic Turks of Bulgaria was formed predominantly on the basis of emigration to the original homeland, Turkey, rather than to Western Europe and the United States. Unlike Albania, a poor isolated country during communism, Turkey was an attractive migrant destination. Yet the borders between Bulgaria, the southern outpost of the Soviet Union in the Balkans, and Turkey, a NATO member, were strictly sealed during the Cold War. It was only possible to leave the country in clandestine ways or through special emigration treaties. A number of such treaties were signed after nationalist domestic pressures in Bulgaria mounted against the ethnic Turkish population. Muslims fled Bulgarian territories during the Balkan wars (1912–1913) and World War I. Ethnic Turks left in waves in the early 1950s, late 1960s, 1978, and 1989.[35] Many assimilated into Turkish society. Even if immigrants harbored a trauma of displacement, especially from the forced assimilation campaign of the mid- to late 1980s, their goal was voluntary assimilation into Turkey, not returning to Bulgaria. Slight changes developed when Bulgaria became an EU member in 2007, as discussed in Chapter 6.

A second plausible explanation posits that diasporas with a high organizational level are more likely to make homeland-oriented claims.[36] If diaspora institutions are developed solely to support a conflict, rather than around a broader scope of activities and appropriated for conflict purposes, they are more likely to have radicalizing effects on domestic conflicts.[37] This explanation is largely irrelevant for the Turks of Bulgaria, who relocated to Turkey and sought to assimilate there. It holds more water for the Albanian diaspora. There was only ad hoc activism in Albanian diaspora circles in Western Europe during communism. The LPK was founded in 1982 by Marxist-Leninist hard-liners in Switzerland and Germany to advocate armed revolt, but many died or were imprisoned for their activities.[38] Major attempts to merge radical groups and consolidate a movement proved futile. Albanian guest workers in Western Europe lacked the institutions to make sustained diasporic claims.[39] The secessionist LDK movement built institutions in exile in the 1990s, but this fact does not account for why the radicalizing effect took place in 1998–1999. The majority of diaspora members pursued nonviolent strategies, while radical elements remained apart through the early to mid-1990s.[40]

The field offers further inconclusive explanations. In an influential large-N study, Collier and Hoeffler demonstrated that conflicts are highly likely to recur if they are linked to large diasporas in the United States.[41] Qualitative evidence from multiple conflicts added that indeed rebels in intrastate conflicts use diasporas—Tamil, Croatian, Albanian, Kurdish—as economic resources to launch and sustain identity-based struggles.[42] Criticized by mounting evidence that diaspora size may not be as important as estimated, Collier et al. used another quantitative study to point out that diasporas can decrease postconflict risks from 40 to 32.8 percent.[43] In this discussion, the mechanisms of diaspora intervention remain understudied. This chapter goes on to determine how the diaspora contributed to the escalation of violence by exerting strong external pressures to the informally institutionalized conflict dynamic in Kosovo, in contrast to the conflicts of Macedonia and Bulgaria where intervention was less pronounced.

Interventions During the Critical Juncture

Early Intervention of Albania and the Albanian Diaspora in Kosovo and Macedonia

Albania underwent three transformations during its transition: from isolation to Western orientation, from totalitarianism to political pluralism, and from a command economy to market pluralism.[44] Albania's transition was belated. While Eastern Europe was shaking from demonstrations and other radical changes that brought down the Berlin Wall in November 1989, Albanian intellectual Ismail Kadare was among the few to advocate more freedom of expression and political pluralism. Communist head of state Ramiz Alia, successor in 1985 to long-time communist dictator Enver Hoxha, initially faced no organized opposition.[45] But he failed to take into account the growing popular discontent, which was first recognized in July 1990, when more than 6,000 Albanians sought refugee status with foreign embassies and fled the country. In December 1990, waves of violent demonstrations and vandalism spread across several cities. Alia was a "reluctant reformer" despite belated attempts to normalize relations with the Soviet Union and the United States. After his party won the 1991 elections, the parliament drafted a constitution that still used the communist designation "people's republic." Political and economic transformations occurred only in 1992, when the opposition democratic forces of Sali Berisha were elected.

State institutions did not remain intact. Albania was the most impoverished state in the communist bloc, and the transition brought almost immediate negative effects to a deteriorating economy and the breakdown of law. By mid-1991 only 25 percent of the productive capacity was functional, about half that of the previous year. Facing skyrocketing foreign debt, the government started printing money, fueling inflation. Property rights were not well defined and quarrels over farmland and property led to destruction of private and state property. The food supply dwindled. Large-scale hunger was only averted by a G-24 humanitarian emergency grant of U.S.$150 million. Italian troops entered the country in September 1991 to ensure distribution of humanitarian aid because of local institutions' declining ability to maintain law and order.

How did Albania react to developing majority-minority relations in Kosovo and Macedonia during the critical juncture? Denying aspirations toward a "Greater Albania," Alia strongly protested Serbian policies toward Kosovo, denouncing them as deliberate discrimination against Kosovo Albanians.[46] Strong statements regarding the changed constitutional status of the Albanians in Macedonia were significantly less prominent. Nevertheless, Albania had to take an official stance about the self-determination processes in its immediate neighborhood, prompted by declarations of independence of countries emerging from the former Yugoslavia in 1991, including Macedonia and Kosovo. The day before the ratification of Kosovo's independence in September 1991, Albanian foreign minister Muhammed Kapllani used the words "Republic of Kosova" for the first time while addressing the UN General Assembly.[47] It was, however, Albania's parliament, not the government, that issued a declaration in support of Kosovo's independence. The pro-independence stance gathered momentum only in 1992 during the presidential campaign of Democratic Party candidate Sali Berisha, when he mentioned the possibility of the unification of Kosovo and Albania. Shortly after he won office, he spoke of Kosovo's right to self-determination[48] and argued that Kosovo Albanians should be entitled to hold free democratic elections as did other breakaway regions of former Yugoslavia.[49]

International pressure against Albania's support for secessionism quickly intensified. Since Berisha's government maintained a pro-Western orientation and was interested in pursuing political and economic reforms, Albania became subject to stringent international control and conditionality. Politically relevant agents such as the United States, the EC, and international financial institutions linked economic aid and promises for political benefits and membership with requirements for democratization and development of a market economy, respect for minority rights, and maintenance of peace and security in the region. This intensified pressure on Albania to reconsider its initial enthusiasm for Kosovo's self-determination. In 1992 German foreign minister Hans Dietrich Genscher promised assistance to Albania while urging Tirana to act in consensus with the principles of inviolability of borders.[50] This statement was rather hypocritical, given that Germany had peacefully unified in 1990 and international law does not forbid peaceful unification of entities. During negotiations at international conferences, Tirana was urged to accept a "minority rights approach" toward the political demands of the Albanians of Kosovo and Macedonia. This approach clashed with the Kosovars, as they considered themselves a "people" with a right to territorial self-determination.[51]

Albania also supported Macedonia's independence in 1991. If Albania were overtly irredentist or interested in fomenting ethnic problems, it could have used this window of opportunity to take an irredentist or pro-secessionist stance. Instead, it was one of the first states to recognize Macedonia without reservations in regard to its constitutionally proclaimed name, Republic of Macedonia.[52] Albania realized that any scenario entailing territorial divisions would have immediate repercussions on Albania and the Albanian minority in Macedonia.[53] Its official policy stance was very close to those of the rest of the international community, seeking preservation of the new Macedonian state above all other scenarios. Shortly after becoming president in 1992, Berisha met with Macedonian president Gligorov. They made a declaration of intent to create a "model" relationship between their two countries.[54] Berisha gave no official encouragement to the national aspirations of the Albanians of Macedonia.[55] He considered domestic Macedonian-Albanian relations an affair of the Macedonian state. Nevertheless, he backed statements of the Albanian PDP party in the coalition government that Albanian population figures were misrepresented and there was insufficient respect for human rights. While advocating peaceful domestic solutions for human rights, Berisha stated that in the case of war, Albania would assist its ethnic brethren.[56]

There were three main reasons why Albania did not advance an irredentist agenda. First, Albania was not driven by internal irredentist processes, but was prompted by demonstration effects from countries in the former communist space that already exercised the right to self-determination. As several scholars observed, the principle of self-determination resurfaced after the end of the Cold War, and became a potent political force for territorial changes.[57] Second, the geopolitical partition of Albanians during more than four decades of communism accounted for the lack of emotional resonance of the pan-Albanian appeal. There is no clear evidence that the two major subgroups among the Albanians in Albania—the lowlander Tosks in the south and the highlander Ghegs in the north—displayed divergent attitudes toward Kosovo at the time. Throughout the 1990s, though, Ghegs became more sympathetic toward the Kosovo struggle, not least because their connections were reinvigorated during the formative period with the Albanians of former Yugoslavia, who were overwhelmingly Ghegs, and facilitated through the porous borders with Kosovo and Macedonia. Third, the national question, though high on Albania's foreign policy agenda, ranked behind obtaining external support for its own democratization.[58] State building was put ahead of nation building. Clearly, instrumental reasons trumped affinitive ones. Geopolitically, Albania wanted to change spheres of influence and become a member of Western institutions, the EU and NATO. Economically, its problems necessitated foreign aid. Its weakness increased its susceptibility to strong international pressures.

Albania's official non-interventionist stance, however, became coupled with a parallel strategy of clandestine support for Kosovo's secession and discontented elements in Macedonia. This dual-pronged strategy started as early as Alia's nonreformed communist rule. His position fluctuated between polemics against curtailment of Kosovo's autonomy and actual support for Kosovo's independence.[59] One of the major indicators of a weak state—widespread corruption—allowed officials in Albania who profited from their position in office to conclude deals with Kosovo rebels across borders. As early as 1990 several Kosovo Albanians went to Albania to begin military training conducted by Albanian army officers, who officially claimed to be "volunteers."[60] Colonel Dilaver Goxhaj, deputy chief of staff of the KLA—which later pursued secessionism through violence—claimed that senior KLA commanders were trained in Albania as of 1991.[61] Former KLA commander Ramush Haradinaj started buying hand grenades, small bombs, and pistols intended for use in Kosovo as of 1991; closely studied the army, police, and "other services"; and established connections with people who could help "at the appropriate time."[62] Pettifer confirmed that future KLA heros such as Zahir Pajaziti received military training at the military academy of Tirana. Unofficial support for secessionism started much earlier than Berisha's arrival on the political scene.[63]

Albania's corruption problems were also linked to Macedonia and to grievances about minority status. The paramilitary conspiracy in the Macedonian army, discovered in 1993, was connected to corrupt officials in Albania.[64] As Ackermann notes, in November 1993 there was an alleged conspiracy that involved two Albanian officials in the Macedonian government, deputy minister of health Imer Imeri and deputy minister of defense Hisen Haskaj. Newspaper reports mentioned that they were among ten ethnic Albanian officials conspiring to establish a paramilitary force referred to as an "All-Albanian Army."[65] Building clandestine alliances across borders was more challenging in this case, since the Albanians of Macedonia became part of the ruling coalition. Nevertheless, the clandestine links to Albania became a major venue for channeling minority discontent due to loss of constitutional status and aspirations for territorial autonomy.

To what degree was the diaspora involved in these early clandestine operations? Some radical diaspora elements associated with the LPK in Western Europe had clandestine members in these training camps. Although minuscule, the LPK consisted of a hard-line Marxist circle that used Leninist theory on how to run clandestine organizations and advocated armed revolt.[66] Radical diaspora elements seem to have briefly cooperated with the nonviolent movement of Rugova in these early years. Perritt writes that "some of the "Peaceful Path Institutionalists" tried to work with the Planners in Exile and the Defenders at Home. They organized training camps in Albania for would-be guerrilla fighters, but the training program was infiltrated by Serb secret police in 1993, and almost all were arrested or dispersed back into exile before they could do anything."[67] The radical diaspora's influence was minimal and did not shape the strength of the minority vis-à-vis the majority in Kosovo during the critical juncture.

Rugova's LDK movement became at the time more influential in diaspora circles. The government in exile started building branches in Western capitals as soon as Kosovo declared independence in 1991, in order to internationalize its claims and create new venues to voice human rights violations.[68] Many branches depended on support from local diaspora communities, which Rugova's network reinvigorated. Peaceful lobbying and not violent action, were characteristics for these early endeavors. One of the most active people at that stage was former U.S. representative Joseph Dio-Guardi, who chaired the Albanian-American Civic League (AACL) and advocated an end to human rights violations in Kosovo. He mobilized several U.S. senators to visit Kosovo in 1990[69] and exerted some impact on the adoption of the 1992 U.S. "Christmas Ultimatum" discussed in Chapter 3.[70] However, initial AACL supporters switched sides and joined LDK after its arrival in the U.S. Harry Bajraktari, an early AACL supporter, claimed that before the LDK arrival DioGuardi was a "hired gun," "paid to work for us, not to tell us what to do."[71]

Early Intervention of Turkey and the Turkish Diaspora from Bulgaria

At the end of the Cold War Turkey went through a strategic reconfiguration of its foreign policy, but did not witness drastic domestic changes associated with transition from communism. Its transition toward political pluralism started in the mid-1950s and has progressed in staggered phases.[72] It never had a command economy, despite strong state interventionism that lasted almost until the economic breakdown in 2001. In the late 1980s Turkey took various steps to increase political pluralism and civic rights, and introduced economic liberalism gradually during the early 1990s.[73] State institutions continued to function despite occasional strong disagreements between elected politicians and the highly autonomous military.[74] By contrast to Albania, Turkey's institutions were never weakened to the point of allowing government officials or non-state agents to form clandestine alliances across borders or highjack official foreign policy. The Balkans was an

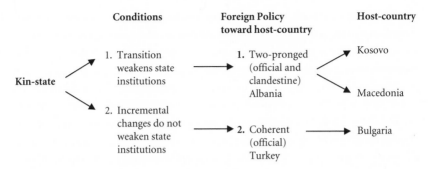

Figure 9. Kin-states during the critical juncture.

area where government, military, and public opinion stood together.[75] Figure 9 visualizes this argumentation.

Turkey's policies toward Bulgaria during the critical juncture took place under president Turgut Özal (1989–1993), one of the most influential figures in Turkish politics after Atatürk. Özal gradually introduced some moderate reforms aimed at political and civil rights and openness to a market economy.[76] In contrast to Albania, these reforms were gradual and initially strengthened the state. Between 1989 and 1993 Turkey's GDP (PPP) grew by 29 percent, from U.S.$256,723 billion to 330,294 billion.[77] Its economy was given an international orientation in the direction of new relationships with Turkic peoples abroad, specifically with the newly independent republics in Central Asia and the Caucasus.[78] Turkey also opened for Black Sea cooperation, including Bulgaria in December 1990, and Turkish trade and investment rapidly expanded in the region.[79] While more democratic pluralism opened opportunities for Islamic and pan-Turkic groups to influence the public opinion domestically,[80] the foreign policy process was dominated by Özal.

How did Turkey react to the changing status of the Turkish minority in Bulgaria? Turkey's relations with Bulgaria were strained during the last years of the Cold War because of the assimilation campaign of the mid-1980s and the expulsion of more than 350,000 Turks in 1989. Yet the political changes in 1990 paved the way for an improved relationship. Turkey maintained a coherent foreign policy dominated by the need to establish and maintain good bilateral relations with Bulgaria while preserving the political and cultural integrity of the Turkish minority. Turkey took seriously the integration of this minority and rapprochement with Bulgaria for two major reasons. It needed to curb immigration because it was overwhelmed by the need to accommodate more than 250,000 Turkish refugees who refused to return to Bulgaria after the regime change. It also sought to minimize its external flashpoints because of security concerns over its borders in the east (conflicts in Armenia and Azerbaijan) and southeast (the Kurdish problem), and the formation of an autonomous Kurdistan region in Iraq after the Gulf War.[81] It also had security concerns about Cyprus and Greece.[82] Turkey backed the integrationist MRF and refrained from developing close ties with the TDP. As discussed earlier, this more radical Turkish formation, not officially registered in Bulgaria, raised occasional demands for autonomy and constitutional changes.[83] No political circles in Turkey identified the autonomy question as a frame for local mobilization that would support ethnic outbidding. The TDP was largely ignored.

A non-interventionist stance toward Bulgaria was enhanced by Turkey's preference for handling foreign relations directly with mainstream Bulgarian politicians rather than through the leadership of the Turkish minority. Central to this dynamic was a leadership issue. Bulgarian media often alleged that MRF leader Dogan had collaborated with the communist regime. It took a special effort to convince Turkish diplomats that he could be trusted in the postcommunist environment.[84] In addition, there was a lack of general interest. Turkey did not respond positively to MRF efforts to broker loans or attract Turkish investment in impoverished minority-inhabited areas.[85] Instead, on several occasions it openly recommended that the Bulgarian state itself take care of its poverty to avert creeping emigration.

Turkey's low-key approach to intervention had limits on occasions when the *political integration* of the Turkish minority was endangered. In 1991 prime minister Mesut Yilmaz wrote a letter to his Bulgarian counterpart Lyuben Berov, recommending that the MRF be allowed to take part in the parliamentary elections.[86] Shortly thereafter, he made an official statement that "the behavior of the Bulgarian government toward the Turkish minority would be a guarantee for Turkish-Bulgarian relations."[87] After the MRF registered and entered the Bulgarian parliament the tone changed, but Turkey still raised international concern about the minority's situation.

Turkey intervened actively in the cultural sphere, particularly in educational and religious affairs, but in line with arrangements brokered with the Bulgarian government. Turkey donated textbooks for the start of mother tongue classes in 1991–1992, which had not been previously offered in Bulgarian classrooms.[88] As of 1992 the MRF became the official distributor of annual stipends for ethnic Turks to study in Turkish universities. Most notable, however, was Turkey's intervention in the religious sphere. Since both Bulgaria and Turkey were interested in preserving the traditional Haneffiya Sunni Islam professed by the ethnic Turks of Bulgaria and the majority of Turks in Turkey, the Bulgarian state was not opposed to Turkey sending trained religious emissaries starting in the early 1990s.

The diaspora of the Turks of Bulgaria was rather passive. There was no serious human rights abuse in Bulgaria to motivate the migrants, and the diaspora adopted an assimilationist attitude toward Turkey. The Kemalist state had been strongly assimilationist since its foundation, so at the time the expelled Turks of Bulgaria had two main options: to return to Bulgaria or assimilate into Turkey. More important, the migrants were not well organized. Although the Federation of the Emigrants from the Balkans, Balgioch, was established in 1985 in Istanbul and the town of Bursa—where more than 60,000 of the refugees from the last 1989 emigration wave had settled, and other minor organizations had developed in Edirne and other towns of Turkey—they were not united internally. The federation was among the first to make international circles aware of the 1989 expulsion campaign.[89] Over time the federation became much more interested in lobbying within Turkey, not externally.[90] In addition, when these organizations rallied over a specific issue, they took into consideration the migrants' conflicting relations with the Bulgarian state rather than the conflicts between ethnic Turks in Bulgaria and the Bulgarian state. The migrants occasionally needed the MRF to lobby for their interests, and they supported it politically by casting absentee votes during elections. Furthermore, this diaspora was economically weak. It was not committed to investing back in Bulgaria, and any investments were in cultural projects, not business enterprises.[91]

To summarize, while the Albanian and Turkish diasporas had little impact on the formation of the conflict dynamic during the critical juncture, toward the end of the formative period in 1992, Albania and Turkey as kin-states established a *set of contextualized relationships* with the minorities in the original homelands. The specific content of these links affected whether more or less conflictual patterns of engagement would consolidate over time. The structure of the links is visible in Figure 10. For the sake of clarity of the overall argument, this figure shows the links between majorities, minorities, and all the external agents (international community, kin-states, diasporas), but concentrates on link D (minority—kin-state) and link E (minority—diaspora).

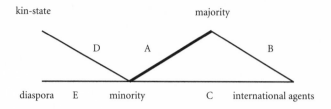

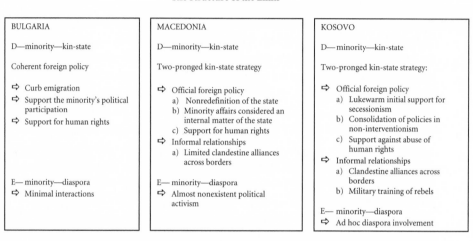

Figure 10. Relationship between minorities and identity-based agents.

Self-Reinforcement Processes: Adaptation
Between Minorities and Kin-States

Adaptive expectations are an important causal mechanism in the perpetuation of relationships between the minority and the kin-state. The content of the links between minorities and kin-states created a bounded rationality for the minorities' behavior. They learned to seek support from the kin-state through specific channels, and acted accordingly. The Albanians of Kosovo and Macedonia adapted to Albania's official foreign policy of non-interventionism but simultaneously sought support for their secessionist and autonomist movements through clandestine channels. The Turks of Bulgaria adapted to Turkey's preference for arranging its relationship directly with the Bulgarian government rather than through the minority leadership, but they could rely on Turkey's support when their political participation and other human rights were endangered, or in cultural projects. By contrast, because the diasporas had little impact on the majority-minority relationship during the critical juncture, they were not subject to these adaptation processes. Hence, where mobilized over time, as in the Kosovo case, the diaspora provided an important external impetus for change of the informally institutionalized conflict dynamic.

Albania and Kosovo's Secessionism

While the transition process allowed international agents to impose an official non-interventionist stance on Albania, domestically there was no clear-cut national doctrine or constitutional clarity on the national question before 1998. The adaptation of Albanian minorities in Kosovo and Macedonia took place amid various formulations of foreign policy alongside the governing elites' ideological orientations, regional/clan affiliations, and particularistic interests.

The 1992–1997 democratic Berisha government was rather supportive of Kosovo's parallel institutions compared to his socialist successors. Berisha considered Ibrahim Rugova and his nonviolent LDK to embody a new democratic doctrine. They had a common interest in challenging the political status quo—socialists in Albania and authoritarian socialist Milosevic in Serbia respectively. Berisha often raised objections in international forums against discrimination and violence against Kosovars, consulted Kosovo leaders on political strategy, concluded economic agreements, and repeatedly warned that Albania would not stand idly by in the event of war in Kosovo.[92] He projected a kin-state commitment to be an external protector for Kosovar human rights. Political factionalism was reinforced by regional and tribal differences, as Berisha derived his support primarily from the Gheg constituency in the north bordering Kosovo. Despite a sympathetic stance toward Kosovo, Berisha eventually toned down his claims under international pressure. In 1993 he abandoned overt calls for independence and suggested a "democratic space in the Balkans" to facilitate regional integration into Europe regardless of international borders.[93] He also arrested a number of KLA leaders advocating armed revolt, including Adem Jasari in 1993, Zahir Pajaziti in 1995, and Hashim Thaci in 1996.[94]

The socialist government that took power in Albania after the collapse in 1997 drew their constituency from the predominantly Tosk south[95] and was less supportive of the Kosovars, and the respective leaders adapted to this. During a 1997 conference in Crete, prime minister Fatos Nano met Milosevic for the first time. Nano spoke about noncontroversial topics such as Balkan integration and economic contacts, while repeating that the dispute over Kosovo should be resolved by Belgrade and Prishtina.[96] This meeting did not improve Albanian-Kosovo relations, and for a long time thereafter the Albanian government solicited information about Rugova from foreign diplomats and the media rather than from direct contacts.[97] The government was reshuffled in 1998 and prime minister Pandeli Majko briefly employed rhetoric abandoning the "minority rights approach" in favor of a secessionist one. Also, a platform issued by the Albanian Academy of Sciences stated that the "rightful aspiration of all Albanians is the unification of all ethnic Albanian lands in a single national state."[98] Yet Albania's connections with the LDK leadership remained weak. An instrumental rather than affinity-based reasoning is transparent here. Majko made a statement in favor of secession only after the warfare in Kosovo intensified in 1998 and threatened to spill over into Albania. He soon succumbed to international pressure again, obliged to weigh the costs of diverting from a non-interventionist path. The pressure intensified to the point that Majko's government was asked to serve as mediator to the 1999 Rambouillet negotiations and unify the highly factionalized Kosovo Albanian movements, while it was prohibited even to mention the word "independence" as an incentive for the Kosovo Albanians.[99] Albania of course stood firmly behind NATO's military intervention in Kosovo.

Although the two parties' ideological competition defined Albania's official stance toward Kosovo, and Kosovo Albanians adapted to the fluctuations of their stances, they also adapted to another more hidden reality—that some Albanian officials were ready to forge clandestine alliances across borders. In 1996 former KLA commander Ramush Hardinaj "employed former and serving officers of the Albanian Army in order to train soldiers and help find routes for moving military equipment."[100] According to Serbian accounts, the primary training camps were in a village near Tirana and three settlements close to the Yugoslav-Albanian border.[101] This is highly mountainous terrain, often considered in the scholarly literature as conducive to the harboring of rebels.[102] As rebel-police collisions intensified in 1996, support for the KLA became more obvious in Albania: large numbers of guerrillas were seen training in the most northern Albanian highlands and relaxing in clubs in Tirana.[103]

Activities across porous borders facilitated the growth of Kosovo's secessionism. Against the backdrop of increasing unemployment the borders offered opportunities for smuggling to flourish. The border point Qafa i Prusht between Kosovo and Albania became well known for trafficking women for prostitution.[104] The mountainous terrain impeded regular monitoring, but evidence also suggests that Albania was not interested in imposing strict controls.[105] As early as 1992, when the European Community wanted to dispatch CSCE monitors to the Albanian-Yugoslav border, foreign minister Rudolf Marku fiercely resisted. Observers would have resulted in a de facto buffer zone formalizing a division of the Albanian nation.[106]

State institutions further declined during Berisha's years in government and reached their nadir in 1997 when finances collapsed. Sham financial schemes flourished with the knowledge of the government and consumed the life savings of more than half the population, causing as a reaction numerous demonstrations, looting, anarchy, and breakdown of the state.[107] During this time, mobs stole around 650,000 weapons and other military items from local armories.[108] Many weapons were directly smuggled into Kosovo, while others were later purchased by militants. In mid-1997 a Kalashnikov AK-47 cost five U.S. dollars.[109] Berisha—feeling vulnerable because of the collapse of his regime and the state—resumed nationalist rhetoric, joining others in criticizing the nonviolent movement in Kosovo and accusing Rugova of passivity.[110] As discussed in Chapter 4, all this was an important external pressure that tilted the conflict dynamic in Kosovo toward more radicalization that eventually led to "internal warfare," although the violence by the Serbian regime in Kosovo remained "extensive" until that period.

Albania and Claims About Autonomy in Macedonia

The argument that ideological ties across borders matter despite an official foreign policy line can also be made with regard to the Macedonian case, but the ideological ties were less salient. From 1994 onward Berisha increasingly supported some radical elements in the governing PDP, who were nationalist in make-up and unhappy with the lack of progress in interethnic relations in Macedonia. Yet these PDP factions also challenged the old postcommunist order, trying to outbid core members of the party whose cadres

had ruled in various capacities in communist Yugoslavia. Berisha was interested in supporting the challengers who opened a parallel Tetovo University
in 1994 to provide Albanian language higher education despite resistance
from the Macedonian state (see Chapter 2). Berisha praised rector Fadil
Sulejmani, who was not recognized as such by the Macedonians in the
coalition government. This move temporarily strained relations with the
government in Skopje.

The response of socialist Fatos Nano toward the 1997 crisis in the
Albanian-inhabited towns in western Macedonia was more muted. When
the police violently crushed an initially peaceful demonstration in support
of raising Albanian flags over the municipalities of Gostivar and Tetovo,
Nano lodged a formal protest with the Macedonian ambassador against use
of excessive force, but made no other protest.[111] Nano embarked on a path
of regional cooperation, visited Macedonia twice in 1998, and signed eight
bilateral cooperation agreements with the coalition government in Skopje,
dominated by the postcommunist SDSM.[112] Moreover, in a meeting in Tetovo he openly discouraged separatism and stressed that Albanians should
view their future in light of regional and European integration.[113] He reinforced an official message from Tirana that human rights should be tolerated, but not autonomist or secessionist movements.

Albania's corruption problems were linked to Macedonia as well. The
Macedonian-Albanian border was patrolled by UNPREDEP troops and
OSCE civilian monitors, but illegal crossings over the mountains still took
place. They intensified after the collapse of the Albanian state in 1997, when
guns were smuggled into Macedonia.[114] Some DPA leaders were rumored
to be involved in clandestine smuggling operations, as some domestic and
international agents observed. The border became even more porous during the refugee crisis of 1999 that followed NATO's bombing in Serbia and
the flight of 400,000 Kosovo Albanians toward the south.

Albania officially maintained distance from the guerrilla insurgency in
Macedonia in 2001, but clandestine currents still exerted an impact. The
radical Albanian National Liberation Army (NLA) in Macedonia initially
claimed it had entirely local roots and was not connected to Albania or
Kosovo, but in fact it had strong support from splinters of the former KLA
and Albanian officials with pan-Albanian sentiments. While media in Albania proper and Kosovo intellectuals accused Albania of a "mute policy"
toward the Macedonian crisis,[115] U.S. secretary of state Colin Powell praised
Albania prime minister Ilir Meta for his public condemnation of ethnic

Albanian extremists.[116] Albania was among the first states to welcome the signing of the Ohrid Framework Agreement in August 2001.

Turkey's Cautious Interventionism in Bulgaria

In the mid- to late 1990s, Turkey continued to be selectively interventionist in Bulgaria in supporting the political integration of the Turkish minority and spreading cultural influences. As Stoyanov notes, in 1994 Turkey pressured the Bulgarian government with a report to the UN and NATO mentioning the article in the Bulgarian constitution prohibiting formation of parties along ethnic and religious lines. This stance was largely hypocritical given that Turkey also bans ethnic and religious parties.[117] During election periods Turkish diplomats visited Turkish-inhabited areas in Bulgaria, and directly or indirectly affected electoral support for the MRF.[118] In 1995, Turkish diplomats also denounced the fraudulent results of the controversial local elections in the southern town of Karzhali, which initially deposed the ethnic Turkish mayor. Whenever state meddling took place in Turkish minority affairs, the MRF raised concerns to Turkey and international organizations.

Although Turkey's generally non-interventionist stance secured stability and good neighborly relations, a slightly revived nationalist understanding of Turkey's relationship with Bulgaria was present as well. New influences, particularly in the cultural sphere, were crucial for Turkey, which exploited internal Bulgarian insecurities in the political, educational and religious spheres to assert its own versions of the issues. Turkey had a similar attitude toward states in Central Asia that were even weaker politically and institutionally. In the cultural sphere, it deepened its relationship with Bulgaria to protect Hannefiya Sunni Islam. Bulgaria had started to fear the uncontrolled Islamic influence of emissaries of non-Sunnite origin and became eager to sign an official agreement with Turkey in 1998 arranging for Muslim religious functionaries in Bulgaria to be officially approved by Turkey's Directorate for Religious Affairs.

In the Bulgarian case, Turkey's foreign policy and non-state agents did not clash but mutually reinforced each other. The influence of some Pan-Turkic and Islamic groups should not be overstated.[119] For example, the highly controversial Islamic movement Gülen maintained a low profile in Bulgaria compared to its much stronger support for Turkic minorities in Central Asia and the Caucasus. Even in Central Asia, the movement's ethnic

sensitivities and national loyalties superseded Islamic frames for mobilization.[120] This suggests that although Turkey's pluralistic society grappled
with various interpretations of Turkey's place in the world after the Cold
War, the relative strength of its secular institutions constrained the development of a schism between state and non-state agents when it came to external ethnic brethren.

External Stimuli for Change: The Albanian Diaspora Intervention and the Radicalization of the Kosovo Conflict

Radical elements in the Albanian diaspora in Western Europe and the
United States were crucial in the radicalization of the conflict in Kosovo in
1998–1999. The diaspora was connected to the conflict but did not experience direct pressures from the international community, as did the majorities, minorities, and kin-states. LDK's diaspora activism until 1995–1996
should be largely viewed as an extension of LDK politics abroad, because
the LDK controlled its branches in the diaspora, and large parts of the diaspora followed its nonviolent strategy. Theirs was a "contained contention."
Radical elements existed but had little following for sustained transborder
mobilization. Because radical elements were not part of the adaptation
processes sustaining the informally institutionalized conflict dynamic, they
turned to be important non-state agents to alter it through "transgressive
contention" in 1998–1999, when two conditions were in place: the moderate LDK lost support for its strategy of peaceful resistance and grave violations of human rights took place in the Drenica region in 1998.

During the initial transnationalization of the conflict, diaspora members engaged primarily with moderate actions, such as financial contributions and lobbying. As Hockenos points out, nowhere outside Kosovo was
the LDK government in exile stronger than in Germany. Of the approxi-
mately 400,000 Albanians in Western Europe, a third lived in Germany and
a quarter in Switzerland.[121] New waves of refugees from Kosovo spread
farther into European countries, such as the UK, where no significant guest
worker communities had existed previously.[122] The major fund-raising effort went through the Fund for the Republic of Kosovo under Bukoshi's
supervision and sustained the parallel institutions in 1992–1995. Bukoshi
and other activists paid numerous visits to cultural societies, guest-worker

clubs, and provincial beer halls to solicit the voluntary 3 percent contributions. The government declared that all Kosovars in the diaspora had a duty to contribute to this fund but there were no reports of violence against members to induce payments, unlike in the case of another prominent diaspora mobilization, the Tamil Tigers in Canada.

The LDK government had a specific strategy about the utility of different diasporas to the secessionist cause. Because of their closer connections and emotional ties with communities at home, the European-based diasporas were targeted primarily for fund-raising, not least because lobbying was more difficult in the European corporatist interest representation systems.[123] As a senior foreign policy advisor to the shadow government explained, the exiled authorities prioritized the United States for lobbying because lobbyists could more easily permeate the pluralist U.S. interest representation system, and because the government was more sympathetic to defense of minority rights than any European government.[124] While some collaboration continued between the LDK and DioGuardi's New York-based AACL, the exiled authorities put more effort into supporting other active House of Representatives members such as Sue Kelly and Eliot Engel, who could better promote Kosovo's independence. The rift between the two groups grew to such an extent that in 1996 the National Albanian American Council (NAAC) was founded with serious LDK support in Washington. DioGuardi remained active on the Kosovo issue, but after 1996 he no longer controlled Kosovo Albanians' lobby politics.[125]

The noninclusion of Kosovo Albanian demands in Dayton in 1995 was a transformative event that started to erode the initial transnational relationships between the weakening LDK and the diaspora. The failure of Dayton to address the Kosovo question, and U.S. and EU reluctance to support the LDK's nonviolent strategy, were clear messages that violence gets attention, while peaceful strategies do not. A rift between Rugova and Bukoshi in 1995–1996 resulted in internal competition for influence in diaspora circles and reduced the diaspora's financial contributions to the parallel institutions.[126] KLA operatives used this rift to infuse their own vision to change strategy from nonviolence to guerrilla warfare. Bukoshi argued that the KLA should join efforts with the exiled government to receive funding and international legitimacy.[127] The KLA rejected his proposal and started building its own networks, saying that "Rugova and company are traitors."[128] Thus, *ethnic outbidding* centered on a *clash of strategies* of the two groups.[129]

Another transformative event in the radicalization of the Albanian diaspora occurred in February 1998, when Serbian military units massacred the extended family of militant KLA leader Adem Jasari in the Drenica region.[130] In response, coordinated demonstrations took place in front of Yugoslav embassies in Europe and major U.S. cities in March, bringing 100,000 people to the streets.[131] At this point, the fund-raising effort moved to the United States, where Albanians were more affluent. As Sullivan noted, New York-based roofer Florin Krasniqi actively raised funds for weapons and military equipment. The Drenica massacre gave additional legitimacy to the emerging radical KLA, because it shifted U.S. public discourse from regarding it as "terrorist" to national liberation movement.[132]

The conjunctural effects of the Drenica massacre, which commanded a strong emotional appeal, and the LDK failure in Dayton, which induced the need to rethink secession strategies, prompted the diaspora in 1998 to shift its extensive support from the shadow government to the KLA and to become more radical.[133] A group of fighters formed the U.S.-based "Atlantic Battalion" that delivered diaspora fighters to Kosovo. At least two buses of volunteers left from the UK, and others were drafted from Germany and Switzerland.[134] Major voluntary contributions started flowing from the U.S., Canada, Australia, Germany, and Switzerland. Single charitable events in New York, Michigan, California, and Alaska raised $16,000–56,000.[135] Diaspora funds were often used to purchase AK-47s. Procured arms helped guerrillas within Kosovo stage attacks on Serbian police stations. As Serbia deployed more military and paramilitary units, Albanian villagers fled and Serbian troops looted their houses. According to a Western diplomat, this tactic served as "the most effective recruitment drive the KLA could have hoped for."[136]

Conclusions

This chapter has demonstrated that kin-states and diasporas contribute to variations in ethnic violence in intrastate conflicts where their ethnic brethren are involved, even if they do not act in outwardly irredentist ways. If a transition drastically weakens the institutions of a kin-state such as Albania, the kin-state may formulate a non-interventionist foreign policy stance with regard to secessionism and autonomy, but its institutions will not be strong enough to implement it. As a result, parallel to official foreign policy, clandestine alliances across borders are formed between kin-state officials and leaders of the secessionist and autonomist movements. The degree of kin-state involvement also depends on the domestic conditions of these intrastate conflicts. It is easier for kin-state officials to forge clandestine alliances when their ethnic brethren experience more human rights violations and where the leadership needs external protection (Kosovo's parallel institutions) versus when their ethnic brethren are in the governing coalition (Macedonia). In contrast, if there is no transition and some reforms are implemented gradually in a kin-state such as Turkey, its state institutions will retain their capacity to enforce official foreign policy. Turkey's foreign policy toward the Turks of Bulgaria offered minimal intervention with regard to political participation while spreading specific cultural and religious influences, but there was no major variation in how kin-state officials pursued their goals.

These findings speak to scholarly accounts on the intervention of identity-based agents in ethnic conflicts in several ways. The importance of kin-state contributions in the formation of the majority-minority relationship during a critical juncture is clear. Scholarly accounts that consider kin-states to behave similarly to diasporas because of their affinity ties miss an important distinction. Since the diasporas were not actively involved in the critical juncture, they did not attract pressure from the international community and did not participate in the same adaptation processes to which majorities, minorities, kin-states, and the international community were bound throughout large parts of the 1990s. With fuller mobilization later, as in the Kosovo case—driven also by the loss of legitimacy of the nonviolent movement and grave human rights violations on the ground— radical diaspora elements and the diaspora which followed it provided a powerful external impetus to challenge the informally institutionalized conflict dynamic and contribute to the conflict escalation in the direction of an "internal warfare." Although instrumental considerations for intervention are more characteristic for kin-states than for diasporas, the specific conditions under which they occur are important. Kin-states act in predominantly instrumentalist ways when they formulate official foreign policies because they need to pursue domestic reforms and obtain aid from the international community. Diaspora entrepreneurs are driven by instrumentalist considerations when ethnic outbidding takes place, as during the competition between LDK and KLA in the diaspora in 1996–1998, but they can be also motivated by strategic reassessments and policy learning, when the nonviolent strategy became dysfunctional. Nevertheless, affinity ties are important as well. In the absence of support from other international agents during the critical juncture, affinity ties established the initial clandestine channels for the Albanian minorities to voice their discontent with the drastic (Kosovo) or more minimal (Macedonia) decrease of constitutional status. Affinity-based ties drove diaspora members to support more radicalism when grave violations took place in their homeland. The times when diasporas learn about human rights violations from family, friends, and the media, provide a potent window for intensive diaspora radicalization.

Finally, this chapter teased out several differences between identity-based agents and the international community as external agents in interventions. Identity-based agents have affinity ties, while the international community is ruled by instrumentalism, normative respect for sovereign states, and aspirations to be a neutral arbiter between majorities and minorities. Kin-states and diasporas are more supportive of altering states. Identity-based agents can influence conflicts in more informal ways: through clandestine channels, sponsoring parallel institutions, fund-raising, gathering fighters from diaspora ranks, and other activities. These findings indicate the need to better understand the future activities of conglomerations of *networks* when researching identity-based agents, rather than the *institutions* usually considered when analyzing the international community.

Chapter 6

Change in Conflict Dynamics

The previous five chapters addressed the book's central question: why did ethnonational conflicts with similar characteristics at the beginning of the transition process lead to different degrees of violence over time? The discussion so far has demonstrated that during a formative period of time (1987/89–1992) when the political and economic systems of Bulgaria, Macedonia, and Yugoslavia were undergoing major transitions from communism, the choices of majorities, minorities, international community, and kin-states were important to establish different conflict dynamics. How majorities approached a change in minority status and reinforcement of the change through co-optation or coercion mechanisms, and how minorities accepted or rejected the state were central to the establishment of conflict dynamics in each case: conflictual in Kosovo, semiconflictual in Macedonia, and cooperative in Bulgaria. International agents added to the evolution of formal and informal relationships in the way they guaranteed the majorities' the preservation of the state, the minorities' political participation in the state institutions, and the international community's own commitment to conflict resolution in these countries. Kin-states also contributed to these dynamics by formulating a clear non-interventionist foreign policy (Turkey) or a foreign policy officially claiming non-interventionism but advancing support for secessionist and autonomist movements in parallel (Albania).

Once the critical juncture ended, these relationships became informally institutionalized through the mechanisms of "advantage of political incumbency," "adaptive expectations," and to a certain degree "learning." Change in conflict dynamics in the direction of higher levels of violence stemmed primarily from exogenous shocks such as the 1995 Dayton Agreement and the 1997 collapse of Albania, and from stimuli by the Albanian diaspora in 1998–1999. In the Bulgarian case there was some influence from long-term EU accession processes toward the consolidation of a non-violent dynamic.

This and the next chapter are connected in their concern with a second important question: why do ethnonational conflicts persevere even after sustained international intervention toward postconflict reconstruction and democratization? This question is central to scholars and policy makers working on postconflict reconstruction in divided places in Africa, Asia, the Balkans, and the Middle East. International administration, peacekeeping, peace building, and democracy promotion efforts have often achieved limited results in fostering interethnic peace and democratization, despite significant resource commitments in blood and treasure. This question is also relevant for scholars on Eastern Europe, who have been preoccupied with demonstrating the benefits of EU integration on majority-minority relations while underestimating the effects of large-scale violence on future EU integration of postconflict countries in the Western Balkans.

What has changed in Kosovo, Macedonia, and Bulgaria over the past decade and why? I argue that "replacement" of the established rules of statehood in Kosovo and Macedonia, where the status of the Albanians was elevated compared to the 1990s, contributed significantly to conflict mitigation throughout the 2000s. The mechanism of "replacement" also altered informal practices in which majorities, minorities, and international agents were earlier locked. These concerned international agents' aversion toward redefinition of the state and long-term commitments to conflict resolution and reform, especially in Kosovo and somewhat in Macedonia. "Layering" of new rules on top of the existing ones through EU "conditionality" and "socialization" mechanisms, but also through formal and informal *practices*, exerted external stimuli for peaceful change in Bulgaria and Macedonia and less so in Kosovo. These changes addressed some aspects of the informally institutionalized conflict dynamics, but they did not overturn the dynamics in their entirety.

The chapter considers the evolution of outcomes of violence in Bulgaria, Macedonia, and Kosovo through the 2000s. It turns to the mechanisms and processes of change through the international community's shift toward redefinition of statehood, its long-term commitment to conflict resolution, democratic reforms, state building, and future EU integration. It concludes with a discussion of the "replacement" and "layering" mechanisms.

Diminished Yet Persistent Ethnonational Violence

Kosovo, Macedonia, and Bulgaria belong to different categories of cases in the 2000s, considering their recent experiences with internal warfare. Kosovo and Macedonia are similar to postconflict Bosnia-Herzegovina, Cambodia, East Timor, Lebanon, Liberia, and Mozambique, where civil wars took place. Bulgaria belongs among cases of peaceful transitions in interethnic relations in other Eastern European countries. This classification is correct but limited, because researchers who study the success or failure of "peace building" or "democratization" as dependent variables rarely examine the actual "levels of violence" across cases central to this book. Figure 11 presents the three cases during the last decade using the operationalization in the Introduction.[1]

"Nonviolent" and "threatened" levels of violence predominated in Bulgaria in the 2000s. The "threatened" level existed in the early 1990s but subsided thereafter. Severe threats resurfaced in 2005–2006: strong public attacks against ethnic Turks and other Muslim minorities were made in the media and during demonstrations by the ultranationalist party Ataka and other more marginal nationalist groups. Threats continued in 2006 with heated anti-Turkish rhetoric during the 2006 presidential campaign. A mosque was set on fire in the town of Kazanlak, which briefly raised the level of violence to "episodic." Pervasive anti-Turkish rhetoric surrounded the 2009 parliamentary elections as well, with numerous cases of vandalism against mosques.

Levels of violence in Macedonia fluctuated in the postconflict period. There was more pervasive "episodic" violence during the 2000s than during the first transition period after 1989. Right after the 2001 "internal warfare," the highest level of violence in the operationalization scheme, the level dropped to "extensive." There were numerous violent attacks and mistreatment of Albanians by the Macedonian paramilitary groups "Lions" and "Tigers," an explosion next to the parliament, shootings of Albanian and Macedonian policemen in separate incidents, attacks on an official in an interethnic relations council, and multiple fights among students in the mixed public schools. The years 2003–2004 were marked by "episodic" violence: public school beatings and tensions continued, Macedonian homes in Skopje were destroyed, and Albanians protested against the commemoration of the killing of two Macedonians in 2001 in the Albanian-dominated village of Čelopek. Tensions were raised by the 2004 referendum

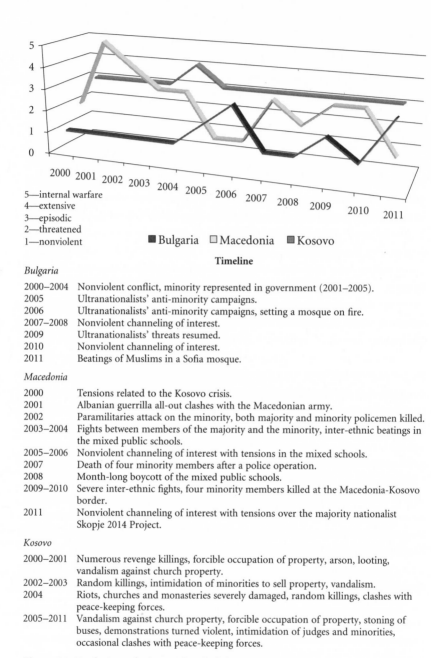

5—internal warfare
4—extensive
3—episodic
2—threatened
1—nonviolent

■ Bulgaria □ Macedonia ■ Kosovo

Timeline

Bulgaria

2000–2004	Nonviolent conflict, minority represented in government (2001–2005).
2005	Ultranationalists' anti-minority campaigns.
2006	Ultranationalists' anti-minority campaigns, setting a mosque on fire.
2007–2008	Nonviolent channeling of interest.
2009	Ultranationalists' threats resumed.
2010	Nonviolent channeling of interest.
2011	Beatings of Muslims in a Sofia mosque.

Macedonia

2000	Tensions related to the Kosovo crisis.
2001	Albanian guerrilla all-out clashes with the Macedonian army.
2002	Paramilitaries attack on the minority, both majority and minority policemen killed.
2003–2004	Fights between members of the majority and the minority, inter-ethnic beatings in the mixed public schools.
2005–2006	Nonviolent channeling of interest with tensions in the mixed schools.
2007	Death of four minority members after a police operation.
2008	Month-long boycott of the mixed public schools.
2009–2010	Severe inter-ethnic fights, four minority members killed at the Macedonia-Kosovo border.
2011	Nonviolent channeling of interest with tensions over the majority nationalist Skopje 2014 Project.

Kosovo

2000–2001	Numerous revenge killings, forcible occupation of property, arson, looting, vandalism against church property.
2002–2003	Random killings, intimidation of minorities to sell property, vandalism.
2004	Riots, churches and monasteries severely damaged, random killings, clashes with peace-keeping forces.
2005–2011	Vandalism against church property, forcible occupation of property, stoning of buses, demonstrations turned violent, intimidation of judges and minorities, occasional clashes with peace-keeping forces.

Figure 11. Evolution of ethnonational violence, 2000–2011.

to challenge the decentralization of Macedonia, but remained mostly confined to threatening rhetoric, with no significant violent incidents. There was a slight drop in the level of violence to "nonviolent" in 2005–2006, when inter-ethnic exchanges were dominated by hate speech and occasional discriminatory incidents against Albanian soldiers in the Macedonian-dominated military. The level then fluctuated between "threatened" and "episodic," but in 2007 escalated to "episodic" when inter-ethnic tensions rose after Macedonian police killed four Albanians in the village of Brodec near the Kosovo border. In 2008 it dropped to "threatened" because of a month-long boycott by Macedonian students and their parents in a Struga school who sought ethnically separated classes. The violence escalated to "episodic" in 2009 because of a severe fight between Albanian and Macedonian soccer fans in Skopje, and remained at this level in 2010 because of the killing of four Albanians implicated in smuggling at the Macedonian-Kosovo border. Interethnic tensions increased after this incident.

Interethnic violence in Kosovo is characterized by two outcomes— "episodic" and "extensive." The extensive level, typical in the immediate aftermath of internal warfare, included the murders of 146 Albanians and 55 Serbs in 2000, and of 92 Albanians and 30 Serbs in 2001. These outcomes are mostly because of revenge violence.[2] In the early 2000s two trends emerged that sustained violence throughout the next decade—Kosovo Albanians attacked Serbian Orthodox Church property, clergy, and returnees, and Kosovo Serbs used violence when seizing the property of Albanians in the divided northern city of Mitrovica. In 2002–2003 the interethnic violence subsided to episodic, with continuing vandalism against churches and pressures for home property sale. The March 2004 riots, broadly covered in the international media, reached an "extensive" level of violence. Eight Serbs and 12 Albanians died and more than 30 Orthodox religious sites and over 900 houses and businesses of ethnic minorities were looted and damaged. Between 2005 and 2008, when Kosovo proclaimed independence, interethnic violence subsided, but remained episodic, with widespread Kosovo Albanian vandalism against Orthodox Church property and stoning of buses, which led to restrictions for freedom of movement to Serbian-dominated areas. In the two years following the 2008 proclamation of independence, violence remained episodic. During this time Kosovo Serbs continued to be subjected to intimidation, with attacks on individuals and church property, but relatively more incidents were reported as initiated by Kosovo Serbs. They included throwing explosive devices at a TV station

and protests against Kosovo Albanian returnees. In the latest incident of
July 2011, a Kosovo police officer was killed, and local Serbs burned a
border post and fired at NATO peacekeepers.[3]

These findings are sobering for all three cases, demonstrating persistent
patterns of violence in each case over a twenty-year period. Nonviolent
and threatened levels predominated in Bulgaria, episodic and threatened in
Macedonia, and a combination of extensive and episodic levels was characteristic for Kosovo. It is critical to explore more deeply the processes and
mechanisms that explain these patterns. In this chapter I further discuss
postconflict change. In the next chapter I turn to the durability of conflict
dynamics.

Changes Toward More Peaceful Majority-Minority Relations

So far, this book has elaborated on the formation and sustenance of informally institutionalized conflict dynamics, combining formal institutions
and formal and informal contextualized practices by multiple agents. I
argue that this offers a different analytical angle to the study of conflicts
from targeting the study of formal institutions (e.g., constitutions, laws,
procedures) or highly fluid strategic interactions among majorities, minorities, and third parties. Informally institutionalized conflict dynamics may
be considered by a broader definition of Mahoney and Thelen, who view
institutions as "enduring features of political and social life (rules, norms,
procedures), that structure behavior and cannot be changed easily and in-
stantaneously."[4] Informally institutionalized conflict dynamics are enduring in political life, their unwritten rules are internalized by the agents
involved, agents act on these rules even if they claim different stances, and
the rules are resistant to change. Hence, discussion about change and continuity of conflict dynamics needs to take these relationships seriously.

In their quest to understand institutional change beyond the effects of
exogenous shocks, Mahoney and Thelen present four mechanisms from
their historical institutionalist perspective:

(1) *displacement* of old institutions, that is, removal of existing rules
    and introduction of new ones;
(2) *layering* of new rules on top of and beside existing ones, and both
    rules coexist;

(3) *drift* from existing institutions when there is a gap between rules and enforcement; and

(4) *conversion*, where rules remain formally the same, but are interpreted and enacted differently.[5]

In the context of this book, the displacement (here "replacement") and layering mechanisms were primarily active to introduce change in the direction of more peaceful majority-minority relationships.[6] "Replacement" worked in Kosovo, which changed the existing rules of statehood; Kosovo was allowed to secede from Serbia de facto but not de jure and became an international protectorate. Macedonia underwent change in which a nation-state became largely consociational under close international supervision. "Replacement" also changed aspects of the informal relationships previously established between international and domestic agents, most notably the former's reluctance to permit restructuring of statehood and guaranteeing its long-term presence on the ground. "Layering" worked when, due to prospects for future EU integration, new legalistic, normative, and practical rules were added to these countries, on top of or next to existing rules. "Drift," in combination with a "reactive sequence," changed the conflicts in a more contentious direction, and will be discussed in Chapter 7 on conflict perpetuation.[7]

The new policies manifested themselves in numerous amendments of constitutions and legislation, the long-term presence of international institutions and peacekeeping forces on the ground, and the opening of a process toward future integration of the Western Balkans into the EU. Toward the end of the 2000s, these changes brought increased minority participation in state institutions, including in Bulgaria, where international commitments were present as of the early 1990s but other problematic practices remained.

The International Community's Shift
Toward Redefinition of Statehood

The international community changed its positions toward the redefinition of statehood in Kosovo and Macedonia, driven by facts on the ground through the activities of what Mahoney and Thelen call "insurrectionaries" as agents of change.[8] The radical formations of KLA in Kosovo and NLA in Macedonia sought "replacement" of the old rules of majority-minority power relations, and actively mobilized against them. In the process they also altered an informal practice in which the majorities and minorities were locked—international agents' reluctance to aid the redefinition of statehood. In Kosovo, redefinition of statehood became more acceptable, especially for Western countries, since Serbia had lost global standing under the repressive Milosevic regime, and Kosovars had forged "friends in high places," unlike other rebel groups across the globe.[9] Shifting international positions opened opportunities for negotiated peace agreements to redress fundamental minority grievances against a relative decrease of minority status, as voiced from 1989 on. In this sense, during the early 2000s a second transition took place in Kosovo and Macedonia, one that concerned statehood, unlike the triple transition at the end of communism, where transformations in political regime and market economy as well as statehood were at stake.

The replacement of statehood rules existing during the 1990s—where Kosovo Albanians in Serbia had façade autonomy but de facto segregation—did not lead immediately to the independence desired by Kosovo Albanians, but did lead to fundamental amendments to the status quo. As Tansey points out, when Serbia agreed to withdraw its troops from Kosovo in 1999, there was still strong international opposition to Kosovo having the right of secession. UN Security Council Resolution 1244 (1999) mandated UNMIK to provide a transitional role before Kosovo's final status, but officially placed Kosovo back in Serbia's legislative domain. The resolution postulated that Kosovars could enjoy "substantial autonomy within the Federal Republic of Yugoslavia."[10] Nevertheless, statehood had been de facto redefined. Serbia was no longer de facto sovereign in Kosovo, but it remained so de jure, whence the prohibition on unilateral secession in 2008. Albanians became a majority and Serbs a minority within Kosovo. The UNMIK became the supreme authority, challenging Serbia's domestic sovereignty. NATO dispatched its peacekeeping troops, Kosovo Force (KFOR), to provide a secure environment, challenging Serbia's legitimate monopoly of force over the territory, although it did not successfully take municipalities inhabited by Serbs in the north and in northern Mitrovica. The new status confused domestic and international agents but effectively paved the way for Kosovo's future independence.

The replacement of existing statehood rules in Macedonia—where Albanian constitutional status was slightly decreased compared to the communist period—took place through the negotiated settlement of the August

2001 Ohrid Framework Agreement (OFA). This peace agreement raised the constitutional status of the Albanians and other minorities. High-ranking EU and U.S. diplomats were directly involved in pressuring and mediating between ethnic group leaders. The OFA "called for a neutral and liberal constitution, thereby eliminating all references to ethnic groups."[11] Nevertheless, there were harsh debates in the Macedonian parliament during the adoption of constitutional changes in November 2001. The new preamble described Macedonia as a state of "citizens of the Republic of Macedonia, the Macedonian people, as well as citizens living within its borders who are part of the Albanian people, Turkish people, the Vlach people, the Serbian people, the Roma people, the Bosniaks people and others."[12] This formulation is still considered somewhat problematic because it "puts ethnic Macedonians in a superior position vis-à-vis the rest of the population"[13] Other reforms introduced more rights for the Albanians, including increased language rights. A minority language (i.e., Albanian) became official if spoken by more than 20 percent of the population. It could be used officially in communications with the central government, and used in parliament with simultaneous interpretation into Macedonian. Laws were to be published in Macedonian and Albanian. However, Macedonian remained the official language for government sessions and foreign relations. Court and parliamentary transcripts continued to be produced only in Macedonian even after the adoption of the 2008 law on language.[14] The special status previously enjoyed by the Macedonian Orthodox Church was diminished when the Islamic Community, Roman Catholic Church, and other religious communities were explicitly mentioned alongside it. A pure Proportional Representation (PR) electoral formula for general elections was introduced in 2002, increasing the proportionality of the vote.[15]

A new voting mechanism was introduced into the parliament in 2001, the "Badinter rule," named after French constitutional lawyer Robert Badinter, who was involved in the EC Arbitration Commission on Yugoslavia that paved the way to Macedonia's independence in 1991 and also in the 2001 Ohrid negotiations. Under this principle, a double majority vote is required, including approval of parliamentary representatives of the smaller ethnic communities, to introduce constitutional changes or laws involving local administration, territorial division, use of languages, flags, and symbols, and protection of cultural identity. The principle requires concurrent Macedonian and Albanian majorities on these subjects, though not on others.[16]

International Long-Term Commitments to Conflict
Resolution and Democratic Reforms

A second major change to the inherited conflict dynamics was the long-term commitment of the international community toward conflict resolution and democratization in Kosovo and to a certain degree Macedonia, starting in 1999 and 2001 respectively. The international community had sought solutions for the conflict in Kosovo during the 1990s, but it had not provided a long-term commitment. In Macedonia there was some commitment to conflict resolution through peacekeeping forces and OSCE conflict-management programs, but not to EU integration. International agents manifested their new commitment through increased presence on the ground, through UNMIK in Kosovo, the EU in Macedonia, and other governmental and nongovernmental organizations; increased state-building efforts, starting from institution building in Kosovo and development of more institutional capacities in Macedonia; and the opening of processes for future EU integration for countries in the Western Balkans.

The long-term international presence on the ground in Kosovo is described by Laitin and Fearon as "neotrusteeship." This term denotes a "complicated mix of international and domestic governance structures" that also evolved in Afghanistan, Bosnia-Herzegovina, East Timor, Iraq, and Sierra Leone, allowing for a "remarkable degree of control over domestic political authority." Under these new forms of rule, "subjects are governed by a complex hodgepodge of foreign powers, international and nongovernmental organizations, and domestic institutions, rather than by a single . . . imperial power."[17] Besides UNMIK, 44,000 NATO forces and 4,700 international police were stationed in Kosovo.[18] The OSCE assumed functions in election monitoring and institution building that it had been unable to perform under the Milosevic regime. In addition, myriad development agencies and international NGOs entered the country, most notably from the U.S., Germany, Italy, and Scandinavian countries, as did human rights organizations, including Human Rights Watch, Amnesty International, and the International Helsinki Federation, which provided much needed oversight over human and minority rights affairs. The international community, driven by lessons from the enormous coordination problems among agencies in Bosnia-Herzegovina, ensured that civilian reconstruction and institution building were placed under the single authority of the special representative to the UN secretary general in Kosovo.[19]

Macedonia was not a neotrusteeship because it retained domestic and international sovereignty and local majority-minority coalitions continued to govern the country. Nevertheless, governance took place under the watchful eyes of international organizations, most notably the EU, which provided a long-term presence, unlike during the pre-conflict period. Hence, some consider Macedonia an EU semiprotectorate.[20] The EU started to become a major player during the 2001 warfare. Its foreign policy representative Javier Solana visited Macedonia three times during the crisis because the EU already had a stake in the country's stability. In early 2001 it signed an SAA with Macedonia.[21] The SAA alone was not a powerful tool for change. The violent crisis continued, even though by signing the SAA and a trade agreement, Macedonia became the first country in the Western Balkans to benefit from an EU preferential trade agreement and to set out on the path to EU integration.[22] Offering the double incentives of future NATO and EU membership, the crisis management team created a broad coalition and broad public support for the OFA.[23]

During the postconflict period, long-term international commitments to Macedonia shifted. The first efforts managed the effects of the armed conflict—100,000 refugees and 70,000 IDPs—and reforms in the security sector and the police,[24] matched by cooperative disarming by the rebels. The UNHCR, EU, U.S., and OSCE were active at this stage, but the OSCE role declined from the previous period.[25] NATO was important as well, with its 4,800 troops[26] and promise of future NATO membership. After 2001, U.S. attention shifted from the Balkans to the Middle East. U.S. officials believed Europe should play a more active role in postconflict reconstruction and mobilize "civilian power" to promote economic reconstruction in the region. The EU, however, also undertook security tasks: it deployed a peacekeeping mission (Concordia), and when the tensions subsided, a police (Proxima) mission to Macedonia. In March 2003 Concordia took command from NATO and deployed 320 EU soldiers and 80 civilians. NATO secretary general Lord Robertson declared that "the EU is demonstrating that its project of a European Security and Defense Policy has come of age."[27] Macedonia was the first country where troops were deployed under the EU flag.[28]

International Commitments to State Building

The international community clearly demonstrated its long-term commitment through support for the state building of Kosovo and Macedonia. Whether this support adequately developed local capacities remains questionable. Engaging with state building is an important element of peace building, since it ideally increases the sense of local ownership, decreases dependency on international donors, and enables further democratization and market reforms to succeed.[29] A comprehensive analysis of state-building efforts in Kosovo and Macedonia is beyond this book's scope, but the most important lines of international engagement are presented below.

In Kosovo, building self-government institutions started from scratch. In other words, the international agents ignored parallel institutions from the 1990s. The activities of several international organizations were centralized under the authority of the UNMIK Special Representative.[30] UNMIK had Security Council-authorized executive, legislative, and judicial authority, and was built on four pillars: police and justice (pillar 1), civil administration (pillar 2), institution building (pillar 3), and economic reconstruction (pillar 4). The UN led primarily pillars 1 and 2, and was responsible for refugee return, civilian administration, international civilian police, and judicial affairs. The OSCE was responsible also for pillar 3, including training of judges, police, and local administrators, political party and media development, and monitoring elections and human rights. The EU was vested also in pillar 4, exerting its economic reconstruction powers, including in the domains of transportation, agriculture, and revenue generation. Following international law on occupied territories UNMIK declared that the pre-1989 legal system of Serbia should be active in the territory.[31]

Between 1999 and 2008, 3.5 billion Euros were spent on Kosovo, much higher per capita aid than for Afghanistan, Bosnia-Herzegovina, East Timor, or Macedonia.[32] Learning lessons from failures in Bosnia-Herzegovina, where the first postconflict elections reinforced nationalist power, the international community inaugurated the first elections in Kosovo almost a year and a half after the hostilities ended. It held them first on the municipal (2000) and then on the national (2001) level, aspiring to build politicians' democratic legitimacy from the bottom up.[33] In line with power-sharing arrangements offering benefits for interethnic peace, the international community built a proportional representation electoral system and minority quotas that allowed for high participation of Serbian and other minorities, regardless of their electoral and other institutional boycotts.[34] It demobilized combatants and then fostered the processes of vetting former KLA soldiers and new applicants under the newly established security institutions, the Kosovo Protection Corps and Kosovo Police Service. It helped build a party system especially within the Albanian majority, parliament, and central and local governments, and assisted in the democratic rotation of parties in power, including by closely monitoring elections.[35] It assisted in building a judiciary, but retained authority in this realm well into 2008. UNMIK was more successful in building viable bureaucracies where it promoted meritocratic recruitment early on—as in police and customs—than in the central administration and judiciary, which it could not isolate from corrupt political influences.[36]

These achievements were accomplished through an intrusive state-building process, brokered with little input from the local elites. As Jens Narten argues, it was only in February 2000 that UNMIK built the Joint Interim Administration Structure, establishing joint consultative bodies. Intrusive control was pervasive and included handpicking members of the Kosovo Transitional Council in July 1999 and issuing the 2001 constitutional framework as a mere regulation, which alienated many local stakeholders.[37] UNMIK had unrealistic expectations with the disputed 2003 policy of "standards before status," where Kosovo governance structures were expected to achieve a level of democratic credentials not reached at the time by Eastern European countries with longer transitions.[38] The policy created pervasive frustration among the Kosovars, who considered it a tool to delay the opening of final status negotiations.

In March 2004 Albanian riots targeted Serbs, UNMIK, and NATO and shook the international community.[39] The riots were initially presented as uncoordinated, spontaneous action, but later turned out to have been planned.[40] It prompted the Kosovo negotiation process to resume in 2005 under UN auspices, with special envoy Martti Ahtisaari authorized to develop a plan for international settlement. Since Kosovars had been highly repressed by Serbia and new institutions had been built, it was extremely unlikely they would settle for any option other than independence.[41] In 2007 Ahtisaari declared that the potential for negotiations was exhausted.[42] He proceeded with a plan for a new international presence in Kosovo, moving toward "supervised independence." This plan did not explicitly touch on the status issue, but implicitly "provided Kosovo with everything it would need for statehood."[43] The Security Council never recognized Kosovo's prospective independence because of resistance from Russia and China, but Kosovars unilaterally declared independence in February 2008. Backed by the U.S. and major European countries, within the first month Kosovo was recognized by 28 states.[44] A Kosovo constitution, drafted under UNMIK auspices, entered into force in June 2008.[45]

The state transformation process of Macedonia was aimed at reforming and strengthening existing institutions. The implementation of the OFA agreement from constitutional amendments to domestic legislation was the centerpiece of these reforms. Further efforts addressed decentralizing power to the municipal level, strengthening the autonomy and capacity of the judiciary, and fighting crime and corruption.[46] The major reforms addressed underlying problems with the functioning of state institutions: the limited Albanian presence in state administration, most notably in the police and military; the lack of independence of the bureaucracies, which acted as extensions of the political parties; and little public confidence in the judiciary, with a long case backlog and pervasive widespread corruption. The OSCE played a key role in police reform and personnel retraining.[47] A 2008 RAND corporation report argued that the EU integrated the state building efforts of other international agents—such as NATO, OSCE, the World Bank, and the U.S.—into an effective effort by deploying a variety of techniques, most notably through the incentive of possible future EU integration.[48]

Commitments to Future EU Integration

The offer of prospective access to the EU occurred at different points in time in the three cases, partly because of their differing levels of political and economic development. In addition to bilateral processes launched with Bulgaria (early 1990s), Macedonia (1999–2001), and Kosovo (after 2008), future integration was envisaged through more regional cooperation. Earlier regional schemes, such as the Royaumont Process (1996) and the Regional Approach (1997), had exhausted their potential to encourage local elites to cooperate for stability, democratization, and market-oriented reforms. The 1999 Stability Pact for Southeastern Europe was established after the Kosovo crisis, under the OSCE auspices, to focus on postconflict reconstruction.[49] The 2003 Thessalonki Declaration provided a comprehensive EU commitment to the Western Balkans, where EU countries pledged that "the future of the Balkans is within the European Union," and that "fragmentation and divisions along ethnic lines are incompatible with the European perspective." Acceleration of the accession processes took place in Bulgaria and Romania during the early 2000s. As Anastakis and Bechev noted, the EU became the "only game in town" for these countries.[50]

Chapter 4 discussed the major EU mechanisms that worked as predicted by the enlargement literature in the Bulgarian case as of the early 1990s. Unlike the pervasive "control" mechanisms used by the UNMIK in Kosovo, "conditionality" and "socialization" in Bulgaria and Macedonia in the

2000s were more consensual but also facilitated incremental change toward more peaceful majority-minority relations. The mechanism of "layering," adoption of rules on top of and beside existing ones, adds to this discussion on long-term change. As Mahoney and Thelen argue, when "layering" occurs, "powerful veto players can protect the old institutions," but they "cannot necessarily prevent the addition of new elements."[51] The powerful veto players here were the nationalist elites that dominated domestic politics. They accepted EU conditions on legislation and to some degree on democratization, but played the nationalist game of rhetorical support while advancing particularistic and nationalist interests. Layering adds value to this discussion by putting "conditionality" and "socialization" alongside old rules and new formal and informal practices. Even if "conditionality" does not always reach its aims for legislative change, or "socialization" for normative change, "layering" new EU rules and practices on top of existing ones aids the internalization of a sense that the EU is the "only game in the town" and creates *new attachments to practices* facilitating non-violent interactions of majorities and minorities. With "layering," "institutional change grows out of the attachment to new institutions or rules onto or alongside existing ones."[52] For example, given Europe's general mistrust of the Albanians but trust for the U.S., which became less interested in the Balkans compared to other conflict regions, "layering" EU rules is important for incremental change.

Bulgaria was the most advanced on the EU integration path, and became a full-fledged member in 2007, together with Romania. Between 2001 and 2007 the EU continued to pressure Bulgarian local governments to pass laws against discrimination, implement the FCPNM (adopted in 1997, ratified in 1999), strengthen the capacity of the National Council on Ethnic and Demographic Issues (NCEDI), and implement a Framework Program on Roma participation in public life. With its regular monitoring reports from 2000 to 2005, the EC reminded Bulgaria that it needed to harmonize its domestic legislation with the EU *acquis communautaire*.[53]

Initially, the Saxcoburggotsky government (2001–2005) gained a good international reputation by including the ethnic MRF in the cabinet, its first opportunity to be in government in Bulgaria's postcommunist history.[54] In 2003 an action plan to implement the FCPNM was adopted, the antidiscrimination law and a law on the ombudsperson were passed, and the NCEDI developed a leaflet to better socialize the public regarding the much feared term "minority." Since these reforms were minimal and adopted only four years after the convention's ratification, a 2004 EU Advisory Opinion concluded that FCPNM implementation remained "problematic" regarding minority languages in public administration and criminal proceedings, topographical indications, and teaching in the compulsory curriculum. In its regular reports the EU also recommended that the NCEDI have more capacity. The government turned the NCEDI administration into a Directorate on Ethnic and Demographic Issues and developed a National Council on Cooperation in the interethnic sphere in 2003, but allowed them only advisory, not executive functions.[55] Since the MRF was again in government between 2005 and 2009, in the coalition of the BSP and Saxcoburggotsky's NDSV, there was a substantial increase of ethnic Turks as ministers and local administrators in the ethnically mixed areas, especially in the towns of Kardzhali and Razgrad. A year before Bulgaria's accession as a member, the EU concluded there had been overall progress, though incomplete, toward protection and integration of minorities.[56]

In Macedonia, OFA implementation became a core component of "conditionality." "Conditionality" was especially successful between 2002 and 2005, when the EU approved Macedonia's application for membership status. This period coincided with the rule (2002–2006) of the coalition government of the SDSM and the DUI, a party that emerged out of the disbanded NLA. This coalition eventually delivered a major legislative package of OFA reforms. According to one DUI politician, the coalition was well suited to introduce reforms. The SDSM preserved the trust of the Macedonians because it was not the party that signed the OFA Agreement. DUI had already demonstrated its strength through warfare and could approach the negotiation table with confidence.[57]

EU "conditionality" worked successfully on several major occasions. One was the pressure to extradite Ljube Bozhkoski, the Macedonian interior minister who had overstepped his powers during the 2001 armed conflict and was indicted in 2005 by the International Criminal Tribunal on Former Yugoslavia (ICTY) for crimes against humanity. Although he was acquitted in 2008, at the time of his extradition he received little defense from the SDSM. The external pressure on the Macedonian government was much less than that exerted on Serbian governments when Radovan Karadzic, Ratko Mladic, and Slobodan Milosevic were indicted. Although the reasons for this SDSM behavior are not entirely clear, one could argue that EU involvement created an incentive for the government to abide by international legal standards.[58]

The EU and other international agents exerted critical pressure for implementation of decentralization reforms in Macedonia. Decentralization laws were approved by parliament in August 2004. They decreased the number of municipalities from 123 to 84 and vested them with authority over culture, primary and secondary education, health care, urban planning, and local policing.[59] As mentioned earlier, these reforms were highly controversial; thus, bold external pressure was necessary because the reforms were considered disproportionally beneficial to the Albanians. Together with diaspora groups, primarily in Australia, the nationalist opposition VMRO-DPMNE organized a referendum to challenge these changes and obstruct the OFA. The referendum asked voters whether they supported a proposal to retain the municipal boundaries before OFA.[60] The EU launched a massive public campaign against popular participation in this referendum, linking nonparticipation with commitment to EU integration. The U.S. provided a highly tangible benefit by recognizing the country with its constitutionally proclaimed name. The referendum went ahead, but gathered only 27 percent turnout, well below the 50 percent threshold.[61] Thus, with joint international effort, the referendum failed and the ruling SDSM-DUI coalition was further enabled to enact laws translating OFA clauses into domestic legislation.

EU "conditionality" worked to a certain degree to reform the judicial, legislative, and educational systems. As a senior ombudsperson observed, a 2003 law gave more competences to the ombudsperson to monitor minority rights. While the OSCE gave this office the most direct external support, the ombudsperson worked within the EU framework for integration.[62] Najceska argues that the EU also supported launching a new police academy in 2003 in coordination with the OSCE, Council of Europe, Europol, and a new Academy for Training of Judges and Prosecutors in 2006. The EU exerted extensive pressure to stop further politicization of religion in 2008, when students were initially allowed to take religious education in primary and secondary schools. Najceska considers this process "the most retrograde," since it allowed religious denominations to actively interfere in secular state affairs and to perpetuate divisions among the communities.[63] In April 2009 the Constitutional Court annulled these provisions.[64] The EU also exerted substantial pressure to adopt the controversial antidiscrimination law in 2010.[65] Finally, international pressures for higher education rights for Albanians in their mother tongue resulted in the 2001 opening of the new South East European University in Tetovo, a long-term project of OSCE's high commissioner on the national minorities Max van der Stoel, and 2004 official recognition of the controversial Tetovo University as a state university.

However, many of these changes were not enforced in practice, suggesting that old rules remained operational. Despite extensive international pressure, participation of minorities in public administration only slightly increased. In 2002, there were 58,348 Macedonian and 8,164 Albanian public employees; in 2006 they numbered 55,086 and 12,397.[66] In 2010, Albanians remained proportionally under-represented in the public administration, especially in the police and military. Excessive use of police force against Albanians and other minorities was common.

Kosovo is the least advanced of the three cases toward EU integration. As mentioned, the EU took an important role in economic reconstruction during the pre-2008-independence period. Unlike other Balkan countries, Kosovo adopted the Euro as the official currency after 2002, replacing the Yugoslav dinar. The EU role dramatically increased only after 2008. Despite the fact that several EU members, including Cyprus, Greece, Romania, Slovakia, and Spain, refused to recognize Kosovo, in July 2008 authorities in Brussels pledged 1.2 billion Euros in aid, of which 358 million was slated for pre-accession funds.[67] The EULEX—directing 3,200 police and judicial civilian personnel—became the largest EU security and defense policy mission to date. It was initially intended to replace the UNMIK, but resistance in the Serbian-dominated areas led to a legal "reconfiguration" under Security Council authority.[68] The EU was reluctant to confront Serbia over Kosovo.

Kosovo's prospects for EU integration remain highly interconnected with Serbia's. Beyond EULEX on the ground, Brussels launched high-level diplomacy shuttles to develop dialogue between the Kosovars and Serbian authorities after 2008, and to facilitate Serbia's recognition of Kosovo, considered crucial for Serbia's EU integration. No breakthrough has been achieved, but a landmark International Court of Justice opinion in July 2010 claimed that Kosovo's declaration of independence "did not violate general international law, Security Council Resolution 1244 (1999) or the Constitutional Framework imposed by the UNMIK."[69] In the aftermath of this decision, pro-democracy Serbian President Tadić was considered "around to the acceptance of consensual separation and mutual recognition."[70] In July 2011 an agreement was reached between the two countries in civil registry, freedom of movement, and acceptance of university and school diplomas.[71]

Although political currents have been slightly changing in Serbia, it has not recognized Kosovo and is far from doing so. Even after Western powers made a landmark decision to end their supervision of Kosovo in September 2012, Serbia dismissed these sovereignty announcements.[72]

"Socialization" was a less powerful mechanism than "conditionality" for change. In contrast to the 1990s, during the 2000s international agents were much closer to the domestic elites due to their increased presence on the ground, numerous workshops, training sessions, and gatherings spreading ideas about liberal democracy and minority rights. Ordinary citizens filed more cases with the European Court of Human Rights against human rights abuses in Bulgaria and Macedonia, demonstrating an increasing belief that justice could prevail through European institutions. Nevertheless, "socialization" was layered over old behavior schemes. Since both the international community and local elites have "locked in" practices often using minority rights discursively rather than substantially, the normative expectations of international agents meant substantially little to the domestic elites. Since domestic elites saw little normative legitimacy in EU policies toward the Western Balkans, they asserted domestic reasons for fake or noncompliance with EU conditions.[73]

Conclusions

During the 2000s, numerous changes took place in the countries of this research related to statehood, long-term international commitments to conflict resolution, democratization, state building, and prospects for EU integration. But the observable implications of violence on the ground spoke of a different phenomenon: patterns of violence continue in spite of many international efforts. Hence, real change of conflict dynamics requires attention, not merely the change of formal institutions on which scholarship usually concentrates. It would be an oversimplification to claim that real change can be easily measured.[74] Nor do I offer a general matrix through which to do so. However, the mechanisms of "replacement" and "layering," used by historical institutionalism, offer leverage on how to think about change of conflict dynamics, when both formal and informal rules need to be addressed.

Replacement—removal of existing rules and introduction of new ones—facilitated more peaceful majority-minority interactions through replacement of both formal and informal rules. An informal aspect of the conflict dynamic in which majorities, minorities, and international community were locked—the international community's staunch opposition to restructuring statehood—started to change under the pressure of insurgents: the KLA in Kosovo and NLA in Macedonia. It was necessary to change this informal relationship first in order to change the formal rules later. New formal rules then became embedded in peace agreements, and followed through constitutional and legalistic reforms that gave the Albanians of Koṣovo and Macedonia increased status and institutional channels to voice their interests. Informal rules facilitated replacement of formal ones also regarding Kosovo's proclamation of independence in 2008. The presence of UNMIK on the ground, the building of Kosovo institutions, as well as the informal knowledge that Kosovo Albanians were extremely unlikely to settle for anything short of independence were driving the formalization of the status quo.

"Replacement" also operated vis-à-vis another aspect of the informally institutionalized relationship in which international agents, majorities, and minorities were locked—the minimal international commitment to conflict resolution and close monitoring of domestic reforms, especially in Kosovo and somewhat in Macedonia. The new rules created a UN protectorate in Kosovo and an EU semi-protectorate in Macedonia. UNMIK received much criticism because of its decisive rule by decree and the EU because of its lack of decisiveness, but their presence throughout the 2000s delivered a clear message to the majorities and minorities: their actions are closely monitored and escalation of violence will not be tolerated.

The "layering" of new rules on top of and beside existing ones worked also as a mechanism of incremental change, primarily in Bulgaria and Macedonia, and will become more relevant for Kosovo in the future. So far my study has confirmed general findings of the existing literature that "conditionality" has been more successful than "socialization" in instigating change. Major achievements in the direction of interethnic peace have led to an increased number of minority persons in government and public administration, and the opening of interethnic institutions and venues for mother tongue education. "Layering" as a mechanism adds value to this discussion, since it views both "conditionality" and "socialization" as mechanisms enforcing new rules—"conditionality" by tackling legislative and "socialization" by tackling normative change. Aside from legislative and normative rules, "layering" includes new formal and informal practices taking place next to existing rules reinforced by nationalists rejecting genuine reforms.

The 2004 referendum in Macedonia demonstrates well how practical attachments to new rules can develop out of the old order. The referendum challenged the implementation of an OFA package aimed at decentralization of Macedonia and increase of Albanian self-government rights. The referendum was strongly opposed by the international community. By practicing minimal voting, the Macedonian population deliberately ignored a democratic procedure that can still reinforce nationalism. The population did not have to make this choice. It was not subject to "conditionality" per se, but the elites were, and it did not have full-fledged liberal values, a result of "socialization." The pressure exerted during the antireferendum campaign, and the informal understanding that Europe is the "only game in town," became important for this practical choice.

Chapter 7

Continuity in Conflict Dynamics

The major changes in the informally institutionalized conflict dynamics during the 2000s have now been outlined. Under pressure from insurgents and delegitimized majority policies, altering statehood became more acceptable to the international agents toward the end of the 1990s. This new attitude was conducive to the "replacement" of old rules of engagement between majorities, minorities, and international agents and the development of new ones. The 2001 Ohrid Framework Agreement and the subsequent constitutional changes in Macedonia elevated the status of the Albanians, and further institutional reforms took place, including decentralization in local government. Although Kosovo remained officially under the international legal jurisdiction of Serbia, a new status quo emerged. The international agents also drastically changed their attitude toward long-term commitment to conflict resolution on the ground. The UNMIK governed in Kosovo, and local institutions were developed. The EU closely monitored the implementation of the Ohrid Agreement in Macedonia. Increased prospects for EU integration also contributed to change by "layering" new EU rules on top of the existing ones, and by giving opportunities to local actors to develop practical attachments to them. These changes were large scale, but they did not overturn the informally institutionalized conflict dynamics in their entirety. As shown in Figure 11 in Chapter 6, specific outcomes continued: "nonviolent" and "threatened" in Bulgaria, "threatened" and "episodic" in Macedonia, and "extensive" and "episodic" in Kosovo.

The aim here is to analyze how residual aspects of the established conflict dynamics continued to operate and contribute to conflict perpetuation during the 2000s. Several questions are considered. How does existing scholarship explain the perpetuation of existing conflicts? How do majorities, minorities, the international community, kin-states, and diasporas alter or perpetuate established conflict dynamics? What mechanisms lead to conflict perpetuation?

I argue that three critical factors continued to incentivize violence.

- Large-scale corruption anchored in minority co-optation and coercion mechanisms of the previous period sustained stability between majorities, minorities, and often the international community. The "normalization of corruption" became a focal point for attacks by agents external to the corrupt political order or who had benefited little from it. They adopted strong anti-corruption claims and attacked minorities and other agents in the process, contributing to low levels of violence.
- Lessons were "learned" from the international community that democratization could be neglected in favor of security and stability concerns.[1]
- Clandestine and often disputed influences remained from kin-states and diasporas, and were sustained by the continuation of adaptation mechanisms.

The causal mechanisms of conflict perpetuation identified here are "drift" in combination with a "reactive sequence," "learning," and "adaptive expectations."

This chapter briefly surveys two clusters of scholarship that seek to explain why ethnonationalist conflicts persist even after strong international commitments to conflict resolution and democratization. I show how the path-dependence perspective adds to this discussion, engage the above-mentioned residual aspects of conflict dynamics, and relate my findings to the literature on conflict perpetuation.

Alternative Explanations to the Durability of Conflicts

Two streams of thought on peace building and power sharing are relevant here to explain why conflicts endure. Scholarship on peace building considers that the immediate aftermath of civil wars creates obstacles to long-term conflict resolution and democratization. "Spoilers" can undermine peace processes by using violence if peace agreements leave them out of the bargaining process. Even if they are included, spoilers can still fail to implement the agreements and slide the polity back into civil war.[2] Failure to provide adequate external security guarantees to disarm and demobilize soldiers can also be a problem.[3] Walter considers 500 or more troops an adequate security guarantee, but in some cases larger numbers of troops have failed to be effective.[4] Trying to implement liberal economic and democratic reforms in a short time span can undermine existing institutions and create competition among elites that ends in violence.[5] The need to start a process of political development quickly can turn rushed founding elections into "a contest between former warring armies masquerading as political parties."[6] Further barriers to implementation of peace agreements include lack of coordination between mediators and implementers and, among the implementing agencies, incomplete fulfillment of mandated tasks, short time horizons, and a limited commitment of implementers.[7]

This scholarship is highly relevant to Kosovo and Macedonia, but some theoretical insights might be rejected. There were no major problems with commitments or security guarantees, since the international community quickly dispatched peacekeeping troops—KFOR in Kosovo and NATO troops and EU's Concordia mission in Macedonia. Demobilization went relatively smoothly, transforming rebel formations into political parties. In Kosovo two major parties emerged out of the radical KLA: Hashim Thaci's Democratic Party of Kosovo (PDK), and Ramush Haradinaj's Alliance for the Future of Kosovo (AAK). In Macedonia, the NLA was transformed into the DUI. Former paramilitaries were redirected toward forming police units, and the Kosovo Protection Corps (KPC) was considered by some a proto-army. Elections did not take place immediately after the warfare, but after interim governments were formed. In Kosovo, more controlled political liberalization was promoted compared to earlier peacekeeping operations.[8] Political and economic liberalization had started in Macedonia in the 1990s.

The peace building literature offers only partial explanations regarding other issues. Collecting small arms during the demobilization process was challenging, and large numbers of weapons remained spread among the population of Kosovo (less so in Macedonia). Some wartime veterans in Kosovo stayed outside the new security structures. Despite strong UNMIK control in Kosovo and incentives for EU integration in Macedonia, coordination problems among local actors and implementing agencies remained. But while the availability of small arms, discontented veterans, and coordination problems provide opportunity structures for local agents to mobilize, it is not clear why and how they would do so. In my account, local agents continue to be bound by the rationality of unreformed aspects of the informally institutionalized conflict dynamics that still incentivize violence.

Works on peace building offer only partial explanations for the continuity of violence for another reason: they want to explain the keeping of "peace," usually measured as the lack of return to war. Lower levels of violence are not considered per se but subsumed under lack of "democratization," the other major variable usually studied. Höchlund is among the few to examine violence in peace-to-war transitions, demonstrating that elections and security sector and media reforms can spark more violence because of enduring legacies and uncertainties in the transition process.[9] Path-dependence takes the "legacies" argument farther by showing how some aspects of informally institutionalized conflict dynamics facilitate conflict perpetuation.

A stream of thought on power sharing is also relevant here, since such arrangements were introduced in Macedonia and Kosovo in the early 2000s.[10] Critics argue that power sharing can create obstacles to peaceful transformations: such arrangements can be good for peace building, but not for consolidating democracies.[11] Rothchild and Roeder claim that problems emerge from "the gap between promises needed to initiate the transition and the performance necessary to consolidate peace and democracy." In the aftermath of civil war, it may be appropriate for the majority to make a commitment to treat the minority fairly, but once leaders turn to consolidating governance, the same institutions can create incentives for conflict escalation. For example, autonomous arrangements brokered earlier could establish the fundamentals for the development of a "state within a state," and extensive veto powers could cause parliamentary deadlocks and other governance failures.[12] In addition, wartime cleavages can become entrenched in the power sharing institutions and electoral politics, creating incentives for the political parties to garner support from their own constituencies and for ordinary citizens to develop little confidence in the new institutions[13] Power sharing agreements could also be a product of "coerced compromise" by international agents, where local ownership is weak in the initial stage and requires significant coercion by the international community in the implementation stage.[14]

Some of these arguments do not find empirical backing in my study. The winners in the first postwar elections were primarily peaceful political alternatives rather than successors of the radical wartime movements. In Kosovo, the LDK, which won the first election, advanced a nonviolent strategy during the 1990s. In Macedonia, the postsocialist SDSM won the elections drawing on the Macedonian Slav constituency. The only exception was the Albanian DUI, a successor of the radical NLA.[15] A "state-within-the-state" argument may work to a certain degree about Kosovo, where fears of secessionism are still grounded for the exclusively Serbian-governed northern areas, but less so for Macedonia, where the Albanians have become bigger proponents of European integration than the Macedonians.

I acknowledge the theoretical validity of other critical arguments about power sharing. Most notably, there has been a fundamental problem of ownership for power-sharing arrangements from the beginning. Macedonian president Boris Trajkovski claimed that the OFA was signed in Macedonia and not at an international peace conference,[16] thus claiming local ownership, but Prime Minister Georgievski of the Macedonian nationalist VMRO-DPMNE argued that "OFA definitely marked the end of Macedonia we remember."[17] Power sharing was also imposed by UN provisions on Kosovo elites without prior consensus by the earlier warring parties.[18] The international agents increased their commitment from the previous period, but also introduced nonconsensual policies to instigate power sharing, rendering the newly established institutions vulnerable to mobilizations from the discontented. Parliamentary deadlocks in Macedonia and Serb boycotts of Kosovo's elections and post-1999 institutions also do not constitute positive effects of power sharing.

Path-dependence finds these explanations complementary. Local agents, who do not accept the new "rules of the game," remain embedded in the existing conflict dynamics. For example, the Serbian minority in postwar Kosovo adopted parallel institutions as a response to their political situation, echoing the response of Kosovo Albanians to their segregation during the 1990s. During the 2000s the Kosovo Serbian minority has been subject to problematic treatment by the new Albanian majority, but not to institutionalized segregation, and could have participated in the new institutions operating under UNMIK. Instead, they mirrored Kosovar behavior of the previous dynamic, and opted for parallel institutions and closer connections with Serbia.

This book contributes to an emerging discussion about the need to rebuild both formal institutions and informal rules during postconflict reconstruction.[19] Some consociationalists argue that informal power sharing norms of inclusiveness need to be introduced *after* the change of formal institutions and beyond the elite level—to penetrate various stakeholders in society, so that power sharing can succeed.[20] Others point to the need for favorable informal rules to be in place *before* formal institutions change during postconflict reconstruction,[21] and that informal rules can limit what peacekeepers can achieve.[22] I take the discussion farther by pointing to the existence of deeply ingrained behaviors of majorities, minorities, and international agents—jointly embedded in the informally institutionalized conflict dynamics—that continue to enable and constrain their behaviors.

Persistence of Conflict Dynamics

The remainder of this chapter focuses on aspects of informally institutionalized conflict dynamics adopted earlier, unaltered by reforms. These residual aspects are embedded in the effects of corruption, anchored in minority cooptation and coercion mechanisms of the early transition period, and are linked to: stability concerns; the lessons that the international community prioritizes security over democratization; the credibility of the international community; and persisting clandestine influences from kin-states and diasporas, which helped perpetuate low to middle levels of violence. The mechanisms of perpetuation identified here are "drift" in combination with a "reactive sequence" on the side of the majorities, and "learning" and "adaptive expectations" continuing since the 1990s. Since the text further discusses numerous domestic agents, Table 4 presents for reference the executive leaderships in Bulgaria, Macedonia, and Kosovo during the 2000s.

Effects of Corruption on Perpetuating Interethnic Violence

Corruption is a major concern of the international community. In 2010 Transparency International ranked Macedonia as 62nd with Croatia and Ghana; Bulgaria as 73rd with El Salvador and Panama; and Kosovo as 110th with Benin, Gabon, and Indonesia.[23] Corruption in the Balkans has been plausibly attributed to a variety of legacies, including antagonism against the state inherited from resistance to Ottoman domination, pervasive corrupt social relationships during the late communist period, and the effects of the international economic embargo on Yugoslavia during the wars of its disintegration. Corruption has been treated as a problem of weak states,

Table 4. Executive Leadership, 2000–2011

Bulgaria

Presidents

1997–2002   *Petar Stoyanov*, Union of Democratic Forces (UDF)

2002–present   *Georgi Parvanov*, Bulgarian Socialist Party (BSP)

Governments

2001–2005   *Simeon Saxcoburggotsky*, National Movement for Stability
                 and Progress (NDSV) in coalition with the ethnic Turkish
                 Movement for Rights and Freedoms (MRF)

2005–2009   *Sergey Stanishev*, Bulgarian Socialist Party in coalition with NDSV
                 and MRF

2009–present   *Boyko Borisov*, Citizens for European Development of Bulgaria
                 (GERB)

Macedonia

Presidents

1999–2004   *Boris Trajkovski*, VMRO-DPMNE

2004   *Lyubcho Jordanovski*, SDSM, acting

2004–2009   *Branko Crvenkovski*, SDSM

2009–present   *Gjorge Ivanov*, VMRO-DPMNE

Governments

1998–2002   *Lyubcho Georgievski*, VMRO-DPMNE in coalition with DPA

2002–2004   *Branko Crvenkovski*, SDSM in coalition with the Liberal
                 Democratic Party (LDP) and the Albanian Democratic Union
                 for Integration (DUI)

2004   *Hari Kostov*, nonpartisan; *Radmila Sekerinska*, SDSM, acting

2004–2006   *Vlado Buckovski*, SDSM in coalition with LDP and DUI

2006–2008   Nikola Gruevski, VMRO-DPMNE in coalition with
                 the Democratic Party of the Albanians (DPA)

2008–present   Nikola Gruevski, VMRO-DPMNE in coalition with DUI

Kosovo (UNMIK-administered until 2008, supervised independence after 2008)

Presidents

2002–2006   *Ibrahim Rugova*, Democratic Movement for Kosovo (LDK)

2006–2010   *Fatmir Sejdiu*, LDK

2010–2011   *Jakup Krasniqi*, Democratic Party of Kosovo (DPK) and Behdjet
                 Pacolli, New Kosovo Alliance, acting

2011–present   *Atifete Jahjaga*, nonpartisan

Table 4. (Continued)

Governments	
2002–2004	*Bajram Rexhepi*, DPK
2004–2005	*Ramush Haradinaj*, Alliance for the Future of Kosovo (AFK)
2005	*Adem Salihaj*, DPK, acting
2005–2006	*Bajram Kosumi*, AFK
2006–2008	*Agim Ceku*, AFK
2008–present	*Hashim Thaci*, DPK

but rarely as an effect of minority coercion and minority co-optation strategies.

Here I argue that pervasive corruption, especially when it incorporates minorities, generates movements among agents who are external to the corrupt political order or have benefited little from it, who then scapegoat minorities and other actors or use violence to thwart minority practices. These agents often assert that stability is maintained by a corrupt political order. This mechanism operates through a combination of "drift" and "reactive sequence."[24] Drift occurs when a gap develops between the established rules and their enforcement. In my account this gap does not contribute to gradual change, as Mahoney and Thelen would argue, but affects the consolidation of political practices in the stasis of "normalization of corruption." A reactive sequence then occurs to reject this normalization of corruption. Unlike the mechanism of "adaptive expectations," which contributes to conflict perpetuation through positive feedback and adaptation of agents to established conflict practices, a reactive sequence does so through rejection of the status quo. Different *pathways* can be demonstrated through which corruption, rooted in majority strategies to deal with minorities during the critical juncture at the end of communism, became an important factor for ongoing low levels of ethnonational violence during the 2000s.

In Bulgaria, the slight increase in minority status combined with co-optation of the MRF leadership in the early 1990s led to the "Bulgarian ethnic peace model," but also to strong antiminority sentiments and low levels of violence in 2005–2006 that continue with occasional flare-ups until the present. The causal pathway started with the Bulgarian constitution's prohibition of ethnic parties, combined with informal arrangements to render the ethnic Turkish MRF the sole legitimate player in ethnic politics. MRF leader Dogan had not been a classic dissident, and was instead tightly connected with the former communist security services that became powerful agents in the redistribution of economic power during the transition period. His role as peaceful political "broker" in the Bulgarian parliament in the 1990s was complemented by participation in economic relationships driven by some of these residual security structures, largely associated with the socialist party. The 1992–1994 technocrat government, which depended on MRF's parliamentary support, was termed "the government of Multigroup," a conglomerate implicated in shady deals and rooted in three former directorates of the communist-era state security services.[25] When the democratic UDF government fought these influences after 1997, the parliament banned several "parliamentary experts" from entering, among them a Multi-group leader and an MRF advisor.[26] By 2001 Dogan did not even hide his strong connections to Multi-group, participating in jointly funded activities.[27]

During the 2000s MRF's participation in two government coalitions (NDSV in 2001–2005 and BSP and NDSV in 2005–2009) allowed its political power to expand. Apart from placing representatives as ministers and in the office of the president, the MRF linked its political influence with businesses related to local administrations, especially in south- and northeastern Bulgaria.[28] Allegations exist that MRF also abused EU funds in MRF-controlled ministries. MRF's financial irresponsibility became widely discussed in the media; Dogan himself made it visible with a statement during the run-up to the 2005 general elections, openly claiming that the MRF was sponsored by a "circle of firms," which was "normal" for each party.[29] President Parvanov and other leaders criticized this statement.

Corruption, coupled with anti-Turkish and anti-Muslim rhetoric, became a centerpiece for popular mobilization against the MRF by Ataka, the nationalist right-wing party at the forefront of the nationalist effort.[30] However, long before the party's "sudden" emergence in the 2005 parliamentary elections, where it received 8.1 percent of the vote, Bulgarian sociologists had warned that there was a strong potential for the development of a nationalist party in the country.[31] Different ad hoc nationalist groups, among them skinheads, competed over who would become Bulgaria's far-right nationalist leader in 2002.[32] Their existence was troublesome, although Ataka outperformed them. Contrary to predictions that the 2005 results would be Ataka's best achievement, in the 2006 presidential elections its leader Volen Siderov received 21.5 percent in the first and 24 percent in the second round of voting. The party performed even better in the general elections of 2009 with 9.4 percent of the vote.[33]

Ataka is not an isolated phenomenon. The radical right contributed to nationalist tensions in Eastern European societies in the mid- to late 2000s, especially in the period around EU membership accession in Bulgaria, the Czech Republic, Hungary, Poland, Romania, and Slovakia. Radical right parties may be charismatic and target minorities and immigrants as "enemies within the state and outside the nation," as Mudde put it.[34] In contrast to the early 1990s, when democratization was at stake in Eastern Europe, by the mid-2000s there was a "death of the liberal consensus," in Krastev's words.[35] The reasons the radical right emerged so suddenly in Eastern Europe include the economic stratification of earlier egalitarian communist societies, which left too many people impoverished during the transition,[36] the exhausted potential of socialist quasi-welfare states to avoid painful restructuring,[37] EU pressures to meet economic convergence[38] and minority rights criteria,[39] demonstration effects from Western Europe and socialization of radical parties within the European Parliament,[40] and widespread corruption, especially in Bulgaria and Romania, that created fertile ground for rallying against the established parties.[41]

While rapid economic stratification and pressures for EU integration are plausible explanations for the renewed nationalist mobilization in Bulgaria, in terms of *timing* these movements emerged shortly after MRF entered government for the first time. Anti-Turkish and anti-Muslim attitudes in Bulgarian society may have been suppressed during the 1990s because of guilt feelings related to the 1980s coercive assimilation campaign and EU integration pressures, but resurfaced in the 2000s with MRF as the target. Nationalist attitudes were carried to a lesser degree by other mainstream parties during the 2000s. Current prime minister Boyko Borisov, of the populist Citizens for the European Development of Bulgaria (GERB) party, who depended until July 2011 on Ataka's parliamentary support for his government, agreed easily to a 2009 proposition of Ataka's Siderov to hold a popular referendum on whether Turkish language broadcasts should continue in the Bulgarian media.[42] This policy had been introduced as an effect of EU conditionality to increase minority representation in the state media. Only a quick outcry from other Bulgarian parties and the European Parliament convinced Borisov to withdraw his support for the referendum.[43]

In a final step on the pathway, the increasing Bulgarian nationalist attacks created a backlash from ethnic Turkish nationalists, who were dissat-
isfied with the MRF's monopoly on minority politics and its lack of concern
for regular members of the Turkish minority, who became further impoverished during the 2000s. The Turkish Democratic Party—banned in the early
1990s—resurfaced briefly in 2000 and again in 2006.[44] Most notably, Millet-
Trakia, a formation under the leadership of Menderes Küngün, emerged in
2006. It launched a petition to adopt Turkish as a second state language and
to have a Turkish-language university education system.[45] It unsuccessfully
attempted to form a party. While BSP prime minister Sergey Stanishev
argued that Ataka and Millet-Trakia mutually reinforced each other.[46] Societal tensions did not disappear even after the demise of Millet-Trakia. In
May and June 2011, Ataka launched demonstrations to eradicate the loudspeakers of the central Sofia mosques; worshipers have been attacked there
and severely beaten.[47] Thus in Bulgaria a co-opted ethnic minority party in
the early 1990s, which became corrupt along with majority parties, facilitated a majority backlash against the minority in the 2000s, not least because reform movements within the minority were blocked.

The pathway through which corruption in Macedonia contributed to
the continuation of conflicts in the 2000s was different. Corruption was
rooted in the decrease of minority status in combination with the co-
optation strategies of the early 1990s, when inter-ethnic coalitions were
induced to cooperate by using the state to divide spoils and clandestine
interactions further drove inter-ethnic polarization. These tendencies
peaked during the 2001 internal warfare, when ideas to divide Macedonia
along ethnic lines existed among the ruling Macedonian and Albanian
elites.[48] These tendencies subsided after 2001, but some continued to exac-
erbate inter-ethnic polarization.[49]

The selective enforcement of official rules had developed the "normalization of corruption" and its wide acceptance by both majorities and minorities. While convenient, a corrupt political order had nevertheless also
facilitated clandestine activities linking Albanians of Macedonia with Kosovo and Albania. Clandestine activities are considered to operate with tacit
political approval. They exacerbated Macedonian fears of Albanian secession and irredentism. Some of the major instances of "episodic violence"
in 2007 and 2010 took place when, rightly or wrongly, police intervened in
response to allegations that Albanians had participated in illegal activities
along the Macedonian-Kosovo border. When tensions flared, police—

predominantly Macedonian—prioritized protecting the state rather than the citizenry and engaged in combat operations, solidifying a one-sided image of acting only on behalf of the Macedonian majority.[50]

Corruption within the Macedonian majority further facilitated tensions and inter-ethnic polarization, albeit more indirectly. The SDSM Crvenkovski government, which introduced the OFA reforms, used privatization to benefit a circle of clients.[51] SDSM's corruption, mixed with resentment about OFA endorsement, became the basis for the anti-SDSM campaign of the nationalist VMRO-DPMNE in the run-up to the 2006 general elections. While one cannot claim that VMRO-DPMNE was external to a corrupt political order—given that joint schemes to divide Macedonia along ethnic lines existed in 2001 when it was in power—throughout the transition processes it had ruled relatively briefly and so was considered less associated with corruption than its ethnic Macedonian rival. VMRO-DPMNE promised economic revival, but its clientelism has reached new levels from 2006 to the present. In a bid to secure public support for his rule, VMRO-DPMNE leader Nikola Gruevski—who also won the 2011 general elections—increased public administration from 95,000 public employees in 2006 to more than 135,000 in 2011.[52]

Having acquired political backing through clientelist channels, Gruevski launched the expensive "Skopje 2014" Project seeking to remodel the state's image through grandiose public buildings in Hellenic style and other monuments of Macedonian nationalism. "Skopje 2014" managed to aggravate not only Greece, but also the Albanians of Macedonia, who consider it a unilateral Macedonian ethnic project. Further tensions arose from a project to build an Orthodox church at a Skopje site claimed to hold remains of the Illyrians, ancient ancestors of the Albanians. The widening polarization between Macedonians and Albanians continues to be demonstrated by a race to build religious buildings—churches and mosques—in Skopje and around the country.[53] In April–May 2012, a wave of sporadic violence was triggered by the killing of five Macedonian fishermen and the arrest of 20 people, among them Albanians, Macedonian and Albanian. Protests brought thousands to the streets of Skopje, Gostivar, Tetovo, and other cities of Macedonia. This wave is considered the worst since the 2001 warfare and is clearly indicative of the potential for the escalation of violence.[54] While corruption per se does not account for these interethnic tensions, it is instrumentalized by nationalist elites gaining support through pervasive clientelism.

In Kosovo, the shadow economy was anchored in the decrease of minority status and majority strategies of coercion of the early 1990s, which prompted the formation of the parallel state that sustained itself primarily through the 3 percent tax imposed on Albanians in Kosovo and the diaspora. However, segregated from official markets, those who worked in Kosovo were often part of the gray economy. The latter flourished under international sanctions and, due to the socioeconomic crisis that engulfed the region, not among Kosovo Albanians only.[55] According to some sources, the KLA profited from contributions of Kosovo Albanian drug traffickers.[56] In contrast to Bulgaria and former Yugoslav successor states, where the shadow economy was linked to the state apparatus and patron-client networks, in Kosovo in the 1990s it was linked to the political opposition and tightly knit into the fabric of extended families and clans.[57] Thus, it became more easily legitimized as a tool against Serbian oppression and an integral part of the conflict.[58]

After NATO's 1999 intervention, the war economy in Kosovo found links to the newly established structures and started exerting a negative impact on inter-ethnic peace. An EU-sponsored report argued that in 2004–2006 the informal economy amounted for 26.7 to 34.8 percent of the GDP.[59] A 2006 investigation of clandestine activities in Italy intercepted phone conversations of local Kosovo Albanian entrepreneurs, who claimed to have contributed to the 2004 ethnic riots when Serbs and the international community were attacked.[60] A Council of Europe investigation suggested that there is a criminal network—supposedly involved in drug trafficking, extortion, and summary executions of Serbian and Albanian civilians during and after the 1999 war, and organ harvesting from murdered civilians for illicit transplants—linked to some circles in government.[61] Furthermore, the shadow economy has eroded the rule of law. The judiciary has been marred by political corruption and a huge backlog of criminal cases, some of which pertain to illegal property seizure from refugees of 1998–1999. Because of corruption, delinquent acts—such as stoning buses or desecrating church property—often go unpunished, furthering insecurity among the Serb community.

The war economy affected the Kosovo Serbs as well. Criminal groups created ethnic tensions around the northern city of Mitrovica, where a de facto ethnic Serbian rule had been established. Local leaders with criminal ties flourished in this area, where the UNMIK and EULEX failed to establish control. For large parts of the 2000s former Serbian paramilitaries and other nationalist elements, called the "bridge watchers," attacked travelers who attempted to cross the bridge linking the northern and southern parts of the city, effectively barring freedom of movement. Although their activities have subsided, threats and attacks against Serbs who cooperate with Kosovo authorities are commonplace.[62] Serbian members of the Kosovo Police Service allegedly report to both Kosovo and Serbia, and judges appointed by the Kosovo government or EULEX are not welcome.[63]

The Kosovo case is indicative of how a decrease of minority status coupled with minority coercion in the early 1990s can unleash a long chain of events whose present outcome is recurring interethnic violence. Although the pathway to this outcome in Kosovo, where the war economy was developed against the state, is different from that in Bulgaria and Macedonia, where joint majority-minority schemes flourished, there is a common denominator regarding how radical claims emerge when corruption is at stake: corruption can be rallied against by radical formations that are not part of the corrupt political order or have benefited little from it. Corruption in Kosovo was a target of two formations—the Kosovo Albanian Vetevendosje (Self-Determination) and war veterans—who had not tapped into any clandestine resources and felt left out of the political process.[64] They wanted independence and used anti-corruption claims, among others, to rally against both the Serbs and the international community.[65]

Perpetuating the Wrong Lessons

In Chapter 4 I mentioned that the mechanism of "learning," usually associated with socialization to liberal norms, can also be operational when securitization of minority rights occurs, and when the international community demotes concerns for democratization in favor of "security" and "stability." When this happens, local agents may learn the lesson that democratization and minority rights are of little importance. As a result, local elites introduce democratic reforms selectively, and often use them as opportunities to advance nationalist goals. This mechanism continued to operate throughout the 2000s, exacerbated by gaps in the international community's credibility, and often tied to problems of personnel appointments, capacities to implement policies, EU's enlargement fatigue, and other case-specific issues.

Although securitization of minority rights did not take place in Bulgaria to the extent that it did in Macedonia and Kosovo, concerns for regional stability and rewards for Bulgaria's support of NATO's 1999 intervention in Kosovo motivated speedy EU accession in 2007. "Learning" that democratization and minority rights were secondary to other political and geostrategic concerns, was thus reinforced throughout the 2000s. The international community showed interest in the Roma and Macedonians of Bulgaria, but less in the actual state of the Turkish minority, considered well integrated in the society because of the MRF participation in government.

This stance was detrimental to democratic development, because it allowed the MRF and other political elites to pursue particularistic interests with minimal consideration of minority rights, and was endorsed by international agents. Some media discussed international pressure to change the constitutional clause prohibiting formation of political parties on an ethnic basis, but those concerns remained discursive and the clause has not been changed as of 2012.[66] The major concern of majority elites was not how to better perform on EU minority rights requirements, but whether growing Bulgarian nationalism and the ultranationalist party Ataka would threaten the country's entry into the EU.[67] EU messages that Bulgaria lagged in the area of minority rights[68] did not affect accession. The EU therefore assisted in sealing the current state of affairs.

Nationalist stances have thrived on certain EU credibility issues. First, European Commission emphasis on the alignment of domestic legislation with the *acquis communautaire* during the pre-accession process gave candidate states a large measure of discretion, because there are no EU minority rights standards aside from the 2000 antidiscrimination directives.[69] Second, because FCPNM adoption and implementation was the major contested reform in Bulgaria, local elites often resisted further minority rights reforms, pointing to the EU double standards: major EU countries, including Belgium, France, and Greece, have not ratified this convention.[70] Third, by 2004 Bulgaria was considered to have fulfilled the Copenhagen criteria, despite unresolved minority rights issues.[71] Fourth, internal inconsistencies in the EU political process created further opportunities to belittle the need for reform. For example, when MEP Els de Groen made an official statement that there were dangers of accession before corruption had been explicitly addressed, the European Parliament voted down some minority-related aspects of her proposal.[72] Political considerations again trumped human and minority rights.

In Macedonia, the authorities used the need for stability guaranteed by OFA as an excuse not to apply meritocratic criteria for employment in public administration, to make changes in the State Judicial Council, or to appoint constitutional judges.[73] Instead, appointments were made with political aims. For example, Idzet Memeti, the ethnic Albanian appointed ombudsman, was not politically neutral but a member of the Albanian DUI party in power. In naming him ombudsman, the parliament violated articles six and eight of the Law on National Ombudspersons.[74] During the privatization reforms the most influential independent daily newspapers— *Dnevnik* and *Utrinski vestnik*—were bought by the German concern VAC, which established a print media monopoly, a development allegedly supported by the government.[75] Members of the Macedonian opposition, aided by the nationalist diaspora primarily from Australia, used constitutional provisions allowing for a referendum if 150,000 people signed a petition in favor of a civil initiative.[76] The organizers of this referendum challenged decentralization and often employed arguments about the need to preserve the country's stability.

The nationalist aversion to genuine reform was supported by claims concerning the EU's lack of credibility. There is a pervasive—and partly correct—argument among Macedonian local elites that the EU has problems implementing its own minority rights policies. For example, the heavily regulated Macedonian electronic media paid considerable attention to interethnic problems in Belgium, which experiences ethnic tensions between its French and Walloon citizens. The lack of credibility argument is often tied to the debate with Greece about Macedonia's name, and with Greece and Bulgaria—both EU members—regarding their Macedonian minorities. During my fieldwork in 2008 several political entrepreneurs argued that if neither Greece nor Bulgaria was able to change its narrow historical vision, why should Macedonia be obliged to support much greater ethnic diversity.

Problems with personnel appointments also exacerbated local elites' ability to play their particularistic game. As an interviewee observed, EU representatives often held short-term contracts, which facilitated loss of institutional memory, especially against the backdrop of an ever-changing union.[77] Moreover, because Macedonia is considered neither a crisis zone nor a case for rapid enlargement, its political situation is stagnant.[78] In such circumstances, knowledgeable personnel move on with their careers and find employment elsewhere.

The EU and the international community have also given signals that help elites exploit the nationalist card. The decision at the 2008 NATO Summit in Bucharest not to offer membership to Macedonia because of the name dispute with Greece, and the EU decision not to give Macedonia a date for the start of accession talks, gave important signals to supporters of isolationism beyond general Euro-fatigue over further enlargement. Thus, instead of advancing on the European agenda, the VMRO-DPMNE government moved in a nationalist direction. Nationalism thrives in times of instability, and ethnic Macedonians have had few coping mechanisms. Macedonians—whether sympathizing with Gruevski's VMRO-DPMNE or its rival SDSM—continue to express the sentiment that the EU has seriously pressured them to implement the OFA, but has shown little appreciation and understanding of what they have done.

In Kosovo, the lessons learned through interaction with the international community during the 1990s continue to condition nationalist behavior despite a drastically changed political landscape. The failure to change the status quo until 2008 out of concern for stability aggravated the radical agents discussed above, for whom corruption and stability were interconnected. In the March 2004 riots, violence reached an "extensive" level because 8 Serbs and 12 Albanians died and more than 30 Orthodox religious sites and over 900 houses and ethnic minority businesses were looted and damaged. Veteran groups and especially the self-determination movement Vetevendosje staged demonstrations in 2006 and 2007 that eventually turned violent. According to the U.S. Department of State, in 2006 the Kosovo Police Service used force to disperse protests and beat demonstrators on at least four occasions. During a November 2006 protest demonstrators threw rocks and bottles of red paint at UNMIK buildings; UNMIK police responded with tear gas and later arrested eight people.[79] During the February 2007 demonstration, which initially started as nonviolent, UNMIK police killed 3 protesters and injured around 80 others. Vetevendosje directed its campaigns against both the Serbs and the international community. Its leader Albin Kurti argued that they both obstructed Kosovo's sovereignty. By "taking over the physical public sphere," he wanted to problematize the international community's approach to stability and tolerance for the corruption of current politicians.[80] Kurti also protested the Ahtisaari plan, especially the vision of decentralization,[81] which he saw not as self-government for the Serbs but as incipient cantonization.

Several credibility problems in the international community further exacerbated nationalist sentiments. Local NGO representatives and self-determination advocates like Kurti noted that the lack of accountability of international organizations to the local population was a major problem. Some international personnel not only were indifferent toward the local corruption, but actively participated in it.[82] In 2002 a senior UNMIK officer committed fraud by assuming a false doctor title and diverting U.S.$4.3 million to a bank account under his control.[83] He was the only one convicted in 2004. Allegations exist that many UN officials mismanaged privatization bids and corporate operations for their own profit, but they were indicted after they were far away from Kosovo.[84] Because of the complicated governance structure, much of the citizenry do not know where to seek responsibility when international officers violate laws and human rights. A self-help mentality prevails, and zero-sum game nationalist politics thrives.[85] As in Macedonia, the short-term contracts of international personnel create gaps of bureaucratic knowledge, allowing for exploitation by domestic elites.

The legitimacy of the international community was questioned by the Serbian community after UNMIK arrived in Kosovo. During the 2000s Serbs lived in their parallel institutions and boycotted elections not organized by Serbia. Serbian parties, the currency (the dinar), and medical and educational institutions sponsored by Serbia operated in the north, the enclaves, and Orthodox monasteries. Apart from Gracanica, an enclave on the outskirts of Prishtina, Serbs live in a string of villages around Prishtina and smaller settlements in the west and the east.[86]

Kosovo's 2008 independence brought a new wave of Serbian resistance against the international community. Clashes in March 2008 left one Ukrainian UNMIK policeman dead and more than 130 people injured, among them 70 Serbs and 63 international police officers.[87] EULEX's "status neutral" position was considered a "cover" for making some facts on the ground prevail. While the international community's legitimacy remains deeply questioned, some Serbian leaders—especially in the enclaves in the Kosovo heartland but not in Mitrovica—have realized that there is a need to reconcile with the new political realities.[88] As a result, campaigning for the first parliamentary elections of postindependence Kosovo in 2010 spread in Gracanica and other Serbian settlements in the south, yet the few people who tried to run for office in the north were severely punished by their own nationalist leaders.[89]

Challenges from Kin-States and Diasporas

During the 2000s, identity-based agents reduced their challenges to the domestic interethnic peace, but residual aspects of the earlier established conflict dynamics remained. The EU integration process created incentives for kin-states to support peaceful domestic and regional integration processes. Albania started negotiations on a Stabilization and Association Agreement in 2003. Turkey was officially recognized as a candidate for full membership in 1999, and negotiations started in 2005. Radicalism from the Albanian diaspora subsided after Kosovo was no longer affected by direct rule from Serbia. Nevertheless, the weakness of the Albanian state, the nonresolution of Kosovo's final status, problems with OFA implementation in Macedonia, and widespread corruption in Bulgaria paved the way for detrimental influences from these identity-based agents, aiding conflict perpetuation.

"Adaptive expectations," as a mechanism for conflict perpetuation that partially sustained the conflict dynamics during the 1990s, continued to operate throughout the 2000s. While the formal rules of engagement between the countries in the region were altered due to prospects for future EU integration, the informal rules remained largely intact. When ethnonational issues were at stake, minorities, kin-states, and diasporas perpetuated the ways they had earlier adapted to each other's policy responses and behaviors.

Albania's Janus-faced approach toward Kosovo and Macedonia continued regarding smuggling, a "bigger Albanian space," and clandestine connections to the Albanian National Army, aiming at unification of all Albanians. First, as the ICG points out, although Albania received large amounts of international aid to curb smuggling of humans, goods, and weapons, challenges persisted, especially in the mountainous regions at the Kosovo-Macedonia border. The local police in the northern areas were largely sympathetic to the aims of the insurgents who continued to operate in this border region, and were susceptible to bribery, while the government was hampered by a small but influential group of military and intelligence officers who deliberately overlooked arms smuggling.[90] Insurgent elements outside the established political structures in Kosovo and Macedonia enjoyed access and moral support.

During my fieldwork five months after Kosovo's independence in 2008, political entrepreneurs, NGO activists, and some local scholars often claimed that Albanians of Kosovo and Macedonia do not want to be a minority in Tirana politics, nor is Albania interested in acquiring more troublesome territories. Nevertheless, different ideas clearly coexisted with theirs. In 2001 the leader of the moderate Tirana-based Democratic Alliance, Arben Imami, claimed that unification between Kosovo and Albania should be a party goal, but his own party members and mainstream politicians quickly criticized him.[91] The idea of building a bigger Albanian space grew during the 2000s, but with a focus on economic and cultural exchanges, especially vis-à-vis future EU integration. Tirana's economic, transportation, and educational exchanges with Kosovo and Macedonia increased.[92] Promoting free movement between the Albanian people "would help to avert pressure from ideas associated with greater Albania," Albanian Prime Minister Nano noted.[93] Instead of seeking to redraw borders, "what is important now is to make borders unimportant," a DUI spokesperson in Macedonia claimed.[94]

It is unclear at this stage whether these statements are separated from intentions for future unification once all candidate countries enter the EU. The idea of a "bigger Albanian space" was not entertained simply for regional integration. In 2003 Nano organized an informal meeting of Albanian political leaders from different parts of the Balkans. While declaring interests in regional integration, the meeting also sought to develop a common agenda if the OFA in Macedonia failed.[95] While DUI leader Ahmeti abstained from taking a stance, DPA leader Xhaferi argued that ethnic Albanians in Macedonia should have the right to self-determination.[96] Frustration with the slow pace of OFA implementation and the ongoing dispute with Greece over the country's official name made some Albanian voices explore more radical ideas. A Greater Albania agenda operated in the background as an alternative in case Kosovo's final status negotiations failed.[97] In 2004 there was strong support for unification with Kosovo in the northern border regions of Albania, partially due to a belief that dissolving the border would bring more economic benefits.[98] A 2005 survey of the Prishtina-based polling agency Reinvest demonstrated that more than 80 percent of the Albanians in the Preshevo Valley in southern Serbia want to join "what many call a union of Albanian territories."[99] A 2010 Gallup Balkan Monitor poll demonstrated that two-thirds of Albanians in Western Macedonia support a common Albanian state, and more than half think that it is likely to happen "soon."[100] In the May 2012 wave of protests, Albanians chanted slogans in favor of Greater Albania.[101]

Seeking Albanian unification in a single state, the Albanian National Army (ANA) had a detrimental impact on inter-ethnic relations in Kosovo and Macedonia. The ANA emerged during the 2001 warfare in Macedonia, and was initially considered a splinter group of NLA, but connections to KLA splinter groups were later found.[102] As the ICG points out, ANA spread its activities through Kosovo, Albania, and the Albanian-inhabited Preshevo Valley. In 2002 two Macedonian reservists and a policeman were killed, and a grenade attack was launched on the newly elected parliament. In 2003 two ANA members were killed in Kosovo, when they attempted to blow up a railway link between Kosovo and Serbia. Serbian civilians and international police were killed, prompting UNMIK to declare ANA a "terrorist organization." A kidnapping incident in Macedonia led to a massive police operation that killed two ANA insurgents.[103] In 2007 the ANA continued to intimidate Kosovo citizens, targeting primarily those engaged in reconciliation processes and Serbian returns.[104]

In a pattern reminiscent of the early 1990s, the ANA was rejected by the official authorities in Tirana, but had a stronghold in Albania. ANA leader Gafur Adili was placed under house arrest in Tirana in 2004, but another leader, Idajet Beqiri, who also headed the small Tirana-based Party of National Unity, was released from prison after a decision of a court of appeals. A third ANA leader was identified as a former Albanian army general.[105] While the strength of the organization seems to have subsided following Kosovo's independence, the organization did not vanish. In April 2010 the ANA was considered responsible for skirmishes on the Kosovo-Macedonian border in which a Macedonian policeman was killed.[106]

The impact of the Albanian diaspora on Kosovo and Macedonia subsided in the aftermath of NATO's 1999 intervention. Priorities shifted for new Kosovo leaders, who started building domestic institutions. Many diaspora members turned their energies away from Kosovo and toward improving their own social situation.[107] Major diaspora personalities—such as U.S.-based KLA representative Dino Asanaj—returned to Kosovo to build new careers. Asanaj became chairman of the Privatization Agency, and inaugurated the construction of a housing complex, International Village, on the outskirts of Prishtina, using cutting edge geothermal technology.[108] Businessman Harry Bajraktari, NAAC member and publisher of the Albanian American *Ilirija* newspaper, launched one of the biggest investment schemes in Kosovo after 1999.[109] KLA fundraiser Florin Krasniqi invested in the energy sector in Decani.[110] Many educated diaspora members, mostly with experience in the information technology sector, returned to Kosovo hoping to find good jobs.[111] The diaspora's strongest impact could be observed in the massive construction that rapidly changed the landscape of both Kosovo and Macedonia. Other diaspora members continued to send remittances to family members or open new small businesses.[112] Given that Kosovo has an official unemployment rate of 40 percent, and Macedonia also has a high unemployment rate, diaspora remittances became a lifeline for the local population.

Elements in the diaspora continued to pose a potential factor for conflict escalation. There are allegations that diaspora radicals have funded the ANA.[113] Former KLA activists voiced threats in a 2005 documentary, stating that arms continued to be shipped to Kosovo on a small scale and that larger repercussions would follow if final status negotiations were not resumed.[114] The Atlantic Battalion issued a similar warning in 2007. Some radical entrepreneurs advocated a unilateral proclamation of independence, while moderates advocated joint action with the international community, which eventually happened.[115] While the diaspora on the whole acted in moderate ways, threats were linked to the stalled progress in the final status negotiations.

Turkey's interference in Bulgaria's inter-ethnic affairs during the early 2000s was minimal, apart from a minor incident in 2000 when authorities quietly asked a Turkish consul to leave the country. The Bulgarian media speculated that the consul had acted in support of the MRF, claiming it was the only party capable of uniting all Muslims in Bulgaria.[116] In line with 1990s patterns of engagement, Turkey became critical when rights of ethnic Turks were threatened, especially after the ultranationalist Ataka party rose to power and openly expressed concern about the proposed referendum on use of Turkish in the media.[117] More recently, Prime Minister Erdogan strongly condemned Ataka's assault on Muslims in a Sofia mosque.[118]

During the 2000s Turkey's relations with Bulgaria were primarily driven by economic interests and Turkey's prospects for EU integration. The former included ongoing initiatives regarding the Nabucco pipeline from the Caucasus to transport natural gas to the EU and decrease EU dependence on Russian gas,[119] an EU-funded cross-border cooperation program,[120] and increasing economic investments, which became Turkey's major strategy to increase its influence in the Balkans.[121]

Nevertheless, Bulgaria's EU accession in 2007 opened avenues for some contentious politics. Since Turkey needed support from other EU members for its own membership, politics in Bulgaria became more important than before. Unresolved issues in the energy sector, water management, and especially compensation for properties of Bulgarian refugees who fled repression in eastern Turkey in the 1910s and 1920s now became conditions for Bulgaria's support.[122] While Bulgaria has so far refrained from officially recognizing the Armenian genocide in 1915—a major roadblock to Turkey's EU accession—after the United States and Sweden recognized it in 2010, there has been a new motion to do so.[123] A 2010 statement by Prime Minister Borisov that Bulgaria could render principled support for Turkey's EU accession was met with fierce resistance from Ataka's Siderov. He staged a show in the Bulgarian parliament and proposed a national referendum on Turkey's accession.[124]

The MRF and the diaspora became important in this process. For example, during a 2011 motion of the Bulgarian parliament on requesting compensation for Bulgarian refugees from eastern Thrace, the MRF boycotted the vote.[125] The MRF had earlier mobilized the diaspora in Turkey to vote in elections in Bulgaria, and to capitalize on their support. In the mid-2000s this trend increased. During the 2005 parliamentary elections, there were claims that ethnic Turks went from Turkey to Bulgaria to vote at their registered address, and then returned to vote in Turkey with their passports.[126] During the 2006 presidential elections irregularities became even more visible when organized busing from abroad took place, referred to as "election day tourism."[127] Multiple voting and vote buying have been a problem. This process continued after 2007, when the ethnic Turkish vote became important for elections for the European Parliament and thus for possible votes supporting Turkey's EU accession. Large-scale vote-buying marred the 2009 European Parliament and parliamentary elections, including busing of voters to different districts.[128] While vote-buying was not an isolated MRF phenomenon and took place among Bulgarian passport holders living in Macedonia as well, it nevertheless aggravated Ataka and other nationalists, who saw in the MRF's successful electoral performance increased chances for Turkey's EU accession, which it resisted fiercely. As a result, Ataka proposed that the parliament restrict voting rights of dual citizens.

Conclusions

This chapter has sought to explain why ethnonational conflicts endure even after strong international intervention for postconflict reconstruction and democratization. Residual aspects of earlier informally institutionalized conflict dynamics largely explain the occurrence of the low to middle levels of violence. Although the international community changed its attitudes toward redefinition of statehood in Kosovo and Macedonia during the postconflict period, and increased its commitments through peace-building and state-building efforts as well as promises for future EU integration, informally institutionalized conflict dynamics continued to operate beneath the surface, and to enable and constrain agents' behaviors.

The effects of corruption, rooted in the cooptation and coercion strategies adopted to deal with minorities during the early 1990s, became detrimental to inter-ethnic peace in the 2000s. A "drift" from the official rules resulted in "normalization of corruption," which was then attacked by majority formations that either were external to the corrupt political order (Ataka in Bulgaria and Vetevendosje in Kosovo), or benefited rather little from it (VMRO-DPMNE in Macedonia). They used the corruption of minority formations together with majority elites (Bulgaria and Macedonia), and corrupt arrangements including local agents and members of the international community (Kosovo), as platforms to launch a nationalist backlash and maintain interethnic tensions.

Domestic elites acted in line with lessons learned from previous interactions with the international community—that stability and security trump democratization—and took advantage of political reforms for their own particularistic benefits, contributing to further interethnic polarization. Local agents resisted reforms, driven by the lack of credibility of international institutions with little capacity to enforce policies, selective adoption of minority rights instruments in their own countries, and stalled interest in EU inclusion of countries in the Western Balkans. Thus "learning" as a mechanism need not be associated primarily with socialization of liberal ideas, but could be based on "wrong" lessons learned in interactions with the international community. Since such lessons became deeply ingrained in the behavior of both local and international agents, they justified the local agents' particularistic behavior and the international community's neglect.

Unreformed aspects of informally institutionalized conflict dynamics related to kin-states and diasporas—especially in the Albanian case—continued to undermine domestic peace as well. When ethnonational issues were at stake, minorities and identity-based actors continued to act alongside their "adaptive expectations" of each other and to perpetuate behaviors similar to those of the 1990s. Unofficial endorsement of radical clandestine formations such as ANA continued with Tirana's involvement. The Albanian diaspora—although acting more moderately—also issued occasional threats. Less problematic was the involvement of Turkey and the Turkish diaspora in Bulgaria, but Turkey's future EU accession, coupled with Bulgaria's EU membership since 2007 amid continuing corruption, allowed for the flourishing of vote-buying schemes that aggravated Bulgarian nationalist formations opposed to EU inclusion of Turkey.

This chapter has developed a new thesis about the effects of informally institutionalized dynamics to explain persistent low to middle levels of violence. My findings build on the literatures of postconflict reconstruction and peace building (Macedonia, Kosovo) and democratization (Bulgaria). I demonstrate that despite significant differences among the cases, informally institutionalized dynamics drive conflict perpetuation. Furthermore, to understand these dynamics, the mechanisms of conflict perpetuation must be examined. The "drift" mechanism in combination with a "reactive sequence" by the majorities, and the continuation of the "learning" and "adaptive expectations" mechanisms observed also during the 1990s have been identified and explored.

Conclusions

Lessons Learned About Informally Institutionalized Conflict Dynamics

Two questions have guided this book in its quest to understand the sources, agents, structures, and mechanisms that drive and sustain ethnonational conflicts over time. Why do ethnonational conflicts reach different degrees of violence? Why do they persevere even after strong international intervention for conflict resolution and institution building? Applying the theoretical approach of historical institutionalism, I derive answers from three cases: Serb-Albanian relations in Kosovo, Macedonian Slav-Albanian relations in Macedonia, and Bulgarian-Turkish relations in Bulgaria. They shared a number of characteristics at the end of communism, including a similar constellation between Orthodox Christian majorities and Muslim minorities, deep penetration of the Communist party into political decision-making processes, and a totalitarian political culture. Yet the conflicts reached different levels of violence over time. Ethnonationalist violence was high in Kosovo, middle range in Macedonia, and relatively low in Bulgaria. It was also puzzling why violence persisted at mid- to low levels during the 2000s, when Kosovo and Macedonia faced postconflict reconstruction along with democratization pressures, whereas Bulgaria was only exposed to the latter. To the dismay of international observers, in all three cases interethnic violence occasionally flared or silently persevered.

This book has argued that these levels of ethnonational violence and their perseverance were anchored in informally institutionalized conflict dynamics between majorities, minorities, and international agents during the formative period—a critical juncture—at the end of communism. At that time drastic shifts on multiple levels in the domestic and international environment allowed contingent events to have major consequences by setting existing conflictual relations onto different political trajectories. At the end of the critical juncture, relationships between majorities, minorities, international agents, and kin-states consolidated in conflict dynamics specific to each case: highly conflictual in Kosovo, semiconflictual in Macedonia, and cooperative in Bulgaria. Causal mechanisms such as "advantage of political incumbency," "adaptive expectations," "learning," and "drift" in combination with a "reactive sequence" from the majorities fostered conflict perpetuation, while "replacement" and "layering" contributed to change toward more peaceful relations. While constitutions, laws, and other policies officially postulated certain behaviors, these informally institutionalized dynamics unofficially conditioned the behaviors. Exogenous shocks from the international environment usually led to drastic change in the direction of higher levels of violence. Both exogenous shocks and mechanisms of change altered some aspects of the conflict dynamics as originally established, but other important residual factors continued to create incentives for conflict perpetuation.

This final chapter summarizes the major arguments, explores the external validity of core claims regarding other conflicts, and highlights their relevance for scholarship on legacies, EU enlargement, informal institutions, and more recent transitions in the Middle East.

Path-Dependence and Conflict Dynamics

Scholars often state that conflicts are path-dependent; some have also used ideas of historical institutionalism.[1] Recently Stroschein argued that historical institutionalism can be applied to understand how repeated protests can create feedback effects, alter minority-related policies, and bring moderation of conflicts.[2] This book emphasizes the analytical leverage of historical institutionalism, unpacks the causal effects of policies and their timing and sequencing during critical junctures, shows the usefulness of positing certain mechanisms for change and conflict perpetuation, and elaborates on the impact of sequences of exogenous shocks for variations in violence. It brings additional rigor to understand *why*, *when*, and *how* these conflicts become path-dependent, that conflicts may progress in a nonlinear manner, and that some formative periods are more important than others for long-term evolution of conflicts. Unlike structural and elite-based explanations that focus on either structure or agency and on simultaneous variations,[3] path-dependence accounts for structure and agency in the same theoretical framework, and captures some of the effects of time on the outcomes of violence.

This book applies historical institutionalism to reshape our understanding of the nature of conflict dynamics. Conflict dynamics are formed through the interactions of majorities, minorities, international agents, and kin-states during a critical juncture. International agents have been discussed in multiple studies on third-party intervention, but the agents' pivotal role during critical junctures has not been adequately addressed.[4] This book argues that after a critical juncture the role of international agents subsides as the agents become part of the adaptation processes that "lock in" the interactions between majorities and minorities. Hence, *conflict dynamics are more static* than predicted in rationalist accounts, and are not merely a function of interlocking and mutually reinforcing civic ties, as other accounts argue. They become informally institutionalized through self-reinforcement mechanisms acting across realms beyond the civic: constitutional, legal, political, linguistic, educational, and religious. This book indicates that conflict dynamics span a spectrum, including conflictual, semiconflictual, and cooperative: they may also persist in conflicts considered less intractable but still posing problems for postconflict reconstruction and democratization.

In the cases discussed here, relationships between majorities and minorities evolved through a similar logic during the critical juncture. The causal chain started with struggles between reformist and conservative communist elites on how to deal with the minorities and their constitutional status. Minorities did not strike first, as security dilemma explanations would suggest;[5] decision-making was firmly located in the communist majorities that controlled both Yugoslavia and Bulgaria during the formative period. The winning faction—nationalists in Kosovo and Macedonia, and reformists in Bulgaria—sealed its vision of how to approach minority status issues. As a result, a first step in a tripartite sequence occurred, as majorities decided to increase (Bulgaria) or reduce (Kosovo, Macedonia) a minority's constitutional status. The *relative* change of status in minority rights mattered, not the *absolute* scope of rights the minorities enjoyed in terms of international norms.

In a second step, majorities moved to reinforce their decision and developed strategies to make minorities comply, whether through co-optation

(Bulgaria, Macedonia) or coercion (Kosovo). Depending on the combination of status change and compliance strategy, minorities reacted in specific ways. Increased status and co-optation produced minority acceptance of the state (Bulgaria). Decreased status and coercion produced rejection of the state by the Albanians, who were a minority in Yugoslavia but a majority in Kosovo, and the building of parallel institutions and society (Kosovo). Decreased status and co-optation for the minority produced a two-pronged strategy of official acceptance and simultaneous clandestine activities (Macedonia).

Prime causal responsibility for variations in violence may be found in the majority-minority relationship, but the intervention of the international community and identity-based agents during this stage was important to establish triangular relationships among local agents and form contextualized conflict dynamics. The intervention of the international community—consisting of international organizations and states that did not share ethnic ties with either majority or minority—was crucial regarding the provision or absence of three types of guarantees. The first was to guarantee to the minorities their political participation in their states (Bulgaria and Macedonia, but not Kosovo). The second was to guarantee to the majorities that the basic premises of statehood (international legal or domestic sovereignty) would not be effectively challenged (guaranteed in Bulgaria, partially in Macedonia, not in Kosovo). The third was credibly to guarantee to both majorities and minorities a long-term commitment to conflict resolution (supplied to Bulgaria, a little in Macedonia, but not Kosovo). International policies differed not simply depending on "how sick was the patient,"[6] or how the majority-minority relationship evolved, but regarding the choices that organizations and states considered important for themselves. The agency of the international community should not be underestimated at this crucial stage. The more it provided these three guarantees, the less likely it was to set up a situation that led to higher degrees of violence over time. With or without its active participation, it did shape the formation of conflict dynamics.

Identity-based agents—especially kin-states—also participated in establishing the "rules of the game" during this formative period. In comparison to the international community their interventions were less formal and clearly favored the minorities with whom they had ethnic ties. If the institutions of a kin-state (Albania for the Kosovo and Macedonian cases) were weakened by transition and unable to enforce a coherent foreign policy of non-intervention for minority secessionism, the kin-state developed a two-pronged strategy toward the conflicts, and contributed to more conflictual dynamics. In these cases, the kin-state formally bowed to international pressures and formulated an official foreign policy of non-intervention while state officials established alliances with secessionist and autonomist movements across borders alongside their own ideological, clan-based, and particularistic interests. In contrast, if the institutions of a kin-state (Turkey in the Bulgarian case) were relatively strong and elites were able to formulate and enforce a coherent foreign policy of non-intervention, then the kin-state was likely to contribute to more cooperative relationships between majorities and minorities.

The impact of diasporas was minimal during the critical juncture, but increased over time. The Albanian diaspora in Western states gradually became involved in the conflicts, especially in Kosovo. The moderate LDK built branches abroad during the 1990s and solicited lobbying and financial support for its nonviolent movement. The diaspora became instrumental for the conflict escalation in 1998–1999, when it backed the radical KLA after the moderate LDK began losing support for its peaceful resistance strategy and grave human rights violations took place in 1998. In contrast, the ethnic Turkish diaspora from Bulgaria was not instrumental in creating inter-ethnic tensions, since it was oriented toward immigration and assimilation in neighboring Turkey, and sporadic support for the ethnic Turkish MRF in Bulgaria during election campaigns. Its electoral support became more pronounced after Bulgaria entered the EU in 2007.

Two causal mechanisms aided the consolidation of informal institutionalization of conflict dynamics after the critical juncture. "Advantage of political incumbency" is a mechanism of amplified reinforcement, where early arrival of certain agents in power allows them to increase power and to consolidate their superiority over the political competition. With a short exception in Bulgaria in 1991–1992, communists or not-so-ex-communists remained in government throughout much of the 1990s. They used their position to exclude the local majority from political, economic, and social life in Kosovo; to postpone or oppose minority rights reforms in language, religious freedoms, education, and decentralization of power in Bulgaria, Macedonia, and Kosovo; and to seek reversal of adopted reforms after returning to power in Bulgaria.

"Adaptive expectations," the second mechanism of amplified reinforcement, worked between majorities and minorities and the international community and kin-states. The agents involved acted on the unwritten rules of "appropriate" behavior regarding other agents. Appropriateness of behavior involved the adaptation of both majorities and minorities to the informal rules. In Bulgaria these rules were preservation of the state, minimal increase of minority status and co-optation, and minority acceptance of the state and its regime—including no constitutional challenges or demands for autonomy. In Macedonia the rules were preservation of the state, minimal decrease of minority status and co-optation, and a two-pronged minority strategy of official participation in governing coalitions, constitutional challenges, and parliamentary boycotts alongside clandestine operations seeking territorial autonomy. In Kosovo, the rules were disputes over preservation of the state, drastic decrease of Albanians' status and coercion, and Albanian rejection of the state and its regime through building parallel institutions.

International and domestic agents also adapted to the informal rules of behavior. The international community and the majorities continued to share interests regarding the territorial integrity of the state. They adapted to specific aspects of the relationship, such as the importance of the international community in establishing prospects for European integration (Bulgaria), provision of security (Macedonia), and formal adoption of major international human and minority rights instruments. Minorities adapted to the international community as well, understanding that they could ally with it on issues of political participation in state institutions and defense of human rights, but not for aspirations for territorial autonomy, challenges to constitutions, or independent statehood. Kin-states better served the latter goals, especially if the kin-state had weak institutions and could not enforce a coherent foreign policy of non-intervention (Albania). Kin-states and minorities adapted to each other, so that minorities did not ask for direct interventions from kin-states but relied on them for diplomatic support, cultural connections (Turkey), and clandestine activities (Albania).

Informally institutionalized relationships are relatively long-lived but undergo change over time. Aspects of these dynamics are altered through both exogenous shocks and gradual transformation. Exogenous shocks occur suddenly, are beyond the control of policy-makers, and often contribute to the escalation of violence by creating incentives for minorities to radicalize their claims. A sequence of two exogenous shocks—the Dayton Agreement (1995) followed by the implosion of the Albanian state (1997)— gave incentives for radical factions to grow within Kosovo and escalated the level of violence to "internal warfare" in 1999. NATO's 1999 intervention was an exogenous shock to established relationships in Macedonia and Bulgaria and increased majority-minority tensions in these countries. In Macedonia it also contributed to further polarization, exploited by radical minority factions who launched the 2001 "internal warfare."

Another mechanism of change is "replacement" of the old rules with new ones. Replacement took place under the auspices of the international community in Kosovo (1999) and Macedonia (2001). Driven by events on the ground and internal warfare, the international community changed its earlier aversion to the nonredefinition of the state, and became instrumental in significant changes. After NATO's 1999 intervention, when Kosovo Albanians became the political majority and Serbs the minority, UNMIK and KFOR dispatched a serious local presence infringing on Serbia's domestic sovereignty, and started building local institutions. In Macedonia, the 2001 Ohrid Framework Agreement was the international agents' response to the armed Albanian insurrection and possible threat from Albanian irredentism, and became the basis of significant constitutional changes that raised the Albanian minority's status, promoted decentralization to the local level, and offered significant linguistic and religious reforms.

Gradual change toward inter-ethnic peace occurred through "layering" of new policies on top of or alongside existing rules, including "conditionality" and "socialization." My analysis confirms the findings of some earlier studies that EU "conditionality" had some beneficial influences, because minority rights became embedded in political requirements for future EU integration, and their progress was monitored on a regular basis in Bulgaria after 1997 and Macedonia after 2001. "Socialization" with liberal norms was less powerful: communities of likeminded individuals with liberal ideas remained confined to human rights activists and some intellectual circles, while political elites often used liberal ideas solely on a rhetorical level.

"Conditionality" and "socialization" with human rights norms occurred along with virulent nationalism. The ultranationalist party Ataka in Bulgaria has won large shares of the vote since 2005, challenging a set of liberal notions and politics. Its challenges to established minority rights commitments continued even after Bulgaria became an EU member in 2007. The Macedonian nationalist party VMRO-DMPNE has been entrenched in power since 2006 and brought nationalism to a new level with the controversial Skopje 2014 project, which alienated both Albanians of Macedonia and Greece, an EU member with which Macedonia remains in a bitter dispute over its history and official name. This dispute continues to hinder Macedonia's progress toward EU integration. In Kosovo, with an intensified policy dialogue with the EU since 2008, some human rights groups are gaining more influence, but anti-liberal sentiments are strong and characterized by an aversion to dealing with the rights of the Serbs.

In contrast to some EU enlargement studies, I argue that "conditionality" and "socialization" should be seen as instances of the overarching mechanism of "layering," since they did not drastically transform political realities but did add new elements of liberalism to the existing nationalist rules of the game. Incumbent elites met some accession conditions—such as adoption of the the Framework Convention for Protection of Minority Rights in Bulgaria and decentralization reforms in Macedonia—but not others. As of 2012, Bulgaria had not changed the constitutional clause prohibiting formation of parties on an ethnic or religious basis, nor had Macedonia accepted Albanian as a second official language. This is so because external conditions are layered over existing dynamics and do not change them drastically, and because the EU uses few direct enforcement mechanisms beyond conditionality.

Nevertheless, "layering" opens opportunities for local agents to develop *practical attachments* to new rules while the old rules are in place. More and more minority individuals—believing in the power of EU institutions—have filed human rights abuse claims in the European Court on Human Rights during the 2000s. Also, many Slav Macedonians did not vote in a 2004 nationalist referendum opposing decentralization that would give Albanians more local power. Individual Macedonian voters were not subject to conditionality, unlike their parties in government, nor were they genuine believers in liberal democracy and multiculturalism, a possible effect of norms socialization. Their decision was *practical*, aimed at supporting the preservation of the fragile Macedonian state through possible future EU integration.

Alongside mechanisms fostering drastic and incremental changes, mechanisms of self-perpetuation sustain the informally institutionalized dynamics. Beyond "advantage of political incumbency," which operated in the 1990s, and "adaptive expectations," which continued to operate throughout the 2000s, this study identified the mechanisms "learning" and "drift," in combination with a "reactive sequence" by the majorities. In contrast to most studies, I demonstrated that "learning" need not be associated only with the acquisition of liberal norms and used as a synonym for "socialization." From the perspective of conflict resolution, local agents may learn from their interactions with the international community that democratization may be trumped by concerns for security and stability, which may be perpetuated through their behaviors. As a result, incumbent agents respond to pressures for democratic reforms selectively, and where possible use them to advance their nationalist or particularistic goals. Also, having exhausted democratization channels to address the political status quo, rebels may use violence strategically. Violence has proved to pay off regarding the international community, which alters its own course in response.

Historical institutionalist accounts view "drift" as a mechanism of gradual change, because a gap develops between formal rules and external conditions, which then facilitates change.[7] This study demonstrates how drift can perpetuate conflict when combined with a "reactive sequence" from the majority. The gap between official rules adopted under international pressure and their minimal enforcement opened opportunities for political practices to consolidate "normalization of corruption" involving majorities, minorities, and sometimes individuals from the international community, while keeping stability intact. Corruption was then challenged with a "reactive sequence" from majority elements who were external to the corrupt political order or did not benefit much from it, and who sought to redress it. They often escalated their nationalist claims and launched attacks against the minority and even against the international community, as in Kosovo in 2004 and 2007. These mechanisms continued to perpetuate conflicts, exacerbated by international community credibility, personnel appointments, capacities to implement policies, and EU enlargement fatigue.

External Validity of Core Theoretical Claims

Like standard historical institutionalist accounts, path-dependence is applicable to real world questions, has historical orientations, and advances meso-level propositions about how durable rules embedded in institutions structure agents' behaviors.[8] This book takes historical institutionalism farther in the direction of conflict analysis by arguing that there are informally institutionalized conflict dynamics beyond existing institutions. It demonstrates how these dynamics are formed, sustained, and changed; how they create a bounded rationality for the behaviors of agents embedded in them;

and eventually how they explain the variation of patterns of violence in long-term conflict processes. Future research can benefit from the awareness that such informally institutionalized dynamics exist in other cases as well; that they often invisibly condition agents' behaviors and thwart efforts for peace building and long-term democratization. To understand these dynamics one needs to analyze:

(1) how sequences of relationships between majorities and minorities are formed during a critical juncture, and how international agents and kin-states participate in them;

(2) how contextually bound relationships are formed between the major agents involved during the critical juncture, and are perpetuated by specific causal mechanisms; and

(3) how other causal mechanisms and exogenous shocks contribute to altering these conflict dynamics, and to political change.

This brings us to the much debated questions of the *falsifiability* and *power of prediction* of path-dependence. Historical institutionalist accounts are often charged as difficult to falsify by general laws about human behavior developed by the social sciences in emulation of the hard sciences. Such criticism emphasizes the historical part of a path-dependence approach and points to the specifics of each case, but downplays the meso-level propositions that can travel beyond specific cases. As Rueschmeyer observed, falsification is more complex than rejection of a single proposition. A long sequence of events approached with the necessary theoretical expectations can eliminate or suggest revision of theories.[9] This book analyzes the outcomes of violence by systematically specifying the validity of theories at different stages of the causal process. Security dilemmas and credible commitment explanations were engaged when discussing critical junctures, theories of third-party interventions regarding conflict escalation and change, and theories on postconflict reconstruction regarding durability of conflicts.

Regarding the predictive power of path-dependence, one needs to be aware that scholars in this tradition are primarily interested in *explaining* outcomes, not predicting them, as Steinmo observed.[10] Because this scholarship is skeptical of the grand ambitions of social science to develop general laws, and sticks to meso-level theorizing, it sees also predictions as proximate. This is not because it dismisses other methods and models, but because it acknowledges that contingency matters during critical junctures, that history is nonlinear and some periods create more causal consequences than others, and that variables are interdependent and conditioned by the specific timing and sequencing of events.

This book develops a few proximate predictions. If majorities and minorities during a critical juncture followed the sequences of relationships discussed here, they would establish the fundamentals of similar conflict dynamics, from more to less conflictual to more cooperative. I do not make the exclusivist claim that such sequences operate at the onset of all ethnonational conflicts, in postcommunist space or beyond. Several cases from the postcommunist world have developed similar sequences starting with relative status change, but the pattern of interactions could evolve differently in other conflict regions. Regardless of the conflict case, however, relative status change will be important and a sequence of interactions during a formative period of time will condition the specifics of informally institutionalized conflict dynamics, which will be perpetuated through various causal mechanisms over time. In many post-totalitarian and post-authoritarian settings when incumbent elites are not completely overturned, one might expect that the mechanism "advantage of political incumbency" would operate at least in the short run. Incumbents' visions on how to approach ethnonational questions would be embedded in legislation as well as informal rules of the game. In contrast, "adaptive expectations" can be expected to sustain conflict dynamics within and across cases and for relatively longer periods of time.

One can also predict that if negative "learning" has occurred in the international community's favoring of stability over democratization, local agents are likely to engage with calls for democratization mostly rhetorically and exploit them for particularistic purposes. Furthermore, "conditionality" and "socialization" alone do not account for the current political changes, but one needs to understand them as part of the overarching mechanism of "layering" of new rules next to or on top of existing ones. Through this mechanism, agents remain embedded in the established conflict dynamics, but can also incrementally build practical attachments to the new rules. Finally, it is important to analyze how exogenous shocks empower agents already adapted to informally institutionalized conflict dynamics, and how aspects of these dynamics change. Conflict scholarship rarely addresses the significance of such exogenous events, instead focusing on rational, structuralist, constructivist, or institutionalist explanations.

This study scrutinized a twenty-year period. This long-term perspective distinguishes path-dependent arguments from others derived and tested through simultaneous variations. Such comparison of variations can focus on short-term periods and on many cases, whereas a path-dependent account needs a longer temporal perspective to confirm or reject theoretical propositions across specific cases. Comprehensive analysis of other cases is obviously beyond the scope of this book, since it requires deep immersion in additional case-based material. This approach is clearly relevant to majority-minority conflicts in polities undergoing transition from totalitarian rule, but could also have much broader applicability. To validate some core theoretical claims, however, the following pages consider some cases to which my arguments could potentially apply. Further inquiry should be regarded as conducting "plausibility probes."

From the postcommunist space I discuss Romania, which underwent nonviolent transition, Bosnia-Herzegovina, which went through civil war, and Georgia, where violent and nonviolent interactions took place over time.

Romania

Romania is a unitary state in Eastern Europe with a sizeable Hungarian minority, 6.5 percent of the total population according to a 2011 census.[11] Hungarians are largely concentrated in Transylvania, a region historically contested between Romania and Hungary. Despite some violent clashes in 1990, ethnonational conflicts evolved nonviolently during the past two decades. With different vigor before and after Romania's integration into the EU in 2007, Hungarians of Romania have voiced calls for autonomy.

To look into sequences of majority-minority relations during the critical juncture (1989–1992), in January 1990 the National Salvation Front of former communist functionary Ion Iliescu aired promises to improve collective rights and freedom for minorities.[12] Other parties rejected this move. As a result two months later a major episode of interethnic violence flared up in the Transylvanian city of Targu Mures.[13] As in the three cases treated extensively above, former communists used exclusionary practices, disregarding the voice of minorities in the legislative process, and adopted the 1991 Romanian Constitution defining Romania as a "unitary nation-state."[14] The early adoption of a constitution during a critical juncture did not guarantee a trouble-free transition, but created incentives for more minority contestation over time. The Hungarian opposition demanded instead "constituent status" in a multinational state.[15]

Serious contention on how statehood should evolve started from this point, with subsequent majority restrictions on Hungarian language education and self-government in the early 1990s and more Hungarian minority demands about the cultural and territorial autonomy of Transylvania. The Democratic Alliance of the Hungarians of Romania (DAHR) was represented consistently in the Bucharest parliament from 1990. Yet co-optation became of serious concern to some Hungarian politicians when the alliance joined a governing coalition for the first time in 1996.[16] In exchange for a government pledge of minority rights and institutional reform, the minority had to suspend its calls for autonomy.[17]

In this case, the *pace* of government response to nonterritorial minority demands also affected whether the minority elite broadens its demands to include territorial demands. In Chapter 2 I argued that if the government postpones such responses, there is a high likelihood that demands will become territorial, as they did in Macedonia. In Romania, the Hungarian minority argued explicitly not for territorial but for communal autonomy with the 1992 Cluj Declaration, yet increased its demands to territorial autonomy in 1993 and 1995.[18] The DAHR made claims against the backdrop of reinforced exclusivist strategies, when members of an ultranationalist Romanian party were appointed to cabinet positions in 1994 and the government proposed that an education law be adopted to restrict the use of minority languages.[19]

Understanding the role of international agents during the formative period must also be taken more seriously in theoretical as well as empirical terms. In Eastern Europe the international community acted in completely different ways during these early stages compared to the Caucasus, for example. In Romania the international community became a guarantor for the political participation of minorities and that there will be no major challenges to the domestic or international sovereignty of the state. International agents gave their credible long-term commitment through conflict resolution initiatives within the OSCE[20] and with regard to larger regional integration processes. Romania applied to join the Council of Europe in 1990 and became part of regional economic agreements.

The credible presence of the international community also created incentives for Hungary to maintain a "remarkably non-interventionist stance" during the formative period, as Jenne noted, apart from the public stance of prime minister Joseph Antall, who in 1990 announced that he considered himself a prime minister "in spirit" of all Hungarians, including five million living outside its post-Trianon borders.[21] A 1990 poll indicated that 85 percent of Hungarians in the kin-state thought their state should assist their ethnic brethren in neighboring countries.[22] Another poll demonstrated that almost 80 percent of the Hungarian public favored Council of Europe, European Community, and NATO accession. The Hungarian government sought to resolve conflicts over the Hungarian minority in Romania by voicing problems through international institutions and bilateral dialogue rather than direct intervention.[23] This made it more susceptible to pressures to sign a bilateral treaty with Romania, which it initially resisted.[24]

After the critical juncture ended, the majorities, minorities, international agents, and Hungary as a kin-state *adapted* to their initial responses and perpetuated a largely cooperative conflict dynamic. "Advantage of political incumbency" was also a mechanism that assisted the consolidation of informal dynamics. The postcommunist government of Ion Iliescu reinforced pressures against the Hungarian minory until the mid-1990s.[25] Majority elites contested minority claims over autonomy, but did not sanction them with violence as in Macedonia. The Hungarian minority found support for their human rights in the international community. Although international agents were more supportive of minority autonomy calls in Romania than in Bulgaria, they did not act in favor of a full-fledged territorial autonomy. The 1993 Copenhagen criteria were also applied toward Romania during the EU accession process, and managed to instill major breakthroughs, such as a minority protection clause in the 1996 friendship treaty between Romania and Hungary, revisions of the 1995 Education Law, initially restricted to mother-tongue education, and provisions for use of minority languages in official contacts in 1998–1999.[26] Nevertheless, a pattern similar to that in Bulgaria occurred: EU monitoring reports were critical of problematic advancement on minority-related issues, but did not envisage concrete mechanisms for implementation or sanctions beyond delaying EU membership. In this case, too, new EU rules were *layered* on top of and next to existing ones, contributing to practical attachments to the new rules but not to concrete policy change.

Hungary's behavior as a kin-state was also not outwardly irredentist, but like Albania it did undergo transition from communism. There are two major differences between Hungary and Albania. First, the transition did not weaken Hungary's institutions to the extent that the actions of individual members of government became uncontrollable. Even when Hungary issued controversial policies regarding minorities abroad—such as the 1996 Budapest Declaration, which obliged the Hungarian government to protect the rights of Hungarians abroad and the 2001 Status Law that granted special benefits and subsidies to Hungarians in neighboring countries—it did so through official foreign policy channels. Second, since Hungary was also in the process of EU accession, such foreign policy channels were officially scrutinized by international agents, and subjected to official pressures with which Hungary needed to comply to enter the EU. Having granted major support to the Hungarian minority in Romania, however, Hungary still participated in the perpetuation of an aspect of the conflict dynamic through which Hungarians in Romania maintain higher expectations about their status. Minority calls for autonomy and their rejection by the majority flared up again in 2003[27] and have continued to shape the conflict dynamic even after Romania became an EU member in 2007.

Bosnia-Herzegovina

Bosnia-Herzegovina is a multinational state in southeastern Europe that includes Bosnian Muslims (Bosniaks), Croats, and Serbs who in 1992–1995 fought the bloodiest war in recent European history. Since the 1995 Dayton Accords put an end to the violence, the state of Bosnia-Herzegovina has been comprised of the Bosniak-Croat Federation of Bosnia-Herzegovina and Republica Srpska. Multifaceted international intervention has been in place under the UN high representative for two decades, but nationalist elites continue to obstruct functioning of a viable state, tensions are high, and calls for secession have increased, especially from Republica Srpska.

Status change was important in the critical juncture (1987/89–1992) when the relations between Bosniaks, Serbs, and Croats were set on a course of war. Status change did not take place in the same manner as in the three cases examined extensively in this book, because Bosniaks, Croats, and Serbs had their own republics within Yugoslavia, and there were no clear political majorities to change the constitutional status of minorities. Yet, both Gagnon and Petersen claim that status changes were a core consideration for why the elites ultimately chose warfare. Gagnon argues that in the collision between reformists and conservatives in the League of Communists in Yugoslavia toward the end of the 1980s, the conservatives of Serbia aspired to centralize Yugoslavia under Serbian leadership.[28] To Bosniaks and Croats this meant their relative status would decrease. The conservatives around Milosevic, who became blatant nationalists, won against the more federally oriented elites, who were more respectful of ethnonational diversity. This triggered reactions: the proclamation of independence of Croatia in 1992 and Bosnia-Herzegovina in 1992, and more autonomous politics in Serbian and Croat ethnic pockets in Bosnia-Herzegovina that sought exclusive ethnic rule.[29] In Petersen's account, nationalist elites opted for the least cooperative option. None of the groups in an ethnically mixed Bosnia-Herzegovina wanted to live as second class citizens governed by groups considered equals in socialist Yugoslavia. Resentment tied to the imminent status change thus motivated many of the elite decisions.[30]

The inaction of the international community with regard to the disintegration of Yugoslavia in the early transition years, and large parts of the 1992–1995 war in Bosnia-Herzegovina has been widely discussed and need not be repeated here.[31] For the transferability of this book's arguments three points are important. First, after the critical juncture ended, international efforts to alter the course of conflict became less effective. The international community did not proactively design the "rules of the game" during the formative period, so it needed to exert much more effort to make a political difference in its aftermath. Second, Dayton's problematic institutional design reinforced the nationalist parties, and so continued to plague the polity despite multiple international calls to redesign the constitution and include more power for the central government.[32] Dayton was created "to end a war," as the book title of Richard Holbrooke, chief U.S. negotiator at Dayton, suggests, rather than to develop the institutions of a viable state.[33] Failure to decide the aim of this peace agreement at yet another critical juncture continues to require negotiation. For example, to respond to multiple policy deadlocks, in 1997 the so-called Bonn powers of the Office of the High Representative were introduced, through which individuals could be removed from office without appeal and laws could be passed by decree.[34] International agents continued to interact with local agents to reinforce stability and maintain the status quo rather than foster genuine reform. As Belloni argues, this focus made international actors prone to support "dysfunctional political structures" rather than "buttress the development of alternative political and social projects in civil society."[35] When international agents advocated reforms, local actors did not take them seriously. They knew that defusing such calls would not have major repercussions, and that they could threaten a serious policy move with secessionist claims.

Some aspects of the informally institutionalized dynamics continue to the present. Without explicitly speaking about the establishment of such informal aspects, Petersen argues that after Dayton the international actors created what he calls "taboos" for the local agents by drawing three lines in the sand: "Croats could not raise the issue of a third entity (to make them equal to the RS), Serbs could not raise the issue of secession, and Bosniaks could not develop a procedure enabling them to outvote the other groups." Local agents broke these "taboos" mostly through boycotts and other forms of defection.[36] Remarkably, these informal rules of what international agents permit and do not permit, and how local agents boycott them, continue to operate in the present. Scholars and policy-makers need to be on alert that adaptation mechanisms are in place that involve both domestic and international agents.

In contrast to the international community, the kin-states Serbia and Croatia had strong impacts on the formation of conflictual dynamics, since they were outwardly irredentists during the critical juncture, and supported to different degrees their brethren and nationalist leaders in Bosnia-Herzegovinia. Numerous Croatian and Serbian leaders, alongside the Bosniak ones, committed crimes against humanity in the Bosnian war and were subsequently indicted by the ICTY.[37] For more than a decade Serbia was accused of shielding two of the most wanted Bosnian Serb leaders, Radovan Karadzic and Ratko Mladic.[38] Karadzic was found in July 2008 in Belgrade working as a new-age healer under an assumed name, and Mladic was found in a village in northern Serbia in May 2011, also with a new identity.[39] Despite domestic opposition and protests, Serbia delivered them to the ICTY driven by its interests in moving toward EU integration.

Serbia and Croatia also harbored large numbers of refugees: 80 percent of Serb refugees went to Serbia proper, and 55 percent of Croat refugees to Croatia, while 95 percent of Bosniak refugees were dispersed across 25 host countries.[40] Hence, the informally institutionalized conflict dynamics in Bosnia-Herzegovina have been clearly intertwined with those of Serbia and Croatia.

The active kin-state involvement in Bosnia does not contradict the findings in the cases I examine, where the kin-states were not outwardly irredentist. Earlier I noted that irredentism has been largely on the decline since the end of the Cold War, but that some countries—among them Serbia, Croatia, and Armenia—have been outwardly irredentist.[41] With regard to path-dependence, active kin-state irredentism during the formative period could explain why internal warfare occurred much more quickly in Bosnia than in Kosovo or Macedonia, hence contributing to a better understanding of the *pace* of reaching warfare after a formative period ends.

A note is necessary about the promises of EU integration. The EU was not a major agent in Bosnia-Herzegovina's reconstruction until the early 2000s. Since 2002 the high representative also served as EU special representative to Bosnia-Herzegovina. After the 2003 Thessaloniki process, when the future of the Western Balkans was pronounced to be in the EU, strengthening governance and state-level institutions became criteria for Bosnia's advancement. The EU stepped farther in. An EU police mission took over from the UN-led International Police Task Force in 2003, and the EU Force Althea, a military deployment similar to the EU Concordia Mission in Macedonia, took over from the NATO-led stabilization force in 2004.[42] Negotiations for signing a Stabilization and Association Agreement—the first milestone toward EU enlargement—started in 2005, but were not concluded until 2008. Throughout this process, the EU signaled mixed messages about its commitment to Bosnia's accession,[43] and tied controversial police reform to the process.[44] The difficult progress toward police reform prompted UN high representative Miroslav Lajcak to assert his office's powers in 2007. His efforts were not entirely backed by the Javier Solana, head of EU's Common Foreign and Security Policy, who tried to diffuse tensions from threats to call a referendum on Republika Srpska's secession.[45] The "watered-down" package finally adopted established a "largely symbolic superstructure" at the state level that would assume power only after constitutional reforms.[46]

Two conclusions emerge here in line with this book's account. First, setting the stage for reforms while reneging on requirements under nationalist threats reinforces existing experience that reform means little and stability reigns. Local elites can view constitutional reforms as rhetorical opportunity structures to exploit for nationalist gains. Second, while "conditionality" and "socialization" are weak, what still takes place in Bosnia is "layering" of EU rules on top of existing nationalist ones. It is unclear to what degree practical attachments to the new rules are bringing in incremental change, but it is clear that the centrifugal tendencies among nationalist elites during the past couple of years have been thwarted by a general vision that each could benefit from EU membership.

Georgia

Georgia is a state in the Caucasus that underwent transition from communism after becoming independent from the Soviet Union in 1991. Adjara was the only region in Georgia that did not experience violent warfare after 1991.[47] There was large-scale violence in two of its three regions—South Ossetia (1991–1992, 2008) and Abkhazia (1992–1993, 2008). With Russia's support, these two regions gained de facto control of their territories in 2008 and started seeking international recognition as independent states.

Adjara experienced a relatively peaceful transition. A combination of preserved but informally increased minority status and co-optation during the formative period facilitated peace in Adjara. Adjara had been an autonomous republic within the Soviet Union because of the Muslim religion of its residents, rather than ethnolinguistic difference, as was commonly the case. During the critical juncture before and shortly after Georgia's independence, the Georgian political scene was dominated by the virulent anti-communism of Zviad Gamsakhurdia. Yet local relationships in Adjara were dominated by the Communist Party.[48] As Toft points out, this brought serious tension, and in 1990 Gamsakhurdia publicly threatened Adjara's autonomous status. Fearing that such threats could become reality, residents voted solidly for the communists, who still had more inclusive visions for minorities, and sidelined Gamsakurdia in the elections.[49] To establish control over the region in an alternative way, Gamsakhurdia decided to co-opt the local communist leader, Aslan Abashidze, trusting that he would abolish autonomy.[50] Abashidze certainly pledged Adjara's allegiance to Georgia, and reiterated that autonomy need not threaten the state's territorial integrity,[51] but he did not abolish it. Instead, as Wheatley points out, he used the 1992 outbreak of war in neighboring Abkhazia to consolidate his autocratic power.

Eduard Shevarnadze, the former communist leader who returned to rule Georgia after 1992, participated in this co-optation scheme by tolerating Adjara's leader because Abashidze provided stability in the region. Despite its officially subordinate status to Georgia, Adjara informally acquired "all the trappings of statehood," claims Wheatley, but not international recognition or UN membership. Abashidze captured the functioning of the entity, and was free to pursue his "foreign policy" toward Russia in a low-key manner. He maintained a corrupt and authoritarian status quo until the 2003 Rose Revolution, when, pressured by mass demonstrations, he stepped down and moved to Russia.[52]

A combination of diminished minority status and coercion led to full-fledged majority rejection of the state in Georgia's autonomous regions of South Ossetia and Abkhazia. The act of diminishing status was more important than the specific rights the regions enjoyed. South Ossetia had a lower status in the Soviet nationalities system as an autonomous *oblast* than Ajara and Abkhazia, which were autonomous *republics*, but Adjara's status was preserved while those of South Ossetia and Abkhazia were annulled in the escalating confrontations. Gamsakhurdia took a special interest in South Ossetia, organizing and participating in Georgian nationalist rallies because he considered the population mere recent immigrants. South Ossetian and Abkhazian elites, by contrast, saw the collapsing central power in Moscow and growing Georgian nationalism as a threat to their position. As Wheatley notes, in 1988 in South Ossetia protests intensified against a state proposal to adopt Georgian as a state language. Thus, their local communist councils pronounced in 1990 that they upgraded the status of their regions to independent republics within the Soviet Union.[53]

Seeking higher status in the Soviet federation resembled Kosovar demands to upgrade Kosovo to a federal unit within Yugoslavia. Georgia adamantly annulled these claims. In 1990 it abolished South Ossetia's autonomy and implemented coercive measures starting with the arrest of the newly elected chairman of the Ossetian parliament. This triggered a civil war that lasted a year and a half and caused hundreds of deaths. In Abkhazia, a temporary power sharing deal was developed for an electoral code to assure adequate representation of Abkhazians and local Georgians, but it was not honored for long. Nominally to protect railway tracks and hostages taken by the internal opposition, Georgian troops entered Abkhazia, and launched an attack on the capital. This coercive measure triggered a civil war that lasted thirteen months and resulted in hundreds of thousands of displaced persons and loss of Georgia's de facto control.[54]

The mechanism of "advantage of political incumbency" was also operational here, although Georgia was a country where the backbone of communism was apparently broken. The previous leader, Shevardnadze, returned quickly to power in 1992 and reinvigorated communist networks, which had already turned nationalist. Hence, Georgia was not an exception in the postcommunist space where unreformed former communists enforced more stringent antiminority policies, because their ideological foundations rejected the liberal paradigm, which included minority rights.

Compared to its involvement in Eastern Europe, the international community's role was minimal in the early conflicts in the Caucasus, leaving a political vacuum to be occupied by Russia. Covertly and overtly Russia intervened on behalf of the independence movements of South Ossetia and Abkhazia but not Adjara. Throughout the 1990s, there was some interest of international agents, but no long-term commitment. Georgia joined NATO's Partnership for Peace mission in 1994 and following the electoral 2003 Rose Revolution sought closer ties and possible NATO membership in the future. It also joined the Council of Europe in 1999, seeking further Western orientation. But from the early 1990s NATO and the EU unofficially considered some post-Soviet space Russia's preserve, allowing it to consolidate its grip over the region.

This book does not seek to diminish the importance of territorial pasts in developing of more radical minority claims as in South Ossetia and Abkhazia, alongside the two other cases just discussed.[55] It does point to the need to look beyond the claim making of nationalist elites and minorities, and to understand how agents adapt to each other's behavior and develop durable informal arrangements that are part of the conflict dynamics. Frozen conflicts in South Ossetia and Abkhazia are also anchored in informally institutionalized relationships established in that period: the regions had de facto independence but no official recognition, though they are currently recognized by Russia. These unofficial arrangements among all the actors involved—the Georgian government, the breakaway regions, the international community, and Russia—established conditions for flare-ups such as the low-level violence in South Ossetia in 2004[56] and the full-scale Georgian-Russian war in 2008. The latter was triggered by Georgia's attempt to reestablish sovereignty over South Ossetia.

When sidelined by Western powers in the negotiations over Kosovo's final status, Russia moved easily toward asserting its power over Abkhazia and South Ossetia. In 2007 foreign minister Sergey Lavrov warned that Kosovo's independence could set a precedent for two hundred other secessionist regions.[57] In early August 2008, six months after Kosovo's proclaimed independence, war broke out. Kosovo's independence was an exogenous shock that changed the equilibrium of the informally institutionalized dynamics. After a cease-fire signed later in August, Russia pulled most troops from the uncontested territory of Georgia but established security zones and checkpoints in Abkhazia and South Ossetia. Some aspects of the conflict dynamic changed, but others remained. The two territories remained largely unrecognized, but informally gained more independence. Russia's security presence remained. Russia recognized the secessionist territories officially, followed by Nicaragua and Venezuela in September 2008.[58]

Beyond the Postcommunist World

Path-dependence propositions can also be applied to other conflict regions. Minority-majority sequences may not evolve in the same manner as in my cases, not all mechanisms of conflict perpetuation and change may be operational in all conflicts, and exogenous shocks may have repercussions on some conflicts but not others. What is highly relevant to other conflicts is a focus on the sequences of agents' relationships during a critical juncture to understand where these relationships will consolidate after the juncture ends, and to factor the relative status change in these sequences. Informally institutionalized dynamics will be formed, be perpetuated in violent and seemingly nonviolent conflicts, and visibly or invisibly condition agents' behaviors. The contextualized aspects of these dynamics and the mechanisms that perpetuate them need to be clearly identified.

"Conditionality" and "socialization" are not unique to the EU, but pursued by major donors such as the IMF and World Bank and by other regional organizations, so one might consider these two mechanisms as instances of "layering" of new rules of the game on or beside existing ones rather than being aimed at policy change. "Layering" is politically attractive for policymakers, since it reduces opposition by agents who would face greater losses if reforms were introduced in their entirety.[59] One must consider also how these mechanisms address motivational structures conditioned by informally institutionalized dynamics. A 2008 Conciliatory Resources report on cases from Africa, Asia, Caucasus, Europe, Latin America, and the Middle East argued that external pressures are more likely to be effective when they respond to "the parties' own motivational structures."[60] These structures may be material or symbolic, as major scholarly accounts maintain. I argue that they also include internalized behavioral patterns over long periods of time, adaptations to relationships with domestic and international agents, and other contextualized specifics rarely discussed by scholars or addressed in policy-making.

Two "lessons" are relevant to other conflicts as well. The lesson that security and stability take precedence over democracy is not unique to the three cases in this book, nor to the postcommunist world. Democracy promotion became a widespread foreign policy tool for the United States and European countries after the end of the Cold War. But its appeal has been taken with cynicism in the developing world, not least because it has often been overridden by strategic concerns. A panel of Middle East experts gathered at Harvard's Kennedy School in April 2011 to discuss the "Arab Spring" reiterated that democracy promotion has for decades been faced with hostility in this region, not only because liberal values are often seen at odds with Islam, but because the word "democracy" has *lost its value* because of the strategic interests attached to it.[61] Democracy promotion may have acquired a slightly better name during the Arab Spring, but deep suspicion in the region remains. The second lesson relates to promoting minority rights while simultaneously securitizing them, especially after the 9/11 attacks. Securitization of minority rights empowers governments and alienates minorities, which often find reasons to exploit democracy for particularistic gains. The international community's behavioral cynicism toward democracy breeds cynicism in the local agents it wants to democratize.

At the time of completion of this work, profound political changes have swept parts of the Middle East, from relatively peaceful departures of long-term dictators in Tunisia and Egypt, to demonstrations that did not bring political change in Bahrain, Oman, and Yemen, to internal wars in Libya and Syria. Critics of historical institutionalism usually voice concern that scholars identify critical junctures ex post rather than ex ante. However, at this stage scholars and policy-makers can identify 2011–2012 as a time of critical juncture, given the fundamental changes destroying political structures and the volatility of relationships among the agents. The outcomes remain uncertain.

Although the focus has been on ethnonational problems and not religious conflicts, which confront much of the Middle East,[62] this work speaks to the political liberalization during the Arab Spring in two major ways. A first implication is that current agents' power advantages—most notably the Muslim Brotherhood, whose representative Mohamed Morsi was elected president of Egypt in June 2012, or militaries that were well organized before the demonstrations—could inaugurate sequences of policy decisions to reinforce majoritarian tendencies and decrease opportunities for

peaceful institutionalization of religious diversity over time.[63] Religious minorities could end up with fewer freedoms than before the regime change.
For example, the Copts of Egypt, a Christian population, fear that democratization could bring more oppression from radical Islamic groups. Muslim-
Christian violence erupted in a poor Cairo neighborhood in May 2011 after
false rumors that a Christian woman was prevented from converting to
Islam. The violence left twelve people dead.[64] Sequences of majority decisions could have major repercussions on how minorities react. The first
troublesome signs have appeared since Copts participated in the early demonstrations in Tahrir Square alongside Muslims, raising democratization
appeals, but after May 2011 their demonstrations accentuated more Christian symbols and rhetoric.

Relevance to Emerging Research Programs

This book's intellectual home lies in conflict studies, and historical institutionalism provided theoretical building blocks for the analysis, but its results are relevant to emerging research programs. It speaks to scholarship
on the former communist world, focusing on *legacies* to explain political
trajectories. The early transition literature was interested in legacies to account for the divergent performance of postcommunist states on the path
to democratization and market-oriented reforms. Several pre-communist
and communist legacies were identified, such as enduring backwardness,
interrupted nation-building, weak party systems during the interwar period, Leninist political legacies, and command economies.[65] With the accession of twelve new Eastern European members to the EU in 2004–2007,
the problematic development of countries in the Western Balkans, and the
consolidation of "competitive authoritarian regimes" in Russia, Central
Asia, and the Caucasus, the variety of political trajectories has grown and
sparked new interest in the causal impact of legacies.[66]

As Wittenberg points out, there are already two postcommunist periods—an early and a more recent one—so it is possible to identify the
uniquely postcommunist legacies that emerged in the 1990s and played
themselves out in the 2000s, in addition to pre-communist and communist
legacies.[67] Legacies are difficult to pin down because of the need to identify

institutions that persist despite different ruptures.[68] Some informally institutionalized conflict dynamics endure as important postcommunist legacies
despite major ruptures such as redefinition of statehood in Kosovo (1999)
and Macedonia (2001) and accession of Bulgaria into the EU (2007). It can
be argued that the continuity of majority-minority relationships is anchored in more durable pre-communist legacies, for example the nation-
building process in the nineteenth and early twentieth centuries.[69] I do not
reject this claim entirely, since nationalism emerged as a phenomenon in
southeastern Europe at that time. This book identifies a new legacy from
the postcommunist period: the international community exerted a unique
impact on majority-minority relations after the Cold War. Neither before
nor during communism was the international community so intensely focused on promoting democracy through a multitude of agents including
NGOs, a rather new political phenomenon. Furthermore, kin-states in Europe were irredentist during the interwar period, largely inactive during
communism, and generally less irredentist after 1989. These new features
of international policies, along with specific sequences of majority-minority
relations, interlocked during the formative period and created postcommunist legacies carried into the twenty-first century.

These new legacies are of utmost importance to the enlargement of the
EU to the Western Balkans. Most early enlargement literature discussed the
accession of the new members, making the assumption that democracy was
"the only game in town." Yet the violent conflicts and weak statehood in
the 1990s provide different initial conditions for EU integration of the
Western Balkans, which may prompt scholars to reconsider their original
assumptions and policy-makers to adopt different approaches. Future research could benefit from understanding the nature of the informally established links between domestic and international agents, and how they create
behavioral incentives toward continuity and change. In practical terms, this
requires a contextualized approach: during field visits to ask questions not
simply about material interests, symbolic politics, and formal institutions,
but about durable informal relationships associated with the conflicts and
how they constrain or enable behavior toward EU integration. Such questions could reveal specific conflict-diffusing informal practices between majorities and minorities,[70] or the existence of conflict networks and their
transnational linkages to other agents beyond the case in question. Such
linkages are invisible when questions traditional to conflict analysis are the

only ones asked. Informal dynamics, especially cross-border informal net-works, render a narrow case-based approach no longer appropriate. Schol-ars face the necessity to integrate transnational influences into scholarship on EU enlargement, not just focus on EU integration policies per se.

Research on informal institutions has been growing in the 2000s and especially after two landmark publications of Helmke and Levitsky in 2004 and 2006.[71] I initially justified the need to think about informally institu-tionalized conflict dynamics based on premises from this literature, arguing that in the postcommunist and developing world informal institutions such as clientelism and corruption abound and provide the actual, not the pre-scribed, rules of the political game.[72] Informal institutions emerge partly because formal institutions are often adopted as a result of pressure from Western liberal democracies and are not adequately adapted to local condi-tions, and partly because most states in these parts of the world lack the capacity to enforce the rule of law. Weak states open political spaces for informal coping strategies that elites and citizens enforce through repeated interactions.[73]

This research agenda, drawing on cases from all parts of the world, has been dominated by interest in explaining democratic performance and, more recently, the functioning of "competitive authoritarian regimes." Helmke, Levitsky, and their collaborators identify several informal institutions that compete with formal ones (corruption, clientelism, patrimonialism) or com-plement them (informal power sharing, shared expectations of politicians' past performance), which affect democratic accountability and governance.[74] As Levitsky and Way argue, informal institutions are a central feature of com-petitive authoritarian regimes, given the disjuncture between formal and actual behavior. Such regimes become sustained by institutionalized corrup-tion, informal mechanisms of repression, privatized violence to suppress the opposition, and strategies such as vote-buying and manipulation.[75]

Informally institutionalized conflict dynamics offer a new dimension when theorizing about democratic performance and competitive authori-tarian regimes. They also contribute to the growing understanding among some scholars working on postconflict reconstruction that informal ar-rangements matter.[76] Informal rules guiding interethnic relations are crucial to many developing societies, but are still marginal to these areas of re-search. In competitive authoritarianism most attention so far has been paid to successor politics, party behavior, media access, and evolution of eco-nomic policies. In postconflict reconstruction some attention has been paid to informal power-sharing norms. Considering informally institutionalized conflict dynamics provides an opportunity to integrate the role of international agents who establish durable informal relationships with domestic agents and support or thwart democratization by being part of path-dependent processes.

A final note is relevant to *policy-makers*. Identifying aspects of informally institutionalized conflict dynamics is crucial in fostering change. Informal relationships are usually dismissed because understanding them requires deep knowledge of a specific context, which international agents— seeking efficiency across multiple conflicts across the globe—have minimal capacity to pursue. Targeting *motivational structures* developed through these informally institutionalized conflict dynamics could offer a possible way out of the current impasse, when international agencies make vast expenditures to resolve conflicts but the conflicts continue to endure.

Notes

Introduction: Applying Path-Dependence, Timing, and Sequencing in Conflict Analysis

1. Republic of Kosovo Assembly, Kosovo Declaration of Independence.
2. Karon, "New Violence in Kosovo."
3. Voice of America, "Kosovo Violence Threatens Serbia's EU Aspirations."
4. Bilevsky, "Fears of New Ethnic Conflict in Bosnia."
5. *European Forum*, "Building of Church in Macedonia Leads to Ethnic Clashes."
6. *RFE/RL*, "Albanian, Macedonian Presidents Call for Calm After Murders."
7. *Novinite*, May 24, 2011.
8. I use the designation "Kosovo" because this wording has gained traction in earlier works on international affairs. Kosova is the designation of the new state-information, which to date has not been fully recognized internationally.
9. For exceptions see Saideman and Ayres, *For Kin or Country*; Jenne, *Ethnic Bargaining*; Toft, *The Geography of Ethnic Violence*; Petersen, *Understanding Ethnic Violence*, and Resistance and Rebellion; Varshney, *Ethnic Conflict and Civic Life*.
10. Fearon and Laitin, "Ethnicity, Insurgency, and Civil War," 88.
11. Lotta Harbom and Peter Wallensteen, quoted in Kalyvas, *The Logic of Violence in Civil War*, 16.
12. On selection bias see King, Keohane, and Verba, *Designing Social Inquiry*; Brady and Collier, *Rethinking Social Inquiry*.
13. On microdynamics of conflicts see Tilly, *The Politics of Collective Violence*; Kalyvas, *The Logic of Violence in Civil War*; Jeremy Weinstein, *Inside Rebellion*; Fujii, *Killing Neighbors*; Stroschein, *Ethnic Struggle*.
14. Gurr, *Peoples Versus States*, 71; Davenport, "The Weight of the Past"; Gurr and Moore, "Ethnopolitical Rebellion."
15. *Novinite*, "Macedonians, Albanians Clash."
16. "International community" designates states and governmental and NGOs not bound by kin to the majority or minority.
17. Pierson, *Politics in Time*; "Big, Slow Moving and Invisible"; "Increasing Returns"; "Not Just What But When."
18. Tilly, *Big Structures, Large Processes, Huge Comparisons*, 14.

19. Collier and Collier, *Shaping the Political Arena*, 27.

20. Capoccia and Kelemen, "The Study of Critical Junctures," 348.

21. On critical junctures as choice points see Mahoney, "Path-Dependent Explanations," 113; on the difficulty of altering trajectories see Pierson, *Politics in Time*, 135.

22. Pierson, "Increasing Returns," 251–52.

23. Pierson, "Not Just What But When," 74.

24. Mahoney, "Path Dependence in Historical Sociology," 526–27.

25. Thelen, "Timing and Temporality," 103; on revolutions: Skocpol, *States and Social Revolutions*; Goldstone, *Revolution and Rebellion*; on democratization and regime change: Mahoney, *The Legacies of Liberalism*; Collier and Collier, *Shaping the Political Arena*; Luebbert, *Liberalism, Fascism, or Social Democracy*; on institutional development: Hall and Soskice, *Varieties of Capitalism*; Ziblatt, *Structuring the State*; Thelen, How Institutions Evolve; Karl, *The Paradox of Plenty*; Pierson, *Dismantling the Welfare State?*

26. On a recent proposition to use historical institutionalism in conflict analysis see Stroschein, *Ethnic Struggle*, 23846.

27. Collier and Sambanis, "Understanding Civil War," 5.

28. Ruane and Todd, "The Roots of Intense Ethnic Conflict"; Hassner, "The Path to Intractability"; rejoinder by Goddard, Pressman, and Hassner, "Time and the Intractability of Territorial Disputes"; Ruane and Todd, *The Dynamics of Conflict in Northern Ireland*.

29. Arifi, "Spontaneous Interethnic Order," 564.

30. Laver and Shepsle, "Events, Equilibria, and Government Survival." On rather exceptional problem-driven research analyzed through rational choice games, see Bates et al., *Analytic Narratives*.

31. Streeck and Thelen, *Beyond Continuity*; Thelen, *How Institutions Evolve*; Crouch and Farrell, "Breaking the Path for Institutional Development"; For conflict analysis see Stroschein, *Ethnic Struggle*.

32. Mahoney and Rueschemeyer, "Comparative Historical Analysis," 11.

33. Pierson, "Not Just What But When," 79.

34. Horowitz, *Ethnic Groups in Conflict*, 85.

35. Kalyvas, *The Logic of Violence in Civil War*, 19.

36. Ibid.; Valentino, *Final Solutions*; Davenport, *Paths to State Repression*.

37. Przeworski and Teune, *The Logic of Comparative Social Inquiry*.

38. George and Bennett, *Case Studies and Theory Development*, 206.

39. Ibid., 157–63.

40. Ibid., 137.

41. I used sources primarily in Bulgarian, English, and Macedonian, but occasionally Bosnian/Croatian/Serbian, German, and Italian.

42. Crawford, *East Central European Politics Today*, 164–69.

43. Schmitter, "Peoples and Boundaries in the Process of Democratization," 6.

44. This is a variation of V. P. Gagnon's argument developed in the context of conflicts in Serbia and Croatia, *The Myth of Ethnic War.*

45. Ibid., 7, 52–86.

46. Gurr, *Why Men Rebel; Peoples Versus States.*

47. Marshall and Gurr, *Peace and Conflict;* Walter, "Information, Uncertainty, and Decision to Secede," 122; Petersen, *Understanding Ethnic Violence.*

48. Basic premises of statehood—internal legal or domestic sovereignty—can potentially be challenged under pressure from minority elites and their external allies. Stephen Krasner (*Sovereignty*, 4) maintains that international legal sovereignty "refers to the practices associated with mutual recognition usually between territorial entities that have formal juridical independence," whereas "domestic sovereignty refers to formal organization of political authority within the state and the ability of public authorities to exercise effective control within the borders of their own polity." I also consider domestic sovereignty under threat when the formal organization of the state remains the same and the state can still exercise control within its borders, but there are well organized clandestine informal groups capable of challenging the existing order.

49. Kymlicka, "Justice and Security in the Accommodation of Minority Nationalism."

50. Koinova, "Kinstate Intervention in Ethnic Conflicts"; Saideman and Ayres, *For Kin or Country.*

51. Axelrod, *Evolution of Cooperation;* Jervis, "Cooperation Under the Security Dilemma"; Fearon and Laitin, "Explaining Interethnic Cooperation"; Glaser, "The Security Dilemma Revisited"; Stuart Kaufman, "Symbolic Politics or Rational Choice?"

52. Varshney, *Ethnic Conflict and Civic Life;* Ruane and Todd, *The Dynamics of Conflict.*

53. Daniel Brinks (2003) quoted in Helmke and Levitsky, *Informal Institutions and Democracy*, 5.

54. Goddard, Pressman, and Hassner, "Time and the Intractability of Territorial Disputes," 197.

55. Helmke and Levitsky, "Informal Institutions and Comparative Politics," 725–26.

56. On "informal institutions" in Latin America see also O'Donnell, "Another Institutionalization."

57. Mitev, "Sociological Study"; Zhelyazkova, "The Bulgarian Ethnic Model"; Paltchev, *Ahmed Dogan.* Bernd Rechel problematized some of these findings in "The Bulgarian Ethnic Model: Ideology or Reality?"

58. On Northern Ireland: Ruane and Todd, *The Dynamics of Conflict;* on intractable conflicts: Hassner, "The Path to Intractability," 128–30.

59. In Pierson the mechanism is called "advantage of political authority" ("Not Just What But When," 81). I slightly adapted the name to point to the incumbency aspect, which can be crucial in a transition process.

60. Mahoney, "Path-Dependence," 523.

61. Peter Hall quoted by Pierson, "When Effects Become a Cause," 613.

62. Mahoney and Thelen, *Explaining Institutional Change*, 21.

63. A 2011 poll showed that 45.4 percent of Macedonians mistrust Albanians, and 43.4 percent of Albanians mistrust Macedonians. Macedonians estimate inter-ethnic relations as similar to prior to the 2001 warfare; Albanians consider them slightly better. See Klekovski, "Inter-Ethnic Relations in Macedonia."

64. Varangis et al., "Exogenous Shocks in Low Income Countries."

65. See Mahoney and Thelen, *Explaining Institutional Change*, 15. I use "replacement" to emphasize new rules in place of old ones, and to avoid associations with displacement of populations within and across borders.

66. Pierson, "Not Just What But When," 72.

67. Zartman, *Ripe for Resolution*; Zartman, "Ripeness."

68. Kriesberg and Thorson, Timing the De-Escalation of International Conflicts.

69. Mansfield and Snyder, *Electing to Fight*, 18.

70. Hassner, "The Path to Intractability," 113, 128–30.

71. Collier and Hoeffler, "On the Incidence of Civil War in Africa"; Elbadawi and Sambanis, "How Much War Will We See?"; Fearon and Laitin, "Ethnicity, Insurgency, and Civil War"; Davenport, Armstrong, and Lichbach, "Conflict Escalation and the Origins of Civil War."

72. Linz and Stepan, "Political Identities and Electoral Sequences," 124–25.

73. Snyder, *From Voting to Violence*, 37–71.

74. Mansfield and Snyder, *Electing to Fight*, 4.

75. Bunce, "Rethinking Recent Democratization," 177.

76. Stroschein, *Ethnic Struggle*, 246.

77. BBC Monitoring Service, October 4, 2001.

78. U.S. Department of State, *Country Reports: Macedonia*, 2004.

79. Minority Rights Group, World Directory, 252.

80. On ethnolinguistic fractionalization see Fearon, Kasara, and Laitin, "Ethnic Minority Rule and Civil War Onset"; Hegre and Sambanis, "Sensitivity of Empirical Results," 515; Fearon and Laitin, "Ethnicity, Insurgency, and Civil War"; Elbadawi and Sambanis, "How Much War Will We See?"; Collier and Hoeffler, "On Economic Causes of Civil War."

81. Walter, "Information, Uncertainty," 111.

82. On ethnic polarization see Montalvo and Reynal-Querol, "Ethnic Polarization, Potential Conflict, and Civil Wars"; Collier, "Implications of Ethnic Diversity"; Reynal-Querol, "Ethnicity, Political Systems, and Civil Wars"; Esteban and Ray, "On the Measurement of Polarization"; Horowitz, *Ethnic Groups in Conflict*, 12.

83. Toft, "Indivisible Territory, Geography, Concentration, and Ethnic War."

84. Critics of the Ethno-Linguistic Fractionalization Index include Kalyvas, "Ethnic Defection in Civil War"; Cederman and Girardin, "Beyond Fractionalization"; Chandra and Wilkinson, "Measuring the Effect of Ethnicity."

85. Kelley, *Ethnic Politics in Europe*; Vachudova, *Europe Undivided*.

Chapter 1. The Majority-Minority Relationship and the Formation
of Informally Institutionalized Conflict Dynamics

1. On minority rights see Thornberry, *Minorities and Human Rights Law*; Miall, *Minority Rights in Europe*; Kymlicka, *Multicultural Citizenship*. On electoral rules see Reilly and Reynolds, *Electoral Systems and Conflict*. On power-sharing and territorial pluralism see Lijphart, *Democracy in Plural Societies*; McGarry and O'Leary, *The Politics of Ethnic Conflict Regulation*; Horowitz, "Democracy in Divided Societies"; Montville, *Conflict and Peacemaking in Multiethnic Societies*; Lapidoth, *Flexible Solutions to Ethnic Conflicts*.

2. O'Leary, "The Realism of Power-Sharing," xviii–xix.

3. Lustick, Miodownik, and Eidelson, "Secessionism in Multicultural States," 223. On increased chances for secessionism Cornell, "Autonomy as a Source of Conflict"; Hale, "The Parade of Sovereignties"; Hechter, "Nationalism and Rationality"; Safran, "Non-Separatist Policies Regarding Ethnic Minorities."

4. Elkins and Sides, "Can Institutions Build Unity in Multiethnic States," 693–94.

5. Snyder, *From Voting to Violence*, 2000; Mansfield and Snyder, *Electing to Fight*, 2005; Hegre, and Sambanis, "Sensitivity," 2006; Ellingen, "Colorful Community or Ethnic Witches Brew?"; Mousseau, "Democratizing with Ethnic Divisions"; Hegre, Ellingsen, Gates, and Gleditsch, "Toward a Democratic Civil Peace?"

6. Offe, "Capitalism by Democratic Design."

7. Gagnon, "Ethnic Nationalism and International Conflict," 132.

8. Snyder and Ballentine, "Nationalism and the Marketplace of Ideas."

9. Rotberg, ed., *State Failure and State Weakness*, 4.

10. Hughes, *Chechnya*, 2–3.

11. Kaplan, *Balkan Ghosts*.

12. Petersen, *Understanding Ethnic Violence*, 23–31.

13. Kalyvas, *The Logic of Violence*.

14. Kaufman, "Symbolic Politics or Rational Choice?" 81–86; Grigorian and Kaufman, "Hate Narratives and Ethnic Conflict."

15. Csergo, *Talk of the Nation*, 5–7.

16. Laitin, "Language Conflict and Violence," 1.

17. Ibid., 1–3; Geertz, *The Interpretation of Cultures*; Horowitz, *Ethnic Groups in Conflict*; Gurr, "Minorities at Risk."

18. Laitin, "Language Conflict and Violence," 1–17; the similarity-breeds-conflict thesis confirmed on interstate level by Henderson, "Culture or Contiguity?"

19. Huntington, "The Clash of Civilizations"; *The Clash of Civilizations and the Remaking of World Order*. On his critics see White, Oates, and Miller, "The 'Clash of Civilizations' and Post-Communist Europe"; Fox, "Two Civilizations and Ethnic Conflict"; Gurr, "Peoples Against the State."

20. This statement was formulated by Catholic Albanian intellectual Pashko Vasa (1825–1892), but was adopted by the majority of Albanians.

21. Collier and Hoeffler, "Greed and Grievance," 2000; Fearon and Laitin, "Ethnicity, Insurgency, and Civil War."

22. Sambanis, "Do Ethnic and Non-Ethnic Civil Wars Have the Same Causes?" 266; Håvard, Ellingsen, Gates, and Gleditsch, "Toward a Democratic Civil Peace?"

23. Collier and Sambanis, "Civil War: A New Agenda," 10.

24. Elbadawi and Sambanis, "How Much War," 307–11.

25. Bhaumik, Kumar, Gang, and Yun, "Ethnic Conflict and Economic Disparity," 756.

26. Ramet, *Nationalism and Federalism*, 199.

27. Konstitutsia na Narodna Republika Bulgaria [Constitution of the People's Republic of Bulgaria] (1971) 25, Art. 45 (7).

28. Dimitrijevic, "The 1974 Constitution as a Factor of Totalitarianism," 15.

29. Constitution of the Socialist Federal Republic of Yugoslavia, 27.

30. Judah, *Kosovo: What Everyone Needs to Know*, 57.

31. Malcolm, *Kosovo: A Short History*, 327.

32. Sluzhben Vennik na Socialisticka Republika Macedonia [Constitution of the Socialist Republic of Macedonia], Preamble.

33. Perry, "The Republic of Macedonia," 253.

34. Poulton, *The Balkans, Minorities and States in Conflict*, 78–79.

35. Ibid.

36. Konstitutsia na Narodnata Republika Bulgaria 25, Art. 49.

37. Eminov, *Muslim Minorities*, 127.

38. Lenkova, *Turks of Bulgaria*.

39. The assimilation campaign has been well discussed by Poulton, *Minorities and States*, 132–35; Eminov, *Muslim Minorities*, 60–61; Crampton, *A Concise History of Bulgaria*, 210; Nedeva-Atanassova, *Assimilating Muslims in Communist Bulgaria*.

40. Höpken, "From Religious Identity to Ethnic Mobilization," 71.

41. Poulton, *Minorities and States*, 65.

42. Schöpflin, "The Rise and Fall of Yugoslavia."

43. Serbian national myth has two historical identity elements related tó Kosovo. The 1389 Battle at Kosovo Polje between Serbs and invading Ottoman Turks is considered a cornerstone in Serbian history and the struggle for national liberation from the Ottomans. During the Serbian medieval empire, the Serbian Orthodox Church Patriarchate was based in Peć in Kosovo and continues to be considered a "holy place" for the Serbs. See Anzulovic, *Heavenly Serbia*.

44. Vickers, *Between Serb and Albanian*, 76.

45. Ibid., 221.

46. Ibid.; Glenny, *The Balkans*, 625.

47. Jansen, "Albanians and Serbs in Kosovo."

48. On April 24, 1987, Milosevic arrived in Kosovo to hear several complaints of local Serbian activists. He intervened in a fight between Serbs and local police, and

gave an emotional speech defending the "sacred" rights of Serbs in Kosovo. Malcolm, *Kosovo: A Short History*, 341–42.

49. Due to its vulnerability to internal and external ethnic conflict with irredentist neighbors, Macedonia's name was used for a "syndrome" in international politics. See Weiner, "The Macedonian Syndrome."

50. The formation of the Macedonian nation is one of the most controversial issues in the study of Balkan nationalisms. Macedonian historiography claims the nation was rooted in ancient times when Alexander the Great ruled over the Macedonian lands; other scholars consider this a nationalist narrative based on mythology, and that Macedonian nationalism was formed during the modernization period. Macedonia was certainly competed over by Bulgarians, Greeks, and Serbs mobilized through their respective Orthodox churches. Scholars argue over whether the Macedonian nation was formed: right after the end of the Russo-Turkish war in 1878 when Macedonia failed to be incorporated into the newly formed Bulgarian state; in 1903 when the Ilinden Uprising took place and the Krushevo Republic was proclaimed; or when the Macedonian language was first officially codified after World War II and Macedonia first allotted territory as a republic in the SFRY. In any case, Macedonian nationalism developed later than many nationalisms of neighboring states, and may be considered "young" in comparison. For more on the history of Macedonia see Danforth, *The Macedonian Conflict*; and Rossos, *Macedonia and the Macedonians*.

51. Poulton, *Minorities and States*, 78.

52. Ibid., 79.

53. Phillips, *Macedonia: Warlords and Rebels in the Balkans*, 45.

54. Poulton, *Who Are the Macedonians?* 128–29.

55. Koinova with Gigova, *Albanians of Macedonia*.

56. Pierson, "Increasing Returns," 251–52.

57. Capoccia and Kelemen, "Critical Junctures," 348.

58. Collier and Collier, *Shaping the Political Arena*, and Mahoney "Path-Dependent Explanations," stress that choices are embedded in antecedent conditions; Pierson, *Politics in Time* and especially Capoccia and Kelemen downplay this aspect.

59. Pierson, *Politics in Time*, 51.

60. Vickers, *Between Serb and Albanian*, 77–94.

61. Judah, *Kosovo: What Everyone Needs to Know*, 41–51.

62. Roeder, "Peoples and States After 1989."

63. Collier and Sambanis, "Understanding Civil War," 5.

64. Koinova, "Kosovo Albanians."

65. Koinova, *Muslims of Bulgaria*.

66. Doder and Branson, *Milosevic: Portrait of a Tyrant*, 45.

67. Mertus, *Kosovo: How Myths and Truths*, 295; Grigoryan, "Third Parties and State-Minority Conflicts," 86.

68. Gagnon, "Ethnic Nationalism," 148.

69. I am grateful to V. P. Gagnon for making this point; personal correspondence, March 2009.

70. Daskalovski, "Democratization in Macedonia and Slovenia," 28.

71. Iso Rusi, Director, Helsinki Committee of Macedonia, telephone interview, April 6, 2009.

72. Ibid.

73. Poulton, *Who Are the Macedonians?* 172–73; Rusi, interview.

74. Rusi, interview.

75. Mihail Ivanov, former advisor to President Zhelyu Zhelev (1990–1997), Lecturer in Ethnic Politics at the New Bulgarian University, and Associate Professor in Physics in the Bulgarian Academy of Sciences, telephone interview, March 29, 2009.

76. Such attempts at nationalist restoration included passage of a declaration that the Turkish language should be used only informally in daily activities, and that old Islamic names should be restored only through the courts, which would create significant obstacles for those affected.

77. Ivanov, telephone interview, March 2009.

78. Krassimir Kanev, Director of Bulgarian Helsinki Committee, email with author, March 24, 2009.

79. Rechel, *The Long Way Back to Europe*, 148.

80. Linz and Stepan, *Problems of Democratic Transition*.

81. Poulton, *Who Are the Macedonians?* 175; Bugajski, *Ethnic Politics in Eastern Europe*, 116–17.

82. Bugajski, *Ethnic Politics in Eastern Europe*, 124.

83. These pressures will be discussed further in Chapter 4.

84. In its statute, the MRF claimed to be an "independent public-political organization." Source: Supreme Court of the Republic of Bulgaria, Decision 636, September 20, 1991. The statute did not mention that the MRF was based in the Turkish minority, but aimed to defend the human rights of the different ethnic communities in Bulgaria. This formulation allowed the opening of legal doors for its registration, though it was widely known that the group was based mainly among the Turkish minority. After serious international pressure by the U.S., EC members, and Turkey the MRF was registered as a "movement" on the basis of the 1990 electoral law, and took part in the founding general elections; Poulton, *Minorities and States*, 167.

85. *Keesing's Record of World Events*.

86. Jervis, "Cooperation Under the Security Dilemma." See also Posen, "Security Dilemma"; Snyder and Jervis "Civil War and the Security Dilemma."

87. Fearon, "Commitment Problems," 108, 121; see also Fearon, "Rationalist Explanations for War."

88. Kostovicova, *Parallel Worlds*, 25.

89. Poulton, *Who Are the Macedonians?* 133.

90. Anonymous, author's interview, August 7, 2008, Sofia.

91. Lijphart and Waisman, eds., *Institutional Design*; Linz and Stepan, *Problems of Democratic Transition*.

92. Elster, "Introduction," 8.

93. Wiatr, "Executive-Legislative Relations in Crisis," 105.

94. Petersen, *Resistance and Rebellion*, 298; Gurr, *Peoples Versus States*, 69; Gurr, *Why Men Rebel*, 24–37.

95. On threshold-based safety calculations by potential rebels when engaging in collective action, see Petersen, *Resistance and Rebellion*, 22–23.

96. The Bulgarian and Macedonian constitutions were passed in 1991, the Serbian one incorporating Kosovo in 1990, and that of Federal Yugoslavia (Serbia and Montenegro) in 1992.

97. Constitution of the Republic of Macedonia, 1991, Preamble.

98. These two issues were amended by the Ohrid Framework Agreement, the peace agreement that ended the 2001 warfare in Macedonia.

99. Constitution of Bulgaria, 1991, Art. 29 (1).

100. Ibid., Art. 54 (1).

101. Anonymous, author's interview, November 2000, Sofia; Krassimir Kanev, Director of the Bulgarian Helsinki Committee, author's interview, Sofia, December 21, 2000.

102. Poulton, *Who Are the Macedonians?* 122.

103. Malcolm, *Kosovo: A Short History*, 343–44.

104. Constitution of Bulgaria, 1991, Art. 11 (4).

105. Constitution of Macedonia, 1991, Art. 13 (3, 4).

106. Constitution of Bulgaria, 1991, Art. 2 (1).

107. Ibid., Art. 36 (2).

108. Constitution of Macedonia, 1991, Art. 48 (4).

109. Constitution of Serbia, 1990, Art. 32 (4).

110. Constitution of Macedonia, 1991, Art. 48 (4); Constitution of Serbia, 1990, Art. 32 (4).

111. O'Leary ("The Elements of Right-Sizing," 38–39) considers both "coercion" and "co-optation" part of the "control" mechanism. To surmount the difficulties with these mechanisms, controllers must "organize the dominant group and disorganize the dominated."

112. International Helsinki Federation, *Annual Report* (1997), 29.

113. Helsinki Watch, *Yugoslavia: Human Rights Abuses in Kosovo*, 17.

114. Human Rights Watch, *Open Wounds*, 61.

115. International Helsinki Federation, *Annual Report*, Art. 298 (1996), 209.

116. Lustick, *Arabs in the Jewish State*, 230.

117. Petai and Hallik, "Understanding Processes of Ethnic Control," 520.

118. Bikov, *Dosieto na Dogan* [Dogan's File].

119. I am grateful to Ivan Krastev, Director of the Center for Liberal Strategies, Sofia, for making this point.

120. Lijphart, *Democracy in Plural Societies*, 25.

121. In 1992, a four-party coalition was appointed consisting of Social Democrats, Liberals, PDP, and Socialists. The Albanians held five ministerial and three deputy posts.

122. O'Leary, "The Elements of Right-Sizing," 43.

123. In Bulgaria, the founding elections for a Grand National Assembly took place under a more open mixed proportional majoritarian formula. Flores Juberias, "Electoral Systems in Eastern Europe," 98; Agh, *Emerging Democracies*, 241

124. Goati, "The Impact of Parliamentary Democracy," 72; Reilly and Reynolds, *Electoral Systems and Conflict*, 15.

125. International Crisis Group, *Macedonia's Ethnic Albanians*, 11.

126. Malcolm, *Kosovo: A Short History*, 346; ICG, "Kosovo Briefing," February 17, 1998, 36.

127. Malcolm, *Kosovo: A Short History*, 347.

128. Kostovicova, *Parallel Worlds*, 37.

129. Lebow, *Forbidden Fruit*, 24.

130. On counterfactuals see also Lebow, "What's So Different About a Counterfactual?" 5.

131. Bugajski, *Ethnic Politics*, 124.

132. Ibid., 116.

133. Daskalovski, *Walking on the Edge*, 62.

134. S. Ramet, *Balkan Babel*, 235.

135. Bugajski, *Ethnic Politics*, 116.

136. For more on the impact of international organizations see Chapter 4.

137. Dogan, *Bulgaria i noviat svetoven red* [Bulgaria and the New World Order].

138. Kanev, "From Totalitarianism to Constitutional State," 62.

139. Krassimir Kanev, interview, Sofia, October 2000.

140. Roeder, "Peoples and States After 1989"; Bunce, "Minority Politics in Ethno-Federal States"; Bunce, *Subversive Institutions*; Beissinger, *Nationalist Mobilization*; Toft, *Geography*.

141. Bunce, "Minority Politics in Ethno-Federal States," 51.

Chapter 2. Self-Reinforcing Processes in the Majority-Minority Relationship

1. See discussion in Introduction, 8.

2. Ruane and Todd, *Dynamics of Conflict*, 3.

3. Hassner, "The Path to Intractability," 113, and response to rejoinders in Goddard, Pressman, and Hassner, "Time and Intractability of Territorial Disputes," 197.

4. On increasing returns see Arthur, *Increasing Returns and Path Dependence*. On applications of economic principles of increasing returns to institution-building see North, "Institutions and Credible Commitment." On application of economic principles on positive feedback to political science see Pierson, "Increasing Returns."

5. See Pierson "Not Just What But When," and discussion in Introduction.

6. Thelen, "Timing and Temporality," 103.

7. "Logic of appropriateness" is used by March and Olsen, "The New Institutionalism."

8. Mahoney, "Path Dependence," 523.

9. For discussion in the Eastern European context see Schimmelfennig and Sedelmeier, *The Europeanization of Central and Eastern Europe*.

10. Eminov, *Turkish and Other Muslim Minorities*, 168.

11. They challenged Art. 11 (4) of the 1991 Constitution, prohibiting formation of political parties on an ethnic or religious basis, and Art. 44 (2) prohibiting formation of organizations that threaten sovereignty and territorial integrity of the state.

12. Eminov, *Turkish and Other Muslim Minorities*, 170.

13. Ibid., 138–40; Kanev, email correspondence, January 20–21, 2001.

14. Bulgarian Helsinki Committee, *Human Rights in Bulgaria in 1996*, 10.

15. UNDP, *Bulgaria 2000*, 21.

16. Anonymous government official, author's interview, September 2000, Skopje.

17. S. Ramet, *Balkan Babel*, 235; Perry, "The Republic of Macedonia," 253.

18. Council of Europe, *The Former Yugoslav Republic of Macedonia*, 23–24.

19. Albert Musliu, Director, Association for Democratic Initiatives, author's interview, September 4, 2000, Gostivar, Macedonia.

20. Abrahams, *A Threat to "Stability"*, 30.

21. Eran Frankel quoted in Koinova, *Muslims of Macedonia*.

22. Najceska, Simoska, and Gaber, "Muslims, State and Society," 84–88; Gaber, "The Muslim Population in FYROM," 106.

23. Maliqi, "Albanians Between East and West," 117.

24. S. Ramet, "The Serbian Church and the Serbian Nation," 118–19.

25. U.S. Department of State, *Annual Report on International Religious Freedom for 1999: Serbia-Montenegro*.

26. Kostovicova, *Parallel Worlds*, 32–35.

27. Lutovac, "All Serbian and Albanian 'Elections' in Kosovo."

28. Lucic, *An Insider Looks at the November 1996 Elections*, 5. The author was a member of the Federal Electoral Commission representing the People's Party of Montenegro.

29. Troxel, "Socialist Persistence," 424.

30. RFE/RL quoted in Troebst, "Nationalismus als Demokratisierungshemmnis in Bulgarien," 211.

31. Anonymous, author's interview, November 2000, Sofia; Kanev interview, 2000, Sofia.

32. Kanev interview, 2000.

33. Turkish Democratic Party, *Program Declaration*.

34. Ljubomir Frckoski, professor of law at Skopje University, former minister of interior, and former presidential candidate, author's interview, September 15, 2000, Skopje.

35. Ministry of Foreign Affairs, *Facts About National Minorities in the Republic of Macedonia*.

36. Fekrat et al. (1999), quoted in Daskalovski, *Walking on the Edge*, 63; for a detailed recollection of the events in Gostivar and Tetovo in 1994–1995 see Nefotistos, *The Risk of War*.

37. HRW, *A Threat to "Stability"*, 51–52.

38. Amnesty International, *Annual Report for 1998*, Macedonia, 240; HRW, *Police Violence in Macedonia*, 19.

39. The first formal discussions of "ethnic outbidding" can be found in Rabushka and Shepsle, *Politics in Plural Societies*.

40. Szajkowski, "Elections and Electoral Politics," 55.

41. Ortakovski, *Minorities in the Balkans*, 353; Poulton, *Who Are the Macedonians?* 97.

42. S. Ramet, "Balkan Babel," 235.

43. Schmidt, "Show Trials in Kosovo," 36–37.

44. Ibid., 37; Orosi, "The Pristina Show Trials," 10.

45. U.S. Department of State, *Annual Report, Serbia, 1999*.

46. According to prime minister in exile Bujar Bukoshi, six ministries existed under his guidance, covering education, health, information, finance, foreign affairs, and justice ("Conversations with Contemporaries," 468). In an explosive situation after Kosovo Albanian medical personnel, teachers, miners, and other laborers lost their jobs under Milosevic's "emergency measures," the parallel institutions provided functional autonomy and a certain degree of stability. President Rugova and Prime Minister Bukoshi played very important roles, as did the educational and medical structures. The parliament and ministries of interior and defense were weak. Sports and arts clubs, media, and trade unions fulfilled mainly organizational functions. Reuter, "Die politische Entwicklung in Kosovo 1992/1993."

47. ICG, *Kosovo Spring*, 16.

48. Bujar Bukoshi, former prime minister of the Government of Kosovo in Exile, author's interview, October 7, 2002, Prishtina.

49. Kostovicova, *Parallel Worlds*, 64.

50. For other sequence-based arguments with regard to the early years of the transition process, see Introduction; Snyder, *From Voting to Violence*; Bunce, "Rethinking Recent Democratization"; Mansfield and Snyder, "Electing to Fight."

51. Kanev, interview, 2001.

52. Lenkova, *Turks of Bulgaria*, 1999.

53. Poulton and Taji-Farouki, *Muslim Identity and the Balkan State*, 81.

54. Kostovicova, *Parallel Worlds*, 43.

55. Gessen, "The Parallel University," 32–33.

56. ICG, *Kosovo Spring*, 28.

57. Ibid.

58. Ibid., 29–30.

59. Judah, *Kosovo: War and Revenge*, 136.

60. Albin Kurti, in his capacity as former leader of the student demonstrations, author's interview, Prishtina, October 3, 2002.

Chapter 3. International Intervention During the Formative Period

1. On interests and internationalization: Carment, James, and Taydas, "The Internationalization of Ethnic Conflict."

2. Relevant works are discussed later in this chapter.

3. Maoz, "Domestic Political Change and Strategic Response," 119.

4. On conflict management: Lake and Rothchild, "Containing Fear"; on democracy promotion: Whitehead, "Three International Dimensions of Democratization"; Schmitter, "The Influence of the International Context."

5. On control (here called "coercive regulation") consent, and contagion: Whitehead "Three International Dimensions of Democratization."

6. On conditionality: Schmitter, "The Influence of the International Context," 29.

7. On early intervention: Edmead, *Analysis and Prediction*; on early warning: Carment and Schnabel, *Conflict Prevention*; on mediation: Northedge and Donelan, *International Disputes*.

8. Regan, "Third Party Interventions and the Duration of Intrastate Conflict," 72. See also Elbadawi and Sambanis, "External Interventions and the Duration of Civil Wars"; Collier et al., *Breaking the Conflict Trap*; Balch-Lindsay, Enterline, and Joyce, "Third Party Intervention and the Civil War Process."

9. On "ripeness" and "mutually hurting stalemate": Zartman, *Ripe for Resolution*; on timing and sequences of developments: Kriesberg, "Introduction."

10. Bercovitch, "Mediation in International Conflict," 145.

11. Regan and Stam, "In The Nick of Time."

12. Jenne, "A Bargaining Theory of Minority Demands."

13. Cetinyan, "Ethnic Bargaining," 647–48.

14. Thyne,"Cheap Signals with Costly Consequences."

15. Grigoryan, "Third-Party Intervention."

16. Schimmelfennig and Sedelmeier, *The Europeanization of Central and Eastern Europe*.

17. Moravcsik and Vachudova, "National Interests, State Power, and EU Enlargement."

18. Jan Zielonka and Alex Pravda, *Democratic Consolidation in Eastern Europe*.

19. Schimmelfennig and Sedelmeier, *The Europeanization of Central and Eastern Europe*.

20. Noutcheva and Bechev, "The Successful Laggards"; Vermeersh, "EU Enlargement and Minority Rights Policies."

21. Kelley, "International Actors and the Domestic Scene," 428; on socialization see also Checkel, "Why Comply?"

22. Kelley, "International Actors and the Domestic Scene," 426; for another account combining the approaches see Schimmelfennig, "The Community Trap."

23. For a skeptical view see Hughes and Sasse, "Monitoring the Monitors."

24. Staff advisor, U.S. Helsinki Commission for Security and Cooperation in Europe, author's telephone interview, November 2008.

25. Eminov, *Muslim Minorities*, 219. An in-depth discussion about the motivations of Turkey follows in Chapter 5.

26. On Germany and the collapse of Yugoslavia see Gow, *Triumph of the Lack of Will*, 168.

27. European Security, "Kosovo."

28. Edita Tahiri, Former Foreign Policy Advisor to LDK President Ibrahim Rugova, currently member of Kosovo Parliament, author's interviews, Prishtina, Kosovo, October 8 and 9, 2002.

29. Bellamy, *Kosovo and International Society*, 17–22.

30. Lulzim Peci, Executive Director, Kosova Civil Society Foundation, author's interviews, Prishtina, Kosovo, October 2 and 4, 2002.

31. HRW, *Bulgaria*.

32. Bulgarian Telegraph Agency, "Na foruma v Paris" [At the Paris Forum].

33. HRW, *Bulgaria*, 1989.

34. Dejan Kiuranov, *Bulgarskite neformali* [The Bulgarian Dissidents], personal archive material, inquiry from 1997.

35. Shopova, "Turski i amerikanski politisti se zastapvat za partiata na Dogan" [Turkish and American Diplomats Intercede for Dogan's Party].

36. Koinova, *Muslims of Bulgaria*.

37. Arbitration Commission of the Peace Conference on the former Yugoslavia (Badinter Commission), Opinion 6 on Macedonia, 1992, http://en.wikipedia.org/wiki/Arbitration_Commission_of_the_Peace_Conference_on_the_former_Yugoslavia.

38. Iso Rusi, director of the Macedonian Helsinki Committee, author's telephone interview, April 6, 2009.

39. Clark, *Civil Resistance in Kosovo*, 89.

40. Senior political advisor to Special Representative of UNMIK secretary general, author's interview, Prishtina, Kosovo, October 3, 2002.

41. Bellamy, *Kosovo and International Society*, 17–21.

42. For Krasner's definitions of international legal and domestic sovereignty, see Introduction, 14 and 233n8.

43. Tahiri, author's interview, 2002.

44. Maliqi, *Kosova: Separate Worlds*.

45. Judah, *Kosovo: War and Revenge*, 92.

46. Tahiri interview.

47. North and Weingast, "Constitutions and Commitment"; Dixit, *The Making of Economic Policy*. On credible commitments and EU institutions see Caballero, Caballero Álvarez, and Losada Álvarez, "Institutions and Credible Commitment."

48. Lake and Rothchild, "Containing Fear."

49. Ackermann, *Making Peace Prevail*, 77, 84.

50. Sokalski, *An Ounce of Prevention*, 96.

51. See ibid.; Ackermann, *Making Peace Prevail*; Vayrynen, "Challenges to Preventive Action"; Lund, "Preventive Diplomacy for Macedonia."

52. Carment and Rowlands, "Evaluating Third Party Intervention."

53. Lund, "Preventive Diplomacy for Macedonia."

54. HRW, *A Threat to "Stability"*, 106.

55. Auerswald and Auerswald, *The Kosovo Conflict*, 65.

56. Clark, *Civil Resistance*, 89.

57. Bellamy, *Kosovo and International Society*, 30–32.

58. Clark, *Civil Resistance*, 91.

59. Bellamy, *Kosovo and International Society*, 43.

60. Ibid., 45.

61. Rechel, *The Long Way Back to Europe*, 166.

Chapter 4. International Agents, Self-Reinforcement of Conflict Dynamics, and Processes of Change

1. On third-party government support and association with civil war duration see Collier, Hoeffler, and Söderbom, *On the Duration of Civil War*. On how biased interventions contribute more than neutral ones to shorter conflict duration, see Regan, "Third Party Interventions." On how external interventions reduce costs for coordinating rebellion, thereby lengthening civil war duration, see Sambanis and Elbadawi, *External Interventions*. On how third-party intervention affects duration until military victory or negotiated settlement, see Balch-Lindsay, Enterline, and Joyce, "Third Party Intervention."

2. Regan and Aydin, "Diplomacy and Other Forms of Intervention."

3. On the long EU shadow see Hughes and Sasse, "Monitoring the Monitors"; and Kelley, "International Actors."

4. See Mahoney and Thelen, *Explaining Institutional Change*, 4. A larger discussion on "layering" as a mechanism follows in Chapter 6.

5. Thelen, "Historical Institutionalism in Comparative Politics."

6. Kin-states and diasporas will be discussed in Chapter 5.

7. This is a plausible cut-off point, since the "opinions" became the first exercise of active EU leverage: Vachudova, "Europe Undivided"; Csergo, *Talk of the Nation*, 78.

8. Hughes and Sasse, "Monitoring the Monitors," 12. For more on inconsistencies in EU conditionality see De Witte, "Politics Versus Law"; Rechel, "What Has Limited the EU's Impact?"

9. Rechel, *The Long Way*, 180.

10. Ibid., 73.

11. Simon, "Bulgaria and NATO."

12. Ackermann, *Making Peace Prevail*, 103–11.

13. Eran Fraenkel, Executive Director, "Search for Common Ground in Macedonia," author's interview, September 11, 2000, Skopje; Frckoski interview, 2000.

14. HRW, *Threat to "Stability,"* 103.

15. Kemp, *Quiet Diplomacy in Action*; Kemp was Van der Stoel's advisor.

16. Anonymous senior official, author's interview, September 7, 2000, Skopje.

17. Teuta Arifi, currently MP elected on the Democratic Union for Integration (in Macedonia) (DUI) ticket, author's interview in her capacity as lecturer at Faculty of Philology, Department of Albanian Language, September 7, 2000, Skopje.

18. Tuerkes and Goekgoez, "The European Union's Strategy."

19. Gjurcilova, *From Co-operation to Membership*, 119–21.

20. Kymlicka, "Justice and Security," 144–75.

21. On securitization of migration discourses: Buzan, "Societal Security"; Roe, "Securitization and Minority Rights."

22. On learning effects and positive feedback, Hall quoted by Pierson, "When Effects Become a Cause," 613.

23. A more detailed discussion on "learning" follows in Chapter 7.

24. Bellamy, *Kosovo and International Society*, 42–51.

25. Kamminga, "State Succession in Respect of Human Rights Treaties."

26. Hughes and Sasse, "Monitoring the Monitors," 6.

27. Keck and Sikkink, *Activists Beyond Borders*; Risse, Ropp, and Sikkink, *The Power of Human Rights*.

28. Ognyan Minchev, Director of the Institute for Regional and International Studies, author's interview, Sofia, July 4, 2002.

29. Nikolova, "Dogan govori dva chasa na evrodiplomati za Kardzhali" [Dogan Talks for Two Hours to Euro-Diplomats About Kardzhali] in *Kontinent* Daily.

30. Eminov, *Turkish and Other Muslim Minorities*, 172–73.

31. Democratsiya "Soczakon za bulgarskia ezik trevozhi DPS" [A Socialist [Draft] Law on the Bulgarian Language Bothers the MRF"; Stoyanov, *Zaplachata* [The Threat], 262.

32. Stefanova, "Dogan topi Bulgaria v Strasbourg za majchinia ezik" [Dogan Complains About Bulgaria in Strasbourg About the Mother-Tongue [Education]."

33. Arifi interview, 2000.

34. Koinova with Gigova, *Albanians of Macedonia*.

35. Bukoshi, interview, 2002.

36. Veton Suroi, editor-in-chief, Albanian daily *Koha Ditore*, author's interview, Prishtina, October 3, 2002.

37. Bukoshi interview, 2002.

38. Tahiri interview, 2002.

39. Clark, *Civil Resistance in Kosovo*, 90.

40. Bukoshi interview, 2002; Suroi interview, 2002.

41. Mahmut Bakalli, Kosovo Parliament, author's interview, Prishtina, October 7, 2002.

42. See Chapter 3, 75.

43. Demolli, "The Mother Teresa Society."

44. Clark, *Civil Resistance*, 170–71.

45. Bob, *The Marketing of Rebellion*, 1–53.

46. Wildmaier, Blyth, and Seabrooke, "Exogenous Shocks or Endogenous Constructions?"; Mabee, "Exogenous Shocks, Institutional Change, and Path-Dependence."

47. Legro, "The Transformation of Policy Ideas," 420.

48. Ibid., 423.

49. Bellamy, *Kosovo and International Society*, 91..

50. Pula, "Modalities of Self-Determination," 391.

51. Peci interviews, 2002.

52. Jenne, "Bargaining Theory," 172–74.

53. Kurti interview 2002.

54. ICG, *Kosovo Spring*.

55. Adem Demaci, former political prisoner, Chair of Council of Human Rights in 1997 and Political Representative of KLA 1998–1999, author's interview, Prishtina, October 10, 2002.

56. Kostovicova, *Parallel Worlds*, 59.

57. For more details see Chapter 5, 149.

58. ICG, "Kosovo Briefing."

59. Kurti interview, 2002.

60. Judah, *Kosovo: War and Revenge*, 136.

61. On historical and legalistic accounts: Weller, *The Crisis in Kosovo*; Auerswald and Auerswald, *The Kosovo Conflict*; journalistic accounts: Pettifer, *Kosova Express*; Judah, *Kosovo: War and Revenge*; on negotiations: Bellamy, *Kosovo and International Society*; Independent International Commission, *The Kosovo Report*; an account of a Kosovo Albanian politician: Tahiri, *The Rambouillet Conference*.

62. Bellamy, *Kosovo and International Society*, 72–77, 80–88.

63. International Commission, *Kosovo Report*, 155.

64. Grigoryan, "Third-Party Intervention," 70–75; Judah, *Kosovo: What Everyone Needs to Know*, 88.

65. U.S. Department of State, *Country Reports on Human Rights Practices: Serbia-Montenegro*, 2000.

66. DiPrizio, *Armed Humanitarians*; Buckley, *Contending Voices*; Hoffmann, *World Disorders*; Chomsky, *The New Military Humanism*.

67. ICG, *Macedonia Towards Destabilization?*

68. Frckoski interview, 2000; Arifi interview, 2000.

69. Elisabeta Georgieva, head of Department of Human Rights, Foreign Ministry of the Republic of Macedonia, author's interview, September 5, 2000, Skopje.

70. Ibrahim Mehmeti, Media Projects Coordinator, "Search for Common Ground in Macedonia," author's interview, September 5, 2000, Skopje.

71. Georgieva interview, 2000.

72. Salehyan and Gleditsch, "Refugees and the Spread of Civil War," 342.

73. Ibid., 346.

74. Lisher, "Collateral Damage."

75. To its credit, the international community adopted multidimensional policies toward the refugee crisis. NATO boosted its military presence in the country. In a major move, on May 5, 1999, an Emergency G-24/Consultative Group meeting chaired by the European Commission and World Bank pledged immediate financial assistance to Macedonia of U.S.$252 million, and promised to shortly close an overall financing gap of over $400 million. In addition to building refugee camps, several international humanitarian organizations provided assistance, most notably the UN High Commissioner on Refugees (UNHCR) and International Committee of the Red Cross. They also supported some local NGOs with humanitarian functions, such as the Muslim El Hilal.

76. Liotta and Jebb, *Mapping Macedonia*, 38.

77. Hislope, "Between a Bad Peace and a Good War," 141.

78. Hislope, "Organized Crime in a Disorganized State."

79. Ethnobarometer, *Crisis in Macedonia*.

80. R. McMahon, "UN: Security Council Alarmed."

81. AP, *Key Events in Macedonia's Standoff*; ICG, *Macedonia: War on Hold*.

82. Hislope, "Corrupt Exchange in Divided Societies," 154.

83. *Balkanalysis*, "Georgievski: Xhaferi and I Had No Deal."

84. On spoilers see Stedman, "Spoiler Problems in Peace Processes."

85. Noutcheva and Bechev, "The Successful Laggards," 121–22.

86. Vachudova, *Europe Undivided*, 65, 105–9.

87. Noutcheva and Bechev, "Successful Laggards," 121.

88. Hughes and Sasse, "Monitoring the Monitors," 22–23.

89. Csergo, *Talk of the Nation*, 80.

90. Rechel, *The Long Way*, 247.

91. On "layering," see more in Chapter 6, 162, 176.

92. Dogan, *Bulgaria i noviat svetoven red* [Bulgaria and the New World Order], 68.

93. Project on Ethnic Relations, "The Bulgarian Ethnic Experience," 21.

94. European Court on Human Rights, *Deloto Hasan i Chaush sreshtu Bulgaria* [The Case of Hassan and Chaush Against Bulgaria].

95. Rechel, "What Has Limited the EU's Impact," 172–73. Current *acquis communautaire* pages in English are estimated in the range of 170,000, more than double the number claimed by the EC and commentators. EUR-LEX legislative database quoted by Open Europe, http://www.openeurope.org.uk/Content/Documents/PDFs/acquis.pdf, accessed June 5, 2012.

Chapter 5. Intervention of Identity-Based Agents: Kin-States and Diasporas

1. Ambrosio defines irredentism as "attempts by existing states to annex territories of another state that their co-nationals inhabit" (*Irredentism: Ethnic Conflict*, 2). O'Leary argues that true irredentism requires that the irredentist state have a partner, a kin-group that wishes to achieve unification or reunification. When the state has no such kin-group, an irredentist posture could be more accurately described as "annexationism." I am grateful to Brendan O'Leary for this comment during personal correspondence on May 21, 2012.

2. Ambrosio, "Irredentism," 20–21.

3. Horowitz, "Irredentas and Secessions," 10–11.

4. Anderson, *The Spectre of Comparisons*.

5. Carment and James, "Internal Constraints and Interstate Ethnic Conflict."

6. On instrumentalist explanations such as political and economic gains, internal politics, and military reasoning: Heraclides, "Secessionist Minorities and External Involvement." On how affinitive ethnic ties become instrumentalized by elites of intervening states: Saideman "Ties that Divide." On affective perspectives, including historic injustice, common identity, religion, racial-cultural affinity and humanitarian considerations: Carment, "The International Dimensions of Ethnic Conflict." On structural considerations including size, concentration, and dispersal of people involved, and porousness of borders: Chazan, ed., *Irredentism and International Politics*.

7. Saideman and Ayres, *For Kin or Country*; Waterbury, *Between State and Nation*.

8. P. McMahon, *Taming Ethnic Hatred*.

9. Saideman and Ayres, *For Kin or Country*.

10. Koinova, "Kinstate Intervention."

11. This argument was first developed by Koinova, "Diasporas and Secessionist Conflicts."

12. Ganguly, *Kin State Intervention*, 13.

13. Adamson and Demetriou, "Remapping the Boundaries of 'State' and 'National Identity'."

14. Under "contained contention" actors use "well established means of claim-making" in episodic, public, collective interactions with other claim makers, often governments. A "transgressive contention" consists of episodic public and collective interactions in which at least some parties are newly identified and use innovative collective action. A contentious repertoire expands to collective claims that incorporate more extreme agendas and "adopt means that are either unprecedented or forbidden," McAdam, Tarrow, and Tilly, *Dynamics of Contention*, 7–8.

15. I have adapted the McAdam et al. concepts in Koinova, "Why Do Conflict-Generated Diasporas Pursue Sovereignty-Based Claims?"

16. Koinova, "Kinstate Intervention," 2008.

17. Xhudo, *Diplomacy and Crisis Management*, 23–25.

18. Koinova, *Muslims of Bulgaria*.

19. Carment and James, *Wars in the Midst of Peace*, 194–231.

20. Anderson, *The New Old World*, 377.

21. Jenkins, "Turkey and Northern Iraq," 4–16.

22. Kramer, *A Changing Turkey*, 151.

23. Trenin and Malashenko, *Russia's Restless Frontier*.

24. Olson, *Turkey's Relations with Iran, Syria, Israel, and Russia*, 181–82.

25. Brubaker, *Nationalism Reframed*.

26. Jenne, "A Bargaining Theory," 729–56.

27. Saideman and Ayres, *For Kin or Country*, 2.

28. Waterbury, *Between State and Nation*.

29. Kelley, *Ethnic Politics in Europe*; McMahon, *Taming Ethnic Hatred*.

30. The argument that transition weakens domestic institutions and contributes to the rise of ethnic conflicts has been discussed from a domestic politics point of view; see Snyder, *From Voting to Violence*; Rotberg, *State Failure*; Mansfield and Snyder, *Electing to Fight*. But it has not been considered for kin-state interventions in Europe.

31. Kaldor, *New and Old Wars*; P. Collier and Anke Hoeffler, "Greed and Grievances in Civil War"; Byman et al., *Trends in Outside Support*; Shain, "The Role of Diasporas"; Sheffer, *Diaspora Politics*; Hockenos, *Homeland Calling*; Adamson, "Globalization, Political Mobilization, and Networks of Violence."

32. Faist, "Transnationalization in International Migration"; Lyons, "Diasporas and Homeland Conflict."

33. Shain, "The Role of Diasporas."

34. Irwin, "Yugoslavia's Relations with European States."

35. Eminov, *Turkish and Other Muslim Minorities*, 79.

36. Shain, "The Role of Diasporas"; Sheffer, *Diaspora Politics*.

37. Fair, "Diaspora Involvement in Insurgencies."

38. Judah, *Kosovo: War and Revenge*, 104–6.

39. Koinova, "Diasporas and Secessionist Conflicts."

40. Koinova, "Four Types of Diaspora Mobilization."

41. Collier and Hoeffler, "Greed and Grievances in Civil War."

42. Byman et al., *Trends in Outside Support*; Kaldor, *New and Old Wars*; Hockenos, *Homeland Calling*; Fair, "Diaspora Involvement in Insurgencies"; Adamson ,"Globalization, Political Mobilization, and Networks of Violence."

43. Collier, Hoeffler, and Soderbom, "Post-Conflict Risks," 472.

44. Offe, "Capitalism by Democratic Design."

45. The following paragraphs build extensively on Pano, "The Process of Democratization."

46. Hedges 1999, quoted in Jenne, *Ethnic Bargaining*, 171.

47. Kola, *The Search for Greater Albania*, 222.

48. Jenne, *Ethnic Bargaining*, 171.

49. Kola, *The Search for Greater Albania*, 206–7, 222, 282.

50. Ibid., 231.

51. Ibid., 309.

52. Perry, "Macedonia: A Balkan Problem," 39.

53. Reuter, "Albaniens Aussenpolitik," 95.

54. Perry, "Macedonia: A Balkan Problem."

55. Gowan, "The NATO Powers and the Balkan Tragedy."

56. Thayer, "Macedonia,"134.

57. Heraclides, "Secessionist Minorities and External Involvement"; Bunce, "The National Idea."

58. Kola, *The Search for Greater Albania.*

59. Zanga, "The Question of Kosovar Sovereignty."

60. Judah, *Kosovo: War and Revenge.*

61. Cota, "KLA Commanders Trained in Albania."

62. Hamzaj, *A Narrative About War and Freedom.*

63. Pettifer, *Kosova Express*, 51.

64. Thayer, "Macedonia," 134.

65. Ackermann, *Making Peace Prevail*, 90.

66. Kusovac, "Round Two: Serbian Security Forces"; Judah, *Kosovo: War and Revenge*, 106.

67. Perritt, *Kosovo Liberation Army*, 8.

68. See Chapter 4, 111.

69. Anonymous source close to UNMIK, author's interview, October 3, 2002, Prishtina.

70. Sullivan, *Be Not Afraid*. See also Chapter 3, 91.

71. Hockenos, *Homeland Calling.*

72. Sunar, "State, Society, and Democracy in Turkey."

73. Fuller, "Turkey's New Eastern Orientation," 39; Dodd, "Developments in Turkish Democracy," 135.

74. Sunar, "State, Society, and Democracy in Turkey," 145; Özcan, "The Military and the Making of Foreign Policy in Turkey."

75. Uzgel, "The Balkans: Turkey's Stabilizing Role," 51.

76. Fuller, "Turkey's New Eastern Orientation," 38.

77. *Index Mundi* 2010, http://www.indexmundi.com/turkey/gdp_(purchasing_power_parity).html.

78. Fuller, "Turkey's New Eastern Orientation," 39.

79. O'Lesser, "Bridge or Barrier," 102.

80. Fuller, "Turkey's New Eastern Orientation," 40.

81. Perry, "Macedonia: A Balkan Problem," 33; Nachmani, *Turkey: Facing a New Millennium*, 41–43.

82. This foreign policy orientation would culminate in the late 2000s with the "no problems with our neighbors" policy of foreign minister Ahmed Davutoğlu.

83. See Chapters 2, 70, and Chapter 3, 93.

84. Ognyan Minchev, Director of the Institute for Regional and International Studies, author's interview, Sofia, Bulgaria, July 4, 2002; see also Bikov, *Dosieto na Dogan* [Dogan's File], which featured documents from Dogan's secret service file. In 2006 a law adopted under EU pressure allowed for opening the archives of the communist secret services.

85. Bulgarian Telegraph Agency, "Gn Ahmed Dogan zamina za Turtsia" [Mr. Ahmed Dogan Left for Turkey]; *Duma* Daily, "Turski holding shte finansira DPS" [A Turkish Holding Will Finance the MRF].

86. *Troud* Daily, "Utchtiv ultimatum ot Ankara" [A Polite Ultimatum from Ankara].

87. *Democratsia* Daily, September 5, 1991.

88. Shopova, "Turski i amerikanski politisti se zastapvat za partiata na Dogan" [Turkish and American Politicians Intervene on Behalf of Dogan's Party].

89. Andaj, "Dogan boikotira izselnitsi v Bursa," [Dogan Boycotts [the Activities] of Emigrants to Turkey].

90. Anonymous source from an organization of ethnic Turks of Bulgaria in Turkey, author's interview, Sofia, June 2, 2002.

91. Antonina Zhelyazkova, Director of the International Center on Minority Studies and Inter-Cultural Relations, author's interview, October 20, 2000, Sofia.

92. Biberaj, "The Albanian National Question," 246; Zanga, "The Question of Kosovar Sovereignty."

93. Kola, *The Search for Greater Albania*, 309.

94. Pettifer, *Kosova Express*, 51.

95. Blumi, "The Commodification of Otherness."

96. Schmidt, "Altered States."

97. Lani, "From Nano-Milosevic to Rugova-Milosevic."

98. ICG, *Pan-Albanianism*, 11.

99. ICG, *Kosovo: Bite the Bullet*, January 22, 1999, no longer available online.

100. Hamzaj, *A Narrative*, 14–15.

101. Pike, "Kosovo Liberation Army."

102. Statistical studies are split on whether mountainous terrain increases the probability of outbreak or duration of civil war by providing sanctuary for rebels. Important for civil war: Buhaug, Cederman, and Rod, "Disaggregating Ethno-Nationalist Civil Wars"; Fearon and Laitin, *Ethnicity, Insurgency, Civil War*," 85; Toft, *Geography of Ethnic Violence*; unimportant for civil war: Sambanis, "What Is Civil War"; Collier and Hoeffler, "Greed and Grievance in Civil War."

103. Vickers, "Tirana's Uneasy Role, 32.

104. Corrin, "Traffic in Women in War and Peace," 180–82; Wennmann, "Resourcing the Recurrence of Intrastate Conflict," 485.

105. Kola, *The Search for Greater Albania*, 261. Kosovo's mountainous terrain was conducive to various smuggling activities, including that of weapons during the 1997

collapse of the Albanian state. Trains of donkeys were used to transfer the weapons in casts covered by other goods. As the 2005 film by Klaartije vividly shows, the use of the mountainous terrain for small arms transfer continued even after NATO's 1999 military intervention. See Klaartije, *The Brooklyn Connection.*

106. Ibid.

107. Nicholson, "The Beginning of the End of a Rebellion."

108. Hedges, "Kosovo Rebels Find Friend in Former Albanian President."

109. Judah, *Kosovo: War and Revenge,* 116–27.

110. Jenne, *Ethnic Bargaining,* 173.

111. ICG, *Macedonia Report.*

112. See Table 2 in Chapter 3.

113. ICG, *Macedonia: New Faces in Skopje,* 34.

114. ICG, *Macedonia Report.*

115. Leka, "Peace in Skopje Accompanied by a Chill."

116. Deutsche Presse Agentur, "Powell Consults Albania's Meta on Balkans."

117. In a similar vein, Turkey in 2003 argued for federalism and ethnofederalism in Cyprus while opposed to federalism in Iraq.

118. Stoyanov, *Zaplachata* [The Threat], 234–44.

119. Winrow, "Turkey and the Newly Independent States," 181.

120. Turam, "A Bargain Between the Secular State and Turkish Islam." On various Islamic influences among Muslims in Bulgaria see Ghodsee, *Muslim Lives in Eastern Europe.*

121. Unless otherwise noted, I base this paragraph section on Hockenos, *Homeland Calling.*

122. Anonymous diaspora entrepreneur in UK, author's interview, July 15, 2009, London.

123. Koinova, "Four Types of Diaspora Mobilization."

124. Anonymous senior foreign policy advisor to Kosovo Exiled Government, author's interviews, October 8, 9, 2002, Prishtina.

125. Koinova, "Four Types of Diaspora Mobilization."

126. ICG, *Kosovo Spring.*

127. Bujar Bukoshi, former prime minister, Government of Kosovo in Exile, author's interview, October 7, 2002, Prishtina.

128. Hashim Thaci, former commander-in-chief of the Kosovo Liberation Army, author's interview, October 8, 2002, Prishtina.

129. Koinova, "Diasporas and Secessionist Conflicts." On "ethnic outbidding" in the diaspora see Adamson, "Diaspora Mobilization and Violent Conflict." The first formal discussions of "ethnic outbidding" can be found in Rabushka and Shepsle. *Politics in Plural Societies.*

130. Amnesty International, *Kosovo: The Evidence.*

131. Hockenos, *Homeland Calling,*

132. Sullivan, *Be Not Afraid.*

133. Koinova, "Diasporas and Secessionist Conflicts."

134. Koinova, "Four Types of Diaspora Mobilization."

135. Judah, *Kosovo: War and Revenge*.

136. Sullivan, *Be Not Afraid*.

Chapter 6. Change in Conflict Dynamics

1. Data on levels of violence are derived from 30 U.S. State Department *Reports on Human Rights Practices* for Bulgaria, Macedonia, and Kosovo, 2000–2010, http://www.state.gov/g/drl/rls/hrrpt/; 2011 data derived from other sources. Bulgaria: *Middle East Online*, "Bulgarian Parliament Condemns a Far-Right Mosque Attack"; Macedonia: ICG, *Macedonia: Ten Years After the Conflict*; Kosovo: ICG, *North Kosovo: Dual Sovereignty in Practice*.

2. Senior UNMIK official (1), author's interview, July 23, 2008, Prishtina; Boyle, "Revenge and Reprisal Violence."

3. *Reuters*, "Violence in North Kosovo Draws EU Warning."

4. Mahoney and Thelen, *Explaining Institutional Change*, 4.

5. Ibid., 5–17.

6. On the rationale for a change of terminology from "displacement" to "replacement" see 234n65.

7. "Conversion" was not operational in the cases described in this book.

8. Mahoney and Thelen, *Explaining Institutional Change*, 28.

9. Coggins, "Friends in High Places."

10. Tansey, "Democratization Without a State," 133.

11. Reka, "The Ohrid Agreement," 57. See also Daskalovski, "Language and Identity," 14.

12. Constitution of the Republic of Macedonia, 2001 Preamble.

13. Daskalovski, "Language and Identity," 12.

14. ICG, "Macedonia: Ten Years After the Conflict."

15. The 1990 electoral law used a majoritarian formula, the 1998 electoral law changed to a mixed system (85 seats by majoritarian vote, 35 seats by PR formula), the 2002 law changed to a pure PR electoral formula. Friedman, "Electoral Systems Design." 386.

16. ICG, *Ten Years After the Conflict*, 3.

17. Fearon and Laitin, "Neotrusteeship and the Problem of Weak States," 7.

18. Skendaj, "Building State Bureaucracies," 65.

19. Ibid., 64.

20. Anastakis and Bechev, "EU Conditionality in South East Europe."

21. The SAA—like agreements with other countries in the Western Balkans and Ukraine—resembled earlier agreements with Eastern European front-runners, but emphasized stability.

22. Hislope, "Between a Bad Peace and a Good War," 142.

23. Reka, "The Ohrid Agreement," 67; Ilievski and Taleski, "Was the EU's Role in Conflict Management in Macedonia a Success?" 57.

24. Dobbins et al., *Europe's Role*, 59.

25. Senior OSCE Official, author's interview, Skopje, July 10, 2008.

26. Dobbins et al., *Europe's Role*, 54.

27. Stuart, "EU Takes over NATO's Mission in Macedonia."

28. Dobbins et al., *Europe's Role*, 71.

29. Paris and Sisk, "Introduction."

30. Narten, "Dilemmas of Promoting Local Ownership," 263.

31. Skendaj, "Building State Bureaucracies," 60.

32. Dobbins et al. *Europe's Role*, quoted in Skendaj, "Building State Bureaucracies," 65.

33. Reilly, "Post-War Elections," 171.

34. Taylor, "Electoral Systems and the Promotion of 'Consociationalism'."

35. De Vrieze, "Building Parliamentary Democracy"; Oliva, "Between Contribution and Disengagement"; Manning, "Party-Building on the Heels of War"; Narten, "Building Local Institutions and Parliamentarism."

36. Skendaj, "Building State Bureaucracies," 3.

37. Narten, "Local Ownership," 265; see also Jarstad, "The Share or to Divide?" 232.

38. UNMIK official on record in Klaartije, *The Brooklyn Connection*.

39. Hehir, "Kosovo's Final Status," 246.

40. Höglund, "Managing Violent Crises,"406.

41. Program coordinator of a Kosovar NGO, author's interview, July 23, 2008, Prishtina.

42. Kostovicova, "Legitimacy and International Administration," 635.

43. Weller, "Kosovo's Final Status."

44. ICG, "Kosovo's First Month," 124. As of June 1, 2012, Kosovo has received recognition from 91 of 193 UN member-states, but not Security Council support and unanimous EU member-state recognition, lacking Cyprus, Greece, Romania, Slovakia, and Spain. Most UN member-states still believe Kosovo should negotiate with Serbia.

45. ICG, *Kosovo's Fragile Transition*, 2.

46. Yusufi, "Assisting State-Building in the Balkans"; Atanasova and Bache, "Europeanization and FYR Macedonia."

47. Senior OSCE official interview, 2008.

48. Dobbins et al., *Europe's Role*, 71.

49. Bechev, "Carrots, Sticks, and Norms." The Royaumont Process (1996) was the first EU initiative aimed at stabilizing the Balkans in support of implementation of the Dayton Accords. The Regional Approach established political and economic conditionality for relations with Albania, Bosnia-Herzegovina, Croatia, Federal Republic of Yugoslavia, and Macedonia. EC, "EU and the Western Balkans."

50. Anastasakis and Bechev, "EU Conditionality in South East Europe" 4.

51. Mahoney and Thelen, *Explaining Institutional Change*, 20.

52. Ibid., 20.

53. Rechel, *The Long Way*, 263. The EU has been an important factor in Roma rights. In the Bulgarian context, some EU criticism was also related to the lack of adequate treatment of Macedonians vs. Roma.

54. Koinova, "Saxcoburggotsky and His Catch-All Attitude."

55. Rechel, *The Long Way*, 244–63.

56. EC, "Monitoring Report: Bulgaria and Romania."

57. DUI official, author's interview, September 19, 2002, Tetovo.

58. Speculation exists that prime minister Branko Crvenkosvki of the SDSM sent Bozhkoski of VMRO-DPMNE to the ICTY to remove him as a possible rival for the presidency, which Crvenkosvki won in 2004. See Koinova, "Challenging Assumptions," 820.

59. Stavrova, "Macedonia: Drawing the Line."

60. Voice of America, "Macedonia Votes on Local Autonomy."

61. *Election Guide*, "Macedonia Referendum."

62. Official, Ombudsperson Office, author's interview, July 16, 2008, Skopje.

63. Mirjana Najceska, professor of sociology and former director of the Helsinki Committee of Macedonia, author's interview, July 10, 2008, Skopje.

64. EC, "The Former Yugoslav Republic of Macedonia Progress Report."

65. The law is still problematic, since it excluded anti-discrimination against sexual orientation.

66. Ministry of Finance of the Republic of Macedonia, quoted by Center for Research and Policy Making, *Budget Watchdogs*.

67. ICG, *Kosovo's Fragile Transition*, 13.

68. Ibid., 15.

69. ICG, *Kosovo and Serbia After the ICJ Opinion*, 1.

70. Ibid., 4

71. CBS News, "EU: Kosovo, Serbia Agree on Practical Issues."

72. BBC, "Kosovo Declared 'Fully Independent.'"

73. Noutcheva, "Fake, Partial, and Imposed Compliance."

74. Caruthers, "Institutional Dynamics."

Chapter 7. Continuity in Conflict Dynamics

1. Regarding Macedonia, this idea was first developed in Koinova, "Challenging Assumptions."

2. Stedman, "Spoiler Problems in Peace Processes," 8.

3. Walter, "The Critical Barrier to Civil War Settlement," 340; see also Söderberg-Kovacs, "When Rebels Change Their Stripes," 138.

4. Stedman, "Introduction," 6–7.

5. Paris, *At War's End*, 5–8.

6. Reilly, "Post-War Elections," 168.

7. Stedman and Rothchild, "Peace Operation"; see also Belloni, "Civil Society in War-to-Democracy Transitions."

8. Paris, *At War's End*, 214.

9. Höglund, "Violence in War-to-Democracy Transitions."

10. Lijphart's original "consociationalism" theory, discussed in Chapter 1, was developed for polities with no recent experience in conflict; most consociational studies today are focused on postconflict cases. See McGarry and O'Leary, "Consociational Theory"; Bieber, "Power-Sharing After Yugoslavia." On limits of consociationalism and power-sharing see Roeder and Rothchild, *Sustainable Peace.*

11. On power sharing and successful peace building see Hartzell and Hoddie, "Institutionalizing Peace."

12. Rothchild and Roeder, "Dilemmas of State-Building," 12–13.

13. Jung, "The Paradox of Institution Building After Civil War," 8–9.

14. Cousens, "From Missed Opportunities to Overcompensation," 538.

15. Call and Cook, "On Democratization and Peace-Building," 237; Pickering, "Explaining Support for Non-Nationalist Parties." 591.

16. Trajkovski, "The Framework Agreement," 55.

17. Georgievski, "Theses for Survival of the Macedonian Nation," 63.

18. Jarstad, "To Share or to Divide," 232.

19. Kumar, *Rebuilding Societies After Civil War*; Fukuyama, *State-Building*; Coyne, "Institutional Prerequisites"; Sisk and Stefes, "Power-Sharing as an Interim Step."

20. Sisk and Stefes, "Power Sharing as an Interim Step," 294.

21. Coyne, "Institutional Prerequisites," 326.

22. Fukuyama, *State-Building.*

23. Transparency International, *Corruption Perception Index,* 2010.

24. On "drift": Mahoney and Thelen, *Institutional Change,* 21, and the discussion in Chapter 6; on "reactive sequence": Mahoney, "Path Dependence in Historical Sociology," and discussion in the introduction.

25. Reneta Indzhova, who led a caretaker government after Berov quit in 1994, called his government a "government of Multi-group." See Bird, Ebel, and Wallich, "Oxford Analytica Reports," 5.

26. Frye, *Building States,* 206.

27. *Novinite,* August 8, 2001.

28. *Monitor,* March 8, 2006; *Ataka,* March 27, 2006.

29. Ganev, "Ballots, Bribes, and State-Building in Bulgaria"; *Ataka,* April 15, 2006.

30. Ghodsee, "Left Wing, Right Wing, Everything."

31. *24 Chasa,* April 4, 2002.

32. *Novinar,* December 3, 2002; *168 Chasa,* May 3–9, 2002.

33. Zhelyazkova, Kosseva, and Hajdinjak, "Tolerance and Cultural Diversity Discourses in Bulgaria."

34. Mudde, *Populist Radical Right Parties,* 63–197.

35. Krastev, "The Strange Death of the Liberal Consensus."

36. Krastev (2006) quoted in Andreev, "The Unbearable Lightness of Membership," 385.

37. Bustikova and Kitschelt, "The Radical Right in Post-Communist Europe."

38. Greskovits, "Economic Woes and Political Disaffection."

39. Taşkin, "Europeanization and the Extreme Right in Bulgaria and Turkey."

40. Mungiu-Pippidi, "EU Accession Is No 'End of History,'" 11.

41. Andreev, "The Unbearable Lightness of Membership," 386; on the link between corruption and state building see Ganev, "Ballots, Bribes, and State-Building in Bulgaria."

42. *Sofia Echo*, December 15, 2009.

43. *Novinite*, December 17, 2009.

44. *Troud*, February 28, 2000; *Ataka*, May 5, 2006.

45. *Troud*, February 21, 2006.

46. *Bulgarian Factor*, February 22, 2006.

47. *Novinite*, May 24, June 23, 2011

48. See Chapter 4, 121–22.

49. Independent political analyst (1), author's interview, July 6, 2008, Skopje.

50. Peake, "Power-Sharing in a Police Car," 21.

51. Independent political analyst (2), author's interview, July 4, 2008, Skopje.

52. Ordanoski, "The Story of Macedonian Populism," 4–5.

53. *The Economist*, "How Many Building Booms Can One City Take?"

54. http://www.euractiv.com/enlargement/protests-macedonia-signal-radica-news-512663, accessed June 30, 2012.

55. Sörensen, "The Shadow Economy," 333.

56. Paoli and Reuter, "Drug Trafficking and Ethnic Minorities."

57. Sörensen, "The Shadow Economy," 338; Yannis, "Kosovo: The Political Economy."

58. Yannis, "Kosovo: The Political Economy."

59. *B&S Europe*, "Survey on the Extent and Prevention of the Illegal Economy," 7.

60. Strazzari, "The Shadow Economy of Kosovo's Independence," 160.

61. Montgomery, "EU Endorses Task Force to Probe Organ Trafficking Allegations."

62. UNMIK official, Office of the Communities, author's interview, July 30, 2008, Prishtina.

63. Hoogenboom, "EU as a Peace-Builder in Kosovo."

64. Representative from a Kosovo anti-corruption NGO, author's interview, July 21, 2008; analyst from a Kosovo think tank, author's interview, July 23, 2008, Prishtina.

65. After Kosovo's 2008 independence, Vetevendosje participated in the 2010 general elections, garnering 12.9 percent of the vote and 14 seats in parliament and becoming the third biggest party after the Democratic Party for Kosovo and Democratic

League of Kosovo. It promised to mix mainstream pragmatic politics and pressure of the streets, and in January 2012 staged new demonstrations against government policy to enter EU-brokered technical negotiations with Serbia before Serbia recognizes Kosovo's independence. Cardias, "Kosovo: Vetevendosje's Determination."

66. *Monitor*, February 17, 2002; *Duma*, April 5, 2002.

67. *Duma*, "Is Bulgarian Nationalism a Threat to Our EU Membership?"

68. *Monitor*, March 10, 2006.

69. Rechel, *The Long Way*, 273.

70. Parliamentary Assembly of the Council of Europe, Document 10961, June 12, 2006.

71. Rechel, *The Long Way*, 273.

72. *European Parliament*, March 7; *Standart*, November 16, 2006.

73. IHF, "Rights in the OSCE Region," 2003.

74. Ibid., 2005.

75. Ibid., 2004.

76. On the referendum see Chapter 6.

77. Senior official at an international organization, author's interview, July 19, 2008, Skopje.

78. Eben Friedman, independent consultant on Romani affairs in Macedonia, author's telephone interview, September 12, 2008.

79. U.S. Department of State, *Human Rights Practices: Serbia (includes Kosovo)*; the use of rocks and bottles with red paint by Vetevendosje was confirmed by senior UNMIK official (2), author's interview, July 25, 2008, Prishtina.

80. Albin Kurti, leader of Vetevendosje, author's interview, July 26, 2008, Prishtina.

81. UNMIK official 2, "interview," 2008.

82. Anti-corruption NGO representative, "interview," 2008.

83. UN General Assembly, *Report of the Secretary-General*.

84. S. Valentino, "Kosovo: UN Leaves, Scandals Stay."

85. Director of a Kosovo-based media network, author's interview, July 22, 2008, Prishtina.

86. Judah, *Kosovo: What Everyone Needs to Know*, 102.

87. *Kosovo Compromise*, "Clashes in Kosovska Mitrovica."

88. Serbian enclave leader, author's interview, July 30, 2008, Gracanica, Kosovo.

89. *BBC*, "Kosovo's Serbs Split by Parliamentary Election."

90. ICG, *Pan-Albanianism*, 13.

91. Ibid., 11.

92. Pettifer and Vickers, *The Albanian Question*, 264.

93. ICG, *Pan-Albanianism*, 11.

94. Judah, *Kosovo: What Everyone Needs to Know*, 121.

95. ICG, *Pan-Albanianism*, 12.

96. Ibid., 19.

97. Perritt, *Kosovo Liberation Army*, 165.

98. ICG, *Pan-Albanianism*, 13.

99. Kamberi and Daliu, "Preševo Valley Albanians Demand Place at Kosovo Talks."

100. ICG, *Macedonia: Ten Years After the Conflict*, 20.

101. *EurActiv*, "Macedonia Protests Signal Surge of Radical Islam."

102. UNHCR, "Albanian National Army Operating in Kosovo."

103. ICG, *Pan-Albanianism*, 8.

104. UNHCR, "Albanian National Army Operating in Kosovo."

105. ICG, *Pan-Albanianism*, 8.

106. *Mondo*, May 2, 2010.

107. Source close to NAAC, author's interview, August 3, 2006, Washington, D.C.

108. *Kosovo Privatization Agency*, http://www.pak-ks.org/?id = 90; Dino Asanaj, author's interview, July 29, 2008, International Village near Prishtina, Kosovo.

109. *Albanian*, "Famous Albanians."

110. World Investment News, *Florin Krasniqi*.

111. International Organization for Migration, "Mapping Exercise Albania."

112. Naim Dedushaj, Director, Kosovo government's diaspora agency, author's interview, July 29, 2008.

113. UNHCR, "Albanian National Army."

114. Quirijns, *The Brooklyn Connection*.

115. Official close to the U.S. government, author's interviews, August 2, 2006 and July 17, 2007, Washington, D.C.

116. *Novinar*, September 29, 2000; *Troud*, October 1, 2000.

117. *Novinite*, December 17, 2009.

118. *News.Az*, "Erdogan Criticizes," May 24, 2011.

119. *Novinite*, July 11, 2011.

120. EU, "Bulgaria-Turkey IPA Cross-Border Programme."

121. *SEETimes*, "The Rise of Turkey in the Balkans."

122. *EUobserver*, "Bulgaria Puts Price on Turkey's EU Membership."

123. *New Europe*, March 21, 2010.

124. *Today's Zaman*, October 7, 2010.

125. *Times.am*, "Bulgaria Has Serious Claims Towards Turkey."

126. The OSCE claimed that its assessment mission received reports about this phenomenon, but that such reports could not be verified or confirmed. OSCE, "Republic of Bulgaria: Parliamentary Elections 2005."

127. U.S. State Department, *Report on Human Rights Practices, Bulgaria*, 2008.

128. U.S. State Department, *Report on Human Rights Practices, Bulgaria*, 2010.

Conclusions: Lessons Learned About Informally
Institutionalized Conflict Dynamics

1. For example, O'Leary and McGarry, *The Politics of Antagonism*, explored unionist-nationalist and British-Irish state relations, considering endogenous and exogenous factors in relation to exogenous shocks and institutional drift.

2. Stroschein, *Ethnic Struggle*.

3. On structural accounts see the discussion of demographic factors in the introduction and civilizational, linguistic, institutional, and economic accounts in Chapter 1. On agency-based accounts see elite-based instrumentalist explanations and economic greed in Chapter 1, third-party intervention in Chapter 3, identity-based agents in Chapter 5, and postconflict reconstruction in Chapter 7.

4. See discussion on third-party intervention in Chapter 3.

5. See Chapter 1.

6. I am thankful to Andrea Ruggeri for making this point.

7. Mahoney and Thelen, *Explaining Institutional Change*, 17.

8. Steinmo, "What Is Historical Institutionalism?"

9. Rueschmeyer, "Can One of a Few Cases Yield Theoretical Gains," 311.

10. Steinmo, "What Is Historical Institutionalism?"

11. Population and Housing Census, *Romania 2011*, 5.

12. Jenne, *Ethnic Bargaining*, 109.

13. Kelley, *Ethnic Politics*, 141.

14. Csergo, *Talk of the Nation*, 37.

15. Ibid., 25.

16. Ibid., 87.

17. P. McMahon, *Taming Ethnic Hatred*, 107.

18. Jenne, *Ethnic Bargaining*, 115.

19. Csergo, *Talk of the Nation*, 63.

20. P. McMahon, *Taming Ethnic Hatred*, 2007.

21. Jenne, *Ethnic Bargaining*, 112, 164.

22. Waterbury, *Between State and Nation*, 58.

23. Jenne, *Ethnic Bargaining*, 112.

24. Saideman and Ayres, *For Kin or Country*, 123.

25. Stroschein, *Ethnic Struggle*; see also Csergo, *Talk of the Nation*; Jenne, *Ethnic Bargaining*; P. McMahon, *Taming Ethnic Hatred*; Waterbury, *Between State and Nation*.

26. Kelley, *Ethnic Politics*.

27. Deets and Stroschein, "Dilemmas of Autonomy," 295.

28. Gagnon, *Myth of Ethnic War*, 87–104.

29. Petersen argues that by 1992 Serbian and Croat nationalists had already claimed parts of Bosnia's territory. In September 1991, months before the start of the war, Serbian political actors developed the Serbian Autonomous Oblasts (SAO): (Eastern and Old Herzegovina, Bosanska Krajina, Romanija SAO, North-east Bosnia); in October they formed the Serbian National Council and an Assembly of the Serb Nation of Bosnia-Herzegovina. In November Bosnian Serbs held a referendum, where they opted for remaining in Yugoslavia. Croats followed the Serbian lead and established autonomous oblasts. See Petersen, *Western Intervention*, 250.

30. Petersen, *Western Intervention*, 250–52.

31. See Burg and Shoup, *The War in Bosnia-Herzegovina*; Cousens, "From Missed Opportunities to Overcompensation."

32. Bose, *Bosnia after Dayton*; Bieber, *Post-War Bosnia*.

33. Holbrooke, *To End a War*; Kurspahic, "From Bosnia to Kosovo and Beyond," 82.

34. Petersen, *Western Intervention*, 261.

35. Belloni, *State Building*, 5.

36. Petersen, *Western Intervention*, 257.

37. On transitional justice and the role of the ICTY see Subotic, *Hijacked Justice*.

38. *The Independent*, "Hunt for Karadzic Ends as Fugitive Is Found."

39. *BBC*, "Profile: Radovan Karadzic"; "Ratko Mladic Arrested: Bosnia War Crimes Suspect Held."

40. Belloni, *State Building*, 126.

41. On variation in irredentism see Saideman and Ayres, *For Kin or Country*.

42. Aybet and Bieber, "From Dayton to Brussels," 9.

43. Belloni, *State Building*, 157.

44. Aybet and Bieber, "From Dayton to Brussels."

45. Petersen, *Western Intervention*, 263.

46. Aybet and Bieber, "From Dayton to Brussels."

47. Toft, *The Geography of Ethnic Violence*, 87.

48. Wheatley, *Georgia from National Awakening*, 58.

49. Toft, *The Geography of Ethnic Violence*, 110.

50. Wheatley, *Georgia from National Awakening*, 58.

51. Toft, *The Geography of Ethnic Violence*, 113.

52. Wheatley, *Georgia from National Awakening*, 71, 115, 196. The "Rose Revolution" involved large-scale grassroots protests that eventually ousted Shevarnadze in 2003. Bunce and Wolchik, *Defeating Authoritarian Leaders*, called such protest movements "electoral revolutions" against consolidated illiberal regimes in postcommunist space. Other such "revolutions" included Slovakia (1998), Croatia (2000), Serbia (2000), Ukraine (2004), and Kyrgyzstan (2005).

53. Wheatley, *Georgia from National Awakening*, 53, 57.

54. Ibid., 53–72.

55. Toft and Csergo develop territorially based arguments on Abkhazia in Georgia and the Hungarians of Romania.

56. Nodia, *The Political Landscape of Georgia*, 12.

57. Bardos, "Regional and International Implications," 56.

58. *RIA Novosti*, "Venezuela Recognizes South Ossetia, Abkhazia."

59. Fioretos, "Historical Institutionalism," 389.

60. Barnes, McKeon, and Griffiths, "Introduction," 6.

61. Dubai Initiative, *Revolution and Reform*.

62. Ethnonational conflicts, though not the majority conflict type in the Middle East, have been quite durable: the Kurdish conflicts in Iraq, Turkey, Syria, and Iran, the Israeli-Palestinian conflict, and Sudan/South Sudan, if we include Sudan as securitized in the Middle Eastern regional complex (see Buzan and Waever, *Regions and Powers*, 188).

63. Trager, "Egypt's Triangular Power-Struggle"; Shenker, "Egypt's Islamist Future."

64. Black, "Egypt Promises Justice."

65. Janos, *East Central Europe*; Ekiert and Hanson, "Introduction," 4.

66. On "competitive authoritarianism": Levitsky and Way, *Competitive Authoritarianism*; on renewed interest on legacies: Capoccia and Ziblatt, "The Historical Turn in Democratization Studies"; contributions of Harris Mylonas and Florian Bieber to the conference Continuity and Change in Southeastern Europe, co-hosted by Kokkalis Program, Kennedy School of Government and Center for European Studies, Harvard University, February 3–4, 2011.

67. Wittenberg, "What Is a Historical Legacy?"

68. Bieber, "Presentation, Continuity and Change in Southeastern Europe.

69. I would like to express gratitude to Grezgorz Ekiert for this point.

70. On how notions of "culture" and "besa" allow for informal inclusion of individual members of the out-group in the in-group, see Neofotistos, "Beyond Stereotypes."

71. Helmke and Levitsky, "Informal Institutions"; Helmke and Levitsky, *Informal Institutions*; Tsai, "Adaptive Informal Institutions"; Kohler, "Authoritarian Elections in Egypt"; Grzymala-Busse, "The Best Laid Plans."

72. O'Donnell, "Another Institutionalization," quoted in Helmke and Levitsky, *Informal Institutions*, 2.

73. Helmke and Levitsky, *Informal Institutions*.

74. Ibid., 13–19.

75. Levitsky and Way, *Competitive Authoritarianism*, 2010.

76. See discussion in Chapter 7, 182–83.

Bibliography

Abrahams, Fred. *A Threat to "Stability": Human Rights Violations in Macedonia*. New York: Human Rights Watch/Helsinki, 1996.

Ackermann, Alice. *Making Peace Prevail: Preventing Violent Conflict in Macedonia*. Syracuse, N.Y.: Syracuse University Press, 2000.

Adamson, Fiona. "Diaspora Mobilization and Violent Conflict." Paper presented at Explaining Diaspora Politics workshop, SOAS, October 30–31, 2009, London.

———. "Globalization, Political Mobilization, and Networks of Violence." *Cambridge Review of International Affairs* 18, 1 (2005): 31–49.

Adamson, Fiona and Madeleine Demetriou. "Remapping the Boundaries of 'State' and 'National' Identity." *European Journal of International Relations* 13, 4 (2007): 489–526.

Agh, Attila. *Emerging Democracies in East Central Europe and the Balkans*. Cheltenham: Edward Elgar, 1998.

Albanian. "Famous Albanians." 2006. http://www.albanian.com/v4/show thread.php?t=8747&page=12.

Ambrosio, Thomas. *Irredentism: Ethnic Conflict and International Politics*. Westport, Conn.: Praeger, 2001.

Amnesty International. *Annual Report for 1998, Macedonia*. http://www .amnesty.org/ailib/aireport/ar98/eur65.htm.

———. *Kosovo: The Evidence*. London: AI, 1998.

Anastasakis, Othon and Dimitar Bechev. "EU Conditionality in South East Europe: Bringing Commitment to the Process." European Studies Center, St. Antony's College, Oxford. April 2003.

Andaj, Ilhan. "Dogan boikotira izselnitsi v Bursa" [Dogan Boycotts [the Activities] of Emigrants to Turkey]. *24 Chasa Daily*, December 19, 1995.

Anderson, Benedict. *The Spectre of Comparisons*. London: Verso, 1998.

Anderson, Perry. *The New Old World*. London: Verso, 2009.

Andreev, Svetlozar. "The Unbearable Lightness of Membership: Bulgaria and Romania After the 2007 Accession." *Communist and Post-Communist Studies* 42 (2009): 375–93.

Anzulovic, Branimir. *Heavenly Serbia: From Myth to Genocide.* New York: New York University Press, 1999.

Arfi, Badredine. "Spontaneous Interethnic Order." *International Studies Quarterly* 44, 4 (2000): 564.

Arthur, Brian. *Increasing Returns and Path Dependence in the Economy.* Ann Arbor: University of Michigan Press, 1994.

Associated Press (AP). *Key Events in Macedonia's Standoff Between Rebels and Government Forces.* August 13, 2001.

Ataka. April 15, 2006. March 27, 2006; April 15, 2006; May 5, 2006.

Atanasova, Gorica and Ian Bache. "Europeanization and FYR Macedonia." *Southeast European and Black Sea Studies* 10, 1 (2010): 85–96.

Auerswald, Philip and David Auerswald. *The Kosovo Conflict: A Diplomatic History Through Documents.* The Hague: Kluwer, 2000.

Axelrod, Robert. *The Evolution of Cooperation.* New York: Basic Books, 1984.

Aybet, Gulnur, and Florian Bieber, "From Dayton to Brussels." *Europe-Asia Studies* 63, 10 (2011): 1911–37.

B&S Europe. "Survey on the Extent and Prevention of the Illegal Economy and Money Laundering in Kosovo." http://www.eulex-kosovo.eu/train ing/police/PoliceTraining/ORGANIZED_CRIME/DOCUMENTS/2.pdf.

Balch-Lindsay, Dylan, Andrew Enterline, and Kyle Joyce. "Third Party Intervention and the Civil War Process." *Journal of Peace Research* 45, 3 (2008): 345–63.

Balkanalysis. "Georgievski: Xhaferi and I Had No Deal to Divide Macedonia." June 3, 2005.

Bardos, Gordon. "Regional and International Implications of Kosovo Independence." *Mediterranean Quarterly* 19, 4 (2008): 54–67.

Barnes, Catherine, Celia McKeon, and Aaron Griffiths, "Introduction." In *Powers of Persuasion: Incentives, Sanctions, and Conditionality in Peacemaking*, ed. Aaron Griffiths and Catherine Barnes. London: Conciliation Resources, 2008.

Bates, Robert, Avner Greif, Margaret Levi, Jean-Laurent Rosenthal, and Barry Weingast. *Analytic Narratives.* Princeton, N.J.: Princeton University Press, 1998.

BBC. "Kosovo Declared 'Fully Independent'." September 10, 2012.

———. "Kosovo's Serbs Split by Parliamentary Election." December 10, 2010.

———. "Profile: Radovan Karadzic." November 5, 2009.

———. "Ratko Mladic Arrested: Bosnia War Crimes Suspect Held." May 26, 2011.

———. "Kosovo Declared 'Fully Independent.'" September 10, 2012.

BBC Monitoring Service. October 4, 2001.

Bechev, Dimitar. "Carrots, Sticks, and Norms: The EU and Cooperation in Southeast Europe." *Journal of Southern Europe and the Balkans* 8, 1 (2006): 27–43.

Beissinger, Mark. *Nationalist Mobilization and the Collapse of the Soviet State.* Cambridge: Cambridge University Press, 2002.

Bellamy, Alex J. *Kosovo and International Society.* London: Palgrave, 2002.

Belloni, Roberto. "Civil Society in War-to-Democracy Transitions." In *From War to Democracy: Dilemmas of Peacebuilding*, ed. Anna K. Jarstad and Timothy D. Sisk. Cambridge: Cambridge University Press, 2008. 182–210.

———. *State Building and International Intervention in Bosnia.* London: Routledge, 2008.

Bercovitch, Jacob. "Mediation in International Conflict: An Overview of Theory, a Review of Practice." In *Peacemaking in International Conflict*, ed. William Zartman and J. Lewis Rasmussen. Washington. D.C.: USIP, 1997.

Bhaumik, Sumon Kumar, Ira N.Gang, and Myeong-Su Yun. "Ethnic Conflict and Economic Disparity: Serbians and Albanians in Kosovo." *Journal of Comparative Economics* 34, 4 (2006): 754–73.

Biberaj, Elez. "The Albanian National Question." In *The New European Diasporas: National Minorities and Conflict in Eastern Europe*, ed. Michael Mandelbaum. New York: Council on Foreign Relations, 2000.

Bieber, Florian. *Post-War Bosnia.* London: Palgrave Macmillan, 2005.

———. "Power-Sharing After Yugoslavia." In *From Power Sharing to Democracy*, ed. Sid Noel. Montreal: McGill University Press, 2005.

———. Presentation, Conference on Continuity and Change in Southeastern Europe, co-hosted by Kokkalis Program, Kennedy School of Government and Center for European Studies, Harvard University, February 3–4, 2011.

Bikov, Toma. *Dosieto na Dogan* [Dogan's File]. Sofia: Millennium, 2009.

Bilevsky, Dan. "Fears of New Ethnic Conflict in Bosnia." *New York Times*, December 13, 2008.

Bird, Richard M., Robert D. Ebel, and Christine I. Wallich. "Oxford Analytica Reports on Red Conglomerates in Bulgaria." *Transition* 6, 3 (1995).

Black, Ian. "Egypt Promises Justice After Copts and Muslims Clash in Cairo." *The Guardian*, May 8, 2011.

Blitz, Brad K., ed. *War and Change in the Balkans: Nationalism, Conflict and Cooperation.* Cambridge: Cambridge University Press, 2006.

Blumi, Isa. "The Commodification of Otherness and the Ethnic Unit in the Balkans." *East European Politics and Societies* 12, 3 (1998): 527–69.

Bob, Clifford. *The Marketing of Rebellion: Insurgents, Media, and International Activism.* Cambridge: Cambridge University Press, 2005.

Bose, Sumantra. *Bosnia After Dayton: Nationalist Partition and International Intervention.* Oxford: Oxford University Press, 2002.

Boyle, Michael. "Revenge and Reprisal Violence in Kosovo." *Conflict, Security, and Development* 10, 2 (2010): 189–216.

Brady, Henry and David Collier, eds. *Rethinking Social Inquiry: Diverse Tools, Shared Standards.* Lantham, Md.: Rowman and Littlefield, 2004.

Brown, Michael E., Owen R. Coté, Jr., Sean M. Lynn-Jones, and Steven E. Miller, eds. *New Global Dangers: Changing Dimensions of International Security.* Cambridge, Mass.: MIT Press, 2004.

Brubaker, Rogers. *Nationalism Reframed: Nationhood and the National Question in the New Europe.* Cambridge: Cambridge University Press, 1996.

Buckley, William, ed. *Contending Voices on International Interventions.* Grand Rapids, Mich.: Eerdman, 2000.

Bugajksi, Janusz. *Ethnic Politics in Eastern Europe: A Guide to Nationality Policies, Organizations, and Parties.* Armonk, N.Y.: Sharpe, 1995.

Buhaug, Halvard, Lars-Erik Cederman, and Jan Rod, "Disaggregating Ethno-Nationalist Civil Wars." *International Organization* 62 (Summer 2008): 531–51.

Bukoshi, Bujar. "Conversations with Contemporaries." In *Kosovo in the Heart of the Powder Keg*, ed. Robert Elsie. New York: Columbia University Press, 1997.

Bulgarian Factor. "Ataka and Millet-Trakia sa Skacheni Sadove" [Ataka and Millet-Trakia go hand-in-hand together]. February 22, 2006, http://www.factor-news.net/index_.php?cm = 2&ct = 1&id = 7047.

Bulgarian Helsinki Committee (BHC). *Human Rights in Bulgaria in 1996.* Annual Report, April 2011. 10.

Bulgarian Telegraph Agency. "Gn Ahmed Dogan zamina za Turtsia" [Mr. Ahmed Dogan Left for Turkey]. March 4, 1993, 63.

———. "Na foruma v Paris" [At the Paris Forum]. BTA Poveritelno Prilozhenie [A Secret Addendum]. June 1989.

Bunce, Valerie. "Minority Politics in Ethno-Federal States: Cooperation, Autonomy, or Secession." Working Paper, Department of Government, Cornell University. June 14, 2006.

———. "The National Idea." *East European Politics and Societies* 8, 19 (2005): 406–42.

———. "Rethinking Recent Democratization." *World Politics* 55 (2003): 167–92.

———. *Subversive Institutions: The Design and the Destruction of Socialism and the State.* Cambridge: Cambridge University Press, 1999.

Bunce, Valerie and Sharon Wolchik, *Defeating Authoritarian Leaders in Postcommunist Countries.* Cambridge: Cambridge University Press, 2011.

Burg, Steven and Paul Shoup. *The War in Bosnia-Herzegovina: Ethnic Conflict and International Intervention.* New York: M.E. Sharpe, 1999.

Bustikova, Lenka and Herbert Kitschelt, "The Radical Right in Post-Communist Europe." *Communist and Post-Communist Studies* 42 (2009): 459–83.

Buzan, Barry. "Societal Security, State Security and Internationalization." In *Identity, Migration and the New Security Agenda in Europe,* ed. Ole Waever, Barry Buzan, Morten Kelstrup, and Pierre Lemaitre. London, Pinter, 1993. 41–58.

Buzan, Barry and Ole Waever. *Regions and Powers: The Structure of International Security.* Cambridge: Cambridge University Press, 2003.

Byman, Daniel, Peter Chalk, Bruce Hoffman, William Rosenau, and David Brennan. *Trends in Outside Support for Insurgent Movements.* Santa Monica, Calif.: Rand, 2001.

Caballero, Gonzalo, Abel Caballero Álvarez, and Abel Losada Álvarez. "Institutions and Credible Commitment in the European Union Institutions." Paper presented at CNISS Seminar, Washington University, St. Louis, November 2004.

Call, Charles and Susan Cook. "On Democratization and Peace-Building." *Global Governance* 9 (2003): 233–46.

Capoccia, Giovanni and Daniel Kelemen. "The Study of Critical Junctures." *World Politics* 59 (2007): 341–69.

Capoccia, Giovanni and Daniel Ziblatt. "The Historical Turn in Democratization Studies: A New Research Agenda for Europe and Beyond." *Comparative Political Studies* 43, 8 (2010): 931–68.

Cardias, Adam. "Kosovo: Vetevendosje's Determination." *Transitions Online*, January 12, 2012.

Carment, David. "The International Dimensions of Ethnic Conflict." *Journal of Peace Research* 30, 2 (1993): 137–50.

Carment, David and Patrick James. "Internal Constraints and Interstate Ethnic Conflict." *Journal of Conflict Resolution* 39, 1 (1995): 82–109.

———. *Wars in the Midst of Peace: The International Politics of Ethnic Conflict*. Pittsburgh: University of Pittsburgh Press, 1997. 194–231.

Carment, David, Patrick James, and Zeynep Taydas. "The Internationalization of Ethnic Conflict." *International Studies Quarterly* 11 (2009): 63–86.

Carment, David and Dane Rowlands. "Evaluating Third Party Intervention in Intrastate Conflict." *Journal of Conflict Resolution* 42, 5 (1998): 572–99.

Carment, David and Albrecht Schnabel, eds. *Conflict Prevention: Path to Peace or Grand Illusion*. New York: UN University Press, 2003.

Carruthers, Bruce. "Institutional Dynamics: When Is Change 'Real' Change?" Comparative-Historical Social Science (CHISS) Working Paper 12–004. Buffett Center, Northwestern University, February 2012.

CBS News. "EU: Kosovo, Serbia Agree on Practical Issue." July 22, 2011.

Cederman, Lars-Eric and Luc Girardin. "Beyond Fractionalization." *American Political Science Review* 101, 1 (2007): 173–85.

Center for Research and Policy Making. *Budget Watchdogs*. Policy Study 6, February 2008. Skopje, Macedonia, http://www.crpm.org.mk/Papers/BudgetWatchdogsENG.pdf.

Cetinyan, Rupen. "Ethnic Bargaining in the Shadow of Third Party Intervention." *International Organization* 56, 3 (2002): 645–77.

Chandra, Kanchan and Steven Wilkinson. "Measuring the Effect of Ethnicity." *Comparative Political Studies* 41, 4–5 (2008): 515–63.

24 Chasa, April 4, 2002.

168 Chasa, May 3–9, 2002.

Chazan, Naomi, ed. *Irredentism and International Politics*. Boulder, Colo.: Lynne Rienner, 1991.

Checkel, Jeffrey. "Why Comply? Social Learning and European Identity Change." *International Organization* 30 (2001): 553–88.

Chomsky, Noam. *The New Military Humanism: Lessons from Kosovo*. Monroe, Me.: Common Courage Press, 1999.

Clark, Howard. *Civil Resistance in Kosovo*. London: Pluto Press, 2000.

Coggins, Bridget. "Friends in High Places." *International Organization* 65, 3 (July 2011): 433–67.

Collier, Paul. "Implications of Ethnic Diversity." *Economic Policy* 16, 32 (2001): 129–66.

Collier, Paul, V. L. Elliot, Marta Reynal-Querol, Anke Hoeffler, and Nicholas Sambanis. *Breaking the Conflict Trap: Civil War and Development Policy*. Washington, D.C.: World Bank, 2003.

Collier, Paul and Anke Hoeffler. "Greed and Grievance in Civil War." World Bank Policy Research Working Paper 2355, 2000.

———. "On Economic Causes of Civil War." *Oxford Economic Papers* 50, 4 (1998): 563–73.

———. "On the Incidence of Civil War in Africa." *Journal of Conflict Resolution* 46, 1 (2002): 13–28

Collier, Paul, Anke Hoeffler, and Måns Söderbom. *On the Duration of Civil War*. Washington, D.C.: World Bank, 1999.

———. "Post-Conflict Risks." *Journal of Peace Research* 45, 4 (2004): 461–78.

Collier, Paul and Nicholas Sambanis. "Civil War: A New Agenda." *Journal of Conflict Resolution* 46, 1 (February 2002): 10.

———. "Understanding Civil War." *Journal of Conflict Resolution* 46, 1 (February 2002).

Collier, Ruth and David Collier. *Shaping the Political Arena*. Cambridge: Cambridge University Press, 1991.

Cornell, Svante. "Autonomy as a Source of Conflict." *World Politics* 54 (2002): 245–76.

Corrin, Chris. "Traffic in Women in War and Peace." *Journal of Contemporary European Studies* 12, 2 (2004): 177–92.

Cota, Lulzim. "KLA Commanders Trained in Albania." United Press International, August 23, 2000. http://www.balkanpeace.org/hed/archive/aug00/hed517.shtml.

Council of Europe. *The Former Yugoslav Republic of Macedonia*. Report by Steering Committee on Local and Regional Democracy (CDLR). Strasbourg: Council of Europe, 1998.

Cousens, Elizabeth. "From Missed Opportunities to Overcompensation." In *Ending Civil Wars: The Implementation of Peace Agreements*, ed.

Stephen Stedman, Donald Rothchild, and Elizabeth Cousens. Boulder, Colo.: Lynne Rienner, 2002.

Coyne, Christopher. "The Institutional Prerequisites for Post-Conflict Reconstruction." *Review of Austrian Economics* 18, 3–4 (2005): 325–42.

Crampton, Richard. *A Concise History of Bulgaria.* Cambridge: Cambridge University Press, 1997.

Crawford, Keith. *East Central European Politics Today: From Chaos to Stability?* Manchester: Manchester University Press, 1996.

Crouch, Colin and Henry Farrell. "Breaking the Path for Institutional Development: Alternatives to the New Determinism." Max Planck Institute Working Paper 02/5, 2002.

Csergo, Zsuzsa. *Talk of the Nation: Language and Conflict in Romania and Slovakia.* Ithaca, N.Y.: Cornell University Press, 2007.

Danforth, Loring. *The Macedonian Conflict.* Princeton, N.J.: Princeton University Press, 1995.

Daskalovski, Zhidas. "Democratization in Macedonia and Slovenia." *South-East European Review of Labour and Social Affairs* 3 (1999): 17–44.

———. "Language and Identity: The Ohrid Framework Agreement and Liberal Notions of Citizenship and Nationality in Macedonia." *Journal on Ethnopolitics and Minority Issues in Europe* 3, 1 (2002).

———. *Walking on the Edge: Consolidating Multiethnic Macedonia.* Skopje: Dominant, 2005.

Davenport, Christian. "The Weight of the Past." *Political Research Quarterly* 49, 2 (1996): 377–403.

———, ed. *Paths to State Repression: Human Rights Violations and Contentious Politics.* Lanham, Md.: Rowman and Littlefield, 2000.

Davenport, Christian, David Armstrong, and Mark Lichbach. "Conflict Escalation and the Origins of Civil War." Working Paper, University of Maryland, 2007. http://www.bsos.umd.edu/gvpt/davenport/dcawcp/paper/111605.pdf, accessed August 2012.

Dawisha, Karen and Bruce Parrott, eds. *Politics, Power, and the Struggle for Democracy in South-East Europe.* Cambridge: Cambridge University Press, 1997.

Deets, Stephen and Sherrill Stroschein. "Dilemmas of Autonomy and Liberal Pluralism." *Nations and Nationalism* 11, 2 (2005): 285–305.

Democratsiya. September 5, 1991. "Soczakon za bulgarskia ezik trevozhi DPS" [A Socialist [Draft] Law on the Dimitar Bulgarian Language Bothers the MRF]. *Democratsia Daily,* July 21, 1995.

Demolli, Gani. "The Mother Teresa Society and the War in Kosovo." Overseas Development Institute, October 9, 2002.

Deutsche Presse Agentur. "Powell Consults Albania's Meta on Balkans." *International News,* May 2, 2001.

De Vrieze, Franklin. "Building Parliamentary Democracy in Kosovo." *Security and Human Rights* 19, 2 (2008): 121–36.

De Witte, Bruno. "Politics Versus Law in the EU's Approach to Ethnic Minorities." European University Institute Working Paper RSC 4. San Domenico: EUI, 2000.

Dimitrijevic, Vojin. "The 1974 Constitution as a Factor in the Collapse of Yugoslavia or as a Sign of Decaying Totalitarianism." European Working Institute Working Paper. Florence: EUI, 1994.

DiPrizio, Robert. *Armed Humanitarians: U.S. Interventions from Northern Iraq to Kosovo.* Baltimore: Johns Hopkins University Press, 2002.

Dixit, Avinash K. *The Making of Economic Policy: A Transaction-Cost Politics Perspective.* Cambridge, Mass.: MIT Press, 1996.

Dobbins, James et al. *Europe's Role in Nation-Building: From the Balkans to the Congo.* Santa Monica, Calif.: RAND, 2008.

Dodd, Clement. "Developments in Turkish Democracy." In *Turkey Between East and West: New Challenges for a Rising Regional Power,* ed. Vojtech Mastny and R. Craig Nation. Boulder, Colo.: Westview, 1997.

Doder, Dusko and Louise Branson. *Milosevic: Portrait of a Tyrant.* New York: Simon and Schuster, 1999.

Dogan, Ahmet. *Bulgaria i noviat svetoven red* [Bulgaria and the New World Order]. Sofia: Friedrich Naumann Foundation and Institute for Liberal Studies, 2000.

Dubai Initiative. Conference, Revolution and Reform: The Historic Transition in the Middle East. April 8–9, 2011.

Duijzings, Ger, Dusan Janjic, and Shkelzen Maliqi, eds. *Kosovo/Kosova: Confrontation or Coexistence.* Nijmegen: Peace Research Centre, 1997

Duma Daily. "Is Bulgarian Nationalism a Threat to Our EU Membership?" Series of interviews with Bulgarian public figures, March 15–24, 2006.

———. "Turski holding shte finansira DPS" [A Turkish Holding Will Finance the MRF], April 28, 1995, 88.

The Economist. "Macedonia's Ethnic Disharmony: How Many Building Booms Can One City Take?" March 1, 2011.

Edmead, Frank. Analysis and Prediction in International Mediation. *New York: Unitar, 1971.*

Ekiert, Grzegorz and Stephen Hanson. "Introduction." In *Capitalism and Democracy in Central and Eastern Europe*, ed. Grzegorz Ekiert and Stephen Hanson. Cambridge: Cambridge University Press, 2003.

Elbadawi, Ibraham and Nicholas Sambanis. "External Interventions and the Duration of Civil Wars." Paper at Workshop on the Economics of Civil Violence, Princeton University, April 18–19, 2000.

———. "How Much War Will We See?" *Journal of Conflict Resolution* 46, 3 (2002): 307–34.

Election Guide. "Macedonia Referendum." November 7, 2004. http://www .electionguide.org/results.php?ID = 280.

Elkins, Zachary and John Sides. "Can Institutions Build Unity in Multiethnic States." *American Political Science Review* 101, 4 (2007): 693–94.

Ellingen, Tanja. "Colorful Community or Ethnic Witches Brew?" *Journal of Conflict Resolution* 44 (2000): 192–206.

Elster, Jon. "Introduction." In *Constitutionalism and Democracy*, ed. Jon Elster and Rune Slagstad. Cambridge: Cambridge University Press, 1988.

Eminov, Ali. *Turkish and Other Muslim Minorities in Bulgaria*. London: Hurst, 1997.

Esteban, Joan and Debraj Ray. "On the Measurement of Polarization." *Econometrica* 62, 4 (July 1994): 819–51.

Ethnobarometer. *Crisis in Macedonia*. Rome: International Research Network on Interethnic Politics and Migration, 2001.

EurActiv. "Macedonia Protests Signal Surge of Radical Islam." May 14, 2012.

European Commission. "EU and the Western Balkans." http://ec.europa .eu/bulgaria/abc/eu_works/enlargement/eu-and-the-western-balkans_ en.htm.

———. "The Former Yugoslav Republic of Macedonia Progress Report." October 14, 2009. http://ec.europa.eu/enlargement/pdf/key_documents /2009/mk_rapport_2009_en.pdf.

———. "Monitoring Report on the State of Preparedness for EU Membership of Bulgaria and Romania." Brussels, September 26, 2006. http://

ec.europa.eu/enlargement/archives/bulgaria/eu_bulgaria_relations_en
.htm.

European Court on Human Rights. *Deloto Hasan i Chaush sreshtu Bulgaria*
[The Case of Hassan and Chaush Against Bulgaria]. The Decision.
Strasbourg: European Court on Human Rights, October 26, 2000.

European Forum for Democracy and Solidarity. "Building of Church in
Macedonia Leads to Ethnic Clashes." February 15, 2011.

European Security. "Kosovo: A Long Road to War. A Chronology 1988–
1991." 2003. http://www.basicint.org/europe/confprev/Kosovo/time
line1.htm, accessed October 2004.

EU. "Bulgaria-Turkey IPA Cross-Border Programme." September 21, 2007.
http://europa.eu/rapid/pressReleasesAction.do?reference = MEMO/09/
39&type = HTML.

EUobserver, "Bulgaria Puts Price on Turkey's EU Membership." January 1,
2010, http://euobserver.com/9/29212.

Fair, Christine. "Diaspora Involvement in Insurgencies." *Nationalism and
Ethnic Politics* 11 (Spring 2005): 127–47.

Faist, Thomas. "Transnationalization in International Migration." *Ethnic
and Racial Studies* 23, 2 (2000): 189–222.

Fearon, James. "Commitment Problems and the Spread of Ethnic Conflict." In *The International Spread of Ethnic Conflict*, ed. David Lake and
Donald Rothchild. Princeton, N.J.: Princeton University Press, 1998.

———. "Counterfactuals and Hypothesis Testing in Political Science."
World Politics 43 (January 1991): 169–95.

———. "Rationalist Explanations for War." *International Organization* 49,
3 (1995): 379–414.

Fearon, James, Kimuli Kasara, and David Laitin. "Ethnic Minority Rule and
Civil War Onset." *American Political Science Review* 101, 1 (February
2007): 187–93.

Fearon, James and David Laitin. "Ethnicity, Insurgency, and Civil War."
American Political Science Review 97, 1 (2003): 75–90.

———. "Explaining Interethnic Cooperation." *American Political Science
Review* 90, 4 (1996): 715–35.

———. "Neotrusteeship and the Problem of Weak States." *International
Security* 28, 4 (2004): 5–43.

Fekrat, Bruce, Jonathan Fox, and Lyubov Mincheva. "Albanians in Macedonia." Minorities at Risk Project, 1999. http://www.bsos.umd.edu/
cidcm/mar/macalban.htm.

Fioretos, Orfeo. "Historical Institutionalism in International Relations." *International Organization* 65 (2011): 367–99.

Flores Juberias, Carlos. "Electoral Systems in Eastern Europe." *Balkan Forum* 17, 4 (December 1996): 87–116.

Fox, Jonathan. "Two Civilizations and Ethnic Conflict." *Journal of Peace Research* 38, 4 (2001): 459–72.

Framework Agreement. August 13, 2001. Ohrid, Macedonia. http://www.venice.coe.int/docs/2001/CDL(2001)104-e.asp.

Friedman, Eben. "Electoral Systems Design and Minority Representation in Slovakia and Macedonia." *Ethnopolitics* 4, 4 (2005): 381–96.

Frye, Timothy. *Building States and Markets After Communism.* Cambridge: Cambridge University Press, 2010.

Fujii, Lee Ann. *Killing Neighbors: Webs of Violence in Rwanda.* Ithaca, N.Y.: Cornell University Press, 2009.

Fukuyama, Francis. *State-Building: Governance and World Order in the Twenty-First Century.* Ithaca, N.Y.: Cornell University Press, 2004.

Fuller, Graham. "Turkey's New Eastern Orientation." In *Turkey's New Geopolitics: From the Balkans to Western China.*, ed. Graham Fuller and Ian O. Lesser. Boulder, Colo.: Westview.

Fuller, Graham and Ian O. Lesser, eds. *Turkey's New Geopolitics: From the Balkans to Western China.* Boulder, Colo.: Westview.

Gaber, Natasha. "The Muslim Population in FYROM (Macedonia)." In *Muslim Identity and the Balkan State*, ed. Hugh Poulton and Suja Taji-Farouki. New York: New York University Press with Islamic Council, 1997.

Gagnon, V. P. "Ethnic Nationalism and International Conflict." *International Security* 19, 3 (1994–1995).

———. *The Myth of Ethnic War: Serbia and Croatia in the 1990s.* Ithaca, N.Y.: Cornell University Press, 2004.

Ganev, Venelin. "Ballots, Bribes, and State-Building in Bulgaria." *Journal of Democracy* 17, 1 (2006): 75–89.

Ganguly, Rajat. *Kin State Intervention in Ethnic Conflicts.* London: Sage, 1998.

Geertz, Clifford. *The Interpretation of Cultures.* New York: Basic Books, 1973.

George, Alexander and Andrew Bennett. *Case Studies and Theory Development in the Social Sciences.* Cambridge, Mass.: MIT Press, 2004.

Georgievski, Lyubcho. "Theses for Survival of the Macedonian Nation and State." In Vladimir Milchin, "Inventory." Skopje: Soros Foundation, 2003.

Gessen, Masha. "The Parallel University." *Lingua Franca* 5, 1 (1994).

Ghodsee, Kristen. "Left Wing, Right Wing, Everything." *Problems of Post-Communism* (May–June 2008): 26–39.

———. *Muslim Lives in Eastern Europe*. Princeton, N.J.: Princeton University Press, 2009.

Gjurcilova, Penelope. *From Co-operation to Membership: The development of Relations Between the European Union and Eastern European Countries Leading to the Stabilization and Association Process, with Special Emphasis on the Republic of Macedonia*. Skopje: EC Delegation, 2005.

Glaser, Charles. "The Security Dilemma Revisited." *World Politics* 50, 1 (1997): 171–201.

Glenny, Misha. *The Balkans: Nationalism, War and the Great Powers 1804–1999*. New York: Viking, 2000.

Goati, Vladimir. "The Impact of Parliamentary Democracy on Ethnic Relations in Yugoslavia, 1989–1995." In *Ethnic Conflict Management*, ed. Dusan Janjic. Ravenna: Longo, 1997.

Goddard, Stacey. Jeremy Pressman, and Ron Hassner. "Time and the Intractability of Territorial Disputes." *International Security* 32, 3 (2007/2008): 191–201.

Goldstone, Jack. *Revolution and Rebellion in the Early Modern World*. Cambridge: Cambridge University Press, 1991.

Gow, James. *Triumph of the Lack of Will: International Diplomacy and the Yugoslav War*. New York: Columbia University Press, 1997.

Gowan, Peter. "The NATO Powers and the Balkan Tragedy." *New Left Review* 234 (March–April 1999).

Greskovits, Bela. "Economic Woes and Political Disaffection." *Journal of Democracy* 8, 4 (2007): 40–46.

Grigoryan, Arman. "Third Parties and State-Minority Conflicts." Ph.D. dissertation, Columbia University, 2008.

———. "Third-Party Intervention and the *Escalation* of State-Minority Conflicts." *International Studies Quarterly* 54, 4 (December 2010): 1143–74.

Grigorian, Arman and Stuart Kaufman. "Hate Narratives and Ethnic Conflict." *International Security* 31, 4 (2007): 180–91.

Grzymala-Busse, Anna. "The Best Laid Plans." *Studies in Comparative International Development* 45, 45 (2010): 311–33.

The Guardian. "EU: Kosovo, Serbia Agree on Practical Issues." July 3, 2011.

Gurr, Ted Robert. *Minorities at Risk: A Global View of Ethnopolitical Conflicts.* Washington, D.C.: USIP, 1993.

———. "Peoples Against the State." *International Studies Quarterly* 38, 3 (1994): 347–77.

———. *Peoples Versus States: Minorities at Risk in the New Century.* Washington, D.C.: USIP, 2000.

———. *Why Men Rebel.* Princeton, N.J.: Princeton University Press, 1970.

Gurr, Ted Robert and Will Moore. "Ethnopolitical Rebellion." *American Journal of Political Science* 41 (1997): 1079–1103.

Hale, Henry. "The Parade of Sovereignties." *British Journal of Political Science* 30, 1 (2000): 31–56.

Hall, Peter and David Soskice. *Varieties of Capitalism: The Institutional Foundations of Comparative Advantage.* Oxford: Oxford University Press, 2001.

Hamzaj, Bardh. *A Narrative About War and Freedom.* Prishtina: Zeri, 1999.

Hartzell, Caroline and Matthew Hoddie. "Institutionalizing Peace." *American Journal of Political Science* 47, 2 (2003): 318–32.

Hassner, Ron. "The Path to Intractability." *International Security* 31 (2006–2007): 107–31.

Hechter, Michael. "Nationalism and Rationality." *Studies in Comparative International Development* 35, 1 (2000): 3–19.

Hedges, Chris. "Kosovo Rebels Find Friend in Former Albanian President." *New York Times,* June 10, 1998.

Hegre, Håvard, Tanja Ellingsen, Scott Gates, and Nils Petter Gleditsch. "Toward a Democratic Civil Peace? Democracy, Political Change, and Civil War 1816–1992." *American Political Science Review* 95, 1 (March 2001): 16–33.

Hegre, Håvard and Nicholas Sambanis. "Sensitivity of Empirical Results on Civil War Onset." *Journal of Conflict Resolution* 50, 4 (August 2006).

Hehir, Aidan. "Kosovo's Final Status and the Viability of Ongoing International Administration." *Civil Wars* 9, 3 (2007): 243–61.

Helmke, Gretchen and Steven Levitsky. "Informal Institutions and Comparative Politics." *Perspectives on Politics* 2, 4 (2004): 725–26.

———. *Informal Institutions and Democracy.* Baltimore: Johns Hopkins University Press, 2007.

Helsinki Watch. *Yugoslavia: Human Rights Abuses in Kosovo 1990–1992.* New York: Helsinki Watch, 1992.

Henderson, Errol. "Culture or Contiguity? Ethnic Conflict, the Similarity of States, and the Onset of War, 1890–1989." *Journal of Conflict Resolution* 41, 5 (2005): 649–68.

Heraclides, Alexis. "Secessionist Minorities and External Involvement." *International Organization* 44, 3 (1990): 341–78.

Hislope, Robert. "Between a Bad Peace and a Good War." *Ethnic and Racial Studies* 26, 1 (January 2003): 129–51.

———. "Corrupt Exchange in Divided Societies." In *Transnational Actors in Central and East European Transitions,* ed. Mitchell Orenstein, Stephen Bloom, and Nicole Lindstom. Pittsburgh: University of Pittsburgh Press, 2008. 142–61.

———. "Organized Crime in a Disorganized State." *Problems of Post-Communism* 49, 3 (May/June 2002): 33–41.

Hockenos, Paul. *Homeland Calling: Exile Patriotism and the Balkan Wars.* Ithaca, N.Y.: Cornell University Press, 2003.

Höpken, Wolfgang. "From Religious Identity to Ethnic Mobilization." In *Muslim Identity and the Balkan State,* ed. Hugh Poulton and Suha Taji-Farouki. London: Hurst, 1997.

Hoffmann, Stanley. *World Disorders: Troubled Peace in the Post-Cold War Era.* Lanham, Md.: Rowman and Littlefield, 1999.

Höglund, Kristine. "Managing Violent Crises." *International Peacekeeping* 14, 3 (2007): 403–41.

———. "Violence in War-to-Democracy Transitions." In *From War to Democracy: Dilemmas of Peacebuilding,* ed. Anna K. Jarstad and Timothy D. Sisk. Cambridge: Cambridge University Press, 2008, 83–90.

Holbrooke, Richard. *To End a War.* New York: Random House, 1998.

Hoogenboom, Jitske. "EU as a Peace-Builder in Kosovo." Paper presented at Civil Society Dialogue Network meeting, Bucharest, June 28, 2011. http://www.eplo.org/assets/files/2.%20Activities/CSDN/CSDN_Romania_PolicyAnalysis_EUasPeacebuilderinKosovo.pdf.

Horowitz, Donald. "Democracy in Divided Societies." *Journal of Democracy* 4, 4 (October 1993): 18–38.

———. *Ethnic Groups in Conflict.* Berkeley: University of California Press, 1985.

———. "Irredentas and Secessions." In *Irredentism and International Politics,* ed. Naomi Chazan. Boulder, Colo.: Lynne Rienner, 1991.

Hughes, James. *Chechnya: From Nationalism to Jihad*. Philadelphia: University of Pennsylvania Press, 2007.

Hughes, James and Gwendolyn Sasse. "Monitoring the Monitors." *Journal of Ethnopolitics and Minority Issues in Europe* 1 (2003).

Human Rights Watch (HRW). *Bulgaria*, 1989. http://www.hrw.org/reports/ 1989/WR89/Bulgaria.htm.

———. *Open Wounds: Human Rights Abuses in Kosovo*. New York: HRW/ Helsinki, 1993.

———. *Police Violence in Macedonia*, April 1998. http://www.hrw.org/ reports98/macedonia.

———. *A Threat to "Stability": Human Rights Violations in Macedonia*. New York: HRW/Helsinki, 1996.

Huntington, Samuel. "The Clash of Civilizations." *Foreign Affairs* 72, 3 (1993): 2–49.

———. *The Clash of Civilizations and the Remaking of World Order*. London: Simon and Schuster, 1997.

Ilievski, Zoran and Dane Taleski. "Was the EU's Role in Conflict Management in Macedonia a Success?" *Ethnopolitics* 8, 3 (2009).

The Independent, "Hunt for Karadzic Ends as Fugitive Is Found." July 22, 2008.

Independent International Commission on Kosovo. *The Kosovo Report*. Oxford: Oxford University Press, 2000.

International Crisis Group (ICG). *Kosovo and Serbia After the ICJ Opinion*. Europe Report 206, August 26, 2010.

———. *Kosovo: Bite the Bullet*. January 22, 1999, not available online.

———. "Kosovo Briefing." February 17, 1998. http://www.intl-crisis-group.org/

———. "Kosovo's First Month." *Europe Briefing* 47, March 2008.

———. *Kosovo Spring* (Part I, II). March 20, 1998. http://www.intl-crisis group.org/.

———. *Kosovo's Fragile Transition*. Europe Report 196, September 25, 2008, 2.

———. *Macedonia: New Faces in Skopje*. Europe Report 51. January 8, 1999.

———. *Macedonia Report: The Politics of Ethnicity and Conflict*. October 21, 1997.

———. *Macedonia: Ten Years After the Conflict*. Europe Report 212, August 11, 2011.

———. *Macedonia's Ethnic Albanians: Bridging the Gulf*. August 2, 2000.

———. *Macedonia Towards Destabilization? The Kosovo Crisis Takes Its Toll on Macedonia.* May 21, 1999.

———. *Macedonia: War on Hold.* Briefing Paper. August 15, 2001. http://www.intl-crisis-group.org/.

———. *North Kosovo: Dual Sovereignty in Practice.* Europe Report 211. March 14, 2011.

———. *Pan-Albanianism.* Europe Report 153. February 25, 2004.

International Helsinki Federation (IHF). "Human Rights in the OSCE Region." *Annual Report.* Vienna: IHF, 1996; 1997; 2003; 2004; 2005.

International Organization for Migration. "Mapping Exercise Albania." Occasional Paper, September 2008, London.

Irwin, Zachary. "Yugoslavia's Relations with European States." In *Beyond Yugoslavia: Politics, Economics, and Culture in a Shattered Community,* ed. Sabrina P. Ramet and Ljubisa S. Adamovic. Boulder, Colo.: Westview, 1995. 349–91.

Janos, Andrew. *East Central Europe in the Modern World.* Stanford, Calif.: Stanford University Press, 2000.

Jansen, Richard. "Albanians and Serbs in Kosovo: An Abbreviated History: An Opening for the the Islamic Jihad in Europe." Colorado State University, Fort Collins, July 22, 2008. http://lamar.colostate.edu/~grjan/kosovohistory.html.

Jarstad, Anna K. "To Share or to Divide: Negotiating the Future of Kosovo." *Civil Wars* 9, 3 (2007): 227–42.

Jarstad, Anna K. and Timothy D. Sisk, eds. *From War to Democracy: Dilemmas of Peacebuilding.* Cambridge: Cambridge University Press, 2008.

Jenkins, Gareth. "Turkey and Northern Iraq: An Overview." Occasional Paper, Jamestown Foundation, February 2008.

Jenne, Erin. "A Bargaining Theory of Minority Demands: Explaining the Dog That Did Not Bite in 1990s Yugoslavia." *International Studies Quarterly* 48, 4 (2004): 729–54.

———. *Ethnic Bargaining: The Paradox of Minority Empowerment.* Ithaca, N.Y.: Cornell University Press, 2007.

Jervis, Robert. "Cooperation Under the Security Dilemma." *World Politics* 30, 2 (1978): 167–214.

Judah, Tim. *Kosovo: War and Revenge.* New Haven, Conn.: Yale University Press, 2000.

———. *Kosovo: What Everyone Needs to Know.* Oxford: Oxford University Press, 2008.

Jung Jai Kwan. "The Paradox of Institution Building After Civil War: A Trade-off Between Short-Term Peacemaking and Long-Term Democracy Building." Ph.D. dissertation, Cornell University, 2008.

Kahler, Miles and Barbara F. Walter. *Territoriality and Conflict in an Era of Globalization, Territoriality, and Conflict.* Cambridge: Cambridge University Press, 2006.

Kaldor, Mary. *New and Old Wars: Organized Violence in a Global Era.* Stanford, Calif.: Stanford University Press, 1998.

Kalyvas, Stathis. "Ethnic Defection in Civil War." *Comparative Political Studies* 41, 8 (2008): 1043–68.

———. *The Logic of Violence in Civil War.* Cambridge: Cambridge University Press, 2006.

Kamberi, Belgzim and Faruk Daliu. "Preshevo Valley Albanians Demand Place at Kosovo Talks." *Balkan Insight*, November 16, 2005.

Kamminga, Menno T. "State Succession in Respect of Human Rights Treaties." *European Journal of International Law* 7, 4 (1996): 469–84.

Kanev, Krassimir. "From Totalitarianism to Constitutional State." In *Bulgaria at the Crossroads*, ed. Jacques Coenen-Huther. New York: Nova Science, 1996.

Kaplan, Robert D. *Balkan Ghosts: A Journey Through History.* New York: St. Martin's, 1993.

Karl, Terry-Lynn. *The Paradox of Plenty: Oil Booms and Petro States.* Berkeley: University of California Press, 1997.

Karon, Tony. "New Violence in Kosovo Could Pose a Quandary for Overstretched NATO." *Time*, July 27, 2011.

Kaufman, Stewart J. "Symbolic Politics or Rational Choice? Testing Theories of Extreme Ethnic Violence." *International Security* 30, 4 (2006): 45–86.

Keck, Margaret and Kathryn Sikkink. *Activists Beyond Borders: Advocacy Networks in International Politics.* Ithaca, N.Y.: Cornell University Press, 1998.

Keesing's Record of World Events. 1990. Section on Bulgaria. 375–44.

Kelley, Judith G. *Ethnic Politics in Europe: The Power of Norms and Incentives.* Princeton, N.J.: Princeton University Press, 2004.

———. "International Actors and the Domestic Scene." *International Organization* 58, 3 (2004): 425–57.

Kemp, Walter. *Quiet Diplomacy in Action.* The Hague: Kluwer, 2001.

King, Gary, Robert Keohane, and Sidney Verba. *Designing Social Inquiry:*

Scientific Inference in Qualitative Research. Princeton, N.J.: Princeton University Press, 1994.

Klekovski, Sasho. "Inter-Ethnic Relations in Macedonia" [in Macedonian]. Skopje: Macedonian Center for Inter-Ethnic Cooperation, June 2011.

Kohler, Kevin. "Authoritarian Elections in Egypt." *Democratization* 15, 5 (2008): 974–90.

Koinova, Maria. "Challenging Assumptions of the Enlargement Literature." *Europe-Asia Studies* 63, 5 (2011): 807–32.

———. "Diasporas and Secessionist Conflicts." *Ethnic and Racial Studies* 34, 2 (2011): 333–56.

———. "Four Types of Diaspora Mobilization: Albanian Diaspora Activism in the US and the UK." *Foreign Policy Analysis*, online, July 12, 2012.

———. "Kinstate Intervention in Ethnic Conflicts." *Ethnopolitics* 7, 4 (2008): 373–90.

———. "Kosovo Albanians and the Solidarity of Their Ethnic Brethren." *Alternative Information Network*, April 30, 1998.

———. *Muslims of Bulgaria.* CEDIME-SE Report, 1999. http://www.greekhelsinki.gr.

———. *Muslims of Macedonia.* CEDIME-SE Report, August 2000. http://www.greekhelsinki.gr.

———. "Saxcoburggotsky and His Catch-All Attitude." *Southeast European Politics* 2, 2 (2001): 135–40.

———. "Why Do Conflict-Generated Diasporas Pursue Sovereignty-Based Claims Through Contained or Transgressive Contention?" Paper presented at Explaining Diaspora Politics Workshop, SOAS, London, October 30–31, 2009.

Koinova, Maria with Irina Gigova. *Albanians of Macedonia.* CEDIME-SE, April 2002. http://www.greekhelsinki.gr.

Kola, Paulin. *The Search for Greater Albania.* London: Hurst, 222.

Kosovo Compromise. "Clashes in Kosovska Mitrovica." March 18, 2008. http://www.kosovocompromise.com/cms/item/topic/en.html?view = story&id = 704&sectionId = 1.

Kostovicova, Denisa. "Legitimacy and International Administration." *International Peacekeeping* 15, 5 (2008): 631–47.

———. *Parallel Worlds: The Response of Kosovo Albanians to Loss of Autonomy in Serbia, 1989–1996.* Keele: University of Keele Research Centre, 1997.

Kramer, Heinz. *A Changing Turkey: The Challenge to Europe and the United States.* Washington, D.C.: Brookings Institution Press, 2000.

Krasner, Stephen D. *Sovereignty: Organized Hypocrisy.* Princeton, N.J.: Princeton University Press, 1999.

Krastev, Ivan. "The Strange Death of the Liberal Consensus." *Journal of Democracy* 18, 4 (2007): 56–63.

Kriesberg, Louis."Introduction." In *Timing the De-Escalation of International Conflicts,* ed. Louis Kriesberg and Stuart Thorson. Syracuse, N.Y.: Syracuse University Press, 1991.

Kriesberg, Louis and Stuart Thorson, eds. Timing the De-Escalation of International Conflicts. *Syracuse, N.Y.: Syracuse University Press, 1991.*

Kumar, Krishna, ed. *Rebuilding Societies After Civil War: Critical Roles for International Assistance.* Boulder, Colo.: Lynne Rienner, 1997.

Kurspahic, Kemal. "From Bosnia to Kosovo and Beyond: Mistakes and Lessons." In *War and Change in the Balkans: Nationalism, Conflict and Cooperation,* ed. Brad K. Blitz. Cambridge: Cambridge University Press, 2006. 76–86.

Kusovac, Zoran. "Round Two: Serbian Security Forces." *Transitions* (September 1998).

Kymlicka, Will. "Justice and Security in the Accommodation of Minority Nationalism." In *Ethnicity, Nationalism, and Minority Rights,* ed. Stephen May, Tariq Modood, and Judith Squires. Cambridge: Cambridge University Press, 2004. 144–75.

———. *Multicultural Citizenship: A Liberal Theory of Minority Rights.* Oxford: Oxford University Press, 1995.

Laitin, David D. "Language Conflict and Violence, or the Straw That Strengthened the Camel's Back." Working Paper 137. Juan March Institute, Madrid, June 1999.

Lake, David and Donald Rothchild. "Containing Fear." *International Security* 21, 2 (Fall 1996): 41–75.

Lani, Remzi. "From Nano-Milosevic to Rugova-Milosevic." *Alternative Information Network (AIM),* May 26, 1998. http://www.aimpress.org/dyn/trae/archive/data/199806/80611–033-trae-tir.htm.

Lapidoth, Ruth. *Autonomy: Flexible Solutions to Ethnic Conflicts.* Washington, D.C.: USIP, 1996.

Laver, Michael and Kenneth Shepsle. "Events, Equilibria, and Government Survival." *American Journal of Political Science* 42, 1 (1998): 28–54.

Lebow, Richard Ned. *Forbidden Fruit: Counterfactuals and International Relations*. Princeton, N.J.: Princeton University Press, 2010.

———. "What's So Different About a Counterfactual?" *World Politics* 52 (July 2000): 550–85.

Legro, Jeffrey. "The Transformation of Policy Ideas." *American Journal of Political Science* 44, 3 (July 2000): 419–32.

Leka, Arjan. "Peace in Skopje Accompanied by a Chill in Relations with Tirana." *Alternative Information Network*, Tirana, August 31, 2001.

Lenkova, Mariana. *Turks of Bulgaria*. CEDIME-SE, December 1999. http://www.greekhelsinki.gr.

Levitsky, Steven and Lucan Way. *Competitive Authoritarianism: Hybrid Regimes After the Cold War*. Cambridge: Cambridge University Press, 2010.

Lijphart, Arend. *Democracy in Plural Societies: A Comparative Exploration*. New Haven, Conn.: Yale University Press, 1974.

Lijphart, Arend and Carlos H. Waisman, eds. *Institutional Design in New Democracies*. Boulder, Colo.: Westview, 1996.

Linz, Juan J. and Alfred Stepan. "Political Identities and Electoral Sequences: Spain, the Soviet Union, and Yugoslavia." *Daedalus* 121, 2 (Spring 1992): 123–39.

———. *Problems of Democratic Transition and Consolidation: Southern Europe, South America, and Post-Communist Europe*. Baltimore: Johns Hopkins University Press, 1996.

Liotta, P. H. and Cindy Jebb. *Mapping Macedonia: Idea and Identity*. Westport, Conn.: Praeger, 2004.

Lisher, Sarah. "Collateral Damage." In *New Global Dangers: Changing Dimensions of International Security*, ed. Michael E. Brown, Owen R. Coté, Jr., Sean M. Lynn-Jones, and Steven E. Miller. Cambridge, Mass.: MIT Press, 2004. 390–411.

Lucic, Zoran. *An Insider Look at the November 1996 Elections*. 1997. http://www.ex-yupress.com/republika/republika1.html.

Luebbert, Gregory. *Liberalism, Fascism, or Social Democracy: Social Classes and the Political Origins of Regimes in Interwar Europe*. New York: Oxford University Press, 1991.

Lund, Michael. "Preventive Diplomacy for Macedonia, 1992–1999: From Containment to National Building.." In *Opportunities Missed, Opportunities Seized: Preventive Diplomacy in the Post-Cold War World*, ed. Bruce Jentleson. Lanham, Md.: Rowman and Littlefield, 2000. 173–208.

Lustick, Ian. *Arabs in the Jewish State: Israel's Control of a National Minority*. Austin: University of Texas Press, 1980.

Lustick, Ian, Dan Miodownik, and Roy Eidelson. "Secessionism in Multicultural States." *American Political Science Review* 98, 2 (May 2004).

Lutovac, Zoran. "All Serbian and Albanian 'Elections' in Kosovo." *Alternative Information Network*, 1997. http://www.aimpress.org/dy/traearchive/data/199705/70523–002-trae-beo.html.

Lyons, Terrance. "Diasporas and Homeland Conflict." In *Territoriality and Conflict in an Era of Globalization*, ed. Miles Kahler and Barbara F. Walter. Cambridge: Cambridge University Press, 2006.

Mabee, Bryan. "Exogenous Shocks, Institutional Change, and Path-Dependence." Paper presented at ISA, Chicago, February 28, 2007.

Mahoney, James. *The Legacies of Liberalism: Path Dependence and Political Regimes in Central America*. Baltimore: Johns Hopkins University Press, 2001.

———. "Path Dependence in Historical Sociology." *Theory and Society* 29 (2000): 526–27.

———. "Path-Dependent Explanations of Regime Change: Central America in Comparative Perspective." *Studies in Comparative International Development* 36, 1 (Spring 2001): 111–41.

Mahoney, James and Kathleen Thelen. *Explaining Institutional Change: Ambiguity, Agency and Power*. Cambridge: Cambridge University Press, 2010.

Mahoney, James and Dietrich Rueschemeyer, "Comparative Historical Analysis." In *Comparative Historical Analysis in the Social Sciences*, ed. James Mahoney and Dietrich Rueschemeyer. Cambridge: Cambridge University Press, 2003.

Malcolm, Noel. *Kosovo: A Short History*. New York: New York University Press, 1999.

Maliqi, Shkelzen. "Albanians Between East and West." In *Kosovo/Kosova: Confrontation or Coexistence*, ed. Ger Duijzings, Dusan Janjic, and Shkelzen Maliqi. Nijmegen: Peace Research Centre, 1997.

———. *Kosova: Separate Worlds*. Prishtina: Dukadjini PH, 1998.

Manning, Carrie. "Party-Building on the Heels of War." *Democratization* 14, 2 (2007): 253–72.

Mansfield, Edward D. and Jack Snyder. *Electing to Fight: Why Emerging Democracies Go to War*. Cambridge, Mass.: MIT Press, 2005.

Maoz, Zeev. "Domestic Political Change and Strategic Response." In *Wars in the Midst of Peace: The International Politics of Ethnic Conflict*, ed. David Carment and Patrick James. Pittsburgh: University of Pittsburgh Press, 1997.

March, James G. and J. P. Olsen. "The New Institutionalism: Organizational Factors in Political Life." *American Political Science Review* 78 (1984): 738–49.

Marshall, Monty and Ted Robert Gurr. *Peace and Conflict, 2003*. Baltimore: CIDCM, University of Maryland, 2003.

Mastny, Voitech and R. Craig Nation, eds. *Turkey Between East and West: New Challenges for a Rising Regional Power*. Boulder, Colo.: Westview, 1997.

May, Stephen, Tariq Modood, and Judith Squires, eds. *Ethnicity, Nationalism, and Minority Rights*. Cambridge: Cambridge University Press, 2004.

McAdam, Doug, Sidney Tarrow, and Charles Tilly. *Dynamics of Contention*. Cambridge Studies in Contentious Politics. Cambridge: Cambridge University Press, 2001.

McGarry, John and Brendan O'Leary. "Consociational Theory, Northern Ireland's Conflict, and Its Agreement." *Government and Opposition* 41, 1 (2006): 43–63.

———. *The Politics of Ethnic Conflict Regulation*. London: Routledge, 1993.

McMahon, Patrice. *Taming Ethnic Hatred: Ethnic Cooperation and Transnational Networks in Eastern Europe*. Syracuse, N.Y.: Syracuse University Press, 2007.

McMahon, Robert. "UN: Security Council Alarmed at Macedonian Violence, Kosovo Role." *RFE/RL Newsline*, July 27, 2001.

Mertus, Julie. *Kosovo: How Myths and Truths Started a War*. Berkeley: University of California Press, 1999.

Miall, Hugh, ed. *Minority Rights in Europe: The Scope for a Transnational Regime*. London: Pinter, 1994.

Middle East Online. "Bulgarian Parliament Condemns a Far-Right Mosque Attack." May 27, 2011.

Ministry of Foreign Affairs, Republic of Macedonia. *Facts About National Minorities in the Republic of Macedonia*. Skopje: Ministry of Foreign Affairs, 1997.

Minority Rights Group. World Directory of Minorities, 1997: Section on Bulgaria (209–13); Section on Macedonia (233–37); Section on Yugoslavia (250–55). London: Minority Rights Group International, 1997.

Mitev, Peter. "Sociological Study." In *Relations of Compatibility and Incompatibility Between Christians and Muslims in Bulgaria*, ed. Antonina Zhelazkova. Sofia: PHARE, 1994.

Mondo, "ONA Odgovorna za Pucnjavu u Makedoniji." [ANA Reponsible for Shooting in Macedonia]. May 2, 2010. http://www.mondo.rs/ s168524/Info/ex-YU/ ONA_odgovorna_za_pucnjavu_u_Makedoniji.html.

Monitor. March 8, 2006.

——. February 17, 2002.

Montalvo, José and Marta Reynal-Querol. "Ethnic Polarization, Potential Conflict, and Civil Wars." *American Economic Review* 95, 3 (June 2003): 796–816.

Montgomery, Michael. "EU Endorses Task Force to Probe Organ Trafficking Allegations in Kosovo." Center for Investigative Reporting, June 9, 2011. http://centerforinvestigativereporting.org/articles/eu-endorses-task-force-to-probe-organ-trafficking-allegations-in-kosovo-4855.

Montville, Joseph. *Conflict and Peacemaking in Multiethnic Societies*. Lexington, Mass.: Lexington Books, 1990.

Moravcsik, Andrew and Milada Vachudova. "National Interests, State Power, and EU Enlargement." *East European Politics and Societies* 17, 1 (2003): 42–57.

Mousseau, Demet. "Democratizing with Ethnic Divisions." *Journal of Peace Research* 38, 5 (2001): 547–67.

Mudde, Cas. *Populist Radical Right Parties in Europe*. Cambridge: Cambridge University Press, 2005.

Mungiu-Pippidi, Alina. "EU Accession Is No 'End of History.'" *Journal of Democracy* 18, 4 (2007): 8–16.

Nachmani, Amikam. *Turkey: Facing a New Millennium*. Manchester: Manchester University Press, 2003.

Najceska, Mirjana, Emilija Simoska, and Natasha Gaber. "Muslims, State and Society in the Republic of Macedonia." In *Muslim Communities in the New Europe*, ed. Gerd Nonneman, Tim Niblock, and Bogdan Szajkowski. London: Ithaca Press, 1996.

Narten, Jens. "Building Local Institutions and Parliamentarism in Post-War Kosovo." *Helsinki Monitor* 17, 2 (2006): 144–59.

——. "Dilemmas of Promoting Local Ownership." In *The Dilemmas of State-Building*, ed. Roland Paris and Timothy Sisk. London: Routledge, 2008.

Nedeva-Atanassova, Ivanka. *Assimilating Muslims in Communist Bulgaria: The Final Stage.* Association of the Study of the Nationalities, Columbia University, New York, 2004.

Neofotistos, Vasiliki. "Beyond Stereotypes: Violence and the Porousness of Ethnic Boundaries in the Republic of Macedonia." *History and Anthropology* 15, 1 (2004): 47–67.

———. *The Risk of War: Everyday Sociality in the Republic of Macedonia.* Philadelphia: University of Pennsylvania Press, 2012.

News.Az. "Erdogan Criticizes Bulgarian Party's Attacks on Muslims." May 24, 2011, http://www.news.az/articles/turkey/37034.

New Europe. March 21, 2010. http://www.neurope.eu/articles/99854.php.

Nicholson, Beryl. "The Beginning of the End of a Rebellion." *East European Politics and Societies* 13, 3 (1999): 543–65.

Nikolova, Galia. "Dogan govori dva chasa na evrodiplomati za Kardzhali" [Dogan Talks for Two Hours to Euro-Diplomats About Kardzhali]. *Kontinent Daily,* June 12, 1995.

Nodia, Ghia. *The Political Landscape of Georgia.* Delft: Eburon, 2006.

Nonneman, Gerd, Tim Niblock, and Bogdan Szajkowski, eds. *Muslim Communities in the New Europe.* London: Ithaca Press, 1996.

North, Douglas. "Institutions and Credible Commitment." *Journal of Institutional and Theoretical Economics* 149 (March 1993): 11–23.

North, Douglas and Barry Weingast. "Constitutions and Commitment." *Journal of Economic History* 49 (1989): 803–32.

Northedge, F. S. and Michael Donelan. *International Disputes: The Political Aspects.* London: Europa, 1971.

Noutcheva, Gergana. "Fake, Partial, and Imposed Compliance." *European Journal of Public Policy* 16, 7 (2007): 1065–84.

Noutcheva, Gergana and Dimitar Bechev. "The Successful Laggards: Bulgaria and Romania's Accession to the EU." *East European Politics and Societies* 22, 1 (2008): 114–44.

Novinar. September 29, 2000.

———. December 3, 2002.

Novinite. August 8, 2001, http://www.novinite.net/view_news.php?id=1341.

———. December 17, 2009, http://www.novinite.com/view_news.php?id=111187.

———. May 24, 2011, http://www.novinite.com/view_news.php?id=128558.

————. June 23, 2011, http://novinite.info/view_news.php?id = 129246.

————. July 11, 2011. http://www.novinite.com/view_news.php?id = 130129.

————. "Macedonians, Albanians Clash in Skopje, Tetovo." March 10, 2012. http://www.novinite.com/view_news.php?id = 137429.

O'Donnell, Guilermo. "Another Institutionalization." Working Paper 222. Kellogg Institute, Notre Dame, Ind., March 1996.

Offe, Claus. "Capitalism by Democratic Design." *Social Research* 58, 4 (1991): 865–92.

O'Leary, Brendan. "The Elements of Right-Sizing and Right-Peopling the State." In *Right-Sizing the State: The Politics of Moving Borders*, ed. Brendan O'Leary, Ian Lustick, and Thomas Callaghy. Oxford: Oxford University Press, 2001.

————. "The Realism of Power-Sharing." Foreword to Michael Kerr, *Imposing Power-Sharing: Conflict and Coexistence in Northern Ireland and Lebanon*. Dublin: Irish Academic Press, 2006. xviii–xix.

O'Leary, Brendan, Ian Lustick, and Thomas Callaghy, eds. *Right-Sizing the State: The Politics of Moving Borders*. Oxford: Oxford University Press, 2001.

O'Leary, Brendan and John McGarry. *The Politics of Antagonism: Understanding Northern Ireland*. London: Athlone, 1993.

O'Lesser, Ian. "Bridge or Barrier." In Graham Fuller and Ian O'Lesser, *Turkey's New Geopolitics: From the Balkans to Western China*. Rand Study. Boulder, Colo.: Westview, 1993.

Oliva, Fabio. "Between Contribution and Disengagement." *Security and Human Rights* 18, 3 (2007): 192–207.

Olson, Robert. *Turkey's Relations with Iran, Syria, Israel, and Russia, 1991–2000*. Costa Mesa, Calif.: Mazda, 2001.

Ordanoski, Sašo. "The Story of Macedonian Populism." In *The Western Balkans and the EU: The Hour of Europe*, ed. Jacques Rupnik. Challiot Paper 126. Paris: EU Institute for Security Studies, 2011.

Orosi, Violeta. "The Pristina Show Trials." In *War Report*. London: Institute on War and Peace Reporting, 1995.

Ortakovski, Vladimir. *Minorities in the Balkans/Maltsinstvata na Balkanot*. Skopje: 2th August St, 1998.

Organization for Security and Cooperation in Europe (OSCE). "Republic of Bulgaria: Parliamentary Elections 2005." November 3, 2005. http://www.osce.org/odihr/elections/bulgaria/16816.

Özcan, Gencer. "The Military and the Making of Foreign Policy in Turkey." In *Turkey in World Politics*, ed. Barry Rubin and Kemal Kirisci. Boulder, Colo.: Lynne Rienner, 2001. 13–30.

Paltchev, Ivan. *Ahmed Dogan and the Bulgarian Ethnic Model*. Sofia: National Museum of Bulgarian Books and Polygraphy, 2002.

Pano, Nicholas. "The Process of Democratization in Albania." In *Politics, Power, and the Struggle for Democracy in South-East Europe*, ed. Karen Dawisha and Bruce Parrott. Cambridge: Cambridge University Press, 1997. 303–16.

Paoli, Leticia and Peter Reuter. "Drug Trafficking and Ethnic Minorities in Western Europe." *European Journal of Criminology* 5, 1 (2008): 31–37.

Paris, Roland. *At War's End*. Cambridge: Cambridge University Press, 2004.

Paris, Roland and Timothy Sisk. "Introduction." In *The Dilemmas of State-Building*, ed. Roland Paris and Timothy Sisk. London: Routledge, 2008. 1–20.

Parliamentary Assembly of the Council of Europe. Document 10961, June 12, 2006. http://assembly.coe.int/Documents/WorkingDocs/Doc06/EDOC10961.pdf.

Peake, Gordon. "Power-Sharing in a Police Car." In *From Power Sharing to Democracy*, ed. Sid Noel. Montreal: McGill University Press, 2005.

Perritt, Henry H., Jr. *Kosovo Liberation Army: The Inside Story of an Insurgency*. Urbana: University of Illinois Press, 2008.

Perry, Duncan. "Macedonia: A Balkan Problem and a European Dilemma." *RFE/RL Research Report* 1, 25 (June 19, 1992): 39.

———. "The Republic of Macedonia: Finding Its Way." In *Politics, Power, and the Struggle for Democracy in South-East Europe*, ed. Karen Dawisha and Bruce Parrott. Cambridge: Cambridge University Press, 1997. 226–82.

Petai, Vello and Klara Hallik. "Understanding Processes of Ethnic Control." *Nations and Nationalism* 8, 4 (2002): 509–29.

Petersen, Roger D. *Resistance and Rebellion: Lessons from Eastern Europe*. Studies in Rationality and Social Change. Cambridge: Cambridge University Press, 2001.

———. *Understanding Ethnic Violence: Fear, Hatred, and Resentment in Twentieth-Century Eastern Europe*. Cambridge: Cambridge University Press, 2002.

———. *Western Intervention in the Balkans: The Strategic Use of Emotion in Conflict*. Cambridge: Cambridge University Press, 2011.

Pettifer, James. *Kosova Express: A Journey in Wartime.* Madison: University of Wisconsin Press, 2005.

Pettifer, James and Miranda Vickers. *The Albanian Question: Reshaping the Balkans.* New York: Tauris, 2009.

Phillips, John *Macedonia: Warlords and Rebels in the Balkans.* New Haven, Conn.: Yale University Press, 2004.

Pickering, Paula. "Explaining Support for Non-Nationalist Parties in Post-Conflict Societies in the Balkans." *Europe-Asia Studies* 61, 4 (2009): 565–91.

Pierson, Paul. "Big, Slow Moving and Invisible." In *Comparative Historical Analysis in the Social Sciences*, ed. James Mahoney and Dietrich Rueschmeyer. Cambridge: Cambridge University Press, 2003.

———. *Dismantling the Welfare State? Reagan, Thatcher and the Politics of Retrenchment.* Cambridge Studies in Comparative Politics. Cambridge: Cambridge University Press, 1994.

———. "Increasing Returns, Path Dependence, and the Study of Politics." *American Political Science Review* 94, 2 (2000): 251–67.

———. "Not Just What But When: Timing and Sequences in Political Processes." *Studies in American Political Development* 14 (2000): 72–92.

———. *Politics in Time: History, Institutions, and Social Analysis.* Princeton, N.J.: Princeton University Press, 2004.

———. "When Effects Become a Cause." *World Politics* 45 (July 1993): 593–628.

Pike, John. "Kosovo Liberation Army." *Federation of American Scientists*, 1999. http://www.fas.org/irp/world/para/kla.htm.

Population and Housing Census. *Romania 2011*, February 2012 [in Romanian]. 5. http://www.recensamantromania.ro/wp-content/uploads/2012/02/Comunicat_DATE_PROVIZORII_RPL_2011, accessed July 4, 2012.

Posen, Barry R. "The Security Dilemma and Ethnic Conflict." *Survival* 35 (Spring 1993): 27–47.

Poulton, Hugh. *The Balkans, Minorities and States in Conflict.* London: Minority Rights Group, 1991.

———. *Who Are the Macedonians?* London: Hurst, 1995, 2000.

Poulton, Hugh and Suja Taji-Farouki. *Muslim Identity and the Balkan State.* New York: New York University Press with Islamic Council, 1997.

Project on Ethnic Relations. "The Bulgarian Ethnic Experience." Round-Table Discussions, June 29–30, 2002, December 18, 2001, 21. http://www.per-usa.org/PER_Bulgaria_9_20_02.pdf.

Przeworski, Adam and Henry Teune. *The Logic of Comparative Social Inquiry*. New York: Wiley, 1970.

Pula, Gazmend. "Modalities of Self-Determination." *Suedosteuropa* 45, 4–6 (1996).

Quirijns, Klaartije, *The Brooklyn Connection*. Documentary, U.S. Premiere July 19, 2005.

Rabushka, Alvin and Kenneth A. Shepsle. *Politics in Plural Societies: A Theory of Democratic Instability*. 1972. New York: Pearson/Longman, 2009.

Ramet, Pedro. *Nationalism and Federalism in Yugoslavia*. Bloomington: Indiana University Press, 1984.

Ramet, Sabrina Petra. *Balkan Babel: The Disintegration of Yugoslavia from the Death of Tito to Ethnic War*. Boulder, Colo.: Westview, 2002.

———. "The Serbian Church and the Serbian Nation." In *Beyond Yugoslavia: Politics, Economics, and Culture in a Shattered Community*, ed. Sabrina Petra Ramet and Ljubiša Adamovich. Boulder, Colo.: Westview, 1995.

Rechel, Bernd. "The Bulgarian Ethnic Model: Ideology or Reality?" *Europe-Asia Studies* 59, 7 (2007): 1201–15.

———. *The Long Way Back to Europe: Minority Protection in Bulgaria*. Stuttgart: Ibidem Vergal, 2008.

———. "What Has Limited the EU's Impact on Minority Rights in Accession Countries?" *East European Politics and Societies* 22, 1 (2008): 171–91.

Regan, Patrick M. "Third Party Interventions and the Duration of Intrastate Conflicts." *Journal of Conflict Resolution* 46, 1 (2002): 55–73.

Regan, Patrick M. and Aysegul Aydin. "Diplomacy and Other Forms of Intervention in Civil Wars." *Journal of Conflict Resolution* 50, 5 (October 2006): 736–56.

Regan, Patrick M. and Allan C. Stam. "In The Nick of Time: Conflict Management, Mediation Timing, and the Duration of Interstate Disputes." *International Studies Quarterly* 44 (2000): 239–60.

Reilly, Benjamin. "Post-War Elections: Uncertain Points of Transition." In *From War to Democracy: Dilemmas of Peacebuilding*, ed. Anna K. Jarstad and Timothy D. Sisk. Cambridge: Cambridge University Press, 2008.

Reilly, Benjamin and Andrew Reynolds. *Electoral Systems and Conflict in Divided Societies.* Papers on International Conflict Resolution 2. Washington, D.C: National Academy Press, 1999.

Reka, Armend. "The Ohrid Agreement." *Human Rights Review* 9 (2008): 55–69.

Republic of Kosovo Assembly, Kosovo Declaration of Independence, February 17, 2008, http://www.assembly-kosova.org/?cid = 2,128,1635.

Reuter, Jens. "Albaniens Aussenpolitik." *Südosteuropa* 44, 1–2 (1995).

———. "Die politische Entwicklung in Kosovo 1992/1993." *Südosteuropa* 43, 1–2 (1994).

Reuters. "Violence in North Kosovo Draws EU Warning. July 27, 2011.

Reynal-Querol, Marta. "Ethnicity, Political Systems, and Civil Wars." *Journal of Conflict Resolution* 46, 1 (2002): 29–54.

RFE/RL. "Albanian, Macedonian Presidents Call for Calm After Murders." May 9, 2012. http://www.rferl.org/content/macedonian_albanian_presidents_call_for_calm/24554051.html.

———. Quoted in Stefan Troebst, "Nationalismus als Demokratisierungshemmnis in Bulgarien" [Nationalism as an Obstacle to Democratization in Bulgaria]. *Suedosteuropa* 41, 3–4 (1992).

RIA Novosti, "Venezuela Recognizes South Ossetia, Abkhazia." September 10, 2008. http://en.rian.ru/world/20090910/156084433.html.

Risse, Thomas, Stephen Ropp, and Kathryn Sikkink. *The Power of Human Rights.* Cambridge: Cambridge University Press, 1999.

Roe, Paul. "Securitization and Minority Rights." *Security Dialogue* 35, 3 (2004): 279–94.

Roeder, Philip. "Peoples and States After 1989." *Slavic Review* 58, 4 (1999): 854–81.

Roeder, Philip and Donald Rothchild. *Sustainable Peace: Power and Democracy After Civil Wars.* Ithaca, N.Y.: Cornell University Press, 2005.

Rossos, Andrew. *Macedonia and the Macedonians.* Stanford, Calif.: Hoover Institution Press, 2008.

Rotberg, Robert, ed. *State Failure and State Weakness in a Time of Terror.* Cambridge, Mass.: World Peace Foundation; Washington, D.C.: Brookings Institution Press, 2003.

Rothchild, Donald and Phillip Roeder. "Dilemmas of State-Building in Divided Societies." In *Sustainable Peace,* ed. Philip Roeder and Donald Rothchild. Ithaca, N.Y.: Cornell University Press, 2005.

Ruane, Joseph and Jennifer Todd. *The Dynamics of Conflict in Northern Ireland.* Cambridge: Cambridge University Press, 1996.

———. "The Roots of Intense Ethnic Conflict May Not in Fact Be Ethnic." *European Journal of Sociology* 45 (2004): 209–32.

Rubin, Barry and Kemal Kirisci, eds. *Turkey in World Politics.* Boulder, Colo.: Lynne Rienner, 2001.

Rueschmeyer, Dietrich. "Can One of a Few Cases Yield Theoretical Gains." In *Comparative Historical Analysis in the Social Sciences,* ed. James Mahoney and Dietrich Rueschmeyer. Cambridge: Cambridge University Press, 2003. 305–36.

Safran, William. "Non-Separatist Policies Regarding Ethnic Minorities." *International Political Science Review* 15, 1 (1994): 61–80.

Saideman, Stephen M. *The* Ties *That Divide: Ethnic Politics, Foreign Policy, and International Conflict.* New York: Columbia University Press, *2001.*

Saideman, Stephen and William Ayres. *For Kin or Country: Xenophobia, Nationalism, and War.* New York: Columbia University Press, 2008.

Salehyan, Idean and Kristian Skrede Gleditsch. "Refugees and the Spread of Civil War." *International Organization* 60 (Spring 2006): 335–66.

Sambanis, Nicholas. "Do Ethnic and Non-Ethnic Civil Wars Have the Same Causes?" *Journal of Conflict Resolution* 45, 3 (June 2001): 259–82.

———. "What Is Civil War." *Journal of Conflict Resolution* 48 (2004): 814–58.

Sambanis, Nicholas and Ibrahim Elbadawi. *External Interventions and the Duration of Civil Wars.* Washington, D.C.: World Bank, 2000.

Schimmelfennig, Frank. "The Community Trap." *International Organization* 55 (2001): 47–80.

Schimmelfennig, Frank and Ulrich Sedelmeier. *The Europeanization of Central and Eastern Europe.* Ithaca, N.Y.: Cornell University Press, 2005.

Schmidt, Fabian. "Altered States." *War Report.* London: IWPR, 1997–1998.

———. "Show Trials in Kosovo." *Transition,* November 3, 1995.

Schmitter, Philippe. "The Influence of the International Context upon Choice of National Institutions and Policies in Neo-Democracies." In *The International Dimension of Democratisation: Europe and Americas,* ed. Laurence Whitehead. New York: Oxford University Press, 1996. 26–54.

———. "Peoples and Boundaries in the Process of Democratization." In *Staat, Nation, Demokratie: Traditionen und Perspectiven moderner Geschallschaften: Festschrift für Hans-Jürgen Puhle,* ed. Marcus Gräser,

Christian Lammert, and Söhnke Schreyer. Göttingen: Vandenhoeck und Ruprecht, 2001.

Schöpflin, George. "The Rise and Fall of Yugoslavia." In *The Politics of Ethnic Conflict Regulation*, ed. John McGarry and Brendan O'Leary. London: Routledge, 1993. 172–203.

SEETimes. "The Rise of Turkey in the Balkans." July 11, 2011. http:// www.setimes.com/ cocoon/setimes/xhtml/en_GB/features/ setimes/arti cles/2011/07/11/reportage-01.

Shain, Yossi. "The Role of Diasporas in Conflict Perpetuation or Resolution." *SAIS Review* 22, 2 (Summer–Fall 2002): 115–44.

Sheffer, Gabriel. *Diaspora Politics: At Home Abroad*. Cambridge: Cambridge University Press.

Shenker, David. "Egypt's Islamist Future." *Los Angeles Times*, July 4, 2012.

Shopova, Milena. "Turski i amerikanski politisti se zastapvat za partiata na Dogan" [Turkish and American Politicians Intercede for Dogan's Party]. *24 Chasa Daily*, July 21, 1999.

Simon, Jeffrey. "Bulgaria and NATO: 7 Lost Years." *Strategic Forum* 142 (May 1998).

Sisk, Timothy and Christoph Stefes, "Power-Sharing as an Interim Step in Peace Building: Lessons from South-Africa." In *Sustainable Peace: Power and Democracy After Civil Wars*, ed. Philip Roeder and Donald Rothchild. Ithaca, N.Y.: Cornell University Press, 2005.

Skendaj, Elton. "Building State Bureaucracies and Democratic Institutions." Ph.D. dissertation, Cornell University, 2011.

Skocpol, Theda. *States and Social Revolutions*. Cambridge: Cambridge University Press, 1979.

Snyder, Jack. *From Voting to Violence: Democratization and Nationalist Conflict*. New York: Norton, 2000.

Snyder, Jack and Karen Ballentine. "Nationalism and the Marketplace of Ideas." *International Security* 21, 2 (1996): 5–40.

Snyder, Jack and Robert Jervis. "Civil War and the Security Dilemma." In *Civil Wars, Insecurity, and Intervention*, ed. Barbara F. Walter and Jack Snyder. New York: Columbia University Press, 1999.

Söderberg-Kovacs, Mimmi. "When Rebels Change Their Stripes." In *From War to Democracy: Dilemmas of Peacebuilding*, ed. Anna K. Jarstad and Timothy D. Sisk. Cambridge: Cambridge University Press, 2008.

Sofia Echo. "GERB, Ataka Join Forces on Holding Referendum on News in Turkish." December 15, 2009. http://sofiaecho.com/2009/12/15/8308 90_gerb-ataka-join-forces-on-holding-referendum-on-news-in-turkish.

Sokalski, Henryk J. *An Ounce of Prevention: Macedonia and the UN Experience in Preventive Diplomacy.* Washington D.C.: USIP, 2003.

Sörensen, Jens. "The Shadow Economy, War, and State Building." *Journal of Contemporary European Studies* 14, 3 (2006): 317–51.

Standart. "European Parliament Turns Down De Groen." November 16, 2006, http://paper.standartnews.com/en/article.php?d = 2006–11–16& article = 1823.

Stavrova, Biljana. "Macedonia: Drawing the Line." *Transitions Online,* August 16, 2004. http://www.tol.cz, pass-protected access.

Stedman, John Stephen. "Introduction." In *Ending Civil Wars: The Implementation of Peace Agreements,* ed. Stephen John Stedman, Donald Rothchild, and Elizabeth Cousens. Boulder, Colo.: Lynne Rienner, 2002.

———. "Spoiler Problems in Peace Processes." *International Security* 22, 2 (Fall 1997): 32–36.

Stedman, Stephen and Donald Rothchild, "Peace Operation." *International Peacekeeping* 3, 2 (1996): 17–35.

Stedman, Stephen John, Donald Rothchild, and Elizabeth Cousens, eds. *Ending Civil Wars: The Implementation of Peace Agreements.* Boulder, Colo.: Lynne Rienner, 2002.

Stefanova, Nina. "Dogan topi Bulgaria v Strasbourg za majchinia ezik" [Dogan Complains About Bulgaria in Strasbourg About the Mother-Tongue [Education]. *Standart Daily,* September 9, 1996.

Steinmo, Sven. "What Is Historical Institutionalism?" In *Approaches and Methodologies in the Social Sciences: A Pluralist Perspective,* ed. Donatella della Porta and Michael Keeting. Cambridge: Cambridge University Press, 2008. 118–39.

Stoyanov, Dimitar. *Zaplachata* [The Threat]. Sofia: Albatros, 1997.

Strazzari, Francesco. "The Shadow Economy of Kosovo's Independence." *International Peacekeeping* 15, 2 (2008).

Streeck, Wolfgang and Kathleen Thelen, eds. *Beyond Continuity: Institutional Change in Advanced Political Economies.* Oxford: Oxford University Press, 2005.

Stroschein, Scherrill. *Ethnic Struggle, Coexistence, and Democratization in Eastern Europe.* Cambridge: Cambridge University Press, 2012.

Stuart, Paul. "EU Takes over NATO's Mission in Macedonia." *World Social-ist Web-site*, 2003. http://www.wsws.org/articles/2003/apr2003/mace-a10.shtml.

Subotic, Jelena. *Hijacked Justice: Dealing with the Past in the Balkans*. Ithaca, N.Y.: Cornell University Press, 2009.

Sullivan, Stacey. *Be Not Afraid for You Have Sons in America: How a Brook-lyn Roofer Helped Lure the U.S. into the Kosovo War*. New York: St. Martin's, 2004.

Sunar, Ilkay. "State, Society, and Democracy in Turkey." In *Turkey Between East and West*, ed. Vojtech Mastny and R. Craig Nation. Boulder, Colo.: Westview, 1996. 141–54.

Szajkowski, Bogdan. "Elections and Electoral Politics in Macedonia." *Tran-sitions* 1–2 (1999).

Tahiri, Edita. *The Rambouillet Conference. Negotiating Process and Docu-ments*. Peje: Dukagjini Press, 2001.

Tansey, Oisin. "Democratization Without a State." *Democratization* 14, 1 (2007).

Taşkin, Yüksel, "Europeanization and the Extreme Right in Bulgaria and Turkey." *Southeastern Europe* 35 (2011): 95–119.

Taylor, Andrew. "Electoral Systems and the Promotion of 'Consociational-ism' in a Multi-Ethnic Society." *Electoral Studies* 24 (2005): 435–63.

Thayer, Bradley. "Macedonia." In *The Costs of Conflict: Prevention and Cure in the Global Arena*, ed. Michael Brown and Richard Rosecrance. Lan-ham, Md.: Rowman and Littlefield, 1999.

Thelen, Kathleen. "Historical Institutionalism in Comparative Politics." *Annual Review of Political Science* 2 (1999): 392–93.

———. *How Institutions Evolve: The Political Economy of Skills in Germany, Britain, the United States, and Japan*. Cambridge: Cambridge University Press, 2004.

———. "How Institutions Evolve." In *Comparative Historical Analysis in the Social Sciences*, ed. James Mahoney and Dietrich Rueshmeyer. Cam-bridge: Cambridge University Press, 2003.

———. "Timing and Temporality in the Analysis of Institutional Evolu-tion and Change." *Studies in American Political Development* 14 (Spring 2000): 101–8.

Thessalonki Declaration. 2003. http://ec.europa.eu/enlargement/enlarge ment_process/accession_process/how_does_a_country_join_the_eu/ sap/thessaloniki_summit_en.htm.

Thornberry, Patrick. *Minorities and Human Rights Law*. London: Minority Rights Group, 1991.

Thyne, Clayton. "Cheap Signals with Costly Consequences: The Effect of Interstate Relations on Civil War." *Journal of Conflict Resolution* 50, 6 (2006): 937–61.

Tilly, Charles. *Big Structures, Large Processes, Huge Comparisons*. New York: Sage.

———. *The Politics of Collective Violence*. New York: Columbia University Press, 2003.

Times.am. "Bulgaria Has Serious Claims Towards Turkey." April 10, 2011. http://times.am/2011/04/10/bulgaria-has-serious-claims-towards-turkey.

Today's Zaman. October 7, 2010. http://www.todayszaman.com/newsDetail _getNewsById.action?load=detay&link=223710.

Toft, Monica. *The Geography of Ethnic Violence*. Princeton, N.J.: Princeton University Press, 2003.

———. "Indivisible Territory, Geography, Concentration, and Ethnic War." *Security Studies* 12, 2 (Winter 2002): 82–119.

Trager, Eric. "Egypt's Triangular Power-Struggle." *Policy-Watch/Peace-Watch*, Washington Institute, July 22, 2011. http://www.washingtoninsti tute.org/templateC05.php?CID=3387.

Trajkovski, Boris. "The Framework Agreement." In *Inventory*, ed. Vladimir Milcin. Skopje: OSI, 2003.

Transparency International. *Corruption Perception Index*, 2010. http://www .transparency.org/policy_research/surveys_indices/cpi/2010/results.

Trenin, Dmitri and Aleksei Malashenko. *Russia's Restless Frontier: The Chechnya Factor in Post-Soviet Russia*. Washington, D.C.: Carnegie, 2004.

Troebst, Stefan. "Nationalismus als Demokratisierungshemmnis in Bulgar-ien." *Suedosteuropa* 41, 3–4 (1992).

Troud. "Utchtiv ultimatum ot Ankara" [A Polite Ultimatum from Ankara]. August 21, 1991.

———. February 28, 2000.

———. October 1, 2000.

———. February 21, 2006.

Troxel, Luan. "Socialist Persistence in the Bulgarian Elections of 1990–1991." *East European Quarterly* 26, 4 (1993): 424.

Tsai, Kellee. "Adaptive Informal Institutions and Endogenous Institutional Change in China." *World Politics* 59, 1 (2006): 116–41.

Tuerkes, Mustafa and Gieksu Goekgoez. "The European Union's Strategy Towards the Western Balkans." *East European Politics and Societies* 20 (2006): 659–90.

Turam, Berna. "A Bargain Between the Secular State and Turkish Islam." *Nations and Nationalism* 10, 3 (2004): 353–74.

Turkish Democratic Party. *Program Declaration*, 1992. Archives of the Bulgarian Helsinki Committee, Sofia.

UN General Assembly. *Report of the Secretary-General.* Agenda item 130. November 13, 2003.

UNDP. *Bulgaria 2000: Doklad za Choveshkoto Razvitie* [Bulgaria 2000: Report on the Human Development: The Municipalities Mosaic]. Sofia: UNDP, 2000.

UNHCR. "Albanian National Army Operating in Kosovo." August 28, 2008. http://www.unhcr.org/refworld/country.IRBC.SRB.49b92b3c7,0 .html.

U.S. Department of State. *Annual Report, Serbia, 1999.*

———. *Annual Report on International Religious Freedom for 1999: Serbia-Montenegro.* http://www.state.gov/www/global/human_rights/irf/irf_rpt/1999/irf_serbiamo99.html.

———. *Country Reports on Human Rights Practices: Macedonia, 2004.* http://www.state.gov/j/drl/rls/hrrpt/2003/27852.htm.

———. *Country Reports on Human Rights Practices: Serbia-Montenegro, 2000.* http://www.state.gov/j/drl/rls/hrrpt/1999/358.htm.

———. *Report on Human Rights Practices, Bulgaria.* March 11, 2008. http://www.state.gov/g/drl/rls/hrrpt/2007/100552.htm.

———. *Report on Human Rights Practices, Serbia (includes Kosovo).* March 6, 2007. http://www.state.gov/j/drl/rls/hrrpt/2006/78837.htm.

———. *Reports on Human Rights Practices for Bulgaria, Macedonia, and Kosovo from 2000–2010.* http://www.state.gov/g/drl/rls/hrrpt/.

Uzgel, Ilhan. "The Balkans: Turkey's Stabilizing Role." In *Turkey in World Politics*, ed. Barry Rubin and Kemal Kirisci. Boulder, Colo.: Lynne Rienner, 2001.

Vachudova, Milada Anna. *Europe Undivided: Democracy, Leverage, and Integration After Communism.* Oxford: Oxford University Press, 2005.

Valentino, Benjamin A. *Final Solutions: Genocide and Mass Killing in the Twentieth Century.* Ithaca, N.Y.: Cornell University Press, 2004.

Valentino, Stefano. "Kosovo: UN Leaves, Scandals Stay." PowerPoint Presentation, Global Investigative Journalism Conference, September 12, 2008, Lillehammer, Norway.

Varangis, Panao, Sona Varma, Angelique de Plaa, and Vikram Nehru. "Exogenous Shocks in Low Income Countries." World Bank Paper, November 20, 2004. http://siteresources.worldbank.org.

Varshney, Ashutosh. *Ethnic Conflict and Civic Life*. Oxford: Oxford University Press, 2002.

Vayrynen, Raimo. "Challenges to Preventive Action." In *Conflict Prevention: Path to Peace or Grand Illusion?* ed. David Carment and Albrecht Schnabel. Tokyo: UN University Press, 2003. 47–69.

Vermeersh, Peter. "EU Enlargement and Minority Rights Policies in Central Europe." *Journal of Ethnopolitics and Minority Issues in Europe* 1, 1 (2003): 1–32.

Vickers, Miranda. *Between Serb and Albanian: A History of Kosovo*. New York: Columbia University Press, 1998.

———. "Tirana's Uneasy Role in the Kosovo Crisis, 1998–1999." In *Kosovo: The Politics of Delusion*, ed. Michael Waller, Kyril Drezov, and Buelent Goekay. London: Frank Cass, 1995.

Voice of America. "Kosovo Violence Threatens Serbia's EU Aspirations." December 11, 2011. http://www.voanews.com/english/news/europe/ Kosovo-Violence-Threatens-Serbias-EU-Aspirations—134860113.html.

———. "Macedonia Votes on Local Autonomy for Ethnic Albanian Minority." July 11, 2004. http://www.globalsecurity.org/military/library/ news/2004/11/mil-041107–357b8ba0.htm.

Walter, Barbara. "The Critical Barrier to Civil War Settlement." *International Organization* 51, 3 (1997): 335–64.

———. "Information, Uncertainty, and Decision to Secede." *International Organization* 60 (2006).

Waterbury, Myra. *Between State and Nation: Diaspora Politics and Kin-State Nationalism in Hungary*. London: Palgrave, 2010.

Weiner, Myron. "The Macedonian Syndrome." *World Politics* 23, 4 (1971): 665–83.

Weinstein, Jeremy. *Inside Rebellion: The Politics of Insurgent Violence*. Cambridge: Cambridge University Press, 2007.

Weller, Marc. *The Crisis in Kosovo 1989–1999*. Cambridge: Center for International Studies, University of Cambridge, 1999.

————. "Kosovo's Final Status." *International Affairs* 84, 6 (2008): 1223–43.

Wennmann, Achim. "Resourcing the Recurrence of Intrastate Conflict." *Security Dialogue* 36, 4 (2005): 479–94.

Wheatley, Jonathan. *Georgia from National Awakening to Rose Revolution.* Aldershot: Ashgate, 2005.

White, Stephen, Sarah Oates, and Bill Miller. "The 'Clash of Civilizations' and Post-Communist Europe." *Comparative European Politics* 1 (2003): 111–27.

Whitehead, Laurence. "Three International Dimensions of Democratization." In *The International Dimensions of Democratization, Europe and the Americas*, ed. Laurence Whitehead. Oxford: Oxford University Press, 1996. 3–25.

Wiatr, Jerzy J. "Executive-Legislative Relations in Crisis." In *Institutional Design in New Democracies*, ed. Arend Lijphart and Carlos Waisman. Boulder, Colo.: Westview, 1996.

Wildmaier, Wesley, Mark Blyth, and Leonard Seabrooke. "Exogenous Shocks or Endogenous Constructions?" *International Studies Quarterly* 51 (2007): 747–59.

Winrow, Gareth. "Turkey and the Newly Independent States of Central Asia and the Transcaucasus." In *Turkey in World Politics*, ed. Barry Rubin and Kemal Kirisci. Boulder, Colo.: Lynne Rienner, 2001.

Wittenberg, Jason. "What Is a Historical Legacy?" Paper presented at 19th International Council of Europeanists, Boston, March 2012.

World Investment News. *Florin Krasniqi*, May 29, 2009. http://www.winne .com/dninterview.php?intervid = 2518.

Xhudo, Gazmen. *Diplomacy and Crisis Management in the Balkans.* London: Macmillan, 1996.

Yannis, Alexandros. "Kosovo: The Political Economy of Conflict and Peacebuilding. In *The Political Economy of Armed Conflict: Beyond Greed and Grievance*, ed. Karen Ballentine and J. Sherman. Boulder, Colo.: Lynne Rienner. 167–95.

Yusufi, Islam. "Assisting State-Building in the Balkans." *Romanian Journal of Political Science* 5, 2 (2005): 71–78.

Zanga, Louis. "The Question of Kosovar Sovereignty." *RFE/RL Research Report* 1, 43 (1992).

Zartman, I. William. *Ripe for Resolution: Conflict and Intervention in Africa.* Oxford: Oxford University Press, 1989.

———. "Ripeness: The Hurting Stalemate and Beyond." In International Conflict Resolution After the Cold War, ed. Paul Stern and Daniel Druckman. Washington, D.C.: National Academy Press, 2000.

Zhelyazkova, Antonina. "The Bulgarian Ethnic Model." *East European Constitutional Review* 10, 4 (2001): 62–66.

———, ed. *Relations of Compatibility and Incompatibility Between Christians and Muslims in Bulgaria.* Sofia: PHARE, 1994

Zhelyazkova, Antonina, Maya Kosseva, and Marko Hajdinjak. "Tolerance and Cultural Diversity Discourses in Bulgaria." *EUI Research Paper*, 2010. http://www.eui.eu/Projects/ACCEPT/Documents/Research/wp1/ACCEPTPLURALISMWp1BackgroundreportBulgaria.pdf.

Ziblatt, Daniel. *Structuring the State: The Formation of Italy and Germany and the Puzzle of Federalism.* Princeton, N.J.: Princeton University Press, 2006.

Zielonka, Jan and Alex Pravda ed., *Democratic Consolidation in Eastern Europe.* Vol. 2: *International and Transnational Factors.* Oxford: Oxford University Press, 2001.

Constitutional Documents

BULGARIA

Konstitutsia na Narodnata Republika Bulgaria [Constitution of the People's Republic of Bulgaria] 1947. Sofia: Izdatelstvo na Natsionalnia Savet na Otechestvenia Front, 1947.

Konstitutsia na Narodna Republika Bulgaria [Constitution of the People's Republic of Bulgaria]. Sofia: Nauka i Izkustvo, 1971.

Constitution of the Republic of Bulgaria, 1991. Article 29 (1), http://www.univ-wuerzburg.de/law/bu00000_.htm.

MACEDONIA

Odluka za Proglasucvanje na Ustavot na Socialistichka Republica Macedonia, [Decision about the Adoption of the Constitution of the Socialist Republic of Macedonia]. Official Gazette, Skopje, February 25, 1974. http://www.slvesnik.com.mk/Issues/0AF2E0456C964935B7705FB5BF6F31F9.pdf.

Constitution of the Republic of Macedonia, 1991, Preamble. http://www.uni-wuerzburg.de/law/ml00000_.htm.

Constitution of the Republic of Macedonia, 2001, Preamble, http://www.sobranie.mk/en/default-en.asp?ItemID = 9F7452BF44EE814B8DB897C1858B71FF.

SERBIA

Constitution of the Republic of Serbia, 1990. http://unpan1.un.org/intradoc/groups/public/documents/untc/unpan019071.pdf.

YUGOSLAVIA

Constitution of the Socialist Federal Republic of Yugoslavia. Belgrade: Yugoslovenski
    Pregled, 1974.
Constitution of the Federal Republic of Yugoslavia, 1992. http://www.worldstatesmen
    .org/Yugoslav_Const_1992.htm

Index

Abkhazia, 221–24. *See also* Caucasus
Acceptance or rejection of the state by the
  minority, 16, 17, Figure 3 (40), 47, 60, 80,
  Figure 6 (102), 206, 208
Ackermann, Alice, 141
Acquis communautaire, 126, 171, 192, 248n95
Adamson and Demetriou, 132
Adaptive expectations (mechanism), 17,
  24–25, 60–62, 68–73, 77, 100–102, 108–9,
  126, 146, 157, 179, 183–85, 196, 201–2, 204,
  207, 213
Adjara, 221–23. *See also* Caucasus
Advantage of political incumbency (mech-
  anism), 17, 24, 60–62, 62–68, 76–77, 157,
  204, 207, 210, 213, 216, 222–23
Affinity-based ties, 129, 130, 148, 155–56
Afghanistan, 3, 85, 166, 168
Africa, 79, 158, 224
Ahmeti, Ali, 197
Ahtisaari, Martti, 169, 194
Albanian-American Civic League (AACL),
  142, 153
Albanian National Army (ANA), 196–99, 201
Alia, Ramiz, 138, 140
All-Albanian Army, 141
Alliance for the Future of Kosovo (AAK), 180,
  Table 4 (185). *See also* Ramush Haradinaj
Amnesty International, 85, 107, 109, 166
"Ancient hatreds" theories, 92
Arab Spring, 27, 81, 225
Asia, 158, 224
Assimilation and expulsion campaign 1984–
  1989, Bulgaria, 35–36, 39, 42–43, 65, 87,
  133, 136, 145, 187
Ataka, 2, 4, 159, 186–88, 192, 199, 201, 209
Atanasov, Georgi, 42
Atatürk, Kemal, 133, 143, 145
Atlantic Battalion, 154, 199
Autonomy, 3, 6, 14, 28, 52, 56, 94, 154,
  221–22; in Bulgaria, 93, 144, 208; in Mace-
  donia, 35, 53, 55, 66, 71, 78, 92, 149, 170,

172; in Kosovo, 37, 39, 46, 48, 50, 86–87,
  91, 109, 140, 141, 164; in Romania, 214–17.
  See also decentralization

Badinter, Robert: Arbitration Commission on
  Yugoslavia, 90, 92; double-majority vote,
  "Badinter rule," in Macedonia, 165
Bajraktari, Harry, 142, 198
Battle of Kosovo, 1389, 36–37, 39
Belgrade, 48, 50, 117, 148, 219
Bellamy, Alex, 91, 117
Berisha, Sali, 138, 139, 140, 147, 149–50
Bieber, Florian, 257n10, 262n32, 263nn66, 68
Borisov, Boyko, Table 4 (184), 187, 200
Bozhkoski, Ljube, 172
Bosnia-Herzegovina, 2, 3, 19, 27, 67, 92–97,
  108, 116–18, 159, 166–68, 214, 217–20
"Brotherhood and Unity" in socialist Yugo-
  slavia, 36
Brubaker, Rogers, 134
Bukoshi, Bujar, Table 2 (64), 72, 111, 152, 153,
  242
Bulgarian Orthodox Church, 65
Bulgarian Socialist Party (BSP), 45, 56, Table 2
  (63), 64, 65, 74, 110, 172, Table 4 (184), 186,
  188
Bunce, Valerie, 21

Carment and Rowlands, 95
Cappocia and Ziblatt, 263n66
Cappocia and Kelemen, 232n20, 237nn57, 58
Caucasus, 79, 143, 151, 199, 221–24, 226. *See
  also* Abkhazia; Adjara; Georgia
Causal mechanism, 10, 27, 60, 100–101,
  113–14, 118, 127, 146, 179
Cederman, Lars-Erik, 252n102, 253n105
Census: in Bulgaria, 22; in Kosovo, 22; in
  Macedonia, 22, 55, 105, 111; in Romania,
  214
Central Asia, 143, 151, 226
Cetinyan, Rupen, 82

Acknowledgments

This book has a long history of travel. I conceived the first ideas in Italy. They matured during the ten years I lived in the United States, and benefited from comparisons between the Balkans and the Middle East during the nine months I spent in Lebanon. The book was completed while my professional life was stretched between the United States and the Netherlands. These acknowledgments were written in the United Kingdom. Throughout this stimulating if often trying academic journey, the support of colleagues and friends has been invaluable.

This research has benefited from generous support from a number of institutions and individuals. I received grants from the European University Institute (EUI); the Italian Foreign Ministry; the World Peace Foundation Program on Intrastate Conflict at Harvard's Belfer Center for Science and International Affairs, the Kokkalis Program on Southeastern and East Central Europe at Harvard, the Open Society Global Supplementary Grant Program; and the Richard C. Welden Foundation. I am also grateful to Harvard's Belfer Center, Davis Center for Russian and Eurasian Studies, and Center for European Studies for giving me institutional affiliations, and to Cornell University and the Dickey Center at Dartmouth College, where many of my ideas ripened.

Academic colleagues gave me outstanding feedback. At the EUI I had the privilege to work with Philippe Schmitter, who inspired me with his passion for political science, freshness of attitude, and support when I was on either side of the Atlantic. Jan Zielonka gave me helpful comments on early versions of this project. Without Robert Rotberg my journey to the United States would not have been possible. He gave me the chance to do my research at Harvard and to participate in a monthly seminar with academic fellows from world class universities. He also read and commented on many drafts of my work. Christianne Wohlforth has been very enthusiastic about this project, and went out of her way to comment on several chapters. Martin Dimitrov, Peter Hall, Erin Jenne, Ned Lebow, Elton Skendaj, and Denise Walsh provided especially helpful comments on various book chapters.

I benefited from the intellectual stimulation of many other scholars. At the EUI I received helpful comments from Svetoslav Andreev, Ivo Banac, Stefano Bianchini, Luisa Chiodi, Verena Fritz, Jonathan Weathley, Senada Selo-Sabic, and Radoslava Stefanova. I am grateful for the outstanding feedback of participants in Harvard's Program on Intrastate Conflict: Fiona Adamson, Roberto Belloni, Marie Besancon, Caty Clement, Fotini Christia, Renske Doorenspleet, Denise Garcia, Arman Grigorian, Sarah Lischer, Neophytos Loizides, Maria Stephan, and Carola Weil. Other scholars at Harvard—Grzegorz Ekiert, Dmitry Gorenburg, Yoshiko Herrera, Greg Mitrovich, Sherrill Stroschein, and Lucan Way—also provided interesting insights. I am also grateful to professors at Harvard's Graduate School of Arts and Sciences: Lars-Erik Cederman, Steven Levitsky, Stanley Hoffmann, Cindy Skach, Pippa Norris, and Daniel Ziblatt, especially to Steven Levitsky for his professional advice. At Cornell, Valerie Bunce and Ken Roberts gave me helpful ideas on how to think about the writing of this book. At Dartmouth I benefited from intellectual exchange with Julie Norman, Ralph Thaxon, and Patrick Forest, and with scholars associated with the International Relations Seminar: Bridget Coggins, Daryl Press, and Benjamin Valentino. Finally, at the University of Amsterdam, Marieke de Goede, Marlies Glasius, Andrea Ruggeri, and Jonathan Zeitlin provided very good ideas on two chapters. Eben Friedman was especially helpful regarding my research on Macedonia.

I very much appreciate the clear interest of Brendan O'Leary in this book, and for his meticulous reading, commenting and outstanding feedback on the entire manuscript. An anonymous reviewer wrote several pages of detailed comments that helped me improve an earlier version. It was a pleasure working with Peter Agree as the editor-in-chief at Penn Press, and with my linguistic editors Debbie West and Alison Anderson.

During my field visits I stayed recurrently with one Macedonian and one Albanian family, who remain anonymous to protect their privacy. They were wonderful hosts with a true sense of hospitality. When living in their homes I could better understand the spoken and unspoken intricacies of inter-ethnic relations, and think about the conflicts from the perspective of human emotions and day-to-day attitudes. During my Kosovo visits I was generously hosted by two members of international organizations, who also remain anonymous. I am very grateful for their personal insights into the conflict, and for the good time we had despite the difficult circumstances. I am also indebted to numerous interviewees who generously offered me their time and ideas, and who also remain anonymous.

I would like to thank Taylor & Francis Ltd. for their permission to reprint information from earlier articles: "Challenging Assumptions of the Enlargement Literature: The Impact of the EU on Human and Minority Rights in Macedonia," *Europe-Asia Studies* 63, 5 (2011): 807–32; "Kinstate Intervention in Ethnic Conflicts: Albania and Turkey Compared," *Ethnopolitics* 7, 4 (2008): 373–90; and "Why Do Ethnonational Conflicts Reach Different Degrees of Violence?" *Nationalism and Ethnic Politics* 15, 1 (2009): 84–108.

I owe many thanks to good friends and family: Sarah Dix, Richard Costa, Ilijan Georgiev, Krum Georgiev°, Liubka Georgieva, Maria Georgieva, Kelly Morgan, Mariana Neisuler, Panayote Dimitras, Nafsika Papanikolatos, Petia Petrova, Gergana Spassova, and Debbie West. Henry Bayerle was an outstanding intellectual partner for six years. Karim Khanipour gave me his warm care and patience during the concluding stages of this project.

I dedicate this book to four people who have most shaped this journey. My late parents Velin and Ivanka ignited me with never-ending love for knowledge, and gave me a wonderful childhood that has been my deepest source of strength. Neda Benova was my mother's caregiver. She took a difficult job and carried it with dignity and stoicism until my mother's passing. She gave me her love and optimism. Elisa Pepe was a true beacon of support during crucial moments in my life. She encouraged me beyond imagination. Thank you so much for all your care and for helping me to make this book possible.